Essays in Contemporary Fields of Economics

Emanuel Thornton Weiler (1914–1979)

Essays in Contemporary Fields of Economics

In Honor of Emanuel T. Weiler
(1914–1979)

Edited by George Horwich and James P. Quirk

Purdue University Press
West Lafayette, Indiana
1981

Portrait of Emanuel T. Weiler by Alfred J. Pounders. Photograph of portrait by permission of Krannert Graduate School of Management.

Library of Congress Catalog Card Number 79-91134
International Standard Book Number 0-911198-59-8
Printed in the United States of America

Contents

vii   PREFACE

ECONOMIC THEORY

3   A Dynamic Process of Exchange
Stanley Reiter

24   The Place of an Individual in an Economy
Edward Ames

41   Technical Change Inclinations of a Resource Monopolist
Morton I. Kamien and Nancy L. Schwartz

54   The Paradox of Voting and Candidate Competition:
A General Equilibrium Analysis
John O. Ledyard

APPLIED ECONOMICS

83   An Empirical Study of Decentralized Institutions of
Monopoly Restraint
Vernon L. Smith

107   The Theory of the Dam: An Application to the Colorado
River
H. Stuart Burness and James P. Quirk

131   Guidelines for a Responsible Natural Resources Policy
Charles W. Howe

152   In Search of the Historical Imperialist
Lance E. Davis and Robert A. Huttenback

168   Professor Hobsbawm on the Evolution of Modern Capitalism
Jonathan Hughes

MACROECONOMICS

191   The Economics of Professor Friedman
John H. Wood

242   The Stability of Macro Models
George Horwich and Sheng Cheng Hu

ECONOMICS EDUCATION

277   The Development of Economics Education through the
      Principles of Economics Course in the United States: Its
      Goal, Content, and Methodology
      Dennis J. Weidenaar

290   Perspectives on Economics
      Leonid Hurwicz

311   Closing the Gap between Frontier Thinking and the
      Curriculum in Economics
      Lawrence Senesh

FOUR MEMOIRS

355   On Forgetting Economics with Em Weiler
      Edward Ames

361   A Note on Early Cliometrica
      Jonathan Hughes

365   "It's Just like New York!"
      Morton I. Kamien

369   Experimental Economics at Purdue
      Vernon L. Smith

375   CONTRIBUTORS

377   AUTHOR INDEX

Preface

Emanuel Thornton Weiler, the founder and first dean of Purdue's School of Management and the Krannert Graduate School of Management, was a pioneer in many areas. A first-rate professional economist, he was an innovator and leader in the field of economics education. He was a gifted academic administrator who was instrumental in developing the management school out of the economics and industrial-management departments he had earlier built. Within ten years of Em Weiler's arrival at Purdue in the early 1950s, both the economics department and the management school were major, nationally ranked organizations.

No simple recital of his achievements, however, conveys the unique quality of Em Weiler's influence and personality. He was a man of keen intellect who could readily navigate the intellectual waters of postwar economic theory. He liked people and intuitively understood their individual personalities. He believed in individual freedom and initiative, both as a political and economic philosophy and as a model for organizational behavior. He could and did communicate with anyone—faculty, students, university administrators, business people, captains of industry. And rarest of all, he was an administrator who took risks, both in terms of programs and of people. Combining his flair for daring entrepreneurship with basic good judgment in scholarship, Em was able to attract talented young academics, offer them moral and financial support, and create a school environment in which each participant was bound only by his or her own imagination and ability.

Em Weiler was born on January 2, 1914 in Chicago, the son of a Mennonite father who had left Pennsylvania to study dentistry in Chicago. The family eventually moved to Elkhart, Indiana, where Em grew up within a large family circle. When his parents migrated to California, following the 1929 financial crash, Em remained in Indiana and enrolled at DePauw University in Greencastle. It was there that he met his future wife, Catherine Reinoehl. They were married in their sophomore year, an act which happened to violate university regulations and led to the young couple's expulsion; they were, however, readmitted. Em supported himself and Cathy by selling typewriters, taking off an entire school year to build their savings. During his senior year, Em discovered his interest in economics and, upon graduating, decided to pursue graduate work at the University of Minnesota. The faculty there was indeed distinguished, including George Garver, Alvin Hansen, George Stigler, and the eminent monetary theorist Arthur Marget, under whom Em later wrote his dissertation. Though Em's undergraduate record at DePauw did not qualify him for an assistantship, his performance in his first year at Minnesota quickly brought him to the faculty's attention. He served as a graduate instructor at Minnesota from 1939 to 1943.

Em's research contributions as a graduate student included an early formulation of the flow-of-funds accounts, a theoretical financial framework that was later to become a major tool of social accounting. Typical of his later interests, he found teaching equally exciting and was particularly "turned on" by a group of unemployed bankers and businessmen to whom he taught economics under a WPA project.

After completing his dissertation, Em joined the wartime migration to Washington, where he served with distinction as an economist, first in the Department of Commerce and later at the Board of Governors of the Federal Reserve System.

Approached after the war by Ohio Wesleyan University, Em undertook his first entrepreneurial venture and agreed to rebuild the university's war-ravished economics department. He created a solid academic tradition at Ohio Wesleyan, which continues to the present day. In 1948 Em accepted a professorship at the University of Illinois, where Howard Bowen, dean of the College of Commerce and Business Administration, was recruiting one of the finest economics departments of the postwar period. Em took responsibility for teaching the introductory course. Among his colleagues on that legendary faculty were Dorothy Brady, Robert Eisner, Everett Hagen, Leo Hurwicz, Franco Modigliani, Don Patinkin, and Margaret Reid. When the Illinois department, having moved too far too rapidly, began to experience internal dissention, the stars left. Em accepted an offer from Purdue to head its economics department and a newly formed department of industrial management and transportation. He arrived on the West Lafayette campus in 1953.

It is doubtful that Em had a fixed blueprint in mind when he began recruiting the new Purdue faculty. His natural tendency was to hire innovative people in any of the subdisciplines of economics and management, letting the curriculum emerge spontaneously. And so it did. While it may not seem a dramatic departure today, the Purdue economics program, both graduate and undergraduate, was unique in being based on the cornerstones of rigorous theory, a solid grounding in econometrics, and quantitative economic history. This was an era in which leading departments of economics each had exactly one "quantitative" faculty member, usually called an econometrician whether he did mathematical economics or econometrics. And the few attempts to establish quantitatively oriented programs, including the one at Illinois and attempts at Chicago and Iowa State during the mobile Cowles Foundation days, had failed. Quantitative economic history was, of course, a completely radical departure from the traditional curriculum.

To compound his risks, Em hired a faculty that had almost no track record. Edward Ames, Jonathan Hughes, and Vernon Smith have contributed brief sketches of the economics program in those early years. Morton Kamien provides the viewpoint of a graduate student of that era. These essays appear at the conclusion of this volume.

The division between economics and management was not tightly drawn. By the late 1950s and early 60s, a distinctive management curriculum, also quantitative and combining aspects of both analytical and case-method teaching, began to take shape. John Day, W. Vern Owen, John Tse, Frank Bass, Edgar Pessemier, Robert Johnson, and Richard Walton were among the early developers of the new program.

The two departments, with financial assistance from the Ford Foundation, merged in 1958 to form a School of Industrial Management, with Em as dean. In 1963 a grant by the Indianapolis industrialist Herman C. Krannert furnished building funds and an endowment for what then became the Krannert Graduate School of Management. Em remained as dean until 1969 when he returned to teaching as the first Krannert Distinguished Professor of Economics and Management.

In the final decade of his life, Em returned to his early interest in the principles course. At Illinois he had published *The Economic System*, a monumental text based on the Walrasian general-equilibrium framework. Though not a best-seller, it led to two other books, *The American Economic System* (coauthored with W. H. Martin) and *Economic Policy* (coedited with William Gramps). His final major writing endeavor was the highly successful text and readings book produced jointly with Dennis Weidenaar, *Economics: An Introduction to the World Around You*. During those last years, Em also served as a director of several major corporations and as a trustee of DePauw University.

Em Weiler died July 1, 1979, leaving his wife, Cathy, and their four children, Peter, Ann, Sarah, and Susan.

The papers collected in this volume were presented at West Lafayette on January 13 and 14, 1978. The occasion was a symposium celebrating Em's twenty-fifth year at Purdue. The range of subjects covered by the papers included the diverse areas of economics that had developed during Em's tenure as department head and dean. The papers are in economic theory, applied economics (including experimental economics and economic history), macrotheory, and, of course, economics education. The editors want to thank all the participants in that program, the reviewers of the papers, and the Krannert School for their assistance in planning the symposium and publishing its proceedings.

Economic Theory

A Dynamic Process of Exchange

Stanley Reiter

The model presented in this paper deals with dynamic behavior of a market not in equilibrium. It is a characteristic feature of markets that are out of equilibrium that opportunities to trade on different terms exist simultaneously. One explanation of how a uniform price comes to prevail in a market is in terms of arbitrage. In broad terms, the model studied here formalizes a dynamic arbitraging process and explores the extent to which that process can bring about results of the kind usually envisaged for it.

The literature on markets that are out of equilibrium contains models which deal with search behavior[1] and models in which a market "process" is formalized as a game.[2] The model studied in this paper differs from these in many details but mainly in two respects. First, the behavior of agents is modeled from a "bounded rationality" point of view, rather than, say, in terms of optimal searching. Second, the main focus is on the dynamic process and its long-run tendency, rather than on a solution concept such as Nash equilibrium or market clearing. In these respects, my viewpoint of 1959 is retained here.[3]

A dynamic market process cannot satisfactorily be based on static excess demand behavior of economic agents (traders, in a pure exchange setting) because it is unsatisfactory to assume that agents will maximize utility, treating the budget constraint as if it were a certainty in a situation in which it is necessarily uncertain. Away from the static equilibrium, no agent can be assured of his opportunities. If the behavior of agents away from equilibrium is qualitatively different from their behavior at equilibrium, they can, in effect, recognize whether the market is or is not in equilibrium. While it is possible that behavior in equilibrium should be in some sense a limit of disequilibrium behavior, we take the view that behavior of agents should, in some sense, be qualitatively the same throughout the process.

The role of information and its effect on the appropriate behavior of agents then becomes important. We try to take account of two aspects of the role of information. First, the institutional structure of the market determines the information agents get from the market process, the "structural" aspect. Second, the restricted capacity of economic agents to handle information restricts behavior, the "bounded rationality" aspect. The structural aspect of information is modeled by looking at an extreme case, one in which

3

each agent acquires information only from his own direct experience—and, at that, only information indispensable to making trades, namely, bids or offers tendered to or by himself. Moreover, trading is assumed to be un-organized and anonymous. Traders meet one another at random, exchange bids, do or do not agree to trade, and then separate, each ignorant of the identity of the other.

The "bounded rationality" aspect enters in two ways. First, in economic life each individual takes part in many different economic activities, includ-ing trading in markets for many different commodities. Each person has limited time and resources, and typically devotes a substantial portion of them to some specialized productive activity, his job, from which he earns his living. Such a person cannot devote a large amount of his time and resources to searching out trading opportunities. If the number of com-modities which an individual trades is large, relative to his capacity, then the individual agent can do relatively little in the way of searching or ac-quiring information in "most" markets. Thus, in any market we may expect to find many agents whose capacities for search are relatively small. In the kind of situation that would typically result, opportunities for arbitrage profit may be expected to exist. Therefore, some agent would have incen-tives to "specialize" in such a market, that is, to devote a large portion of his resources to trading in that market and in effect make trading his "job." Such considerations led to the formulation of a pure exchange model in which there are two types of agents, those with relatively large capacity and those with low capacity, and correspondingly, with different appropriate behavior.

Second, the behavior of each type of agent is itself restricted by restricted capacity to process information in the face of complex and changing cir-cumstances. Explicitly to derive and characterize rules for fully rational behavior in such circumstances is a difficult problem. Instead, the model specifies certain plausible modes of behavior supported only by heuristic arguments. This leads, as will be seen below, to behavior involving stochastic elements.

More specifically, the process is as follows. A market consists of a finite collection of agents.

The *market process* goes on in time, which is discrete, consisting of a se-quence of periods. Contact among agents takes place at random during each period.

There are two types of agents. One is characterized by low capacity for contact per period (reflecting a low allocation of information-processing capacity to this market). The other is characterized by a high capacity for contact per period. There are many low-capacity agents and a few high-capacity ones.[4] I shall call the agents *consumers* and *traders* respectively.

The situation envisaged was one in which the various agents, having very little information about opportunities, might be prepared to trade on very different terms. This is a situation in which the possibility of arbitrage profit exists.

When a trader and a consumer meet, some form of bargaining takes place. Because of the trader's high capacity for contact, he is likely to be better off devoting his capacity to seeking arbitrage profits than to spend scarce time in hard bargaining with a single consumer, from whom he is likely to make a relatively small gain, at best. This is modeled as follows. When trader and consumer meet, the consumer makes a bid. The trader either accepts it or rejects it and moves on to another consumer. Thus, each participant makes and receives a bid as a result of each contact he makes. These bids are the sole basis of the information acquired from the market.

I turn next to the behavior of agents. First, the consumers. The specification of rational behavior for a consumer presents an interesting and largely unsolved problem of behavior under uncertainty. In the nature of the case, a consumer can have at best an estimate of the alternatives confronting him. The only point that he can be certain is available to him is the point involving no trade. His problem is complicated by three factors. First, the set of alternatives facing him may change from time to time. Second, his ability to acquire information and, hence, the rate at which he acquires information may be slow, relative to the rate at which the set of alternatives is changing. This means that aging information becomes increasingly irrelevant. Third, each "observation" involves both information and payoff. The means of acquiring information is the making and receiving of offers. The process involves the risk of making deals. In this respect the consumer's problem is like problems of the "two-armed-bandit" class.

In view of these difficulties, we shall prescribe intuitively appealing modes of behavior for consumers, the rationality of which is supported only by heuristic arguments.

Roughly speaking, each consumer selects his current bid probabilistically, on the basis of the current state of his information about his opportunities.

Now, the traders. Each trader, in pursuit of arbitrage profit, accepts or rejects the bids received by him, using a decision rule that is chosen at the beginning of the current period and maintained unchanged through that period. Thus, a trader is assumed not to be able to respond to variations in the pattern of bids received which take place within a period. That is, he cannot condition his response to a bid on the basis of the other bids received before it in the same period. Such a restriction on behavior reflects considerations of "bounded rationality." The specification of rational behavior for a trader presents difficulties similar to those already mentioned in connection with the same problem for consumers. Our approach is the same in this case as in that: we prescribe intuitively appealing modes of behavior supported by heuristic arguments. The prescribed behaviors represent conjectured solutions to a problem of statistical decision theory, namely, this particular form of the two-armed-bandit problem.

The difference between traders and consumers is the higher capacity for contact enjoyed by traders. This makes it plausible for traders to attempt to take advantage of the possibility for profit inherent in the simultaneous existence of offers on different terms. In such circumstances it is possible for a trader to find several transactions the net effect of which is preferred by him to no trade, while no single one of them is so preferred. Therefore, the behavior of traders, being directed toward finding advantage in the sum of many transactions, does not depend on an evaluation of each offer individually, with immediate reference to his own preferences.

In addition, the asymmetry between traders and consumers provides a basis for strategic behavior. A trader, knowing that he is a trader, may consider that he has a degree of monopoly power, namely, the power to control the information received by individual consumers and, thereby, to influence the perception on the part of consumers of the opportunities in the market. One type of monopoly power—or perhaps it is better to say one source of monopoly power—is the ability of an agent to distort the "true" opportunities confronting the others. In this view the stick-up man who holds a pistol to his victim's head and says "Your money or your life!" exercises a kind of monopoly power not so different from that, say, of a product monopolist, who presents consumers with marginal rates of transformation different from those determined by the technology. A consumer, knowing that he is a consumer in a world in which there are traders, also has a strategic problem. These will be explored below.[5]

In what follows, the behavior of agents is stated more precisely. A stochastic process, resulting from the behavior of agents and their interactions, represents the market process. The long-run behavior of this process is studied. The main results are stated in propositions 1 and 2.

Generally, we expect arbitraging to eliminate price differences within a market, and for the resulting allocations to be "optimal." For instance, a process based on recontracting à la Edgeworth has been shown to lead to Core allocations.[6] In the present model, the unorganized structure of the market and the restricted capacity of agents to make contacts limit the allocations achievable by the process. Specifically, the process cannot be guaranteed to achieve Core allocations. Rather, the process tends toward allocations in the K-core. (The K-core is the set of allocations which cannot be blocked by coalitions involving fewer than $K + 1$ agents, where K, one of the parameters of the model, is a positive integer.[7]) If a core allocation results, it is essentially accidental. The results contained in propositions 1 and 2 are established in a model in which each agent acquires very little information about what is happening in the market generally. However, these results would remain even if agents were provided with information about all transactions. They depend on the restricted capacity of traders to make contacts. As long as individual arbitrageurs are small, relative to the market, a process of unorganized arbitrage, such as the one in this model, cannot guarantee Core allocations, or competitive ones. Thus, it appears that some organized market institution is needed. "Natural" arbitrage is not enough. Furthermore, increasing the number of traders will not save the situation. Increasing the number of competing arbitrageurs seems to lead to a sort of monopolistically competitive solution rather than one in which full equalization of opportunities prevails.

Agents are of two kinds: *consumers* and professional traders or intermediaries, called *traders*. Let

$$\mathscr{C} = \{1, \ldots n\}$$

be the set of consumers and let

$$\mathscr{T} = \{n + 1, \ldots, m\}$$

be the set of traders. Then the set of agents I is given by

$$I = \mathscr{C} \cup \mathscr{T}.$$

Let $\overline{X}$ be the commodity space. I shall suppose that $\overline{X}$ is a (countable) discrete subset of $I\!R^\ell$. The role of this assumption is to avoid technical complexities connected with probability and measure, while retaining the main ideas.

Consumer i is characterized, as usual, by his consumption set $Y^i \subseteq \overline{X}$; his initial endowment $\omega^i \in Y^i$ and his preferences, $\succeq_i$, assumed to be represented by a utility function. Correspondingly, the trade space of consumer i is

$$X^i = Y^i - \{\omega^i\} = \{x \in I\!R^\ell \mid \omega^i + x \in Y^i\}.$$

A preference relation $\succeq_i$ on Y^i induces a preference relation $\succeq_i$ on X^i in the usual way, that is, $\bar{x}^i \succeq_i \bar{\bar{x}}^i \Leftrightarrow \bar{x}^i + \omega^i = \bar{y}^i, \bar{\bar{x}}^i + \omega^i = \bar{\bar{y}}^i$, and $\bar{y}^i \succeq_i \bar{\bar{y}}^i$.

I assume that $\succeq_i$ is represented by a utility function $U^i : X^i \to I\!R$, where $\succeq_i$ is strictly monotone for each $i \in \mathscr{C}$, and $U^i(0) = 0$; $\succeq_i$ is automatically continuous since X^i is discrete.

BIDS

Each agent makes *bids*. The bid of consumer i is a point of X^i.

Denote by $b^i(t)$ the *bid* of consumer i at time t. Let $b(t) = (b^1(t), \ldots, b^n(t))$ be the vector of bids of consumers, where $b^i(t) \in X^i$.

Traders respond to bids received. The response of trader j is a function,

$$\beta^j : \overline{X}^n \to \overline{X}^n$$

defined as follows.

First, let

$$\rho^j : \overline{X}^n \to \overline{X}^n$$

where $\rho^j(b^1, \ldots, b^n) = (b^{1j}, \ldots, b^{nj}) = b^j j \in \tau$ and

$$b^{ij} = \begin{cases} b^i \text{ if } i \in \mathscr{C}_j \text{,}^8 \\ 0 \text{ otherwise.} \end{cases}$$

Thus, $\rho^j(b) = b^j$ is the vector of bids received by trader j when b is the vector of bids made by the consumers. The response β^j of trader j to each bid received is either that bid, indicating that he accepts the bid, or the zero vector in $\overline{X}$, indicating that he rejects that bid. Thus, when the consumers bid b, $\beta^j(b^j) = a^j$, where $a^{j\cdot} = (a^{j1}, \ldots, a^{jn})$ and

$$a^{ji} = \begin{cases} b^{ij} \text{ if } b^{ij} \neq 0 \text{ and } b^{ij} \text{ is accepted; that is, if } j \text{ receives } i\text{'s} \\ \quad \text{bid } b^i \text{ and accepts it} \\ 0 \text{ otherwise.} \end{cases}$$

The functions β^j must also satisfy the following condition. For trader j there is a scalar c^j, which may be interpreted either as representing j's costs of being a trader or, alternatively, as representing trader j's aspirations to monopoly profit. It is required that trader j accept only sufficiently profitable trades; that is, if

$$\beta^j(b^j) = (a^{1\cdot}, \ldots, a^{n\cdot}) = a,$$

then $\sum_{i=1}^{n} a \leq - c^j \cdot 1 < 0$, where $1 = (1,1, \ldots, 1) \in \overline{X} \subset I\!\!R^\ell$.

Anonymity of trading imposes a further restriction on the responses β^j, as follows. If $b^j = (b^{1j}, \ldots, b^{nj})$ is an array of bids received by j, and if

$$\overline{b}^j = (b^{i_1 j}, \ldots, b^{i_n j})$$

where $i_1, \ldots, i_n$ is the permutation of $(1, \ldots, n)$, given by

$$\begin{pmatrix} 1, \ldots, n \\ i_1, \ldots, i_n \end{pmatrix}$$

then

$$\beta^j(\overline{b}^j) = \beta^j(b^j).$$

Thus, trader j's responses to a given array of bids received must be independent of who made those bids. Note that j's response to a bid depends on the array of bids received, not just on the individual bid.

To express the idea that agents have limited capacity to contact other agents, I shall assume that consumers can make, at most, one contact with another agent in each period and that traders can make some given finite number: $k^j \geq 1$ for trader j. I assume further that the nature of the (random) meeting process is such that consumers meet only traders and vice versa. Thus there is a positive integer k^j, such that trader j can receive no more than k^j bids in any period. Then if k^j is the number of non-zero bids in b^j, 2^{k^j} is the number of different functions β^j which satisfy the anonymity condition; only some of these will meet the profitability condition. I shall suppose that trader j chooses his response to bids received, b^j, probabilistically, from the set of possible responses satisfying the requirements of anonymity and profitability, given b^j. We may identify a function β^j with its graph in $X^n \times X^n$, that is, with the (discrete) set

$$\{(a^{j\cdot}, b^j \in X^n \times X^n \mid a^{j\cdot} = \beta^j(b^j)\}$$

and the response of trader j may be represented as a (discrete) conditional probability measure:

$$p^j(\cdot|x) = p^j(x)$$

where $p^j(y|x) = \text{Prob.} \{\beta^j(b^j) = y|b^j = x\}$.

Thus, $p^j(x)$ is a discrete measure non-zero on the set of vectors $y = (y^1, \ldots, y^n)$, such that $y^i = x^i$ or $y^i = 0$.

Let $\mathcal{P}^j$ be the set of all these conditional probabilities:

$$p^j : X^n \times X^n \to [0,1].$$

Thus, an *action* of trader j at time t is a function, $p^j_t \in \mathcal{P}^j$.

The information that trader j has about his trading opportunities may be described by a function which assigns a subjective probability to each bid he might conceivably receive.

Let $\hat{Q}^j$ denote the class of functions

$$\hat{q}^j : x^j \to [0,1] \qquad j \in \mathcal{T}$$

where X^j denotes the trade set of trader j. Thus, if $a \in X^j$, $\hat{q}^j_t(a)$ is the subjective probability that trader j has in mind at time t to receive the bid a.[9]

The behavior, or strategy, of trader j is given by a function:

$$\varphi^j : \hat{Q}^j \to \mathcal{P}^j.$$

These functions will be specified further below.

BIDDING OF CONSUMERS

Bids of a consumer are chosen probabilistically. Let Q^i denote the set of probability measures on X^i. Thus, if $q^i \in Q^i$, then

$$q^i : X^i \to [0,1] \qquad \text{for } i \in \mathcal{C}$$

is a probability measure; $q^i_t(x^i)$ is the probability that $b^i_t = x^i \in X^i$.

The *action* of consumer i in period t is q^i_t.

This is interpreted and justified as follows. If consumer i knew his present and future trading opportunities for sure, he would select a bid which would maximize his utility, given his opportunities. However, in the present context he cannot in general know his opportunities. He is uncertain about them and must use his meetings with traders to explore those opportunities, that is, to search. Consumers use randomized bidding to try to avoid being trapped in a mistakenly perceived set of opportunities. However, a consumer also uses the information so acquired to guide his further exploration in directions of advantage to him.

I shall suppose that consumer i's state of knowledge about his trading opportunities is represented by a subjective conditional probability function, as follows.

Let $\mathcal{P}^i$ denote the class of functions

$$\hat{p}^i : X^i \to [0,1] \qquad i \in \mathcal{C}.$$

Then $\hat{p}_t^i \in \mathscr{P}^i$ for $i \in \mathscr{C}$ and $t = 0,1, \ldots$. The interpretation of this function is

$\hat{p}_t^i(x) = Prob.$ {x is accepted by the trader i meets at t, given that b_t^i equals x}.

A behavior rule or strategy for consumer i is a way of choosing his action, that is, bidding distribution q^i on the basis of his knowledge of his opportunities $\hat{p}^i$. Thus, a behavior rule of agent i is a function:

$$\varphi^i : \mathscr{P}^i \to Q^i \qquad i \in \mathscr{C}$$

where

$$q^i = \varphi^i(\hat{p}^i) \qquad i \in \mathscr{C}$$

is the bidding distribution of i, chosen when $\hat{p}^i$ summarizes his current knowledge. I shall specify the function φ^i more particularly below.

THE MEETING PROCESS

Each time t agents meet one another according to a random process. Denote by $\mathscr{C}_j(t)$ the set of consumers who meet trader j at t. Here $j \in \{n + 1, \ldots, m, m + 1\}$, where $\mathscr{C}_{m+1}(t)$ is the set of consumers who fail to meet anyone at time t.

I shall assume that $\mathscr{C}_{n+1}(t), \ldots, \mathscr{C}_{m+1}(t)$ constitutes a random partition of $\mathscr{C}$. This expresses the assumption, made above, that each consumer can make at most one contact per period.

Let $\pi(i,j;m,n,I\!K)$ denote the probability that agent i meets agent j (assumed to be independent of t) for given values of the parameters $n,m,I\!K$, where $I\!K = (K^{n+1}, \ldots, K^{m+1})$ and $K^{m+1} \geq n$. For notational simplicity, I shall assume $K^j = K$ for all $j \in \mathscr{T}$; that is, all traders have the same capacity.[10]

Let $m_{ij}(t) = \begin{cases} 1 \text{ if } i \in \mathscr{C}_j(t) \\ 0 \text{ otherwise} \end{cases}$

and let $((m_{ij})) \equiv M$.

I assume that $\pi(i\,j;m,n,I\!K) = 0$ if $i, j \in \mathscr{C}$ or if $i, j \in \mathscr{T}$ (that is, only a meeting between a consumer and a trader is possible) and that $\pi(i,j;m,n,I\!K)$ is positive for $i \in \mathscr{C}$ and $j \in \mathscr{T}$.

When consumer i and trader j meet, i's bid b_t^i becomes a component of the bid received by j, and the ith component of j's response is the bid received by i.

STRUCTURE OF OBSERVATION

The potentially observable events in the market consist of
   (i)   The matrix M, describing the meetings that take place,
   (ii) the bids made by each consumer, $b = (b^1, \ldots, b^n)$, and
   (iii) the responses made by each trader,
         $(a^{n+1}, \ldots, a^{m\cdot}) = (a^{m+1,1}, \ldots, a^{m+1,n}; \ldots; a^{m1}, \ldots, a^{mn})$.
Let E be the (discrete) space of possible observations, (M,b,a), and denote by $\underset{\sim}{E}$ the set of subsets of E.

Given the actions of each agent and the probabilities of meetings, the meetings which take place and the bids made by consumers are probabilistically determined, hence, so are the bids received by traders and so are their responses. Thus, given π, the actions (q,p) together determine a probability measure on E. Thus,

$$\Pi: Q^{(n)} \times \mathcal{P}^{(m-n)} \times E \rightarrow [0,1],$$

where $\Pi(q,p,e)$ is the probability of the point $e \in E$, given q,p, where $q = (q^1, \ldots, q^n)$ and $p = (p^{n+1}, \ldots p^m)$.

Because

$$q^i = \varphi^i(\hat{p}^i) \text{ for } i \in \mathcal{C}$$

and

$$p^j = \varphi^j(\hat{q}^j) \text{ for } j \in \mathcal{T},$$

we may write:

$$\Psi((\hat{p}^i),(\hat{q}^j),e) = \Pi((\varphi^i(\hat{p}^i)),(\varphi^j(\hat{q}^j)),e).^{11}$$

I next define a stochastic process that represents the market process, using the stochastic kernel Ψ as its transition kernel. The states of the process are

$$s = ((\hat{p}^i),(\hat{q}^j)), i \in \mathcal{C} j \in \mathcal{T}.$$

Thus, $\mathcal{S} = \mathcal{P}^n \times \hat{Q}^{m-n}$ is the set of states, and their projections are

$$\mathcal{S}^i = \begin{cases} \hat{\mathcal{P}}^i \text{ if } i \in \mathcal{C} \\ Q^i \text{ if } i \in \mathcal{T}. \end{cases}$$

To complete the specification of the process, define the function

$$\lambda^i : \mathcal{S}^i \times E \rightarrow \mathcal{S}^i \text{ for } i \in I,$$

as follows. Let

$$\eta^i : E \rightarrow D^i \, i \in I$$

denote the function which associates with each point in E the datum observed by i when that event occurs. Thus, if e obtains, then i observes $\eta^i(e) = d^i \in D^i$.

On the basis of this "new" information, i can revise his state of knowledge. Let

$$\bar{\lambda}^i(\hat{p}^i_t, d^i_t) = \hat{p}^i_{t+1} \, i \in \mathcal{C}$$

and

$$\bar{\lambda}^i(\hat{q}^j_t, d^i_t) = \hat{q}^j_{t+1} \, j \in \mathcal{T}$$

be the functions which represent this "learning" process. Then

$$\lambda^i(s,e) = \bar{\lambda}^i(s^i,\eta^i(e)), \text{ for } i \in I,$$

where

$$s = (s^1, \ldots, s^m)$$

and

$$s^i = \begin{cases} \hat{p}^i \text{ for } i \in \mathcal{C} \\ \hat{q}^i \text{ for } i \in \mathcal{T}. \end{cases}$$

The Markov process just defined is given by the mappings

(1) $\psi : \mathcal{S} \times \underline{E} \rightarrow [0,1]$

and

(2) $\lambda : \mathcal{S} \times E \to \mathcal{S}$

where $\lambda = \lambda^1 \times \ldots \times \lambda^m$.

I am interested in several variants, each of which is in the class of Markov processes given by (1) and (2).

If we impose some additional properties on the mappings (1) and (2), certain general theorems could be applied to establish the existence of stochastic equilibria for these processes (for an exposition of these theorems see Futia). However, those theorems do not provide the kind of information we would like to have about the set of states to which the system tends in the long run. Therefore, my approach is to specify more particularly the behavior of the various agents in the process and to study the long-run behavior of the process more directly.

The following example helps make clear some of the motivations for the specifications made below.

AN EXAMPLE

Suppose the number of commodities and the number of consumers is 2, that is, $\ell = n = 2$, and that there is just one trader, that is, $m = 3$. Given their characteristics, we can represent the economy, consisting of the two consumers, in an Edgeworth box, as in figure 1. As the trader views this

Figure 1

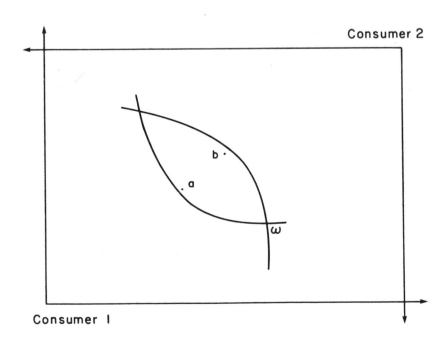

situation, he, seeking arbitrage profits, can assure himself of a permanent flow of profit, for example, by inducing the consumers to make bids corresponding to a and b respectively. The trader can do this by adopting an action which gives positive probability only to accepting the bids corresponding to a and b. If the consumers give positive probability to bids a and b, respectively, they will acquire data which reinforce the belief that their opportunities include a and b, respectively, and nothing else but the initial endowment.

In terms of trades, as shown in figure 2, the trader can ensure a profit of $(a - \omega^1 + b - \omega^2) < 0^{12}$ by allowing the consumers to "learn" that their opportunities are confined to a, b, and the initial endowment.

Figure 2

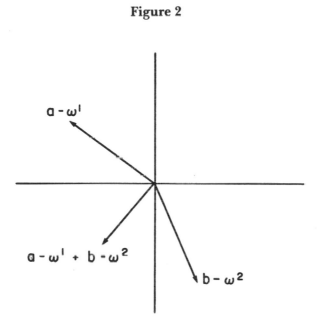

Consider next a two-commodity economy, consisting of four consumers. Represented in the Edgeworth box in figure 3 are the four consumers. It is assumed that there are two pairs, each with the same initial endowment but different preferences. Thus, the indifference curves, labeled 1, 2, 3, and 4, refer to different agents. The single trader facing this situation could make a profit of $a + b + c + d$, if he could induce the agents to make those bids persistently. However, if he accepts only the bids a and b, he must forgo the profit, $c + d$. If he always accepts $c + d$, since he cannot identify the agents who are bidding, he will allow agents 1 and 3 to learn that c and d are acceptable bids. They will, therefore, tend not to bid a and b, but rather bid *c* and *d*. In that case, the trader's arbitrage profit may be expected to tend to $2(c + d)$.

Figure 3

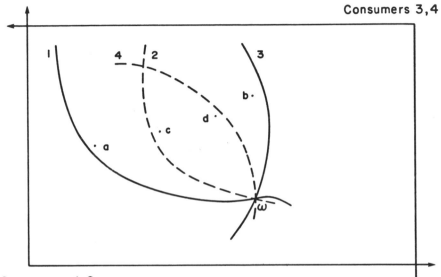

If, however, by sometimes rejecting bids *c* and *d*, he can "teach" consumers 1 and 2 that the probability of acceptance of *c* and *d* respectively is so small that it is worthwhile for them to continue bidding *a* and *b*, at least sometimes, then the trader can make a long-run profit between $a + b + c + d$ and $2(c + d)$. Thus, by falsifying the "true" terms of trade in the economy, a trader can make persistent monopoly profit. He might do this by randomizing his acceptance of bids received.

The question is whether any behavior is open to the consumers which protects them against the trader(s). There is indeed such a course of behavior, and it, in part, motivates the behavior rules prescribed for consumers. We turn now to these specifications.

The functions φ^i and λ^i must be specified more closely. I consider consumers first.

Let
$$\mathcal{G}^i : \mathbb{R}_+ \to X^i \qquad i \in \mathcal{C}$$
be the correspondence that associates to each non-negative utility level of

consumer i the (upper contour) set of trades, individually feasible for i, which afford him at least that level of utility, that is, for $r \in I\!R_+$:
$$\mathcal{G}^i(r) \equiv \{x^i \in X^i \mid U^i(x^i) \geq r\}.$$
Also, define
$$C^i : X^i \to X^i \qquad i \in \mathcal{C}$$
by
$$C^i(y^i) = \mathcal{G}^i(U^i(y^i)).$$
Next, define
$$\mathcal{V}^i(\hat{p}^i) \equiv \max_{x^i \in X^i} \hat{p}^i(x^i) U^i(x^i)$$
and denote the value of $\mathcal{V}^i(\hat{p}^i_t)$ by
$$v^i_t \equiv \mathcal{V}^i(\hat{p}^i_t) \qquad \text{for } t \geq 1 \text{ and } v^i_0 = 0.$$
Then v^i_t is the maximum expected utility level that consumer i considers available to him at time t. That $v^i_0 = 0$ is implied by setting
$$\hat{p}^i_0(x^i) = \begin{cases} 1 \text{ if } x^i = 0 \\ 0 \text{ otherwise.} \end{cases}$$

ASSUMPTION I. (1) For all $\hat{p}^i \in \hat{\mathcal{P}}^i$ and $i \in \mathcal{C}$, if $q^i = \varphi^i(\hat{p}^i)$, then the support of q^i is $\mathcal{G}^i(v^i)$ where $v^i = \mathcal{V}^i(\hat{p}^i)$. That is, for any subset $A \subset X^i$, $\varphi^i(\hat{p}^i)(A \cap \mathcal{G}^i(v^i)) > 0$ and $\varphi^i(\hat{p}^i)(A \cap \text{comp. } \mathcal{G}^i(v^i)) = 0$.

(2) For each $i \in \mathcal{C}$, $\hat{p}^i_0(x^i) = \begin{cases} 1 \text{ if } x^i = 0 \\ 0 \text{ otherwise.} \end{cases}$

Thus, initially, q^i_0 is positive on $\mathcal{G}^i(0)$ and, subsequently, bids are selected from a set which i regards as affording him a sure utility at least as great as the highest level of expected utility he thinks available to him.[13]

Figure 4 shows this assumption for the case in which X^i is one dimensional (a case not naturally interpreted in terms of trades, but easy to see).

DEFINITION. We say that $x^i \in X^i$ is a *basis for* q^i, or that q^i *is based on* x^i if supp $q^i = C^i(x^i)$, that is, if supp $q^i = \mathcal{G}^i(v^i)$ and $U^i(x^i) = v^i$.

We say that the joint bidding distribution $q = (q^1, \ldots, q^n)$ is based on $x = (x^1, \ldots, x^n)$ if q^i is based on x^i for each $i \in \{1, \ldots, n\}$.

Let q^i_t be based on x^i_t with $U^i(x^i_t) = v^i_t$. If $v^i_{t+1} > v^i_t$ and x^i_{t+1} are such that $U^i(x^i_{t+1}) = v^i_{t+1}$, then $\mathcal{G}^i(v^i_{t+1}) \subset \mathcal{G}^i(v^i_t)$. Let q^i_{t+1} be the conditional measure on $\mathcal{G}^i(v^i_{t+1})$, corresponding to q^i_t. Thus, if $A \subseteq \mathcal{G}^i(v^i_{t+1})$, then

$$q^i_{t+1}(A) = \frac{q^i_t(A)}{q^i_t[\mathcal{G}^i(v^i_{t+1})]}.$$

LEARNING

Let B^i_t denote the response received by consumer i to his bid at t. Then,
$$B^i_t = \begin{cases} b^i_t \\ 0 \end{cases}$$
depending on whether i's bid b^i_t is or is not accepted by the trader whom he

Figure 4

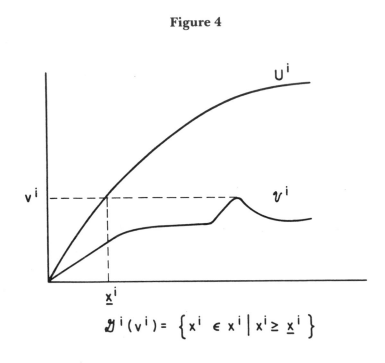

$$\mathcal{D}^i(v^i) = \left\{ x^i \in x^i \mid x^i \geq \underline{x}^i \right\}$$

meets at t. The function η^i, which represents the structure of observation in the market, determines what agent i observes as a result of his participation in the process. In the present case, for each $i \in \mathcal{C}$

$$\eta^i(M,b,a) = (b^i, B^i)$$

where

$$B^i = \beta^j(p^j((b^i))) = \begin{cases} x^i \text{ if } m_{ij} = 1 \text{ and } \beta^j (p^j((b^i))) = x^i \\ 0 \text{ otherwise.} \end{cases}$$

Thus,

$$d_t^i = \begin{cases} (b_t^i, 0) \text{ if } b_t^i \text{ was bid by } i \text{ at } t \text{ and rejected} \\ (b_t^i, x^i) \text{ if } b_t^i \text{ was bid by } i \text{ at } t \text{ and } x^i = b_t^i \text{ was accepted.} \end{cases}$$

I consider two types of learning. The first, which may be called *probability matching*, has two properties.

(1) The revised estimate $\hat{p}^i$ is monotone with respect to d^i in the following sense.
If $d_t^i = (b_t^i, x^i)$, then $\lambda^i(\hat{p}_t^i, d_t^i) = \hat{p}_{t+1}^i$ is such that $\hat{p}_{t+1}^i(x^i) > \hat{p}_t^i(x^i)$
$(0 < \hat{p}_t^i < 1)$, and if $d_t^i = (b_t^i, 0)$, then $\hat{p}_{t+1}^i(x^i) < \hat{p}_t^i$ for $x^i = b_t^i$, and all $t \geq 0$.
That is, an accepted bid leads to increased perceived probability of acceptance of that bid, while a rejected bid leads to a decrease in that probability.

(2) Let $\bar{p}_t(x^i)$ denote the "objective" probability that a bid $x^i = b_t^i$ will be accepted at t; that is, that i will meet some trader j who will accept x^i in combination with some array of bids received from others. This is just a complicated combination of the true acceptance probabilities (p^j) of traders.

If

$$\bar{p}_t^i(x^i) = \bar{p}^i(x^i) \text{ for all } t > \bar{t} \text{ and } x^i \in X^i$$

then

$$\hat{p}_t^i(x^i)_t \to \bar{p}^i(x^i).$$

Thus, the probability matching type of learning is one in which the consumer responds to positive and negative reinforcement in such a way that his estimate of the objective probability of acceptance he faces would converge to the true probability, if it were constant, given sufficient time.

The second type of learning, which may be called *defensive* (or *strategic*), ignores rejection of offers and responds only to bids accepted. In this case,

$$\lambda^i(\hat{p}_t^i, d_t^i) = \hat{p}_{t+1}^i$$

where $\hat{p}_{t+1}^i(x^i) > \hat{p}_t^i(x^i)$, if and only if $d_t^i = (b_t^i, x^i)$, where $x^i = b_t^i$, and $\hat{p}_{t+1}^i(x^i) = \hat{p}_t^i(x^i)$, if $d_t^i = (b_t^i, x^i)$ and $x^i \neq b_t^i$.
A particular function with this property is

$$\lambda^i(\hat{p}^i, d)(x^i) = \begin{cases} \hat{p}^i(x^i) + \theta^i(1 - \hat{p}^i(x^i)) & 0 < \theta^i < 1 \\ \text{if } d^i = (b^i, x^i) \text{ and } x^i = b^i \\ \hat{p}^i(x^i) & \text{otherwise.} \end{cases}$$

According to this learning rule, consumer i increases his estimate of the probability that a bid of his will be accepted only when such a bid is accepted and never decreases his estimate of such a probability.

Such learning behavior may be partly justified, as follows. If the consumer is aware that he is dealing with traders who may be attempting to take advantage of him by misrepresenting trading opportunities, as in the example, he can realize that, in order to profit from transactions with him, a trader will have to accept his bid sometimes. He might then ignore all rejections as attempts to confuse him and give consideration only to acceptances. He does not take "no" for an answer.[14]

BEHAVIOR OF TRADERS

Bidding

The behavior of traders is directed toward arbitrage profit. As the examples above suggest, a trader may attempt to exploit his position by sometimes refusing profitable bids so as to mislead consumers.

ASSUMPTION II. The action p_t^j of trader j at time t satisfies the following condition.

(1) Let $x_t = (x_t^1, \ldots, x_t^n)$ be the bid received by trader j at t, if y_t is a possible response of j to x_t, that is, $y_t^i \in \{x_t^i, 0\}$, and

$$\sum_{i=1}^{n} y_t^i \leq -c^j \cdot 1;^{[15]} \text{ then } p_t^j(y_t|x_t) \geq \delta > 0.$$

I consider two cases:
1. $c^j = 0$
2. $c^j > 0$.

Regarding the learning behavior of traders, I assume that it is of the probability matching type. Thus, for $j \in \mathcal{T}$,

$$\gamma^j(\hat{q}^j_t, d^j_t) = \hat{q}^j_{t+1}$$

satisfies the monotonicity and consistency conditions above. Here $d^j_t = (\beta^j_t(p^j(b_t), p^j(b_t)))$; that is, trader j observes the bids he receives and his response to them.

(Since β^j_t is not permitted to depend on the identity of the consumers who make the bids, we may regard $p^j(b_t)$ as a representative element of the equivalence class, consisting of all bids received which are obtained from $p^j(b_t)$ by permutation of the names of consumers.)

The learning behavior of traders is not significant in the models considered here, because only the restriction of φ^j by assumption II will play a role. This restriction is to the effect that any sufficiently profitable array of bids received has a positive probability of being accepted.

What is the long-run behavior of this process? First, if the consumers use the probability matching type of learning, depending on the specific properties of λ^i, $i \in \mathcal{C}$ (and λ^j for $j \in \mathcal{T}$), the process may or may not converge. Clearly, however, it is possible that the process has recurring states in which the trader(s) earn monopoly profit. This is suggested by figure 3. Given the four utility functions (U^i $i = 1, 2, 3, 4$) of consumers and the points a, b, c, d, it is possible to find probabilities $\bar{p}(a)$, $\bar{p}(b)$, $\bar{p}(c)$, $\bar{p}(d)$, such that

$$\mathcal{V}^1(a) = \mathcal{V}^1(c) \quad \mathcal{V}^2(c) \geqq 0 \quad \mathcal{V}^3(b) = \mathcal{V}^3(d) \quad \mathcal{V}^4(d) \geqq 0.^{16}$$

Suppose the (sole) trader uses these values $\bar{p}(\cdot)$ as his acceptance probabilities. Suppose further that all consumers meet the trader in each period. Then each consumer will eventually learn the objective probabilities $\bar{p}$; that is, $\hat{p}^1(a) = \bar{p}(a)$, $\hat{p}^1(c) = \bar{p}(c)$, etc. Consequently, $q^1(a) > 0$, $q^1(c) > 0$, $q^2(c) > 0$, $q^3(b) > 0$, $q^3(d) > 0$, and $q^5(d) > 0$.

It is not difficult to construct a numerical example in which the average profit of the trader is strictly greater than $2(c + d)$. If there is more than one trader, the acceptance probabilities that face each consumer are a mixture of the acceptance probabilities of traders, the same for each consumer. From their point of view, it is as if there is one trader.

Consider next the case of defensive learning by consumers. Given the current array of bids of consumers $b_t = (b^1_t, \ldots, b^n_t)$ and the current matrix of meetings M_t, the behavior of traders determines an array of bids accepted. Call this array the *current trades* and denote it by $y_t = (y^1_t, \ldots, y^n_t)$,

$$\text{where } y^i_t = \begin{cases} b^i_t \text{ if there exists } j \text{ such that } i \in \mathcal{C}_j(t) \text{ and} \\ \qquad b^i_t \text{ is accepted by } j \\ 0 \text{ otherwise.} \end{cases}$$

DEFINITION. Let z and x and w be allocations. We say that z *K-dominates* x *from* w if there exists a subset $\{i_1, \ldots i_r\} \in \mathscr{C}$ where $r \leq K$, such that

$$\sum_{v=1}^{r} z^{i_v} \leq \sum_{v=1}^{r} w^{i_v}$$

and

$$U^{i_v}(z^{i_v}) \geqq U^{i_v}(x^{i_v}) \text{ for each } v \in \{i, \ldots, r\}$$

with strict inequality for at least one value of v. Let $y_1 = x - w$ and $y_2 = z - w$. We say that y_2 K-dominates y_1 from w if z *K-dominates* x from w.

PROPOSITION 1. Under assumptions I (defensive learning) and II, with $c^j = 0$ for $j \in \mathscr{T}$, let $\{s_t : t \geqq 0\}$ be a sequence of states and let

$$q_t = \varphi(s_t) \ t \geqq 0$$

be the corresponding bidding distributions of consumers. Suppose that for some $t \geqq 0$ there are two distinct allocations x and z such that (i) the bids $y_1 = x - w$ and $y_2 = z - w$ are each in the support of q_t and (ii) y_2 K-dominates y_1 from w; *then* s_t is a transient state.

PROOF OF PROPOSITION 1. To show that s_t is a transient state, it suffices to show that for some consumer i and for some trade y^i and time $t' > t$, $\hat{p}^i_{t'}(y^i) \neq \hat{p}^i_t(y^i)$. This suffices because $\hat{p}^i$ is monotone.

Since y_2 K-dominates y_1, there is a subset $\{i_1, \ldots, i_r\}$ of consumers such that

$$\sum_{v=1}^{r} y_2^{i_v} \leq 0 \text{ and } U^{i_v}(y_2^{i_v}) \geqq U^{i_v}(y_1^{i_v}), \ \forall \ v \in \{1, \ldots, r\} \text{ und } y_2^{i_v}$$

is individually feasible for i_v from w.

Since $r \leq K$, the probability $\{i_1, \ldots, i_r\} \subset \mathscr{C}_j(\tau)$ is a positive constant (independent of τ) for each j.

If $\hat{p}^i_\tau \neq \hat{p}^i_t$ for some i and $\tau > t$, then s_t is transient. Hence consider the case $\hat{p}^i_\tau = \hat{p}^i_t$ for all i and for all $\tau \geqq t$. But that implies that $\hat{p}^i_\tau$ is constant for $\tau \geqq t$. It follows that $q^i_\tau = \varphi^i(\hat{p}^i_t) = \varphi^i(\hat{p}^i_t) = q^i_t$ for all $\tau \geqq t$, and for all i. In particular, $q^{i_v}_\tau = q^{i_v}_t$ for $v \in \{1, \ldots, r\}$ and all $\tau \geqq t$.

By hypothesis, $y_2^{i_v} \in \text{supp } q^{i_v}_t = \text{supp } q^{i_v}_\tau$ for all $\tau \geqq t$. Hence, the probability that $b^{i_v}(\tau)$ equals $y_2^{i_v}$ is a positive number, the same for all $\tau \geqq t$. Hence, the probability that both $b^{i_v}(\tau)$ equals $y_2^{i_v}$ and that $\{i_1, \ldots, i_r\} \subset \mathscr{C}_j(\tau)$ for a given $j \in \mathscr{J}$, is the product of two positive constants (these events are independent) and, hence, is also a positive number and the same for all $\tau \geqq t$.

Under assumption II, the probability that the combination of bids $(y_2^{i_1}, \ldots, y_2^{i_v})$ will be accepted by j, given that it is received by him as a positive number bounded away from 0. It follows that the waiting time until the bid containing $(y_2^{i_1}, \ldots, y_2^{i_v})$ is made to and accepted by the given trader j is finite, with probability 1, since the probability of that event at any one time is bounded from below by a positive constant.

Therefore, with probability 1 there exists some $t' > t$, such that $\hat{p}^{i_v}_{t'} \neq \hat{p}^{i_v}_t$ for $v \in \{1, \ldots, r\}$, and hence $s_{t'} \neq s_t$.

Under assumption I, because of monotonicity, supp $q_\tau^{iv} \nsubseteq$ supp q_t^{iv} for all $\tau \geqq t' > t$. Hence, the state s_t never recurs.

DEFINITION. The K-core from w is the set of feasible allocations which are not K-dominated from w.

PROPOSITION 2. The set of states s, such that the corresponding bidding distributions $q = \varphi(s)$ are based on allocations in the K-core from ω, is an absorbing set.

PROOF OF PROPOSITION 2. Suppose s is a state such that $q = \varphi(s)$ is based on an allocation $x \in$ K-core from ω. In order to leave s, there must exist a set of consumers $\{i_1, \ldots, i_r\}$ with $r \leq K$ and a set of trades $y^{i_1}, \ldots, y^{i_r}$, such that $\sum_{v=1}^{r} y^{iv} \leq 0$ and such that $y^{iv} \in$ supp q^{iv}. But since supp $q^{iv} = C^{iv}(x^{iv})$, $U^i(y^{iv}) \geq U^i(x^{iv})$ for $v = 1, \ldots, r$. Hence the allocation z, where

$$z^i = \begin{cases} \omega^i + y^i \text{ if } i \in \{i_1, \ldots, i_r\} \\ \omega^i \quad \text{ if } i \notin \{i_1, \ldots, i_r\}, \end{cases}$$

K-dominates x from ω, which contradicts the hypothesis that $x \in$ K-core from ω.

Furthermore, under the assumptions on preferences of consumers used in Hurwicz, Radner, and Reiter, we conjecture that the reasoning used there can be employed to show that this process actually converges to its set of absorbing states, namely, those based on the K-core from ω.

When the cost of trading is positive, that is, $c^j > 0$ for $j \in \mathcal{T}$, trader j will accept only such combinations of bids that yield at least $c^j \cdot 1$ profit. This is based on costs being costs per period rather than costs per transaction. (If the costs are related to the number of transactions, say by $c^j \cdot \|\{i \in \mathcal{C}_j(t)) \mid b_t^i$ is accepted$\}\|$, then accepted bids must satisfy the condition

$$\Sigma y_t^i \leq - c^j \| i \in \mathcal{C}_j(t) \mid y_t^i \neq 0\} \| \cdot 1.$$

Hence, c^j is the cost per transaction.)

The arguments used in the proofs of propositions 1 and 2 can, with appropriate modification, be applied to the case where $c^j \geqq 0$ for $j \in \mathcal{T}$ to establish analogous results. In essence, let s be a state such that the bidding distribution of consumers is based on a point from which an r-lateral trade, $r \leq K$, is possible which yields at least $- c^j \cdot 1$, where $c = \min_{j \in \mathcal{T}} c^j$, the analogue of proposition 1 states that s is a transient state.

Similarly, in place of proposition 2 is a result to the effect that states which do not permit the type of improvement just described form an absorbing class.

The quantities $c^j, j \in \mathcal{T}$ can be interpreted in another way. Each trader may regard himself as having monopoly power, that is, the power to misrepresent to consumers the "natural" terms of trade. One way of doing this is for j to choose a value $c^j > 0$ and accept with non-zero probability only combinations of bids that yield a profit at least $(- c^j \cdot l)$.

It is easy to see that when $\mathcal{T}$ consists of more than one trader and when consumers bid defensively, if for some $j \in \mathcal{T}$, $c^j > c = \min_{j \in \mathcal{T}} c^j$, then the average profit per period of trader j will fall to zero. This follows from proposition 1 in the case $c^j \neq 0$, because states such that profits of any trader are more than c are transient.

Suppose that the number of traders is fixed and that the c^j, $j \in \mathcal{T}$ are chosen, once and for all, at the beginning of trading. Then, the long-run behavior of this process will be one in which all traders j whose $c^j = c$, the minimum profit level, will share equally, on average, in the monopoly profits thereby determined, while traders with $c^j > 0$ will get no shares.

If we imagine that the choice of c^j can be modified, then "competitive pressure" exists, tending to drive c^j and hence, c to the level of the minimum cost of being a trader, say c^*. However, with a fixed number of traders, many stable situations can exist in which all traders choose $c^j = c \geq c^*$. We suppose that if the number of traders increases relative to the number of consumers, then—while each period in which a transaction takes place yields the transacting trader a profit of $-c^j \cdot 1$—the average profit per period tends to zero as the number of traders increases.

It would be useful to explore the consequences of different structures of information (representing different institutional arrangements in the market). Public information about transactions or about bids and transactions might be made available to consumers and traders. For example, market reports, similar to the stock exchange reports published in newspapers, might be made available. One interesting question is whether making additional information available to consumers can, by itself, overcome the effects of anonymous trading and insufficient capacity of individual traders in restricting the optimality of the allocations achievable by the process to the K-core. (Allowing supplementary trading among traders is another interesting possibility.)

It appears to be the case that, in general, if $K < n$, this process cannot be guaranteed to achieve core allocations. In general, multilateral trades involving all n consumers are needed to achieve core allocations. Furthermore, this situation is not improved by having a large number of traders. Only if the capacity of at least one trader exceeds the number of consumers can we be sure that the process does not get stuck at states such that the (joint) bidding distribution of consumers is based on an allocation that is not in the core.

Even if more information is made available to consumers—for example, if the structure of observation is such that consumers observe all transactions that take place (or all bids and transactions, for that matter)—we cannot be sure that the process does not get stuck at a non-core state. Based on the greater information, consumers may simultaneously aspire to utility levels which cannot be achieved as a result of K-lateral trades which yield a non-negative arbitrage profit. It appears to be essential that there be an institution which permits n-lateral trades to be achieved by several simultaneous K-lateral ones. This is, of course, what trading at constant known prices permits.[17]

Another approach to studying this process, though in a different spirit, would be to set it up as a game in which the learning functions or perhaps the mappings φ^i are strategies of the players and to study the Nash equilibria of that game.

NOTES

I have benefited from discussions with Ehud Kalai, Glenn C. Loury, and Michael Magill, and from comments by Truman Bewley, Hugo Sonnenschein, and an anonymous referee.

1. A bibliography of the job search literature may be found in Lippman and McCall (1976). For a reference on market search, see Rothchild (1974).

2. See Schmeidler (1976) and Shapley and Shubik (1976).

3. This paper is a revision of Reiter (1959), whose basic objective was to investigate the equilibria of a process of exchange in unorganized markets. The ideas of bounded rationality, of stochastic behavior as a way of coping with insufficient information, and the stochastic nature of equilibrium are all taken from it, although the present formulation is different.

4. In Reiter (1959), the low-capacity agents were called "flounders" and the high-capacity ones "sharks." The process was visualized as taking place in an ocean in which the flounders form a numerous collection of widely separated and slow-moving individuals, while the sharks circulate among them at high speed. It was assumed that each flounder can make at most one contact per period while each shark is restricted to some number greater than 1.

5. The monopolistic aspects of this process were not explored in Reiter (1959).

6. See Green, 1974.

7. The K-core is a concept closely related to Ψ-stability (Luce and Raffer, 1958). Here the function Ψ allows all changes resulting in a coalition of no more than K players. The connection with Ψ-stability was pointed out to me by L. Hurwicz.

8. The symbol $\mathscr{C}_j$, defined in "The Meeting Process" section which follows, denotes the subset of consumers who meet trader j.

9. If trader j knows the meeting process, and if he assumes individual bids to be independent, he can calculate the probability of receiving a given vector of bids from knowledge of $\hat{q}^j$. An alternative formulation would express traders' information in the latter form to begin with, that is, by a subjective probability measure over the vector of bids received.

10. Recall that k^j is the number of contacts trader j can make in a period.

11. The notation (x^i) denotes the vector whose components are x^i, where it is understood that $i = 1, \ldots, n$. Similarly for (x^j), where it is understood that $j = n+1, \ldots, m$. No confusion need result from this abuse of notation.

12. Profit to the trader is measured here from the viewpoint of the consumer; that is, a negative quantity indicates a net flow from consumers to trader.

13. Notice that if consumer i is certain of his alternatives, his bidding distribution is positive on the set of trades, at least as preferred by him as the best trade available to him in a form of the static demand responses.

14. A class of learning behaviors "between" defensive and probability matching is also possible. It would be interesting to investigate such cases.

15. The number 1 denotes the vector whose total components are unity.

16. $\mathcal{V}^1(a)$ denotes $\mathcal{V}^1(p_a)$ where $p_a(a) = 1$; $p_a(x) = 0$ if $x \neq a$.

17. Vernon Smith pointed out to me that the international gold market is similar to the process presented here. In that market the institution which permits full multilaterial clearing to be achieved with traders who deal with only part of the market is a final stage, consisting of a tâtonnement among the traders.

REFERENCES

Futia, Carl A. "A Stochastic Approach to Economic Dynamics." Murray Hill, N.J.: Bell Telephone Laboratories. Mimeographed.

Green, Jerry R. "The Stability of Edgeworth's Recontracting Process," *Econometrica* 42:21 (Jan. 1974).

Hurwicz, Leonid; Radner, Roy; and Reiter, Stanley. "A Stochastic Decentralized Resource Allocation Process: Part II," *Econometrica* 43:3 (May 1975), pp. 363–393.

Lippman, Steven A., and McCall, John J. "The Economics of Job Search: A Survey," *Economic Inquiry* (June 1976), pp. 155–189.

Luce, D., and Raiffa, H. *Games and Decisions.* New York: John Wiley and Sons, Inc., 1958, pp. 220–236 (chapter 10).

Reiter, Stanley. "A Market Adjustment Mechanism," Institute Paper No. 1, School of Industrial Management, Purdue University, West Lafayette, Indiana (Dec. 1959).

Rothchild, M. "Searching for the Lowest Price When the Distribution of Prices Is Unknown," *Journal of Political Economy* (July-Aug. 1974), pp. 189–212.

Schmeidler, D. "A Remark on Microeconomic Models of an Economy and a Game: Theoretic Interpretation of Walras Equilibrium," Minneapolis (Mar. 1976). Mimeographed.

Shapley, L., and Shubik, M. "Trade Using One Commodity as a Means of Payment," Disc. Paper No. R-1851-NSF (Apr. 1976), Rand Corp., Santa Monica, California.

The Place of an Individual in an Economy

Edward Ames

This paper is a narrative of the discovery of Generalized Non-Hicksian Utility Functions (GNHUFs). Theorists will, for this reason, consider it fictional, apocryphal, anecdotal, unscientific, and unscholarly. A longtime student of economic systems other than our own, I originally drafted a properly abstract, formal, and arid account of the matter. Theorists told me it was useless: it is well known all consumers are Hicksian. So my result was uninteresting.

I need not argue the first point. To a systems economist, however, the possibility of yet another system is news. The little green men, who come in their saucers to visit the ETHIC Laboratories, may not frequent Marshall Field, General Mills, route 128, or other haunts of terrestrial economic life, but their economies have unexpected features.

A GNHUF is a special kind of price-dependent utility function (see Pollak, 1977). Prices are the essential data from competitive price economies. To say a GNHUF consumer has a price-dependent utility function means that his preferences change with his economic surroundings. His liking for gasoline is really affected when there is a new oil crisis—he does not simply buy less because the price has gone up. An economy of such people is different.

Although price-dependent utility functions are well known and frequently difficult to analyze, GNHUFs have not hitherto been noticed and some have very simple properties. To anticipate, it takes five things to characterize a GNHUF consumer: (1) the n-vector x, which one must choose—an ordinary commodity bundle; (2) an $(n + 1)$—vector (p, y), an ordinary price-income vector; (3) a map of f from R_t^{n+1} to R_t^n, called the *lifestyle*, a rule of behavior which the consumer prefers to all other rules of behavior. The only restrictions upon f are that $f_i \geq 0$, and $\sum_i^n p_i f_i \equiv y$. The ith component of f, say f_i, is the individual's demand function for good i; (4) a function $v(x,f)$, $v \leq 1$, $v = 1$ if and only if $x = f$. Given v, it is convenient to name $1 - v$ the frustration, for it measures the loss of welfare the consumer suffers if he is unable to set $x = f$; and (5) a nonnegative perception function $g\ (p,y)$ which measures the way the consumer's economic surroundings affect his well-being. (This consumer *does* look at prices, including the price of his own

24

services as basic social valuations.) Finally, then, a GNHUF is written $U = V(x / f(p,y))g(p,y)$.

Two GNHUF consumers may have the same lifestyle, but have different frustration and perception functions; they may have different lifestyles, but share either frustration or perception functions, or both. There are, thus, three sets of reactions by which GNHUF consumers may be described, and these are independent of each other. It will be shown that there are non-countably many GNHUFs for any lifestyle.

Hicksian consumers must have lifestyles (demand functions) which satisfy Slutsky's condition. GNHUF consumers might, but need not, have such lifestyles. They might have money illusion, or other peculiar behavior. In particular (since their preferences are defined over lifestyles and not commodity bundles), they need not feel that "more is better." All in all, economics of GNHUF consumers may make different social choices from economies with similar resources and institutions which are populated by Hicksian consumers. Section III will give a simple example of this basic result.

Without claiming in any way that a GNHUF consumer lives on this planet, or that the luxuriant flowering of Hicksian utility theory of the past forty years is about to be withered by the icy blast of non-Hicksian theory (turning microtheorists into technological dinosaurs), I shall proceed with a narrative of the discovery of GNHUFs.

I

The only economic systems studied so far are those of *Homo sapiens*, and, perhaps, bees, the latter of whom are thought to be strictly nonlearning creatures. For this reason, the declassification of the archives of the Laboratories for the study of Extra-Terrestrial Hyper-Intelligent Creatures (ETHIC) will be welcomed by economists everywhere. There is now a modest (though intriguing) body of information about intelligent, inhuman species and their economic systems. The following discussion will present some of these data, collected from studies of ETHIC guests.[1]

A brief summary of ETHIC procedures will help the discussion. Once linguistic problems have been reduced to manageable levels, guests are given a daily "income" (plastic tokens) which they may "spend" at a commissary.[2] The goods "sold" there vary according to the needs of the guests and may, when appropriate, include iron filings (dietary supplement, junk food), methane or ammonia (atmospheric enrichment), garments of appropriate configuration (where feasible and appropriate), rental of computer terminals or dice (for entertainment), and so on. Prices and incomes vary randomly from day to day, on the vertices, and faces of a hypercube in a price-income space of suitable dimension. Individual demand functions can efficiently be estimated under these controlled conditions. All transactions are photographed, so that guests and commissary personnel can be interviewed about incidents of interest. In addition, questions of economics always arise in regularly scheduled interviews.

In what follows, an individual is designated by a superscript number referring to his group. ETHIC has found that a group is composed of "like" individuals, while different groups are "unlike." (Different groups are composed of different biological species while members of a group are members of one species.) For any group i, ETHIC seeks to identify (a) a preference ordering p^i, utility function U^i, and a set f^i, which will be called a *lifestyle*. That is, f^i is an element of F, with

$$F = \{f^i | f^i = (f^i_1, \ldots, f^i_n); f^i_j \equiv f^i_j(p_1, \ldots, p_n, y) \equiv f^i_j(q); f^i_j \geq 0; \sum_{j=1}^{n} f^i_j p_j = y\}.$$

An element of F is, thus, a vector of demand functions, which use up all of the individual's income, whatever prices may prevail.

A simple extension of this concept of lifestyle makes $f^i = (f^i_1, \ldots, f^i_n)$ into a supply and demand system: (a) $f^i_j \equiv f^i_j(p_i \ldots p_n)$ and (b) $\sum_i f_i p_i \equiv 0$ for every vector $(p_1 \ldots p_n)$. Then $f^i_j \geq 0$ is referred to as a demand function and $f^i_j \leq 0$ as a supply function; evidently, an individual may supply a particular good under certain price conditions and demand it under others. Thus, the property "j is a commodity demanded" (f^i_j is a demand function) may only hold in certain subsets of the non-negative orthant of prices.

The records of ETHIC have isolated a class of utility function found among some of its visitors, but hitherto not known in human populations. It is useful to present briefly some of the evidence which led to the identification of these Generalized Non-Hicksian Utility Functions. This section will describe the way in which the biological existence of these functions was discovered, and will give some of their elementary properties. (They turn out to be a special form of what Pollak [1977] has termed "price dependent preferences.") Section II will discuss whether one should regard GNHUFs as being genetically determined or in some sense learned. Section III will indicate that economic systems of GNHUF individuals may make social choices which organizations of Hicksian individuals would never make.

Omitting some details, we first outline the sequence of events which led to the discovery of the GNHUF, beginning with group 7.

Group 7

Group 7, an early group of visitors was very difficult to deal with and left ETHIC prematurely, leaving behind a trail of unanswered but disturbing questions. One cannot be certain that GNHUF individuals were involved, but detailed examination of the interview reveals the following passage. An interview was in progress, in which guests were asked to make binary comparisons of commodity bundles:

Q. Now please place a check mark opposite the bundle you would prefer in list 1, page 4.
A. I can't, obviously.
Q. Do you mean that the instruction is not clear? Let me repeat. Look at . . .
A. No, idiot, the instruction is clear but impossible.
Q. Do you mean that you are indifferent among the bundles?
A. Fool, you haven't given me enough information.
Q. What more do you need?
A. Take me to the commissary, and I'll give you my preference there.
Q. Why can't you answer the question here, but can answer it there? Is our description of the goods inadequate?
A. Description, shmescription. You haven't told us the values of the goods.
Q. But surely . . .
A. Prices arc fundamental information about the stupid values which your idiotic society places upon the commodities. How can I choose rationally among things if I don't know what they are worth?
Q. Are you the sort of creature who buys expensive things just to show off to his neighbors? [Q. is breaking training rules, but he has been provoked.—E.A.]
A. In an economy of a wise species, society values precious things highly; a foolish species will value precious things cheaply. Knowing you, I can safely prefer the goods which you consider worthless.

The interview terminated untidily. Group 7 clearly had some sort of price-dependent preferences. ETHIC suspected *ex post* that observed preferences would be distorted from their standard by the bad relations between the group and the laboratories. ETHIC perceived that group 7's preferences (which they had hitherto considered Veblenesque) were, in fact, Hayekite[3]: prices are the (marginal) social valuations of a competitive price economy; they provide a consumer with information about the opinions of mankind; and a consumer with a decent respect for the opinions of his fellows will take prices into account in his preferences.

Group 19

Group 19, more cooperative than group 7, had a technically intractable behavior. Consider the following tape.

Q. I apologize for taking up your time, but our econometrician has a problem. Do you mind?
A. Certainly not. What is it?
Q. He has plotted your demand functions by our normal procedure, but your interviews bother him.
A. Why so?
Q. Well, Tuesday you said you preferred bundle A to bundle B, and on Wednesday you preferred bundle B to bundle A.
A. What is the difficulty?

Q. Well, if your preferences really changed on Wednesday, then, he says, his estimation technique must be applied separately to separate subperiods.

A. But no. My demand behavior remained the same throughout. My preferences changed from day to day, because prices changed from day to day. Surely my behavior is a more fundamental attribute of mine than my preferences, which are mainly unrealizable states of mind!

At this time, ETHIC economists began an investigation of the class of preference orderings which were compatible with a given demand system. But the only tractable cases seemed to be those which merely made monotone transformations of Hicksian utility functions. ETHIC found it could only map price-income changes into monotone transformations of a given Hicksian utility function.

A later group of visitors (group 23) made, in effect, the same point as had group 17. Moreover, their demand system, f^{23}, failed to satisfy Slutsky's condition. (ETHIC econometricians were convinced that their techniques were capable of distinguishing Slutsky from non-Slutsky behavior.) Theorists were once again uncertain how to interpret their observations.

Group 31

Group 31 consisted of five members with very clearly defined patterns of consumption, and their ship had, in effect, customized service facilities for each crew member. Members of the group could make binary preference comparisons of commodity bundles, but only if (a) prices and incomes were given to them, and (b) they were also able to communicate with each other before making the comparison.

Group 31, like group 19, used prices as social valuations in their binary rankings of bundles. They were indifferent among points on their individual demand functions. That is to say, if q and q' are two price-income combinations yielding different values $f(q)$ and $f(q')$ for the individual's lifestyle, individuals talked as if they were indifferent between $f(q)$ and $f(q')$. *However,* this was not strictly the case. Individual i was indifferent between $f(q)$ and $f(q')$ if, and only if, the incomes of other members of the group were simultaneously changed in an appropriate way. Given a pair of commodity bundles (x,x') and price-income combinations (q,q'), the members of the group could make a binary choice between x and x' only if they exchanged information on each other's incomes. No other information was exchanged.

All that members of group 31 could say about their perceived welfare was: "We each have a role in operating our craft. We are unhappy if we cannot carry it out. Moreover, in any event, our welfare depends on our status." ETHIC believes that when members of this group change jobs (for whatever reason) they change their lifestyles.

These examples will be concluded with the following.

Group 73

One day, after group 73 had been at ETHIC for some time, the commissary called urgently for a doctor. A guest was lying on the floor; it had changed in color, emitted a cloud of brownish, malodorous vapor, and shrunk by about one-quarter of its normal volume. Staff members were greatly concerned. Another member of the group arrived with the doctor and seemed quite calm. He went to his afflicted comrade, spoke gently with the victim, and then asked the doctor if he was allowed to remove a small amount of good j from the victim's shopping cart. When it did so, the victim visibly relaxed, struggled to its "feet," and apologized for the tumult. In a matter of half an hour, it had returned to normal size and hue, and by the next day was ready to be interviewed about its experience.

From an economist's point of view (disregarding medical details), its story was as follows: "I have [it said] a very well-established lifestyle, described by the function $f^{73}(q)$. Whenever I am able to 'do my thing,' then I am happy; if I cannot, I am miserable, with the effects which you saw. I realized, leaving the commissary, that I had been given more of good j than I had ordered. I was miserable, for I thought I was required (for some unknown reason) to keep the excess. I would have been just as unhappy if I had received *less* of good j than I wanted."

A member of group 73, it turned out, could be represented by a demand system, f^{73}, and the price-dependent utility function: U^{73}:

$$U^{73}(x|f(q)) = \begin{cases} \overline{U} \text{ if } x = f(q) \\ \underline{U} \text{ otherwise.} \end{cases} \quad \overline{U} > \underline{U}; \ f \text{ a demand system}$$

That is to say: Suppose an individual confronts the given price income vector $\overline{q} = (\overline{p}_1, \ldots, \overline{p}_n, \overline{y})$; he maximizes his utility if he selects the consumption vector x, so that $x = f^{73}(\overline{q})$. If he does so, his utility function has the value $\overline{U}$; otherwise it has the value $\underline{U} < \overline{U}$.

The price-dependent utility function U^{73} is an example of a Generalized Non-Hicksian Utility Function. More formally:

DEFINITION 1. Let $f \in F$ be a lifestyle and $X = \{x | x \in R_+^{n+1}\}$ be the set of vectors of (non-negative) consumptions. Then any mapping $U(x|f): R_+^{n+1} \to R$, such that (a) at every $q \in \{(p_1, \ldots, p_n, y) | p_i, y \geq 0\}$, $U(x|f(p_1, \ldots, p_n, y)) \leq U(f(p_1, \ldots, p_n, y) | f(p_1, \ldots, p_n, y))$ and equality implies $x = f(q)$ is a *Generalized Non-Hicksian Utility Function*. Two examples follow.

EXAMPLE 1'. Let $U(v_1, \ldots, v_n)$ be a real-valued function attaining a global maximum at the point $(0,0, \ldots, 0)$. Then $U(x_1 - f^j_1, x_2 - f^j_2, \ldots, x_n - f^j_n)$ is a Generalized Non-Hicksian Utility Function for a consumer with demand system $f^j = (f^j_1, \ldots, f^j_n)$.

EXAMPLE 1''. Let $U(v, \ldots, v_n)$ be a real-valued function attaining a global maximum at the point $(1,1, \ldots, 1)$. Then $U(x_1/f^j_1, x_2/f^j_2, \ldots, x_n/f^j_n)$ is a Generalized Non-Hicksian Utility function for a consumer with demand system $f^j = (f^j_1, f^j_2, \ldots, f^j_n)$.

DEFINITION 2. U_f is the set of GNHUF corresponding to the demand system $f \in F$.

The following lemma characterizes U_f. The proofs, being elementary, are omitted.

LEMMA 3. Let U_f be the set of GNHUF's for $f \in F$ and let G: $\{g(p_1, \ldots, p_n, y) | (p_1, \ldots, p_n, y) \in R_+^{n+1}\} \to \cdot R_+^1$. Then

(a) If $U_1, U_2 \epsilon U_f$ then $(U_1 + U_2) \epsilon U_f$

(b) If $U_1, U_2 \epsilon U_f$ then $U_1 U_2 \epsilon U_f$

(c) If $U_1 \epsilon U_f$, $g \epsilon G$ then $g U_1 \epsilon U_f$

(d) If $g_1, g_2 \epsilon G$, then $g_1 + g_2 \epsilon G$

(e) If $g_1, g_2 \epsilon G$, then $g_1 g_2 \epsilon G$

(f) If $g \epsilon G$, then $1/g \epsilon G$.

There are, therefore, at least as many elements in U_f as there are mappings from R_+^{n+1} into R_+^1. This is a larger number than can be counted on the fingers of even the most exotic ETHIC guest. It is easily verified that GNHUFs are a subclass of the functions "rationalizing price dependent preferences" (Pollak, 1977). Thus when Pollak notes that "surprisingly enough . . . the price-dependent preference orderings which rationalize the [normal price] demand function is not unique," he has made a masterly understatement.

DEFINITION 4. Let $U \epsilon U_f$. Then U is said to be *written in standard form* if
$$U = gV$$
for

$$g \epsilon G, \text{ and } V \equiv \frac{U(x|f)}{U(f|f)}.$$

If U is written in standard form, then it is the product of two factors: one is a function which attains a maximum value equal to 1 at any point $x = f(q)$; the second is some non-negative function of q. For U in standard form, V_U will be termed the *fulfillment factor* and g_U the *perception factor*.

EXAMPLE 5. ETHIC does not know the preferences or utility function of group 31, but it would now rationalize the latter in the following simple spirit. Imagine that the *fulfillment factor* of group 31 were that of group 73:

$$V^{31a} = \begin{cases} 1 \text{ if } x = f(q) \\ V < 1 \text{ otherwise} \end{cases} \text{ (a hypothetical case)}$$

and imagine that each member k of the group defines its "status" by the perception factor.

$$g^{31a,k} = \frac{y^k}{\dfrac{1}{n-1}\sum_{i \neq k} y^i} \quad (n \text{ is the crew size}).$$

(That is, by the ratio of its income to the average incomes of other group members).

Then

$$U^{31a} = g^{31a,k} V^{31a}$$

formally interprets their verbal description: "We each have a role [f] in operating our craft. We are unhappy [$V = \underline{V}$] if we cannot carry it out. Moreover, in any event, our welfare [the value of U] depends on our status

$$[y^k \mid \frac{1}{n-1} \sum_{i \neq k} y^k].\text{"}^4$$

ETHIC's understanding of the GNHUF consumer owes a good deal to group 144, which included a widely-traveled professional economist. Before leaving ETHIC, he presented a useful lecture series, parts of which may be summarized as follows:

> Consider a GNHUF in standard form. A consumer is dissatisfied ($V < 1$) if prevented from following its lifestyle. In a competitive price economy, dissatisfaction may arise because some existing price sector $\bar{p} \equiv (\bar{p}_1, \ldots, \bar{p}_n)$ is not market-clearing. Then at least one consumer is forced to behave suboptimally. Even if $\bar{p}$ is market-clearing ($\sum_{j=1}^{m} f^j_i - 0$ for all i), moreover, there may be imperfections in some market k, so that consumer j cannot find a consumer j' with whom to trade. In this case, $x^j_k \neq f^j_k(\bar{p})$ and $x^{j'}_k \neq f^{j'}_k (\bar{p})$, even though $\sum_r f^r_k(\bar{p}) = 0$.
>
> Thus dissatisfaction exists because the competitive price economy is not in a state of equilibrium. Any disequilibrium state is Pareto inferior to some equilibrium state.

Again:

> Some species on some planets have GNHUFs for which the function $g(p,y)$ attains a maximum for a particular value $\bar{y}$ of current income. In this case, it is straightforward to show that certain initial allocations of resources are Pareto-inferior to others. Indeed, it may even be possible to find a unique initial allocation which is Pareto superior to every other one. . . . It is not clear why this idea causes such difficulties [to ETHIC economists]. Prices are social valuations, and an individual's income is the social valuation which society places on the individual's contribution to society. Your psychologists tell us that many humans have only limited estimates of their own worth; evidently such people will be at odds with a society which persistently ranks their services more highly than they themselves do.

A final observation:

> It is curious that humans should have evolved the elegant theory of the competitive price system, when they have always known that it is not individually incentive compatible. You have Hicksian utility functions, so that your consumers always have constrained optima. This means, as you know, that it is to your advantage to misrepresent your preferences and demand functions.[5] At a more fundamental level, it is always to your advantage to steal, rather than to agree to the budget constraint which the competitive price mechanism imposes on you. What collective masochism causes you to praise the competitive mechanisms and to abominate theft, given your Hicksian natures? If you were GNHUF consumers, if you followed your lifestyle in a competitive price system, you would be at a local bliss point,[6] and you would not wish either to lie or to steal. You would provide an individually incentive compatible environment for a competitive price system. In equilibrium, scarcity would not exist for anyone. I do not wish to offend you, my generous hosts, but your welfare economics seems inappropriate to your basic natures.

II

The discovery of GNHUFs and their analysis by the remarkable lecturer from group 144 led to lively debate and even scholarly acrimony within ETHIC. The cautious viewpoint was that terrestrial utility functions were certainly Hicksian, but there was no reason why extraterrestial utility functions should not be of the GNHUF type. But an inquiry began, among the more adventurous, to determine whether one class of utility function would not suffice for all biological species.

A first study (*ETHIC 1048/2*) argued very simply: the purpose of consumer theory is to account for demand behavior. If individual lifestyles could be estimated directly from market data, it was known that they could be generated by a nondenumerable infinity of utility functions of which one or none was Hicksian (depending on whether the Slutsky equation was or was not met) and the remainder were GNHUF. No further interest attached to the question.

A second paper (*ETHIC 2236/2*) established that GNHUFs were generated by preferences over social states, on the following basis. Let $I\!R^m_+$ be the space of final allocations for individuals, and $x = (x^1, x^2, \ldots, x^m)$, ϵR^m_+, with x^i the allocation to individual i. Now consider individual 1, who has a complete preference ordering on vectors of the form x of the following sort: individual 1 is indifferent between $x = (x^1, x^2, \ldots, x^m)$ and $y = (x^1, y^2, \ldots, y^m)$, if and only if the adjustment mechanism generates the same price vector $p = (p_1, \ldots, p_n)$ for x and y. (One of these prices is the price which rewards consumer 1 for his services.) Then individual 1 has a complete preference ordering on vectors $x^1 \epsilon I\!R^m$ for every price vector p. If this ordering has a (unique) maximal element x^* for each p, this is identified with the value $f(p)$, required by GNHUF theory.

Opponents were quick to object (*ETHIC 2413/3*) on two grounds. First (they said), the GNHUF consumer had preferences defined over lifestyles and not commodity bundles. It would be an interesting *theoretical* question to find out if there were any sort of relation between the two classes of preference orderings; but even if there were, it would be a theoretical curiosity, since the lifestyle is what really counts for these strange beings. Second, they argued, suppose that one brings a subject directly from the commissary to the laboratory, and questions him about his preferences. How can one tell whether his responses reflect the hypothetical situations described by the questioner rather than the real satisfactions (or disappointments) he has just experienced in looking over the commissary price list?

Meanwhile, ETHIC's Skinnerian experimental psychologists entered the battle. Look, they said, at the GNHUF $U(x|f(p))$. If $f(p)$ represents learned behavior, then in principle this behavior can be modified. Let us inquire whether any future groups of GNHUF visitors have had their behavior modified. This proposal, of course, met with general approval, but the findings are mixed. If one supposes that something akin to hypnosis has been used on some visitors, however, interview techniques would underestimate the cases of successful modification. Some visitors said, "But of course our behavior is taught us in schools, in order that it be pleasing to our wise rulers, and through them, to the gods." (*ETHIC 3757/3* has analyzed this case from the point of view of radical political economy.) Other visitors, asked about behavior modification, simply shuddered. (*ETHIC 5879/4* interprets these cases from a reactionary, Orwellian perspective.)

From a Heisenbergian point of view, another paper (*ETHIC 7792/3*) has argued that the act of measuring a GNHUF would induce a change in the demand system $f(p)$. "One cannot suppose that all of these visitors came from planets with competitive price mechanisms. Being intelligent, however, they quickly mastered the rules of our economy. Thus if they came from an economy in which there was central planning, they used a behavior function $g(p_1, \ldots, p_m)$, where p_g was their plan for good g, not its price; they merely transformed some g into the function f which we observed" (Ames, 1976).[7]

To this, however, came the stern reply of the contingent with Ph.D.s from a celebrated Midwestern institution (*ETHIC 9956/4*): "Since the competitive price system is obviously the most natural and most perfect of all mechanisms, and since our visitors are all of intelligence at least equal to our own, we must conclude that their economic systems are at least as natural and perfect as our own, which, as everyone knows, is a competitive price system."

The ETHIC anthropologists, however, objected (*ETHIC 9630/5*) to this view that utility functions might be innate. If understanding of the competitive price mechanism were innate (presumably of genetic origin), they argued, then a taste for colored television sets must also have been programmed into our ancestors, living in the Olduvai Gorge—so that, without knowing it, they must have secretly longed for someone to invent them. It seems unlikely, they argued, that this can have been the case—even though if it were, economists could regard technological change as really endogenous and biologically predetermined, with only matters of timing being left as economic phenomena.

These various points of debate have certainly not yet been resolved. There was a consensus that investigations should be vigorously pursued. The next section reports on a case which casts some doubt upon the universality of the Hicksian hypothesis. It involves a problem of social choice in which GNHUF-like optimization led to an outcome which would have been impossible had the subjects been Hicksian.

III

It is well known but worth repeating that the problem of designing an economic system[8] is as follows: one is given an environment e in some class E. This environment is an assignment of tastes (utilities), technologies, and resource endowments to a set of individual agents. For each such environment $e \epsilon E$, one selects a criterion so as to identify the set of desirable actions $P(e)$ which economic activity might bring about. Then one seeks to construct an appropriate message set M, such that the agents in question can use M to reach an agreement (find an equilibrium message), which will in turn bring about an action in the set $P(e)$. Thus systems design has to do with constructing message sets and means of translating equilibrium messages with actions which are desirable for each environment in some class E of environments.

Once it became clear that a number of groups of ETHIC guests consti- tuted unfamiliar and distinctive economic environments, it was natural to investigate the decision-making systems which had brought them to ETHIC. A representative account of one such system follows.

The head of the ETHIC engineering division approached the economics division with a problem. The craft of group 97 appeared to have functioned in an impossible way, and the economists were asked to study the decision making structure of this group. Here was the situation:

The group consisted of an engineer (E) and a researcher (R). Each was given control of a single instrument with three settings.[9] If E selected setting a^{E_i} and R selected setting a^{R_j}, the pair (a^{E_i}, a^{R_j}) of settings induced a perform- ance $(x^{E_{ij}}, x^{R_{ij}})$. Immediately on takeoff, E received a matrix printout X^E and R a matrix printout X^R; each used his information to select a setting, without any exchange of information with the crewmate. Later, however, a discus- sion took place, and a mid-course correction was permitted. The two mat- rices in question were

$$X^E = \begin{pmatrix} 0 & 9 & 4 \\ 7 & 1 & 8 \\ 6 & 7 & 2 \end{pmatrix} \qquad X^R = \begin{pmatrix} 8 & 6 & 4 \\ 0 & 8 & 3 \\ 7 & 1 & 9 \end{pmatrix}$$

For E, choosing a setting meant choosing a row of X^E; for R, choosing a setting meant choosing a column of X^R. As it happened, E had chosen setting 3, R had chosen setting 1, and the performance was thus $(6,7)$. The engineers were certain that the performance of both engineering and research func- tions in the craft were accurately measured by the numbers X^E and X^R, respectively.

The problem was the following. The crew asserted flatly that it had no communication with Flight Control over its choice of instrument setting. The data in each matrix could only be calculated, by instruments on board, after takeoff. The performance matrix (X^E, X^R) led to the ordinary (vector) partial ordering:

(9,6)	(6,7)	(2,9)
>	>	>
(8,3)	(4,4)	(1,8)
>		>
(7,1)		(0,8)
>		
(7,0)		

If each crew member adopted a Max Min strategy, the crew would select setting (3.3) on takeoff. Since the corresponding payoff (2,9) is Pareto optimal, no course correction would be needed. Evidently, this did not happen.

Imagine, however, that there had been some centralization of decision making. If Flight Control had forbidden E to use setting 3 on takeoff, E would then have used setting 2; if R were forbidden to use setting 3 on takeoff, he also would have used setting 2. Thus,

If E alone is restricted, E selects 2 and R selects 3; the outcome is (8,3).

If R alone is restricted, R selects 2 and E selects 3; the outcome is (7,1).

If both E and R are restricted, both select 2; the outcome is (1,8).

In the first two cases, midflight correction would produce (9,6); in the third, it would produce (2,9). Indeed, only if Flight Control forced E to use setting 1 would the observed outcome (6,7) have been observed. The crew, however, insisted that theirs was a decentralized decision-making process, in which Flight Control played no part.

Naturally, the Economics Division of ETHIC was interested in the problem, and (after verifying the reasoning of the engineers) decided to interview group 97 directly. After suitable clarification of terms, the group made the following statement:

If this [decision-making system] generated only an empty set of feasible actions, we could never have got here. We were, of course, constrained by the tub we came in (our initial resource endowment). Our instruments measure our individual performances on a scale of 0 to 10. We each can perform at all levels on this scale, but E most prefers $X^E = 6$ and R most prefers $X^R = 7$. We also prefer to behave efficiently, other things being equal. Let $P(X^E,X^R)$ be the cardinality of the upper contour set of (X^E,X^R)—i.e., $P(8,3) = 2$; $P(0,8) = 3$, etc. We have the utility functions,

$$U^E(X^E,X^R) = \frac{(X^E)^{.6}\,(10\text{-}X^E)^{.4}}{P(X^E,X^R)}$$

$$U^R(X^E,X^R) = \frac{(X^R)^{.7}\,(10\,X^R)^{.3}}{P\,(X^E,X^R)}$$

and you may easily see that what we did was this: at takeoff, we set our instruments at random. Later, when we have time, we can easily calculate that (6,7) is the best choice for us to make. Nobody told us what to do and what not to do.

This seemed to ETHIC[10] a straightforward response, for by that time it was getting used to GNHUF agents. But one of its economists was led to ask group 97 the following question: "Suppose the exponents of E's utility function had been .2 and .8, and that the exponents of R's utility function had been .9 and .1. Then would you have decided on performance vector (2,9)?" Back came the surprising response, "No, you can't ask that question. Nor can you ask about E's exponent values (.9,.1) and R's exponent values (.6,.4)." Asked why these questions were inadmissible, group 97 replied as follows. "(A) Engineering setting 2 takes us to a place where there is nothing interesting to research; (B) research setting 9 requires that on arrival our research must be of quality 9, which is not acceptable to the hypothesized researcher, so the project is infeasible. Those two crews would never be formed."

This response puzzled ETHIC, which knew the (New)^2 Welfare Economics. The procedure of this study was to select an environment (a pair of utility functions and an initial resource endowment—in this instance a saucer), compute a class of desirable actions (in this case, the class has one element); then one constructs an information system which will realize the optimal action.[11] All at once they are told by group 97 that the approach is backward. One selects a desired action, here (6,7), and then finds a crew which will want to carry out this action; if an action is *a priori* undesirable, here (2,9) and (9,6), one refrains from forming a crew which will execute it. Thus the home of group 97 transforms the design of economic systems into a matter of personnel selection.

Reference has already been made to the economist of group 144. His lecture to ETHIC contained the following comments about group 97.

> It is reasonable to regard group 97 as a coalition, producing a mixture of engineering and research services. An engineer (or a researcher) without a saucer to travel in is obviously less productive than a coalition of an engineer and a researcher using a saucer, providing their joint efforts can maneuver the craft to and from a spot in which research of adequate quality can be done. Consider an economic environment consisting of three engineers having utility functions with exponents (.9,.1), (.6,.4), (.2,.8) and three researchers having utility functions with exponents (.6,.4), (.7,.3), and (.9,.1). You have been told that only the crew which selects performance (6,7)—that is, a crew with engineers and researchers having exponents (.6,.4) and (.7,.3) respectively—will take the craft to any point worth going to. You may wish to conclude that the other four individuals will stay home and tend to whatever passes for their knitting back on their home planet.
>
> But there is a difference between mathematical and other forms of existence. Do these other four individuals have any existence other than mathematical (in which they are useless as space travelers)? Consider two planets I have visited, located at points X and Y. Residents of X are made from instructions coded on DNA molecules, just as you are. It has been determined that their utility functions are determined by proteins located at 1,111 positions on the molecule, and it is known how to produce an individual having any desired utility function. At Y, on the other hand, utility functions are psychologically determined, and may be altered by a process which you would call "deep hypnosis." If you ask an individual agent from either X or Y what his utility function is, he will tell you truthfully. He may have been purposefully designed to have that utility function, but that (so to speak) is no concern of his.[12] If you know no more about group 97 than you have here set down, you cannot tell whether your friends E and R were especially designed so that they would wish to visit ETHIC. You know, after all, that their resource endowment (the saucer) was designed to bring them here, and it is equally reasonable to suppose the crew was similarly designed. In that sense, they are biological realizations of a mathematical existence. Remember that your own social and intellectual conditioning processes (though cruder than those at X and Y) are designed to train individuals for tasks which your economy needs to have executed. Part of the training involves persuading individuals to want to execute these tasks.

IV

This brief raid upon the bulging ETHIC archives suggests that the further study of GNHUF species will prove a rich mine for exoeconomists. The study of systems where scarcity is present only in disequilibrium conditions is bound to alter their views about many questions. The concluding remarks which follow, however, are more closely related to the present literature on the human consumer and his economic organizations.

One can determine that an individual is *not* Hicksian by showing that his lifestyle does not satisfy the Slutsky conditions. If it meets those conditions, however, one cannot conclude whether the consumer is Hicksian or GNHUF. The only way to tell is by a very careful test to determine whether his lifestyle originates in a preference ordering of commodity bundles or a preference ordering of lifestyles.

Some GNHUF consumers have lifestyles which are incompatible with a more-is-better Hicksian preference ordering. Decision-making systems, made up of some agents, may make choices which no similar organization of Hicksian agents would make (see section III). Thus, in some cases, one can distinguish between social choices of GNHUF and of Hicksian consumers as well as their individual choices.

For example, Hurwicz (1972) has shown that a competitive price mechanism is incentive incompatible for Hicksian consumers. It is incentive compatible for GNHUF consumers. The GNHUF consumer would be tempted to steal (i.e., to violate the budget constraint) only in a general disequilibrium, whereas the Hicksian consumer will always be tempted to steal. Thus if one could determine that no theft occurred during periods of general equilibrium, one could conclude that an economy had GNHUF consumers.

The lifestyle of a GNHUF consumer obviously is influenced by his economic surroundings. The function f, considered here, would have no meaning in an economy without prices. Unless one assumes that there is some *biological* necessity for prices to exist, one must regard the lifestyle as something learned and not innate. It thus seems natural to think of modifying part or all of a GNHUF. Since the preferences, utility functions, and demand functions of Hicksian consumers all change at once, the corresponding modification of lifestyle is much more of an "identity crisis" for Hicksian consumers.

This remark is conjectural, but it serves to introduce a comment about economic adjustment. The usual problem of economic adjustment is to take a collection of agents with given preferences and to design for them a mechanism which will lead *them* to make socially optimal (i.e., undominated) choices. But there is an inverse to that problem: given a mechanism and a particular choice, to "find" a collection of agents for whom that choice, given that mechanism, will be optimal. The expression "to find" can include the concept "to modify."

In the twentieth century, various governments have chosen objectives, designed mechanisms, and talked of the "perfectibility of man." This sounds like the inverse problem just outlined. In practice, they have instituted forced labor camps because their population otherwise would not operate the mechanism as desired. The forced labor camp seems to be a constraint upon agents rather than a modification of the preferred behavior of agents. For if modification of lifestyles had actually taken place, the camps would not be needed.

It may be that these economic systems must use force because their subjects are Hicksian and have fixed ability function. On other planets, with GNHUF residents, governments might have to use the equivalent of forced labor camps for a different reason: although the lifestyles of their subjects can be changed, governments have wrongly calculated the properties of lifestyles which would enable their economic mechanisms to attain the goals desired. In such economies, the question "How should our subjects behave?" would be meaningful and operational.

One of the good ways of determining the boundaries of the class of feasible mechanisms to be operated by Hicksian consumers is to consider the mechanisms which can efficiently be operated by GNHUF consumers with endogenous lifestyles. In the limit, one might say, GNHUF consumers go to fixed lifestyles. This limit should turn out to be the boundary of the class of mechanisms which Hicksian consumers could operate efficiently.

That is why the study of little green men is not only of biological interest but also of practical concern for students of economic systems populated by *Homo sapiens*.

NOTES

Some of this material has appeared previously (see entries under my name in References); I am indebted to Alain Cotta (1974) for comments on this. I also thank Robert Clower for helpful comments on an earlier version of this paper. Finally, I have been influenced by the doctoral research of David Conn, Mo-Yin Tam, Willie R. Taylor, and Bengt-Arne Wickstrom. None of them, however, should be blamed for either my views or my mistakes.
  1. It may be useful to regard ETHIC guests as little green men in flying saucers, even though they are of varied sizes, colors, and sexes and travel in many kinds of vehicles.
  2. The published literature relevant to this subject relates to situations in which subjects are either psychiatric patients (Ayllon and Azrin, 1968; Kazdin, 1977) or laboratory animals (Kagel et al., 1975; Kagel and Winkler, 1972). ETHIC visitors were neither of these, and some were undoubtedly emotionally more stable and intellectually superior to their hosts. They were, however, subjected (voluntarily, of course) to an intensive study under controlled conditions.
  3. The welfare of a Veblenesque consumer depends on the consumption of other individuals, as well as on his own. A Hayekite consumer uses prices as a measure of the value which society places upon goods (von Hayek, 1945).

4. My paper (1972) gives a detailed analysis of a GNHUF's having marginal rates of substitution everywhere defined.

5. Hurwicz (1972) uses the term "incentive compatible" to describe economic systems in which, broadly speaking, it is not in the self-interest of individuals to break the rules. He shows, in competitive price mechanisms, individuals who misrepresent their demand functions (and implicitly their utility functions) may end up better off than individuals who do not. Evidently, however, it did not occur to this law-abiding professor that in such an economy individuals had an incentive to violate the budget constraint by stealing.

6. That is to say, at the point $x = f(p)$, marginal utilities vanish, and behavior is (locally) unconstrained. This is the property of GNHUFs which violates the Hicksian axiom $x > x'$ implies $U(x) > U(x')$.

7. Compare the GNHUF for a planned economy in my book (1976) with the analogous GNHUF for a competitive price economy in my paper (1972).

8. Here we summarize Reiter's (1977) "triangular diagram."

9. There is a remarkable similarity between this decision problem and example 3 in Camacho (1972).

10. An ETHIC economist with academic experience claimed (without proof) the following. How, he asked, do undergraduates select the grade point index they wish? The student takes n courses, receiving a grade of x_i in course i ($i = 1, \ldots, n$). The lowest and highest grades given by faculty are a and c. If the student's utility function is

$$U = (\frac{1}{n} x_i - a)^b (c - \frac{1}{n} \Sigma x_i)^{1-b}$$

it is easily shown that the optimal index for the student is

$$\frac{1}{n} \Sigma x_i = bc + (1-b)a.$$

The parameter b is the result (he claimed) of social pressure from parents (who try to increase b) and fellow students (who try to lower b). Thus GNHUF behavior is found among humans, to the extent that undergraduates are human.

11. I give an illustration of a GNHUF individual (Ames, 1976) in a planned economy, who (because of a budget constraint) may be unable to behave optimally. Moreover, Cotta (1974) has considered various constraints upon a central planner which may prevent him from selecting that plan which elicits optimal performance from the other agents in the economy.

12. An ETHIC economist who had once been employed in a business school remarked, "What is odd about all this? Scruffy seniors are admitted into M.B.A. and economics graduate programs. Within a year's time, their clothing will have become differentiated, as they have learned what kind of demand functions they must acquire in their coming careers."

REFERENCES

Ames, E. "*A Class of Non-Hicksian Utility Functions*," Stony Brook Working Paper No. 55 (Apr. 1972) (mimeo).

_____. "A Priceless Planned Economy," in J. Thornton, ed., *Economic Analysis of the Soviet-Type System*. Cambridge: Cambridge University Press, 1976, pp. 75–89.

Ayllon, T., and Azrin, N. *The Token Economy: A Motivational System for Therapy and Rehabilitation*. New York: Appleton-Century-Crofts, 1968.

Camacho, A. "Centralization and Decentralization of Decision-Making Mechanisms: A General Model," in *Jahrbuch der Wirtschaft Osteuropas*. Munich: Olzog, 1972, 3:45–66.

Cotta, A. "Le Pouvoir et la strategie du chef dans un systeme centralise," *Revue d'Economie Politique*, 84 (1974), 399–415.

Hurwicz, L. "On Informationally Decentralized Systems," in C. B. McGuire and R. Radner, eds., *Decision and Organization*. Amsterdam: North Holland, 1972, pp. 1–29.

Kagel, J. H.; Battalio, R. C.; Rachlin, H.; Green, L.; Basmann, R. L.; and Klemm, W. R. "Experimental Studies of Consumer Demand Behavior Using Laboratory Animals," *Economic Inquiry*, 13 (1975), 22–38.

Kagel, J. H., and Winkler, R. C. "Behavioral Economics: Areas of Cooperative Research between Economics and Applied Behavioral Analysis," *Journal of Applied Behavior Analysis*, 5 (1972), 335–342.

Kazdin, A. E. *The Token Economy: A Review and Evaluation*. New York: Plenum, 1977.

Pollak, R. A. "Price Dependent Preferences," *American Economic Review* (Mar. 1977), pp. 64–75.

Reiter, S. *Information and Preference in the (New)^2 Welfare Economics*. American Economic Association Papers and Proceedings (1977), pp. 226–234.

von Hayek, F. A. "The Use of Knowledge in Society," *American Economic Review*, 35 (1945), 519–530.

Technical Change Inclinations of a Resource Monopolist

Morton I. Kamien and Nancy L. Schwartz

Firms try to influence demand for their products through marketing efforts and research and development activity. They advertise, develop new uses for their products, and modify existing applications. While the bulk of these activities are directed toward increasing demand, some are intended to reduce peak demand and, thereby, "smooth" sales.

Our particular interest is in a monopolistic owner of a nonrenewable resource, such as fossil fuel. In the very long run, the public or private sector may develop a substitute for the irreplenishable resource (see Dasgupta and Heal, 1974, and Kamien and Schwartz, 1978). In the interim, modest technical advances influence the depletion rate of the resource. The main questions addressed in this paper are the direction of technical change (resource using or resource saving) most profitable for the monopolistic resource owner and its compatibility with "society's" interests. The broad research context of which this paper is a part is described in Howe's review in this volume and in the survey by Peterson and Fisher (1977).

Although previously assumed to be an exogenous event, technical advance has more recently been regarded as an endogenous variable, motivated by the quest for profit and responsive to resource allocation. Thus some recent work has focused on the incentives in a market environment for developing a substitute for an exhaustible resource. Optimal usage of the resource, perhaps mindful that a substitute may appear eventually, is also investigated, especially under uncertainty regarding the total stock of the resource (see Kemp, 1976; Cropper, 1976; Gilbert, 1979; and Loury, 1978).

This work is in the spirit of the foregoing efforts, in that we consider both the optimal rate of resource depletion when its total stock is uncertain and also the type of technical advance that may be sought in response to its increasing scarcity. It also differs in a number of significant ways.

A monopolist owns a resource stock and wishes to deplete it at an expected profit-maximizing rate. The resource is not consumed directly; it is a factor of production. A manufacturing industry buys the resource competitively and combines it with another factor to turn out a final good, according to a Cobb-Douglas production function with constant returns to scale. Hence the demand the monopolist faces is affected by the demand for the final

41

good and also by the technology governing the resource's use in production. Our analysis is partial equilibrium, focusing on the exhaustible resource and taking as given the supply of the other productive factor and the demand for the final good.

The paper is organized as follows. The model is presented as an optimal control problem under uncertainty and the solution found. The optimizing extraction plan is discussed at some length (as it is of interest in its own right) before the main thrust of the paper. The technical change inclinations of the monopolist are then considered and compared with those of society. The impact on this assessment of an artificially foreshortened time horizon is also considered. Further support is lent to the generality of the findings by the discovery that the same conclusions emerge even if the supposition about the probability distribution is altered substantially.

Within the context of our model, we show that if the expected resource stock is relatively small (large), both the resource owner and his customers will benefit from a technical change that causes the resource to be used less (more) rapidly. There is an intermediate range of resource stock size for which the interests may conflict; the resource monopolist would benefit from a technical change leading to more rapid use of the resource, while "society" would be harmed thereby. A number of other observations on optimal resource exploitation under uncertainty also emerge from our study.

THE MODEL

The total quantity of the resource held by the monopolist is uncertain. The probability density over the total quantity is assumed to be uniform over an interval about S, the expected quantity at the moment of planning $t = 0$. In particular, letting $F(x)$ denote the probability that the initial reserve does not exceed x, we assume

$$F(x) = \begin{cases} 0 & 0 \leq x < S - n \\ (x+n-S)/2n & S - n \leq x < S + n \\ 1 & S + n \leq x \end{cases} \tag{1}$$

so

$$F'(x) = \begin{cases} 1/2n & S - n \leq x \leq S + n \\ 0 & \text{elsewhere.} \end{cases} \tag{2}$$

Thus there is at least $S - n$ and no more than $S + n$ of the resource, and a uniform density is ascribed over the interval spanned by these limits. We suppose $S > n$. The width of the interval of uncertainty is $2n$; so n measures the extent of uncertainty. A better measure of the degree of uncertainty is n/S, which gives the uncertainty relative to the expected total. If the initial reserve is known exactly, $n = 0$.

The resource is employed as a factor of production. The resource-using industry has a Cobb-Douglas production function for output Q in two factors; capital K and the irreplenishable resource R:

$$Q = AR^aK^{1-a} \qquad\qquad 0 < a < 1. \tag{3}$$

The capital stock grows or declines exponentially, according to

$$K(t) = K_o e^{bt}. \tag{4}$$

The constant b may be positive, zero, or negative. We take the price of the production sector's output to be unity. The resource is employed at a rate so that its marginal product equals its price p:

$$p = \partial Q/\partial R = aA(K/R)^{1-a}. \tag{5}$$

In view of (4) and (5), the cash flow to the resource-supplier at time t (prior to exhaustion) is

$$p(t)R(t) = Be^{b(1-a)t}R^a(t) \tag{6}$$

where

$$B \equiv aAK_o^{1-a}. \tag{7}$$

It is assumed that the resource can be extracted without cost at any rate before it is exhausted. The probability that exhaustion has not occurred by t is $1 - F(x(t))$. The resource supplier seeks an extraction plan to maximize the present value of the expected cash flow:

$$\max B \int_0^T e^{(b(1-a)-r)t} R^a(t)(1-F(x(t))dt \tag{8}$$

subject to

$$x'(t) = R(t) \tag{9}$$
$$x(0) = 0 \tag{10}$$
$$x(T) = S+n \tag{11}$$
$$R(t) \geq 0 \tag{12}$$

where r is the discount rate. We assume

$$r > b(1-a). \tag{13}$$

This means that the capital stock grows no faster than a certain multiple of the interest rate. It also insures convergence of the integrand in (8).

Note that the constant B, defined in (7), affects the value of the optimal policy, but not its selection. Constraints (10) and (9) say that cumulative extraction is zero initially and that it grows with depletion. Extraction is nonnegative, (12). Time T, to be determined optimally, is the date by which the resource is exhausted with certainty; note constraint (11). While an optimal extraction plan is to be determined up to T, it can be followed only until the resource is exhausted, which is some unknown time prior to T.

THE SOLUTION

Define the "current value" Hamiltonian for problem (8)–(12) as

$$H = R^a(1-F) + mR$$

where $m(t)$ is the "current value" multiplier associated with (9). Necessary conditions are that

$$\partial H/\partial R = aR^{a-1}(1-F(x)) + m \leq 0, \; R\partial H/\partial R = 0 \tag{14}$$

$$m' = (r - b(1-a))m - \partial H/\partial x = (r - b(1-a))m + R^a F'(x) \qquad (15)$$
$$H(T) = 0. \qquad (16)$$

Condition (16) arises from the fact that T is to be chosen optimally.

The solution to these conditions is conveniently stated in terms of two constants, defined as follows:

$$S^* \equiv S - (1-a)n/(1+a) \qquad (17)$$
$$k \equiv r/(1-a) - b. \qquad (18)$$

It turns out that there is no finite time by which the resource is optimally exhausted with certainty; that is,

$$T = \infty. \qquad (19)$$

The extraction path takes different functional forms during the initial period when $x < S - n$, so the probability of immediate exhaustion is zero, and subsequently when that probability becomes positive. Denoting the optimal switching time between these two phases as t_1, we have

$$t_1 = -k^{-1} \ln (2an/S^*(1+a)). \qquad (20)$$

The optimal plan calls for

$$R(t) = \begin{cases} kS^* e^{-kt} & 0 \le t < t_1 \\ (2nak/(1+a))e^{-ka(t-t_1)/(1+a)} & t_1 \le t \end{cases} \qquad (21)$$

$$x(t) = \begin{cases} S^*(1 - e^{-kt}) & 0 \le t < t_1 \\ S + n - 2ne^{-ak(t-t_1)/(1+a)} & t_1 \le t \end{cases} \qquad (22)$$

$$m(t) = \begin{cases} -a(kS^* e^{-kt})^{a-1} & 0 \le t < t_1 \\ -a^a[(1+a)/2nk]^{1-a}e^{-ka^2(t-t_1)/(1+a)} & t_1 \le t \end{cases} \qquad (23)$$

$$1 - F(x(t)) = \begin{cases} 1 & 0 \le t < t_1 \\ e^{-ak(t-t_1)/(1+a)} & t_1 \le t. \end{cases} \qquad (24)$$

The extraction plan $R(t)$, and also $x(t)$ and $m(t)$, are continuous throughout, including at t_1.

A more compact view of the solution is through the proportionate rates of change:

$$R'(t)/R(t) = \begin{cases} -k & 0 \le t < t_1 \\ -ka/(1+a) & t_1 \le t \end{cases} \qquad (25)$$

$$m'(t)/m(t) = \begin{cases} k(1-a) & 0 \le t < t_1 \\ -ka^2/(1+a) & t_1 \le t \end{cases} \qquad (26)$$

$$(dF(x(t))/dt)/(1-F) = \begin{cases} 0 & 0 \le t < t_1 \\ ka/(1+a) & t_1 \le t \end{cases} \qquad (27)$$

$$p'(t)/p(t) =$$

$$(1-a)(K'/K - R'/R) = \begin{cases} r & 0 \le t < t_1 \\ r - (1-a)k/(1+a) & t_1 \le t. \end{cases} \qquad (28)$$

DISCUSSION

Inspection of the upper branch of (21) shows that S^* defined in (17) is the certainty-equivalent stock of the resource. The firm's optimal extraction plan during phase I (the interval $0 \le t < t_1$) under uncertainty (1) is precisely the same as if the initial resource stock were known to be exactly S^*. Since $S^* < S$, the extraction rate is lower during phase I, when there is uncertainty, than when the reserves are known precisely (and the expectation is the same). Indeed, since S^* is decreasing in n, it follows that the more uncertainty n, *ceteris paribus*, the slower the resource depletion.

The proportionate rate of resource exhaustion [see (25)] is independent of both the level of reserves and the extent of uncertainty. It depends on the interest rate r, the rate of growth or decline b of the other factor capital, and the elasticity of derived demand for the resource R:

$$- (dR/dp)p/R = 1/(1 - a). \tag{29}$$

The percent decline in phase II (the interval $t_1 \leq t$) is slower than in phase I. Accordingly, the resource price grows at the rate of interest during phase I and more slowly during phase II [see (28)]. It is interesting to note from (27) that during this phase, the realized conditional probability density of immediate exhaustion, given that exhaustion has not yet occurred, is constant and independent of S.

The multiplier m reflects the marginal opportunity cost of extracting a unit of the resource. According to (14), one extracts at a rate such as to equate the marginal opportunity cost of depleting the reserves with the expected marginal profit from sale. During phase I, there is no possibility of immediate exhaustion and the optimal extraction rate declines; thus, the marginal profitability of a unit rises. During phase II, conflicting forces determine the expected marginal profitability. Extraction is declining and, therefore, realized marginal profitability is rising. On the other hand, the probability of realizing profits is falling as the probability of exhausting the reserves grows. As it turns out, the latter effect dominates. The marginal opportunity cost, or marginal expected profitability of extraction, falls during phase II [see (26)].

REMARKS

Feedback Form

The optimal extraction plan can also be stated in terms of the current state rather than time, that is, in so-called feedback form. This gives further insight into the solution and highlights the intertemporal consistency of the solution. That is, recomputation of the optimal path at any $t' > 0$ confirms the optimality for $t \geq t'$ of the path generated at $t = 0$.

Let S_t denote the expected stock of the resource reserves remaining at t, given that exhaustion has not yet occurred by t. In particular, $S_o = S$ and

$$S_t \equiv \begin{cases} S_o - x(t) & 0 \leq t \leq t_1 \\ (S_o + n - x(t))/2 = n e^{-ak(t-t_1)/(1+a)} & t_1 \leq t. \end{cases} \tag{30}$$

During phase I, the expected remaining stock is the amount originally expected, less the amount withdrawn. During phase II, the probability distribution over the remaining stock (given survival to date) is uniform, so the expected remaining stock is half the maximum remaining stock. Also, let S_t^* be the corresponding certainty-equivalent stock at $t \leq t_1$:

$$S_t^* \equiv S_t - (1-a)n/(1+a) = S_o^* e^{-kt} \qquad\qquad 0 \leq t \leq t_1. \qquad (31)$$

The equations in (30) and (31) follow on substituting from (22) for $x(t)$.

With (30) and (31) in (21), the optimal extraction rate at t, $R(t)$, can be written in terms of the contemporaneous certainty-equivalent remaining stock for $t < t_1$ and in terms of the conditional expected remaining stock for $t \geq t_1$:

$$R(t) = \begin{cases} kS_t^* & 0 \leq t \leq t_1 \\ (2ak/(1+a))S_t & t_1 \leq t. \end{cases} \qquad (32)$$

This is the form sought. It is now readily seen from (32) that so long as the probability of immediate exhaustion is zero, the optimal extraction rate is a constant multiple k of the remaining certainty-equivalent resource stock. Once the probability of immediate exhaustion is positive, the optimal extraction rate is a constant fraction (smaller than k) of the expected remaining stock.

Time Horizon

The maximum life of the resource stock has been chosen optimally and it is not finite in this model. Koopmans (1978) and Howe (this volume) have warned that in the distant future, the extraction rate approaches zero, and, generally, we are carried beyond regions of the model for which we have solid empirical knowledge to date. The merits of the Cobb-Douglas function representation, for example, are unknown in the corners. As an attempt to check on how our conclusions are affected by the long, narrow tail that results when $T \to \infty$ is permitted, we solve (8)–(12) with a maximum horizon of $\overline{T} < \infty$ specified. Conditions (14)–(15) are then necessary, but (16) is not.

The resulting $T = \overline{T}$ and the switching time t_1 between phase I and phase II is given implicitly by

$$(1 - e^{-kt_1})/(1 - e^{-kT}) = (S - n)/S^* \qquad (33)$$

where S^* is the certainty-equivalent stock defined in (17). The planned cumulative extraction path is

$$x(t) = \begin{cases} S^*(1 - e^{-kt})/(1 - e^{-kT}) & 0 \leq t \leq t_1 \\ S + n - 2n((e^{-kt} - e^{-kT})/(e^{-kt_1} - e^{-kT}))^{a/(1+a)} & t_1 \leq t \leq \overline{T}. \end{cases} \qquad (34)$$

The proportionate rate of change of current extraction is

$$R'(t)/R(t) = \begin{cases} -k & 0 \leq t \leq t_1 \\ -k[(1 - 1/(1+a))(1 - e^{-k(T-t)})] & t_1 \leq t \leq \overline{T}. \end{cases} \qquad (35)$$

During phase I, the extraction pattern is the familiar one, but the level will be higher if the horizon T is shorter. During phase II, the pattern is modified to assure the resource is depleted by T. The extraction rate will rise throughout phase II in case T is so small that

$$T < k^{-1} \ln (1 + (1+a)S^*/2a^2n). \qquad (36)$$

If (36) does not hold, the extraction rate will continue to fall in phase II, but there will be a final interval of time

$$T - k^{-1} \ln((1+a)/a) < t \le T$$

during which the planned extraction rate rises.

Utility from Resource Consumption

A number of previous studies have assumed, in effect, that the irreplenishable resource could be consumed as a final good yielding utility. See, for example, Kemp (1976), Cropper (1976), and Loury (1978). The optimal extraction path for a society with constant elasticity of marginal utility, $U(R) = R^a$, and a probability distribution (1) over total reserves is immediate. Setting $b=0$ and $B=1$ in the problem statement (8) gives the present case. The solution is read from (21)–(24) with $k = r/(1-a)$. Indeed, all of our results given above apply immediately with $b=0$ and $B=1$.

Certainty-Equivalent Resource Stock

The generality of our finding of a certainty-equivalent resource stock is noted next. Suppose it is known that the resource stock is at least $x_1 > 0$ and the reward function and probability distribution over reserves have general form. We then show that, so long as immediate exhaustion is impossible (i.e., while $0 \le x(t) < x_1$), (1) the form of the optimal extraction path is invariant to the extent of uncertainty and (2) a single parameter in the solution will capture the entire impact of the uncertainty.

To see this, let the reward from extraction and sale at rate R be $g(R)$, where g is a concave function with $g'(0) > 0$. Let $F(x)$ be the probability that the initial reserve does not exceed x and suppose $F(x) = 0$ for $0 \le x < x_1$. We seek to

$$\max \int_0^T e^{-rt} g(R(t))(1 - F(x(t)) dt$$

$$s.t. \; x'(t) = R(t) \quad x(0) = 0.$$

The current value Hamiltonian for this problem is

$$H = g(R)(1 - F(x)) + mR$$

where m is the current value multiplier. Necessary conditions include

$$\partial H/\partial R = g'(R)(1 - F(x)) + m \le 0 \quad R(\partial H/\partial R) = 0$$

$$m' = rm + g(R)F'(x).$$

So long as $0 \le x(t) < x_1$, we have $F'(x) = F(x) = 0$.

If $R > 0$, these conditions imply that

$$g'(R(t)) = -m(0)e^{rt} \quad \text{while} \quad 0 \le x(t) < x_1.$$

Hence, we have the result familiar from analyses of the certainty case. The marginal profitability of extraction rises at the discount rate so long as immediate exhaustion is not possible, even if the total stock is not known exactly. The impact of uncertainty is wholly contained in the multiplicative constant $m(0)$. Thus, as claimed, the *form* of the extraction path during the period that immediate exhaustion is not possible depends only on the reward function g. The *level* of the extraction path, reflected in $m(0)$, is, of course, affected by the probability distribution over reserves.

TECHNICAL CHANGE INCLINATIONS

We now determine the maximum expected value (8) to the monopolist of the optimal policy and the direction of technical advance that will increase it. The technology parameters affecting demand for, and profits from, the resources are A and a. The resource's elasticity of derived demand, $1/(1-a)$, depends on its output elasticity a.

The maximum expected value, to be denoted V, is obtained by evaluating (8) with (21), (24), and (7), yielding

$$V = aAK_o^{1-a}S^{*a}/k^{1-a}. \tag{37}$$

Appreciation of this form may be enhanced by recalling that if a resource, R, is employed according to production function (3), and is priced to equal the value of its marginal product (5), then the revenue received will be

$$pR = aAK^{1-a}R^a. \tag{38}$$

Compare (37) and (38), noting that (37) gives the present expected value of a stream of receipts while (38) is a static current return only. Both the initial capital stock and the certainty-equivalent resource stock are raised to the appropriate power. The multiplicative factor aA appears in both expressions. Finally, recall that k is a capitalization factor.

We next inquire about the direction of technical advance in the client industry that would be preferred by the resource supplier. Only once-for-all exogenous, *ceteris paribus* shifts at $t=0$ are to be considered. It is apparent from (37) and (21) that an increase in the general efficiency parameter, A, will increase V, but not alter R. That is, if the user experiences a general increase in productivity and continues to price its own product at unity, then the resource supplier does not alter its supply, but its profits increase.

Whether the resource supplier would favor an increase in the elasticity of demand for its product depends on the magnitude of the stock. Differentiate (37) logarithmically:

$$\partial \ell n\, V/\partial a = 1/a + \ell n(kS^*/K_o) + 2an/S^*(1+a)^2 - r/k(1-a). \tag{39}$$

Since $S - n = S^* - 2an/(1+a)$ and $S > n$ have been assumed, it follows that

$$S^* > 2an/1+a). \tag{40}$$

Now (39) is increasing in S^* since (40) is satisfied:

$$\frac{\partial}{\partial S^*} (\partial \ell nV/\partial a) = S^{*-1}(1 - 2an/S^*(1+a)^2) > a/(1+a)S^* > 0. \tag{41}$$

The first inequality of (41) was obtained by replacing the S^* in parentheses by its lower bound in (40). Thus (39) is increasing in S^*. Further, evaluating (39) for both small S $(> n)$ and for large S indicates that (39) may take both signs: $\partial V/\partial a < 0$ for small S and $\partial V/\partial a > 0$ for large S.

Thus, it has been shown that the resource supplier with a large initial reserve will find it advantageous to increase its output elasticity and thereby increase its elasticity of derived demand. On the other hand, if the supplier has but small reserves, he would favor a reduction in the resource's output elasticity and a consequent reduction of its elasticity of demand.

An increase in the output elasticity a causes the resource to be used more rapidly, in the sense that total consumption by any time $t' < t_1$, $x(t') = S^*(1 - e^{-kt'})$, is an increasing function of a. This follows from the observations that both the certainty-equivalent stock S^* and the factor k increase with a. The result of the last paragraph may be reinterpreted as follows: A resource supplier with relatively large (small) reserves will profit by technical advance that causes the reserves to be depleted more (less) rapidly. (Note the supplier in each case has equivalent market power.)

The technical advance that is favored by the resource supplier may be compared with the technical advance that others favor. In particular, let us consider the extraction policy that will maximize the present expected value of the area under the demand curve for the resource, the "consumer" surplus, and then ask how it would be affected by technical change. Since

$$p = aA(K/R)^{1-a} = Be^{b(1-a)t}R^{a-1}$$

the area under the demand curve at t is

$$\int_0^R p\,dy = \int_0^R Be^{b(1-a)t}y^{a-1}dy = Be^{b(1-a)t}R^a/a$$

and the present expected value of this stream of areas through time is

$$\int_0^\infty (e^{-rt}(1 - F(x(t))Be^{b(1-a)t}R^a/a)dt. \qquad (42)$$

But this is just a multiple ($1/a$) of the monopolist's objective (8). Since, in addition, the constraints are precisely the ones the monopolist faces, the optimal extraction path for (42) is precisely the one the monopolist would choose! This result is a consequence of the Cobb-Douglas assumption: we showed in (1977a) that a resource monopolist will choose the same extraction path as would a competitive supplier of the resource, in case the resource is used as a factor of production and the production function is Cobb-Douglas (since then the elasticity of demand is constant with respect to time). We shall henceforth identify objective (42) as the objective of "society."

Let us denote the maximum value of (42) as V_s. Then

$$V_s = V/a. \qquad (43)$$

Direct manipulation of (43) confirms that

$$\frac{\partial V/\partial a}{V} - \frac{\partial V_s/\partial a}{V_s} = 1/a > 0$$

so that

$$\frac{\partial V/\partial a}{V} > \frac{\partial V_s/\partial a}{V_s}.$$

Thus, for any given set of parameters, whenever "society," identified with (42), would prefer a technical advance that causes the resource to be used more rapidly ($\partial V_s/\partial a > 0$), a monopolist would have a similar preference ($\partial V/\partial a > 0$). Likewise, whenever the monopolist would prefer a technical advance that would lead to a slower use of the resource, "society" will concur. There is also, however, a set of parameter configurations such that the monopolist would prefer an increase in the parameter a so that the resource would be used more rapidly, while "society" would prefer a reduction in a and slower depletion of the resource.

The preferences of a resource monopolist with an imposed finite horizon can likewise be determined. Let V_T denote the maximum value of (8) if a horizon T is set. Then, evaluating (8) with (34) gives

$$V_T = V(1 - e^{-kT})^{1-a}. \tag{44}$$

Differentiating (44) with respect to a and combining the result with our earlier findings gives

$$\frac{\partial V_T/\partial a}{V_T} > \frac{\partial V/\partial a}{V} > \frac{\partial V_s/\partial a}{V_s}. \tag{45}$$

Thus, the results obtained when the horizon could be chosen optimally are strengthened if the horizon is finite.

In sum, for any given set of parameters under our assumptions, the monopolist will exploit the resource optimally from the viewpoint of society as well. For a wide range of parameter values, the direction of technical advance favored by the two will also coincide. Yet it is possible that the monopolist would be eager to promote technical change that would lead to more rapid exhaustion of the resource, while society's interests are in the opposite direction. If the monopolist is shortsighted for some reason, there is a tendency for this disparity of interests to occur for a wider range of parameter values.

FURTHER REMARKS

Exponential Distribution of Reserves

Our results are corroborated by considering the probability distribution over the level of resource reserves to be exponential with mean s. Then the probability that the stock exceeds x is

$$1 - F_e(x) = e^{-x/s} \tag{46}$$

and the density is

$$F_e'(x) = e^{-x/s}/s. \tag{47}$$

Note that the conditional probability of exhaustion, given reserves of at least x, is constant:

$$F_e'(x)/(1 - F_e(x)) = 1/s.$$

This distribution has the further property that the expected remaining stock is always s, no matter how much has been extracted, provided the reserves are not exhausted. We use a subscript e to refer to functions and results under the present hypothesis (46).

Solving problem (8)–(13) with specification (46) leads to necessary conditions (14)–(16) as before. We find that

$$T = \infty \tag{48}$$

and that

$$R_e = aks \tag{49}$$
$$x_e(t) = akst \tag{50}$$
$$m_e(t) = -a^a(ks)^{a-1}e^{-akt} \tag{51}$$
$$1\text{-}F_e(x(t)) = e^{-akt} \tag{52}$$
$$V_e = a^{a+1}AK_o^{1-a}s^a/k^{1-a} \tag{53}$$

where k is as defined in (18). These results should be compared with the corresponding findings under the assumption of the uniform distribution. The extraction rate is constant. It is a fixed fraction ak of the expected remaining stock [cf. (32)]. Cumulative extraction grows linearly. The implicit cost of withdrawing reserves falls exponentially toward zero. The probability that reserves will not be exhausted by any time t is exponential; the conditional probability of immediate exhaustion, given survival to t, is a constant ak that is independent of s [cf. (24) and (27)]. Finally, the maximum expected value of (8) under specification (46) is (53), which should be compared with (37).

To find the direction of technical change preferred by the resource supplier, we differentiate (53) with respect to a:

$$\frac{\partial V_e/\partial a}{V_e} = \ell n\,(aks/K_o) + (a+1)/a - r/k(1-a).$$

Therefore,

$$\partial V_e/\partial a \lessgtr 0 \text{ according as } s \gtrless (K_o/ak)e^{r/k(1-a)-(1+a)/a}.$$

Thus, the qualitative conclusion under the supposition of a uniform distribution is affirmed in the case of an exponential distribution. A resource supplier with a relatively large expected reserve prefers to increase the output elasticity of his resource and thereby increase both its elasticity of derived demand and its depletion rate. If the resource supplier has a relatively small expected stock s, he will gain by a reduction in the parameter a, reducing both the elasticity of derived demand and the rate of depletion.

Sales Tax

Imposition of a constant ad valorem sales tax τ on the resource will reduce the profit of the resource supplier, but will not alter either the extraction path or the technical change inclinations, under our assumptions. If the purchaser pays unit price p and the supplier gets unit gross receipts of $p(1-\tau)$, then the objective (8) is reduced to a fraction $1-\tau$ of its former value. This constant factor joins B in front of the integral in (8) and has the same impact, say, as a reduction in the purchaser's general efficiency parameter A. Invariance of the solution with respect to the sales tax may be attributed to the assumption of the Cobb-Douglas form.

SUMMARY

We have studied the technical change preferences of a monopolist of a nonrenewable resource and compared them with society's. To determine these preferences, we analyzed the optimal extraction plans for a given technology under the assumptions that the resource stock magnitude is uncertain and that the resource is a factor of production. We found that when the expected stock of the resource was relatively large, a technical change that accelerates its depletion would increase the present value of the expected profit stream, generated by the optimal extraction policy, and therefore would be preferred by the monopolist. On the other hand, if the expected resource stock is relatively small, a technical advance that slows down its depletion is desirable. The technical change preferences of the monopolist and society may, but need not, coincide. Disagreement, if it occurs, would be that the monopolist prefers a technical advance that accelerates extraction while society prefers the opposite.

The optimal extraction plan falls into two phases. In the first phase, during which it is known that the resource stock will not be exhausted, the optimal extraction rate coincides with the optimal policy if the stock were known and equal to a specific magnitude. This specific magnitude, which we called the "certainty-equivalent stock," is smaller than the expected stock of the resource, and the corresponding extraction rate is slower than it would be under certainty. Thus, uncertainty regarding the magnitude of reserves slows depletion even when there is no fear of imminent exhaustion. In the second phase, during which imminent exhaustion is possible, extraction is slower than in the first phase. The resource price rises at the rate of interest in the first phase and at a slower rate in the second phase.

Several additional observations deserve mention. First, our results on optimal extraction can be readily applied to the case studied by others, that the resource is a final good and that the marginal utility of consumption is constant. The optimal extraction rate is a constant multiple k of the remaining certainty-equivalent stock while imminent exhaustion is impossible, and is a smaller constant multiple of the expected remaining stock once immediate exhaustion is possible. Second, imposition of a finite time horizon generally leaves the qualitative conclusions intact. Third, the results appear robust with respect to the choice of probability distribution over reserves.

REFERENCES

Cropper, M. L. "Regulating Activities with Catastrophic Environmental Effects," *Journal of Environmental Economics and Management*, 3 (1976), 1–15.

Dasgupta, P., and Heal, G. "The Optimal Depletion of an Exhaustible Resource," *Review of Economic Studies* (symposium) (1974), pp. 3–28.

Gilbert, R. J. "Optimal Depletion of an Uncertain Stock," *Review of Economic Studies* (Jan. 1979), pp. 47–57.

Howe, Charles W. "Guidelines for a Responsible Natural Resources Policy" (this volume).

Kamien, M. I., and Schwartz, N. L. "A Note on Resource Usage and Market Structure," *Journal of Economic Theory* (Aug. 1977), pp. 394–397.

——. "Disaggregated Intertemporal Models with an Exhaustible Resource and Technical Advance," *Journal of Environmental Economics and Management* (1977), pp. 271–788.

——. "Optimal Exhaustible Resource Depletion with Endogenous Technical Change," *Review of Economic Studies* (Feb. 1978), pp. 179–196.

Kemp, Murray C. "How to Eat a Cake of Unknown Size," ch. 23 in M. C. Kemp, ed., *Three Topics in the Theory of International Trade* (New York: North-Holland Pub. Co., 1976).

Koopmans, T. C. "The Transition from Exhaustible to Renewable or Inexhaustible Resources," Cowles Foundation Discussion Paper No. 486 (Feb. 1978).

Loury, Glenn C. "The Optimum Exploitation of an Unknown Reserve," *Review of Economic Studies* (Oct. 1978), pp. 621–636.

Peterson, F. M., and Fisher, A. C. "The Exploitation of Extractive Resources: A Survey," *Economic Journal* (Dec. 1977), pp. 681–721.

The Paradox of Voting and Candidate Competition: A General Equilibrium Analysis

John O. Ledyard

Conventional analysis of the decision of expected utility maximizing agents to vote has concluded that it is irrational to vote unless voters have a distorted view of their individual impact or place a direct value on the act of voting.[1] On the other hand, mathematical analyses of the electoral process (see, for example, Davis, Hinich, and Ordeshook, 1970) have usually assumed that all voters vote.[2] Each theory is incorrect, in the sense that in actual elections turnout is neither zero nor 100 percent.

In this paper we will argue that previous analyses of expected utility maximizing voters stopped too soon, because of the partial equilibrium approach, and that if each voter considers the simultaneous reactions of all voters in a "rational" manner, then, depending on the location of the candidates' platforms, turnout will usually be positive but less than 100 percent. In particular, we will derive a (probabilistic) vote supply function, given a distribution of voters and the choice of platforms of candidates, which has the property that—even with costs of voting (unless the candidates have identical platforms)—the expected turnout is positive. The model and these results are presented in sections IA and IB.

Since Ferejohn and Fiorina (1974 and 1975) have presented persuasive theoretical and empirical arguments that another form of rational behavior, "minimax regret," is realistic and has the property that turnout is positive (unless platforms are identical), we will spend some time comparing the implications of their model and ours. Essentially, we claim that our model predicts larger turnout than their model when preferences (ideal points) are symmetrically distributed, candidates' platforms are close, and the variance of tastes is small (with concave utility functions) or large (with a type of convex utility function). Predicted turnout is larger in their model for opposite values. Thus, neither dominates the other with respect to predicted turnout. This is discussed in detail in section IC.

The results concerning turnout and voter behavior in both models depend on the candidates' choices of their platforms. Thus a natural question is, What will candidates do, given our model of voters? This furthers the move to a general equilibrium approach since candidates' and voters' behavior now are simultaneously determined. Using expected plurality max-imizing behavior for two-candidate elections, we obtained mixed results in our investigation. For concave utility functions and symmetrically distrib-uted ideal points, equilibrium occurs with both candidates' choosing the median ideal point and no voter voting (since platforms are identical). Fur-ther, if ideal points are asymmetrically distributed in the tails of the distri-butions (that is, at extreme distances from the median), usually no general equilibrium will exist. These results appear in sections IIA, IIB(i), and IIB(ii).

On the other hand, if utility functions are convex on each side of the ideal point and if tastes are unimodal and not too asymmetric, a general equilib-rium exists with candidates choosing identical platforms at the *modal* ideal point and no voter voting. These results are included in section IIB(iii).

A summary of results is provided in section IIC, with some additional remarks. One deserves emphasis. In general equilibrium, with expected plurality maximizing candidates, the outcome is identical for two models of voter behavior: ours and minimax regret. That is, both models predict, in equilibrium, identical candidate platforms and no voter turnout if costs of voting are positive.

In section III we consider three additional problems: (a) the implications of vote maximizing candidates—turnout is positive in equilibrium if it exists; (b) M candidate elections for $M \geq 2$, although no general equilibrium results are presented where candidate behavior is included; and (c) some remarks on testing models of simultaneous voter and candidate behavior—particu-larly our model. This section concludes the paper.

I. VOTER (PARTIAL) EQUILIBRIUM: TWO CANDIDATES

We begin with the conventional analysis of the voting decision of a single voter in the spirit of Downs, Tullock, Riker-Ordeshook, and Ferejohn and Fiorina. In this model, candidates A and B select platforms Θ_A, Θ_B ε H, an "issue space." A voter than votes for (say) A, if and only if the expected utility outweighs the expected utility from voting for B or from abstaining.

A. The Conventional Analysis

We consider a model with $n + 1$ voters, indexed by $i = 1, 2, \ldots, n + 1$. Each voter has preferences over a set of possible issues, H. Two candidates are indexed $j = A, B$, where Θ_j ε H is j's platform. When a voter votes for a particular candidate (or abstains), he is implicitly selecting a gamble, since at the time of the decision he does not know how other voters will vote. We make the standard assumption that the voter who makes the decision under uncertainty acts as if he maximizes expected utility.

ASSUMPTION 1. With each voter i is associated a utility function U^i on H, such that

(a) (candidate irrelevance) i prefers candidate A to B if and only if $U^i(\Theta_A) > U^i(\Theta_B)$, and

(b) (expected utility hypothesis) letting $(\Pi_A, \Pi_B, \Theta_A, \Theta_B)$ represent the gamble that j is elected on platform Θ_j with probability Π_j (for $j = A, B$), voter i prefers $(\Pi_A, \Pi_B, \Theta_A, \Theta_B)$ to $(\Pi_A', \Pi_B', \Theta_A', \Theta_B')$ if and only if $\Pi_A \cdot U^i(\Theta_A) + \Pi_B \cdot U^i(\Theta_B) > \Pi_A' \cdot U^i(\Theta_A') + \Pi_B' \cdot U^i(\Theta_B')$.

To ease the exposition and pave the way for later analysis, we make the additional assumption that each voter's (expected) utility function can be parameterized. That is, we let D be a space of voters' characteristics and let $U^i(\Theta) = U(\Theta, d^i)$ be the utility of i for Θ if his characteristic is $d^i \; \varepsilon \; D$. Three simple examples may help the reader understand the notation.

Example 1 (Type I preferences).[3] Let $H \equiv R^L$, the L dimensional Euclidean space. Let $D \equiv R^L$ and let $U(\Theta, d^i) = -(\Theta - d^i)'(\Theta - d^i) = -\Sigma_{\ell=1}^L (\Theta_\ell - d_\ell^i)^2$. Thus, every voter has a quadratic utility (loss) function, whose ideal point is d^i, over L issues measured as real numbers.

Example 2 (Simple social choice). Let $H = \{x_1, x_2, x_3\}$. That is, there are only three alternatives. Let $D \equiv R^3$ and let $U(x_k, d^i) = d_k^i$ for $k = 1,2,3$. Thus $d^i = (d_1^i, d_2^i, d_3^i)$, where d_k^i is i's utility for alternative k.

Example 3 (Type II preferences). Let $H \equiv R^L$, $D = R^L$ and $U(\Theta, d^i) = -[(\Theta - d^i)'(\Theta - d^i)]^{\frac{1}{m}}$, $m > 1$. As for type I preferences, each voter has an ideal point d^i. However, while type I preferences are concave utility functions, type II preferences are convex, on each side of d^i. As we will see, the behavior implied by type II preferences is significantly different from behavior implied by type I preferences.

A digression. Assumption 1(a) can be weakened, in what follows, to allow voter identification of candidates to be important. For example, suppose i believes *ex ante* that if j adopts the platform Θ_j, then j will implement the platform γ, if elected, with probability $\ell^j(\gamma, \Theta_j, d^i)$. Then i's *ex ante* utility for j, given the platform Θ_j, is $W^j(\Theta_j, d^i) = \int U(\gamma, d^i)\ell^j(\gamma, \Theta_j, d^i)d\gamma$. Thus, i prefers A to B if and only if $W^A(\Theta_A, d^i) > W^B(\Theta_B, d^i)$, and even if $\Theta_A = \Theta_B$, i may prefer A to B. Since this does not explain where the $\ell^i(\cdot)$ likelihood functions come from, and since this generality tends to obscure the main issues, we will reconsider it only if it has some significant bearing on the results to be derived.

One characteristic (in addition to d^i) which we also need to consider is the cost of voting, c^i. We will assume that $0 < \underline{c} \le c^i < \infty$ for all i; that is, all voters must incur a cost if they vote, and these costs are bounded away from zero by $\underline{c}$. For shorthand purposes only, we will let $e^i = (d^i, c^i)$ and $E^i \equiv D \times (c, \infty)$.

ASSUMPTION 2 (No income effects). If candidate j wins, then voter i, with characteristic e^i, receives utility $U(\Theta_j, d^i) - c^i$ if he votes and $U(\Theta_j, d^i)$ if he abstains.

Another digression. Assumption 2 could be weakened to i receives $U(\Theta_j, c^i, d^i)$ if i votes and j wins, while i receives $U(\Theta_j, 0, d^i)$ if j wins and i abstains. Unfortunately, this complicates the analysis somewhat. Further, as far as I can tell, this weakening does not seem to alter the equilibrium results below. I will therefore stay with assumption 2 to ease exposition and to remain as close as possible to the standard framework.

We are now ready to analyze the voters' decision. A voter has three possible acts: vote for A, vote for B, or abstain. There are, essentially, five states of the world which must be considered. Let n_j be the number of votes cast by the other n voters for $j = A, B$. (Since we allow abstentions, $n_A + n_B < n$ is possible.) The five states are S_1, where $n_A > n_B + 1$; S_2, where $n_A = n_B + 1$; S_3, where $n_A = n_B$; S_4, where $n_B = n_A + 1$; and S_5, where $n_B > n_A + 1$. Let p^i be the probability of state k from i's point of view.

Lemma 1 (Ferejohn and Fiorina, 1974). If tied elections are decided by a fair coin toss, then, given Θ_A, Θ_B, e^i, and $p^i = (p^i_1, \ldots, p^i_5)$, voter i maximizes expected utility by (deleting the i on p^i_k):

$$\text{voting for } A \text{ if } W(\Theta, e^i) > \frac{1}{p_3 + p_4} \tag{1a}$$

$$\text{voting for } B \text{ if } -\frac{1}{p_2 + p_3} > W(\Theta, e^i) \tag{1b}$$

$$\text{abstaining if } -\frac{1}{p_2 + p_3} < W(\Theta, e^i) < \frac{1}{p_3 + p_4} \tag{1c}$$

$$\text{where } W(\Theta, e^i) \equiv \frac{U(\Theta_A, d^i) - U(\Theta_B, d^i)}{2c^i}.$$

For precision, the boundary cases in Lemma 1, when $W(\Theta, e^i) = \dfrac{1}{p_3 + p_4}$ or $W(\Theta, e^i) = -\dfrac{1}{p_2 + p_3}$, should be dealt with. At these values, i is indifferent between voting and abstaining. Thus one should make some assumption about the actual act chosen. Fortunately, this boundary situation will usually occur (below) with probability zero and may safely be ignored. If not, we will point out the implications at the appropriate time.

At this point, the conventional analysis notes that both $p_3 + p_4$ and $p_2 + p_3$ are objectively very small and, unless voters inflate their estimates or receive a direct utility gain from voting, a rational expected utility maximizing citizen will decide to abstain. This contradicts empirical evidence, since people *do* vote. As a solution to this apparent dilemma, Ferejohn and Fiorina suggest that instead of maximizing expected utility, voters act according to Savage's minimax regret criterion. It is useful for later analysis to summarize their results in our notation:

Lemma 2 (Ferejohn and Fiorina, 1974). If tied elections are decided by a fair coin toss, then, given Θ_A, Θ_B and e^i, voter i minimizes his maximum regret by:

$$\text{voting for } A \text{ if } W(\Theta, e^i) > 2 \tag{2a}$$

$$\text{voting for } B \text{ if } W(\Theta, e^i) < -2 \qquad\qquad (2b)$$
$$\text{abstaining if } -2 < W(\Theta, e^i) < 2. \qquad\qquad (2c)$$

We note that this is equivalent to expected utility maximizing if and only if

$$p_2 + p_3 = \frac{1}{2} = p_3 + p_4.$$

B. Full Rationality

In this section we consider an alternative to both models discussed in IA. In particular, we propose and analyze a solution to the paradox of voting suggested by Ferejohn and Fiorina but never followed up.[4] The solution is brought about by assuming that each voter is rational and that each assumes the others also are rational. This will allow us to calculate precisely what $p_2^i + p_3^i$ and $p_3^i + p_4^i$ are in the mind of each voter i. Further, we will be able to make some statements about expected turnout (which will, in general, be non-zero).

ASSUMPTION 3. (a: Each voter assumes all voters are rational). Each voter i believes all other voters follow the (expected utility maximizing) decision rules in lemma 1. (b: Independent-identical beliefs). Each voter i believes other voters' characteristics are independently and identically distributed on E, according to the probability measure μ.

Thus, although i doesn't know h's characteristic and, therefore, doesn't know how h will vote, he does know how h will vote (or abstain) if h has the characteristic e^h. He also believes that e^h is a random variable drawn from μ. For full rationality (as in a rational expectations equilibrium), one might want to assume that μ was the empirical distribution. Below, it will be helpful to have μ "continuous," and, thus, we usually assume that the true distribution of characteristics is approximated by a continuous density function. For large electorates this is not a severe limitation.

Another digression. The assumption of independent and identical beliefs is not crucial for much of what follows but *does* allow for considerable simplification of the analysis. We could replace A3 with the following weaker expectations hypothesis. Let $z^i = [d^1, \ldots, d^{i-1}, d^{i+1}, \ldots, d^n]$ and assume each i believes the others' characteristics, z^i, are distributed according to the measure $\Psi^i(e^i)(z^i)$ if i's characteristic is e^i. In this case, i's expectations can depend on e^i, whereas in assumption 3 they are independent of e^i. This is followed up in section IIIB.

Lemma 3. Under assumptions 1–3, given Θ_A, Θ_B, μ, and p^i, voter i believes the probability q_j, that an arbitrary voter h ($h \neq i$) votes for $j = 0, A, B$ ($j = 0$ means abstention), is (assuming $p^i = p^h$):

$$q_A = 1 - G(\frac{1}{\alpha}, \Theta_A, \Theta_B) \qquad\qquad (3a)$$

$$q_B = G(-\frac{1}{\beta}, \Theta_A, \Theta_B) \qquad\qquad (3b)$$

$$q_o = G(\frac{1}{\alpha}, \Theta_A, \Theta_B) - G(-\frac{1}{\beta}, \Theta_A, \Theta_B) \tag{3c}$$

where $\alpha = p_3^i + p_4^i$, $\beta = p_2^i + p_3^i$, and $G(r, \Theta_A, \Theta_B) = \mu(\{e^i \in E \mid W(\Theta_A, \Theta_B, e^i) \le r\})$ [assuming that $\mu(\{e^i \in E \mid W(\Theta, e^i) = \frac{1}{\alpha}, W(\Theta, e^i) = -\frac{1}{\beta}\}) = 0]$.

Proof. Straightforward application of assumption 3 and lemma 1.

Notice that if μ is concentrated on a finite number of points (say, $n + 1$) then the last qualifying phrase, needed for the case of indifference between voting and abstaining, may be false. We will assume shortly that μ, Θ_A and Θ_B are such that G is continuous in r. This will rule out μ concentrated on a finite number of characteristics and make the qualifying clause unnecessary.

Now if voter i knows q_A, q_B, and q_o, he is in a position to calculate $\alpha = p_3 + p_4$ and $\beta = p_2 + p_3$.

Lemma 4. Given q_A, q_B, and q_o,

$$\alpha = f(q_A, q_B) \tag{4a}$$
$$\beta = f(q_B, q_A) \tag{4b}$$

where $f(x,y) = \sum_{k=0}^{\left[\frac{n}{2}\right]} \binom{n}{k}\binom{n-k}{k} x^k y^k (1-x-y)^{n-2k} +$

$\sum_{k=0}^{\left[\frac{n-1}{2}\right]} \binom{n}{k}\binom{n-k}{k+1} x^k y^{k+1} (1-x-y)^{n-2k-1}$, and $[v]$ is the largest integer that is no greater than v.

Proof. For n voters, let $(n_A, n_B, n-n_A-n_B)$ be the event where n_A vote for A, n_B vote for B, and $n-n_A-n_B$ abstain. Given q_A, q_B, and q_o, plus the independence assumption, the probability of $(n_A, n_B, n-n_A-n_B)$ is calculated to be $\binom{n}{n_A}\binom{n-n_A}{n_B} (q_A)^{n_A}(q_B)^{n_B}(1-q_A-q_B)^{n-n_A-n_B}$ from the trinomial distribution. The rest follows easily.

At this point it can be seen that q_A, q_B, α, and β are simultaneously determined and that all voters' decisions (as described in [1]) and expectations will be consistent and in equilibrium if, and only if, (3) and (4) are jointly satisfied.

Definition. A (symmetric) *voters' equilibrium* for $(\Theta_A, \Theta_B, \mu)$ is a 4-tuple $(q_A^*, q_B^*, \alpha^*, \beta^*)$, such that (3a), (3b), (4a), and (4b) are simultaneously satisfied.

Remarks. (1) The qualifier "symmetric" refers to the fact that all voters are assumed to have identical decision rules, (1), and identical expectations.

(2) This concept of equilibrium is a special case of a Bayes equilibrium in strategies, S^i; $E \to \{0, A, B\}$, where, for each e^i, $S^i(e^i)$ maximizes i's conditional expected utility, given the strategies $(S^1, \ldots, S^{i-1}, S^{i+1}, \ldots, S^n)$ of the other voters. This is explored more fully in section 3b.

Of interest, of course, is whether a voters' equilibrium exists and what its properties are. The second question is more difficult, primarily because of the cumbersome form of $f(x,y)$ in lemma 4, but as will be seen, we can say some things about it. The first is easy and so we turn to it now. We state a simple and somewhat uninteresting result.

Proposition 1. Given $(\Theta_A, \Theta_B, \mu)$, such that $G(1, \Theta_A, \Theta_B) - G(-1, \Theta_A, \Theta_B) = 1$, $(q_A^*, q_B^*, \alpha^*, \beta^*) = (0, 0, 1, 1)$ is the unique symmetric voters equilibrium.

Proof (Existence). One can easily show by substitution into (3) and (4) that $(0, 0, 1, 1)$ is an equilibrium under the assumption on G.

(Uniqueness). Under the assumption on G, it follows from (3) that $q_A = q_B = 0$ for any values of $\alpha, \beta \varepsilon [0,1]$. Thus by (4), $\alpha = \beta = 1$ must hold.

Remarks. Several remarks are in order. First, if $\Theta_A = \Theta_B$, then $G(1, \Theta) - G(-1, \Theta) = 1$ and the proposition applies. Second, if μ is sufficiently dispersed, then $G(1, \Theta) - G(-1, \Theta) = 1$ only if $\Theta_A - \Theta_B$ is small. For example, consider the type I preferences of example 1 when there is a single issue, $H \equiv R^1$. Let $\Theta_A - \Theta_B = \varepsilon$ and $\dfrac{\Theta_A + \Theta_B}{2} = \overline{\Theta}$, let c be fixed, and assume d is distributed normally with mean 0 and variance 1. Then $G(1, \Theta)$

$$- G(-1, \Theta) = \frac{1}{\sqrt{2\pi}} \int_{\overline{\Theta} - \frac{c}{|\varepsilon|}}^{\overline{\Theta} + \frac{c}{|\varepsilon|}} e^{-\frac{x^2}{2}} \, dx < 1$$ whenever $\varepsilon > 0$. For type II pref-

erences[5] with $U(\Theta, d) = -|\Theta - d|^2$, $G(1, \Theta) - G(-1, \Theta) = 0$ if $|\Theta_A - \Theta_B| = |\varepsilon| \le 4c^2$. Otherwise, $G(1, \Theta) - G(-1, \Theta) > 0$.

Another thing to notice is that if $G(1, \Theta) - G(-1, \Theta) = 1$, then expected turnout is always zero since no voter ever has preferences d and costs c which provide any gain from voting, even if all others abstained. Finally, notice that it is also true that expected turnout is zero under minimax regret behavior (from lemma 2) if $G(1, \Theta) - G(-1, \Theta) = 1$. Thus, this situation is somewhat uninteresting, except that it exactly describes the equilibrium if $\Theta_A = \Theta_B$. As we will see below, candidate competition may well produce $\Theta_A = \Theta_B$ as a final result and, therefore (by proposition 1), no turnout.

Proposition 2. Given $\Theta_A, \Theta_B, \mu)$, if $G(r, \Theta_A, \Theta_B)$ is continuous in $r \varepsilon (-\infty, \infty)$, there is a symmetric voters' equilibrium for $(\Theta_A, \Theta_B, \mu)$.

Proof. Let $h^\alpha(\alpha, \beta) = f[q_A(\alpha), q_B(\beta)]$ and $h^\beta(\alpha, \beta) = f[q_B(\beta), q_A(\alpha)]$, where $q_A(\alpha) = 1 - G[\dfrac{1}{\alpha}, \Theta]$ and $q_B(\beta) = G(-\dfrac{1}{\beta}, \Theta)$. Then $q_A(\cdot), q_B(\cdot)$ are defined for $\alpha, \beta \varepsilon (0, 1)$. Let $q_A(0) = 0$ and $q_B(0) = 0$. It is then easy to show that the function $h(\alpha, \beta) = [h^\alpha(\alpha, \beta), h^\beta(\alpha, \beta)]$ continuously maps $[0, 1] \times [0, 1]$ into itself, since G and f are continuous respectively in r and (α, β). By Brouwer's theorem, there is a fix-point (α^*, β^*). Let $q_A^* = q_A(\alpha^*)$ and $q_B^* = q_B(\beta^*)$. Then $(q_A^*, q_B^*, \alpha^*, \beta^*)$ is an equilibrium.

Remarks. There are a variety of easily acceptable assumptions on $U(\Theta, d)$ and μ, such that $G(r, \Theta)$ is continuous in r. For example, let $D \equiv R^k$, $k < \infty$, and assume (1) $U(\Theta, d)$ is continuous in Θ for all $d \in D$ and (2) for each Borel subset $R \subseteq D \times (\underline{c}, \infty)$, $\mu(R) = \int_R h(e)de$, where h is a continuous density function such that $h(e) > 0$ for all $e \in E$. In fact, these conditions are stronger than necessary.

Perhaps unfortunately, if there are only a finite number of types in E (that is, E is a finite set), it is usually the case that G is not continuous in r. This does not mean there is no equilibrium; however, proposition 2 does not cover this case.

A simple corollary of proposition 2 is that if there is a positive probability that someone will vote if all others abstain, expected turnout [that is, $(n + 1)(q_A^* + q_B^*)$] is positive in equilibrium.

Corollary 2.1. Given $(\Theta_A, \Theta_B, \mu)$, such that G is continuous in r and $G(1, \Theta) - G(-1, \Theta) < 1$, then a voters equilibrium exists and $q_A^* + q_B^* > 0$.

Proof. If $q_A^* + q_B^* = 0$, then $q_A^* = q_B^* = 0$ and $\alpha^* = \beta^* = 1$. But then $q_A^* + q_B^* = 1 - G(1, \Theta) + G(-1, \Theta) > 0$ by assumption. QED.

C. Comparison to Minimax Regret

As an interesting side issue, one might wish to compare expected percentage turnout, $q_A^* + q_B^*$, in this expected utility model with that predicted by the minimax regret model of Ferejohn and Fiorina. The first obvious fact is that if $\alpha^*, \beta^* \leq \frac{1}{2}$, then $t_E \geq t_M$. If one is tempted to conclude from this that "since α and β are small, $t_M > t_E$," one would be wrong. To see why, consider type I preferences on a single-dimensional issues space, $U(e, \Theta) = -(a - \Theta)^2$. Let $c = 1$ (that is, normalize u by c) and assume a is normally distributed with mean 0 and variance σ. Further assume $\Theta_A = \frac{d}{2}$ and $\Theta_B = -\frac{d}{2}$. Then in voters' equilibrium $\alpha = \beta$ and $q_A(\alpha) = q_B(\alpha) = 1 - \frac{1}{\sqrt{\pi}}\int_0^{\frac{1}{\alpha d\sigma}} e^{-\frac{x^2}{2}}dx = q(\alpha d\sigma)$. Thus, implicitly, $\alpha = f[q(\alpha d\sigma), q(\alpha d\sigma)]$, or explicitly: $\alpha = h(d\sigma)$. Now $h(o) = 1$ and $h'(d\sigma) = \frac{(f_x + f_y)q'}{1 - (f_x + f_y)q'} < 0$, since $q' > 0$ and[6] $f_x + f_y < 0$. Further, $\lim_{d\sigma \to \infty} h(d\sigma) \cong \frac{\sqrt{2}}{n\pi}$ for large n. Thus for small values of σd, $\alpha^* > \frac{1}{2}$, which implies $t_E > t_M$, while for large values of σd, $\alpha^* < \frac{1}{2}$, which implies $t_M > t_E$. I have not calculated the value of $d\sigma$ for which $h(\sigma d) = \frac{1}{2}$. In any case, with symmetric type I preferences, close and symmetric platforms, and small variances in tastes, higher turnout is predicted by this model than by the minimax regret model. Large variances and distant platforms lead to the opposite conclusion.

If we consider type II preferences where $U(\Theta, a) = - |\Theta - a|^{\frac{1}{2}}$ and let $\Theta_A = \dfrac{d}{2}$, $\Theta_B = - \dfrac{d}{2}$ and a be distributed normally with mean 0 and variance 1, then we find again, that for small values of d, α is near 1. For $d \le 2\, c^2$, $\alpha = 1$. However, now $\dfrac{d\alpha}{d\sigma} > 0$ and therefore large values of σ imply $\alpha > \dfrac{1}{2}$. Thus, in the case of type II preferences, close and symmetric platforms and large variance in tastes lead to a higher prediction of turnout than under minimax regret behavior. That is, the effect of the variance of the tastes of voters is exactly opposite under type I and type II preferences.

In summary, given platforms, Θ_A and Θ_B, and a distribution of preferences and costs, μ, a voters' equilibrium can be defined and shown to exist if G is continuous. In general, expected turnout seems to be positive, although no precise figures were calculated. Further, whether more or less turnout is predicted by this model, as opposed to the minimax regret model, depends on the specific values of Θ_A and Θ_B, the form of preferences, and their variance. Since the choice of platforms is so crucial to that question, we turn now to modeling how they are chosen.

II. ELECTORAL EQUILIBRIUM: TWO CANDIDATES

A. Definition of Equilibrium

From section I, given $(\Theta_A, \Theta_B, \mu)$, a natural concept of voters' (partial) equilibrium arises from which one can infer, for each voter, (q_A^*, q_B^*, q_o^*): their probabilities of voting for A or B, or abstaining. Thus, given $(\Theta_A, \Theta_B, \mu)$, one can compute, assuming voters are in equilibrium, such things as (i) the probability that A wins, which is

$$\text{prob}\,\{n_A > n_B\} + \frac{1}{2}\,\text{prob}\,\{n_A = n_B\} =$$

$$\sum_{k=0}^{\left[\frac{n}{2}\right]} \sum_{r=1}^{n-2k+1} \binom{n+1}{k+r}\binom{n-k-r+1}{k} (q_A)^{k+r}\,(q_B)^k\,(1-q_A-q_B)^{n-2k-r+1}$$

$$+ \frac{1}{2} \sum_{k=0}^{\left[\frac{n+1}{2}\right]} \binom{n+1}{k}\binom{n-k+1}{k}(q_A)^k (q_B)^k\,(1-q_A-q_B)^{n-2k+1}$$

or (ii) A's expected plurality, which is $(n+1)(q_A - q_B)$, or (iii) A's expected vote, which is $(n+1)\, q^A$. Each of these has been proposed, along with others,[7] as a possible objective function for candidate A. We will begin by considering expected plurality and will reserve comment on the others until later in section IIIA.

ASSUMPTION 4. (a: Expected plurality hypothesis). Given $(\Theta_A, \Theta_B, \mu)$, both candidates act as if they wish to maximize expected plurality under the assumption that voters are in equilibrium. (That is, A desires to maximize $(n + 1) [q_A^* (\Theta_A, \Theta_B, \mu) - q_B^* (\Theta_A, \Theta_B, \mu)]$.)

(b: Existence of voters' equilibrium). Given $(\mu, \Theta_A, \Theta_B)$, either $G(1, \Theta) - G(-1, \Theta) = 1$ or $G(r, \Theta)$ is continuous in r.

Under this assumption, there is a natural concept of electoral equilibrium.

Definition. The 4-triple $(\hat{\Theta}_A, \hat{\Theta}_B, \hat{q}_A, \hat{q}_B)$ is an *electoral equilibrium* for μ if (a) there are α and β, such that $(\hat{q}_A, \hat{q}_B, \alpha, \beta)$ is a voters' equilibrium for $(\hat{\Theta}_A, \hat{\Theta}_B, \mu)$, and (b)

$$W^A(\hat{\Theta}_A, \hat{\Theta}_B) \geq W_A(\Theta_A, \hat{\Theta}_B) \ \forall \ \Theta_A \ \varepsilon \ H$$
$$W^B(\hat{\Theta}_A, \hat{\Theta}_B) \geq W^B(\hat{\Theta}_A, \Theta_B) \ \forall \ \Theta_B \ \varepsilon \ H$$

where $W^A (\Theta_A, \Theta_B) = q_B(\Theta_A, \Theta_B, \mu) - q_A(\Theta_A, \Theta_B, \mu)$, $W^B(\Theta_A, \Theta_B) = - W^A(\Theta_A, \Theta_B)$, *and* $[q_A(\Theta_A, \Theta_B, \mu), q_B(\Theta_A, \Theta_B, \mu), \alpha, \beta]$ for some (α, β) is a voters' equilibrium for $(\Theta_A, \Theta_B, \mu)$.

Thus, $(\hat{\Theta}_A, \hat{\Theta}_B)$ is a Nash equilibrium of the (zero-sum) game in which candidates' payoffs are their expected plurality under the assumption that voters will vote as if in voters' equilibrium.

B. Existence of Equilibrium

It is easy to show that if $q_A(\Theta_A, \Theta_B, \mu)$ is concave in Θ_A and convex in Θ_B and if $q_B(\Theta_A, \Theta_B, \mu)$ is concave in Θ_B and convex in Θ_A, then an electoral equilibrium exists. However, these concavity properties need not be valid for arbitrary classes of preferences, $U(\Theta, d)$, and priors, μ. Therefore we need to explore for what preferences and priors an equilibrium *does* exist. It turns out that both the question of existence and the character of equilibrium depend crucially on the concavity properties of the utility functions and the symmetry (or lack of it) of the prior distribution. Thus, we need to consider several cases.

(i) CONCAVE UTILITY: SYMMETRIC PRIOR. We first prove that if tastes are concave in Θ and the prior, μ, is symmetric around $\hat{\Theta}$, then $\Theta_A = \Theta_B = \hat{\Theta}$ and $q_A = q_B = 0$ is an electoral equilibrium. We will then discuss the implications of weakening some of the assumptions.

Proposition 3. If

(i) $H \equiv R^k, k < \infty$.

(ii) (concave utility). For each $d \ \varepsilon \ D$, $U(\Theta, d)$ is concave in, and $\nabla U = [\partial U/\partial \Theta_1, \ldots, \partial U/\partial \Theta k]$ exists for all $\Theta \ \varepsilon \ H$.

(iii) (symmetric priors). There is a $\hat{\Theta}$ such that, for all $\gamma \ \varepsilon \ R^k$, $\mu(\{e \varepsilon E| \nabla U(\hat{\Theta}, d) \cdot \gamma \leq - c\}) = \mu (\{e \varepsilon E| \nabla U(\hat{\Theta}, d) \cdot \gamma \geq c\})$, then $(\Theta, \Theta, 0, 0)$ is an electoral equilibrium.

Proof. Let $\Theta_A = \Theta_B = \hat{\Theta}$. Then, by definition of voters' equilibrium and proposition 1, $q_A(\Theta_A, \Theta_B, \mu) = q_B(\Theta_A, \Theta_B, \mu) = 0$ and $\alpha(\Theta_A, \Theta_B, \mu) = \beta(\Theta_A, \Theta_B, \mu) = 1$. We must show that there do not exist $\lambda > 0$, γ, ε, R^k, such that

$1 - G(\frac{1}{\hat{\alpha}}, \hat{\Theta} + \lambda\gamma, \hat{\Theta}) - G[-\frac{1}{\hat{\beta}}, \hat{\Theta} + \lambda\gamma, \hat{\Theta}] > 0$, where $\hat{\alpha} = \alpha(\hat{\Theta} + \lambda\gamma, \hat{\Theta})$

and $\hat{\beta} = \beta(\hat{\Theta} + \lambda\gamma, \hat{\Theta})$. A symmetric argument will cover B. By concavity of U in Θ, $U(\hat{\Theta} + \lambda\gamma, d) \leq U(\hat{\Theta}, d) + \lambda\nabla U \cdot \gamma$ for all $\lambda > 0$. From this, it is

easy to show that $G(r, \hat{\Theta} + \lambda\gamma, \hat{\Theta}) = \mu (\{e \mid \dfrac{U(\hat{\Theta} + \lambda\gamma, d) - U(\hat{\Theta}, d)}{2c} \leq r\})$

$\geq \mu(\{e \mid \dfrac{\lambda\nabla U \cdot \gamma}{2c} \leq r\})$, since $e \, \varepsilon \, \{e \mid \lambda\nabla U\gamma \leq 2rc\}$ implies $e \, \varepsilon \, \{e \mid U(\hat{\Theta} + \lambda\gamma, d)$

$- U(\hat{\Theta}, d) \leq 2rc\}$. Thus, if $1 - G(\frac{1}{\hat{\alpha}}, \hat{\Theta} + \lambda\gamma, \hat{\Theta}) - G(-\frac{1}{\hat{\beta}}, \hat{\Theta} + \lambda\gamma, \hat{\Theta}) > 0$,

then $1 - \mu(\{e \mid \lambda\nabla U\gamma \leq \dfrac{2rc}{\hat{\alpha}}\} - \mu(\{e \mid \lambda\nabla U \cdot \gamma \leq -\dfrac{2c}{\hat{\beta}}\}) > 0$. By condition (iii),

this implies

$$1 - \mu(\{e \mid \dfrac{\lambda\nabla U \cdot \gamma}{2c} \leq \dfrac{1}{\hat{\alpha}}\}) - \mu(\{e \mid \dfrac{\lambda\nabla U\gamma}{2c} \geq \dfrac{1}{\hat{\beta}}\}) > 0. \tag{5}$$

Now from (4), $\hat{\alpha} - \hat{\beta} = f(q^A, q^B) - f(q^B, q^A) = (q^B - q^A) \, \Gamma(q^A, q^B)$, where[8] $\Gamma(\cdot)$

> 0. Therefore, if $q^A(\hat{\Theta} + \lambda\gamma, \hat{\Theta}) - q^B(\hat{\Theta} + \lambda\gamma, \hat{\Theta}) > 0$, then $\hat{\alpha} < \hat{\beta}$ or $\dfrac{1}{\hat{\alpha}} >$

$\dfrac{1}{\hat{\beta}}$. But then it is true that $\mu(\{e \mid \lambda\nabla U\gamma \leq \dfrac{1}{\hat{\alpha}}\}) + \mu(\{e \mid \lambda\nabla\gamma \geq \dfrac{1}{\hat{\beta}}\}) \geq 1$, which

contradicts (5). *QED.*

Let us look at each assumption to check its severity. Condition (i) rules out, for instance, the social choice example and others where the alternative set is finite. It also implies that issues can be measured. This is unfortunate, but standard, in spatial election models. Condition (ii) is also standard in these models, natural to an economist, and allows type I preferences: $[U(\Theta, d) = -(\Theta - d)'(\Theta - d)]$. However, as we will see later, there is some question about the empirical validity of these preferences. Further, the entire character of equilibrium is altered if preferences are not concave. We will look at these issues in detail in section IIB (iii).

Given the assumption of concave preferences, condition (iii) is the crucial restriction. Let us first see what it requires. If μ comes from a continuous density on E (that is, $\mu(R) = \int_R h(e)de$), then a sufficient condition for (iii) is the existence of $\hat{\Theta}$, such that for all $d \, \varepsilon \, D$ there is $d' \, \varepsilon \, D$, such that $\nabla U(\hat{\Theta}, d) = -\nabla U(\hat{\Theta}, d')$ and $h(d, c) = h(d', c)$ for all c. For type I preferences with a shift parameter, $U(\Theta, d) = -(d - \Theta)'A(d - \Theta) + \gamma\Theta$ where (A, γ) is fixed and A is symmetric positive definite, $\nabla U = 2A(d - \Theta) + \gamma$. In this case, if d is distributed by the continuous density (h) symmetrically around $\hat{d}$ (that is,

$h(d + \hat{d}) = h(\hat{d} - d)$) and independently of c, then $\hat{\Theta} = d + \dfrac{1}{2}A^{-1}\gamma$ satisfies (iii). Thus $\hat{\Theta}$ is the ideal point of the median voter type, $\hat{d}$. In general, condition (iii) does not seem to imply a median voter outcome because of the role of c; however, if c is independently distributed from d, then (iii) requires the existence of a median voter of type $\hat{d}$ and a platform $\hat{\Theta}$ where $\nabla U(\hat{\Theta}, \hat{d}) = 0$ ($\hat{\Theta}$ is d's ideal point).

(ii) CONCAVE UTILITY: ASYMMETRIC PRIOR. Now (iii) is clearly not a necessary condition for existence. Let us see what happens if (iii) is weakened by considering a class of examples. In particular, we return to type I preferences on a single issue, $U(\Theta, d) = -(\Theta-d)^2$. Assume c is identical and known across all voters. Let d be distributed according to the continuous density function

$$h(d) = \begin{cases} \dfrac{a}{a+1} e^d & d \le 0 \\[4mm] \dfrac{a}{a+1} e^{-ad} & d \ge 0 \end{cases}$$

where $a > 0$. We will consider different values of a and note that condition (iii) of proposition 3 is satisfied if and only if $a = 1$, in which case $\hat{\Theta} = 0$. For this class of examples we can prove

Proposition 4. If $H - [\quad m_1, m_2]$, $m_1, m_2 > 0$ and if (Θ_A^*, Θ_B^*) is an electoral equilibrium for the above example, then

$$\Theta_A^* = \Theta_B^* = \begin{cases} 0 & \text{if } a = 1 \\[3mm] m_2 & \text{if } a < 1 \\[3mm] -m_1 & \text{if } a > 1 \end{cases}$$

Proof. If $a = 1$, proposition 3 applies. If $a > 1$, let $\Theta_A^* > -m_1$ be arbitrary and suppose Θ_A^*, Θ_B^* is an electoral equilibrium. Then $W^B(\Theta_A^*, \Theta_B) \le 0$ for all Θ_B. Let $\Theta_B = \Theta_A^* - \varepsilon$ where $\varepsilon > 0$. $G(r, \Theta_A^*, \Theta_B) = H(\Theta_A^* - \dfrac{\varepsilon}{2} + \dfrac{rc}{\varepsilon})$ where

$$H(d) = \begin{cases} \dfrac{a}{a+1} e^d & \text{if } d < 0 \\[4mm] 1 - \dfrac{1}{a+1} e^{-ad} & \text{if } d > 0. \end{cases}$$

Thus for ε near zero,

$$W^B = (\dfrac{a}{a+1}) \exp\left[-a(\Theta_A^* - \dfrac{\varepsilon}{2} - \dfrac{c}{\beta\varepsilon})\right] - (\dfrac{1}{a+1}) \exp\left[-a(\Theta_A^* - \dfrac{\varepsilon}{2} + \dfrac{c}{\alpha\varepsilon}\right].$$

We will show that for some ε near zero $W^B > 0$, and therefore $\Theta_A^* > m_1$ cannot be an equilibrium. Suppose $W^B \leq 0$ for all $\varepsilon > 0$. Then for all

$$\varepsilon > 0, \ a \ exp \ (\Theta_A^* - \frac{\varepsilon}{2} - \frac{c}{\beta\varepsilon}) \leq exp \ [-a(\Theta_A^* - \frac{\varepsilon}{2} + \frac{c}{\alpha\varepsilon})]$$

or

$$\Theta_A^* - \frac{\varepsilon}{2} - \frac{c}{\beta\varepsilon} + ln \ a \leq - a(\Theta_A^* - \frac{\varepsilon}{2} + \frac{c}{\alpha\varepsilon}).$$

This implies

$$\Theta_A^* \leq \frac{\varepsilon}{2} + \frac{c}{\varepsilon(1+a)} [\frac{1}{\beta} - \frac{a}{\alpha}] - ln \ a.$$

We remind ourselves that as $\varepsilon \to 0$, $q_A \to 0$ and $q_B \to 0$. Thus as $\varepsilon \to 0$, $\alpha \to 1$ and $\beta \to 1$. Since $a > 1$, $\overset{lim}{\varepsilon\to0} \frac{1}{\varepsilon}[\frac{1}{\beta} - \frac{a}{\alpha}] = -\infty$. Thus, if $a > 0$ and $\Theta_A^* > m_1$, there is some ε near zero such that $\Theta_B \ \varepsilon \ H$ and $V^B > 0$. This establishes the proposition for $a > 1$ since a symmetric argument applies for $\Theta_B^* > -\infty$. For $a < 1$ as similar proof applies. *QED.*

The key fact to note, in understanding why the proposition is true, is that if Θ_A and Θ_B are very close to each other, then, because of the type I (quadratic loss) preferences, it is only the voters in the tails of the distribution (the extreme positive and negative values of d) who will vote.[9] Thus, for example, if $a > 1$, then voters with extreme negative d are more likely [10] than voters with extreme positive d. Thus, platforms move in a negative direction. This observation extends to more general density functions and to multidimensional issue spaces.

The problem with this fact is that boundary points cannot be equilibria.

Corollary 4.1. For the class of examples covered in proposition 4, if m_1 and m_2 are large enough, an equilibrium exists if and only if $a = 1$.

Proof. (if) follows from proposition 3. (only if) Suppose $a > 1$. If (Θ_A^*, Θ_B^*) is an equilibrium, then $\Theta_B^* = -m_1$. Let $\hat{\Theta}$ be such that $\frac{a}{a+1} e \hat{\Theta}$ $= \frac{1}{2}$. That is, $\hat{\Theta}$ is the median voter's ideal point, $\frac{1}{2} \leq ln \ \frac{a+1}{2a} < 0$ for $a > 1$.

Let $\Theta_A = \Theta_B + \varepsilon = -m_1 + \varepsilon$ and let $- m_1 + \frac{\varepsilon}{2} + \frac{c}{\alpha\varepsilon} = \hat{\Theta}$. Thus $\Theta_A = - \hat{\Theta} - \sqrt{(m_1 - \hat{\Theta})^2 - \frac{2c}{\alpha}}$. (By m_1 "large enough," we mean that $(m_1 - \hat{\Theta})^2 > \frac{2c}{\alpha}$.) Then $q_A = 1 - G(\frac{1}{\alpha}, \Theta) = 1 - H(\Theta_B + \frac{\varepsilon}{2} + \frac{c}{\alpha\varepsilon}) = \frac{1}{2}$. $q_B = H(\Theta_B + \frac{\varepsilon}{2} - \frac{c}{\beta\varepsilon}) < \frac{1}{2}$. Therefore, $q_A > q_B$ and $\Theta_B^* = -m_1$ cannot be an equilibrium. A similar argument follows for $0 < a < 1$. *QED.*

One must conclude that symmetric tails are a necessary condition for the existence of an equilibrium. Is this sufficient? Surprisingly, it seems so, subject to a precise definition of "tails." Returning to a single issue space with

$$U = -(\Theta - d)^2, \text{ remember that } V^A = q_A - q_B = 1 - H(\overline{\Theta} + \frac{c}{\alpha\varepsilon}) - H(\overline{\Theta}$$

$$- \frac{c}{\beta\varepsilon}) \text{ where } \varepsilon = \Theta_A - \Theta_B > 0 \text{ and } \overline{\Theta} = \frac{\Theta_A + \Theta_B}{2}. \text{ Now consider } \partial V^A/\partial\Theta_A$$

$$= -h(\overline{\Theta} + \frac{c}{\alpha\varepsilon})[\frac{1}{2} - \frac{c}{\alpha\varepsilon^2} - \frac{c}{\alpha^2\varepsilon}\frac{\partial\alpha}{2\Theta_A}] - h[\overline{\Theta} - \frac{c}{\beta\varepsilon}] \times [\frac{1}{2} + \frac{c}{\beta\varepsilon^2} + \frac{c}{\beta^2\varepsilon}\frac{\partial\beta}{\partial\Theta_A}].$$

For ε large enough $\partial V^A/\partial\Theta_A < 0$. In particular, if $\frac{1}{2} - \frac{c}{\alpha\varepsilon^2} - \frac{c}{\alpha^2\varepsilon}\frac{\partial\alpha}{\partial\Theta_A} > 0,$

then A will want to decrease Θ_A. Similarly, B will want to increase Θ_B if $\frac{1}{2}$

$- \frac{c}{\beta\varepsilon^2} - \frac{c}{\beta^2\varepsilon}\frac{\partial\beta}{\partial\Theta_B} > 0$. Since $\alpha = \beta \le 1$ at equilibrium, we know that there

is an $\hat{\varepsilon}$ such that if $1 - H(\hat{\Theta} + \frac{c}{\varepsilon}) = H(\hat{\Theta} - \frac{d}{\varepsilon})$ for all $0 < \varepsilon \le \hat{\varepsilon}$, then an

equilibrium exists at $\hat{\Theta}$. Another way of stating this is that $h(d) = h(-d)$ for

all $d \ge \hat{\Theta} + \frac{c}{\hat{\varepsilon}}$.

It should be noted that the more concave the $U(\cdot)$ are, the larger the tail which must be symmetric. Thus, for example, if $U(\Theta, d) = -(\|\Theta - d\|)^v$ for $v \ge 1$ where $\|x\| = (\Sigma x_\ell^2)^{1/9}$, then larger v require larger $\hat{\varepsilon}$. In the best case ($v = 1$) with a single issue, $\hat{\varepsilon} = 0$; that is, no symmetry is required for

existence at the median. In this case, for $A > B$, $q_A = \mu(\{e \mid \frac{A-B}{2c} \ge \frac{1}{\alpha}$ and

$d \ge \frac{A+B}{2} + \frac{1}{\alpha}\})$ and $q_B = \mu(\{e \mid \frac{A-B}{2c} \ge \frac{1}{\beta}$ and $d < \frac{A+B}{2} - \frac{1}{\beta}\})$. If $A = \hat{\Theta}$

where $\mu(\{e \mid d \le \hat{\Theta}\}) = \frac{1}{2}$, then, for all $B < A$, either $q_A = q_B = 0$ (when

$\frac{A-B}{2c} < 1$) or $q_A \ge \frac{1}{2}$ and $q_B \le \frac{1}{2}$ and, therefore, $V^A(\Theta_A, \Theta_B) \ge 0$ for all Θ_B

$\ne \Theta_A = \hat{\Theta}$. The conclusion one draws from all of this is that if preferences are concave, a sufficient amount of symmetry of tastes must occur if an equilibrium is to exist. This lack of robustness of the model is somewhat discouraging.

However, one must recognize that type I preferences, as well as strictly concave utility functions, imply a form of behavior which seems to be empirically invalid. I refer, in particular, to a stylized empirical fact: abstentions increase with alienation. That is, as both candidates' platforms move away from a voter's ideal platform, the voter is more likely to abstain. With concave and type I preferences, however, just the opposite is predicted. This is easiest to see by writing $\Delta = U(\Theta_A, d) - U(\Theta_B, d) = -(-\Theta_A + d)^2 + (-\Theta_B + d)^2 = 2(d\varepsilon - \overline{\Theta}\varepsilon)$, where $\varepsilon = \Theta_A - \Theta_B$ and $\overline{\Theta} = \dfrac{\Theta_A + \Theta_B}{2}$. Now $\dfrac{\partial\Delta}{\partial\overline{\Theta}} = -2\varepsilon\,\overline{\Theta}$. If $\varepsilon > 0$, $\dfrac{\partial\Delta}{\partial\overline{\Theta}} < 0$ and, therefore, as $\overline{\Theta}$ declines, this voter is more likely to vote for A. From our model (assuming α and β constant for now), a voter abstains if $-\dfrac{1}{\beta} < \dfrac{\Delta}{2c} < \dfrac{1}{\alpha}$ or $-\dfrac{1}{\beta} < (d - \overline{\Theta})\,\varepsilon < \dfrac{1}{\alpha}$. Thus abstentions occur for small values of $|\overline{\Theta} - d|$ and not for large values. This is contrary to the stylized fact. We thus turn to a consideration of other types of preferences.

(iii) NONCONCAVE UTILITY: EXAMPLES. As an alternative to type I preferences we consider those of type II, or $U(\Theta, d) = -\|\Theta - d\|^{1/2}$. These are convex functions on each side of the ideal point d, even though they are not convex over all Θ. Assume $\Theta_A > \Theta_B$ and let $r = \dfrac{2c}{\alpha}$ and $s = \dfrac{2c}{\beta}$. If $H = R^1$ (a single issue), then a voter with parameters (d, c)

    (i) votes for A if $\Theta_A - \Theta_B > r^2$ and $\Theta_A - z(r) \le d \le \Theta_A + x(r)$
    (ii) votes for B if $\Theta_A - \Theta_B > s^2$ and $\Theta_B - x(s) \le d \le \Theta_B + z(s)$
and (iii) abstains otherwise,
where

$$z(w) = \frac{\Theta_A - \Theta_B}{2} - w(\frac{\Theta_A - \Theta_B}{2} - \frac{w^2}{4})^{1/2}$$

and

$$x(w) = (\frac{\Theta_A - \Theta_B}{2} - \frac{w^2}{2})^2\, w^{-2}.$$

Notice that if $\Theta_A - \Theta_B$ is fixed and if Θ_A and Θ_B simultaneously move far enough away from d, the voter will abstain. Let $H(\cdot)$ be the distribution function of d (and $h(\cdot)$ the density function) and assume c is fixed and identical for all voters. Then the probability that a voter votes for A is

$$q^A = \begin{cases} h(\Theta_A + x(r)) - H(\Theta_A - z(r)) & \text{if } \Theta_A - \Theta_B > r^2 \\ 0 & \text{otherwise} \end{cases}$$

and the probability that a voter votes for B is

$$q^B = \begin{cases} H(\Theta_B - x(s)) - H(\Theta_B + z(s)) & \text{if } \Theta_A - \Theta_B > r^2 \\ 0 & \text{otherwise.} \end{cases}$$

The following proposition can be established for this class of examples.

Proposition 5. If $H(\cdot)$ is continuous and unimodal at Θ_m (i.e., $h'(d) \ge 0$ for $d \le \Theta_m$ and $h'(d) \le 0$ for $d \ge \Theta_m$) and if Θ_A^*, Θ_B^* is an equilibrium for h, then $\Theta_m - 4c^2 \le \Theta_A^*$, $\Theta_B^* \le 4c^2 + \Theta_m$.

Proof. Suppose $\Theta_B^* < \Theta_m - 4c^2$. Then there is $\varepsilon > 0$ such that $\Theta_A \equiv \Theta_B + 4c^2 + \varepsilon < \Theta_m$. Now $\varepsilon \to 0$ implies $x \to 0$ and $z \to 0$, since $\varepsilon \to 0$ implies $r \to 2c$ and $s \to 2c$ (because $\alpha \to 1$ and $\beta \to 1$). [Note that for $\varepsilon > 0$, $\Theta_A - \Theta_B > r^2$ and $\Theta_A - \Theta_B > s^2$, since otherwise $q_A = q_B = 0$, which implies $\alpha = \beta = 1$, which implies $\Theta_A - \Theta_B > r^2, s^2$.] Assume $s = r$. There exists $\varepsilon > 0$ such that $\Theta_A(\varepsilon)$ $+ x(\varepsilon) < \Theta_m$. Therefore $h(t) \geq h[\Theta_A(\varepsilon) - z(\varepsilon)]$ for all $t \, \varepsilon[\Theta_A - z, \Theta_A + x]$ and, since $\Theta_B + z \leq \Theta_A - z$, $h(t) \leq h(\Theta_B + z) \leq h(\Theta_A - z)$ for all $t \, \varepsilon[\Theta_B - x, \Theta_B + z]$. Thus $q_B(\Theta_A(\varepsilon), \Theta_B^*) < q_A(\Theta_A(\varepsilon), \Theta_B^*)$ if $r = s$. Suppose $r \neq s$ and $q_B > q_A$. At a voters' equilibrium[11] if $q_B > q_A$, then $s > r$ since $\beta < \alpha$. Now

$$\partial x/\partial s = - \frac{1}{2s^3}(\frac{\Theta_A - \Theta_B}{2} - \frac{s^2}{2})^2 - \frac{1}{s}(\frac{\Theta_A - \Theta_B}{2} - \frac{s^2}{2}) < 0 \text{ and } \partial z/\partial s = -$$

$$(\frac{\Theta_A - \Theta_B}{2} - \frac{s^2}{4})^{1/2} + (\frac{s}{2})^2(\frac{\Theta_A - \Theta_B}{2} - \frac{s^2}{4})^{-1/2} < 0 \text{ since } - [\frac{\Theta_A - \Theta_B}{2} -$$

$$\frac{s^2}{4}] + \frac{s^2}{4} = -(\frac{\Theta_A - \Theta_B}{2} - \frac{s^2}{2}) < 0.$$

Thus $\partial q_B/\partial s = h(\Theta_B + z) \cdot \partial z/\partial s + h(\Theta_B - x) \, \partial x/\partial s < 0$. Therefore $q_B(h) < q_B(r) < q_A(r)$ implies that if $\Theta_B^* < -4c^2 + \Theta_m$, there is $\Theta_A < \Theta_m$ such that $q_A > q_B$. Thus Θ_B^* cannot be an equilibrium platform. A similar proof works for $\Theta_A > 4c^2 + \Theta_m$ and symmetry implies the rest of the proposition. QED.

We have shown that for a unimodal distribution of tastes and $U = -|\Theta - d|^{1/2}$, any equilibrium must be concentrated around the *mode*.[12] Since this equals the median only for symmetric distributions, we immediately see that non-concavities produce qualitatively different equilibria.

Although proposition 5 contains necessary conditions for equilibrium platforms, they are not sufficient. In fact, if the mean and the mode are too far apart (relative to $4c^2$) or—what is the same thing—if the distribution of tastes is too skewed, there may be no equilibrium. Consider the following continuous, asymmetric density function for d.

$$h(d) = \begin{cases} S \cdot e^{bd} & \text{if } d \leq 0 \\ (1 - \varepsilon d)S & \text{if } 0 \leq d < R \\ e^{-a(d-R)}S(1 - \varepsilon R) & \text{if } d \geq R \end{cases}$$

where $S = [\frac{1}{b} + R(1 - \frac{\varepsilon}{2}R) + \frac{1}{a}(1 - \varepsilon R)]^{-1}$, $b, \varepsilon, a, R > 0$, and $1 - \varepsilon R > 0$. Note that h is unimodal, where $d = 0$ is the mode. Let $\Theta_A = \Theta_B + \eta$ and assume that $r = s$. Then $x = \frac{1}{r^2}(\frac{\eta}{2} - \frac{r^2}{2})^2$. For (η, R) such that $x > 4c^2$, and $R \geq x$, if $\Theta_B \leq \Theta_m + 4c^2 = 4c^2$, then

$$q^A - q^B =$$

$$S \cdot [(\Theta_A + x)(1 - \frac{\varepsilon}{2}(\Theta_A + x)) - (\Theta_A - z)(1 - \frac{\varepsilon}{2}(\Theta_A - z)) -$$

$$((\Theta_B + z)(1 - \frac{\varepsilon}{2}(\Theta_B + z)) + \frac{1}{b}) - \frac{1}{b}e^{+b(\Theta_B - x)}] = \frac{1}{b}S(1 + e^{+b(\Theta_B - 2)}) +$$

$$S[x - \Theta_B] - \frac{\varepsilon}{2}S[(\Theta_A + x)^2 - (\Theta_A - z)^2 - (\Theta_B + z)^2] > 0,$$

if $x - \Theta_B > \frac{\varepsilon}{2}[(\Theta_A + x)^2 - (\Theta_A - z)^2 - (\Theta_B + z)^2].$

Since $x - \Theta_B > 0$, we can choose $\varepsilon > 0$ as well as η and R, such that, for all $\Theta_B \leq 4c^2$, $q_A - q_B > 0$. Therefore, from proposition 5, if ε is small enough and R is large enough, there can be no equilibria, since there are enough voters to the right of B (relative to those to the left of the median) to enable A to always collect a majority of those who vote.

One can state (overly strong) sufficient conditions for the existence of an equilibrium in this class of examples.

Proposition 6. If $h(d)$ is continuous and unimodal, $U = - |\Theta - d|^{1/2}$, d, $\Theta \varepsilon R'$, and c is fixed, let $\hat{\Theta}$ maximize $H(\Theta_A + 4c^2) - H(\Theta_A - 4c^2)$. Let $P(\hat{\Theta}) = H(\hat{\Theta} + 4c^2) - H(\hat{\Theta} - 4c^2)$. If $P(\hat{\Theta}) \geq H\hat{\Theta} - 4c^2)$ and $P(\hat{\Theta}) \geq 1 - H(\hat{\Theta} + 4c^2)$, then $\Theta_A^* = \Theta_B^* = \hat{\Theta}$ is an equilibrium.

Proof. Let $\Theta_A = \hat{\Theta}$ and $\Theta_B < \Theta_A$. If $\Theta_B \geq \Theta_A - 4c^2$, then $q_A = q_B = 0$. If $\Theta_B < \Theta_A - 4c^2$, one can show $\Theta_B + z \leq \Theta_A - 4c^2 < \Theta_m$. If $x \leq 4c^2$, then $h(r) \geq h(\Theta_B + z)$ for all $v = \varepsilon [\Theta_A - z, \Theta_A + x]$ and $h(t) \leq h(\Theta_B + z)$ for all $t \varepsilon [\Theta_B - x, \Theta_B + z]$. Therefore $q_A > q_B$. If $x \geq 4c^2$, $q_A - q_B = H(\Theta_A + x) - H(\Theta_A - z) - H(\Theta_B + z) + H(\Theta_B - x) \geq H(\Theta_A + 4c^2) - H(\Theta_A - 4c^2) + H(\Theta_B - x) - H(\Theta_A - z)$. By assumption, $P(\Theta_A) \geq H(\Theta_A - 4c^2) \geq H(\Theta_A - z)$. Thus, $q_A > q_B$. A similar argument follows for $\Theta_B = \hat{\Theta}$ and $\Theta_A > \Theta_B$. QED.

One is led naturally to the following

Conjecture. If $U = - \|\Theta - d\|^{1/n}$ for $n > 1$, Θ, $d \varepsilon R^k$, $\|x\| = (\Sigma x_k^2)^{1/2}$ and if the density on (d, c) is $h(d)g(c)$ where h is continuous and unimodal [i.e., $\exists \Theta_m \varepsilon \nabla h(d)\cdot(\Theta_m - d) > 0 \ \forall \ d$] and, letting $\bar{p} = \max_{\Theta} \mu(\{(d,c) \mid \dfrac{\|\Theta - d\|^{1/n}}{2c}$

$\leq 1\})$ and $\hat{\Theta}$ be the solution, if $\hat{p} \geq \mu(\{(d,c) \mid \alpha(d - \hat{\Theta}) \geq 0$ and $\dfrac{\|\hat{\Theta} - d\|^{1/n}}{2c}$

$> 1\})$ for all $\gamma \neq 0$ then $\Theta^A = \Theta^B = \hat{\Theta}$ is an equilibrium.

Thus, if this conjecture is correct, then when preferences are of the form $- \|\Theta - d\|^{1/n}$, $(n > 1)$, and the distribution of tastes is unimodal and not too asymmetric, equilibrium exists where $\Theta_A = \Theta_B$, $q_A = q_B = 0$, and Θ_A and Θ_B are somewhere near the mode.

C. Summary and Comments

We can summarize the results of this section in several brief statements.

1. If utility functions are concave and tastes are continuously and symmetrically distributed, then an electoral equilibrium exists, with both candidates selecting the *median* voter's ideal point, and no one votes.

2. If utility functions are concave and tastes are asymmetrically distributed in the tails, then an electoral equilibrium will not exist.

3. If preferences are of type II (convex on each side of an ideal point) and if tastes are continuously, unimodally, and not too asymmetrically distributed, then an electoral equilibrium exists, with both candidates choosing the *modal* voter's ideal point, and no one votes.

Several comments about these results seem to be in order. First, if we were to substitute minimax regret behavior for our fully rational expected utility model of voters, nothing substantive with respect to the existence of electoral equilibrium or modality of candidates platforms would be altered. None of the arguments in this section would be affected if we let $\alpha = \beta = \frac{1}{2}$. Thus *both models of behavior produce identical outcomes in equilibrium.*[13] They are, therefore, significantly different in their predictions of disequilibrium phenomena only if candidates maximize expected plurality.

Second, the role of the assumption of candidate irrelevance should not be ignored. If different voters have different beliefs about the likelihood of candidates' postelection positions, then, even if candidates were driven (by expected plurality maximization) to choose identical positions, there may be a positive probability of turnout. Further, it is highly likely, if the candidates' names (reputations) count, that equilibria with differentiated platforms and positive turnout will exist.

Third, we have not considered the implications for existence and characterization of equilibria of the assumption that preferences might be a mixture of type I and type II. It would be interesting to know, for example, the outcome (equilibrium) predicted by this model when "Republicans" have type I preferences and are concentrated to the "right" of the median voter and "Democrats" have type II preferences and are concentrated to the "left" of the median voter. Technically, one could consider a distribution of preferences constructed as a convex combination of type I and type II. For example, let $h^I(d)$ be a density of type I preferences and $h^{II}(d)$ be a density of type II preferences, and consider the implications if the actual density of tastes is $\lambda\, h^I(d) + (1 - \lambda)\, h^{II}(d)$ for some $\lambda\ \varepsilon\ [0, 1]$. We leave this exercise to the interested reader.

Fourth, we have not explored the implications of this model for the standard social choice problem with a finite set of alternatives. A reasonable approach to that problem would be to imbed that set of alternatives in the real line, extend the preferences of voters over the line, and then apply the results of this section. This is in the spirit of single-peak preferences (a property that both type I and type II preferences have on the line—although not if the issue space is multidimensional) and, of course, the method of imbedding is crucial.[14]

Finally, although I have used the phrase "general equilibrium" in the title, I have ignored at least one set of important actors and one type of candidate decision. The missing actors are political activists who donate funds (to change voters' likelihood beliefs?) and who, by ringing doorbells, can raise the cost of not voting and thereby raise turnout. The missing decision is the issue of whether to run or not. Entry into electoral competition has been ignored.

We turn next to some generalizations of the model and to the implications which arise when candidates adopt behavior other than expected plurality maximization.

III. EXTENSIONS AND ALTERATIONS
A. Other-Candidate Objective Functions

In section IIA we indicated that candidates might wish, for example, to maximize the probability of winning or their expected vote. We now consider each of these in turn.

Let us consider a scoring function where $s^i = 1$ if voter i votes for A, 0 if they abstain, and -1 if they vote for B. Then the probability that A wins is simply $P_A = \text{prob}\{\sum_{i=1}^{n} s^i > 0\} + \frac{1}{2}\text{prob}\{\sum_i s^i = 0\}$, or $\text{prob}\frac{1}{n}\sum_{i=1}^{n} s^i > 0\} + \frac{1}{2}\text{prob}\{\frac{1}{n}s^i = 0\}$, where $q_A = \text{prob}\{s^i = 1\}$ and $q_B = \text{prob}\{s^i = -1\}$. Since each voter is independently and identically distributed,[15] as $n \to \infty$ prob $\{|\frac{1}{n}\sum_i s^i - (q_A - q_B)| > \varepsilon\} \to 0$ for all $\varepsilon > 0$. Thus for large electorates, a reasonable approximation of the maximization of P_A is the maximization of expected plurality.[16]

One expects, therefore, that if candidates maximize their probability of winning, the outcome in large electorates will be the same as that which occurs if they maximize expected plurality.

If, on the other hand, candidates maximize expected votes, the outcomes are significantly different because of the role of abstentions. For example, there is no tendency for platforms to converge; in fact, candidates will constantly try to differentiate themselves from their opponents.

Lemma 5. If there is an $\varepsilon \geq 0$ such that $G(1, \hat{\Theta}_A, \hat{\Theta}_B) - G(-1, \hat{\Theta}_A, \hat{\Theta}_B) > 0$ whenever $\|\Theta_A - \Theta_B\| > \varepsilon$, and if Θ_A^*, Θ_B^* is an electoral equilibrium under vote maximization, then $\Theta_A^* \neq \Theta_B^*$.

Proof. If $\Theta_A^* = \Theta_B^*$, then $q_A^* = q_B^* = 0$. But either A or B can change Θ_j such that $q_j^* > 0$. *QED.*

I have not characterized further (much less established the existence of) electoral equilibrium under vote maximization. It may, however, be informative to consider an example, and so we return to a single-dimensional issue space with type I preferences and c fixed and known across all voters. As before, if $\Theta_A > \Theta_B$, $\overline{\Theta} = \frac{\Theta_A + \Theta_B}{2}$ and $\varepsilon = \Theta_A - \Theta_B$, then $G(r, \Theta) = H(\overline{\Theta} + \frac{rc}{\varepsilon})$ where H is the distribution function of ideal points, d. We consider only equilibria for which $q_A = q_B$ (whether there may be others is an open question). Under the appropriate differentiability and symmetry conditions on H, a necessary condition[17] at equilibrium is that $\frac{\partial q_A}{\partial \Theta_A} = 0$ and $\frac{\partial q_B}{\partial \Theta_B} = 0$.

Thus, $\frac{1}{2} = \frac{c}{\alpha \, \varepsilon^2} = \frac{c}{\beta \, \varepsilon^2}$ and $q_A = 1 - H(\overline{\Theta} + \frac{\varepsilon}{2}) = H(\overline{\Theta} - \frac{\varepsilon}{2})$. If H is

symmetric around $\hat{\Theta}$, then $\Theta_A = \hat{\Theta} + \frac{1}{2}\sqrt{\frac{2c}{\alpha}}$ and $\Theta_B = \hat{\Theta} - \frac{1}{2}\sqrt{\frac{2c}{\alpha}}$ where

$\alpha = f(q_A, q_B)$. [For minimax regret behavior $\alpha = \frac{1}{2}$ and $\Theta_A = \hat{\Theta} + \sqrt{c}$, $\Theta_B = \hat{\Theta} - \sqrt{c}$.] Although α cannot be easily solved for, we know (since $q_A = q_B$) that $\frac{n!}{(n/2)!(n/2)!}(\frac{1}{2})^n \le \alpha \le 1$. By Stirlings formula, for large n, $\sqrt{\frac{2}{n\pi}} \le \alpha \le 1$. Therefore, at a vote maximizing electoral equilibrium, $(\sqrt{2c})(\frac{n\pi}{2})^{1/4} \ge \Theta_A - \Theta_B \ge \sqrt{2c}$. These are not very tight bounds, but whatever $\Theta_A - \Theta_B$ is, there is always positive turnout in this type of equilibrium.

It should be emphasized that, even for the example, only necessary conditions have been examined. I have not yet found additional conditions which guarantee that these are sufficient. Thus it is possible that an electoral equilibrium, with vote maximizing behavior on the part of the candidates, does not exist.

B. More Candidates and Non-identical Beliefs

Rather than proceed through a variety of special cases, we turn to a description of the general model of voter behavior under the extension of rationality that we have proposed. To do so, we must introduce some new notation and recall some old:

$i = 1, \ldots, n + 1$	voters	$(0 < n < \infty)$,
$j = 1, \ldots, m$	candidates	$(z \le m \le \infty)$,
$\Theta_j \, \varepsilon \, T$	j's platform	
n_j	the number of votes for j,	
δ^i	i's decision function where $\delta^i = (\delta^i_o, \ldots, \delta^i_m)$ and if i votes for j ($j = 0$ is abstention), then $\delta^i_j = 1$ and $\delta^i_k = 0$ for $k \ne j$. We will let $\delta^i(j) = (0, \ldots, 0, 1, 0, \ldots, 0)$ be i's decision to vote for j,	

$\Omega_n = \{\underline{n} \, \varepsilon \, R^{m+1} \mid n_j \text{ is a non-negative integer and } \Sigma^m_{j=0} \, n_j = n\}$.
Ω_n represents all possible election outcomes in terms of votes if there are n voters,

$\Theta = (\Theta_1, \ldots, \Theta_m)\varepsilon \, T^m$,	
$h: T^m \times \Omega \to M(T)$	where $M(T)$ is the space of probability measures on T and h is the outcome rule specifying the probability of the winning platform, if candidates have platforms $(\Theta_1, \ldots, \Theta_m)$ and voters vote $(n_o, \ldots, n_m)$.

Remark. In section II, where $m = 2$,

$$h(\Theta, \underline{n}) = \begin{cases} \Theta_A \text{ if } n_A > n_B \\ \Theta_B \text{ if } n_B > n_A \\ \Theta_j \text{ with probability } \frac{1}{2} \text{ if } n_A = n_B. \end{cases}$$

Using the above, we see that $V(\Theta, n, d^i) = \int_H U(\gamma, d^i)dh(\Theta, n)$ is i's expected utility if platforms are Θ and votes are n.

A voting strategy for voter i is a mapping from voter characteristics (d^i, c^i) to decisions. That is, $\delta^i: E \to \{\delta^i(o), \delta^i(1), \ldots, \delta^i(m)\}$. We let $Z^i = E^1 x \ldots x E^{i-1} x E^{i+1} x \ldots x E^n$ be the space of others' characteristics and represent i's beliefs about $z^i \varepsilon Z^i$ by a mapping $\Psi^i: E^i \to M(Z^i)$. Thus if i has characteristic e^i, he believes that others' are distributed according to $\Psi^i(e^i)$. With these beliefs and with knowledge of the strategies of others, $\delta^{)i(} = (\delta^1, \ldots, \delta^{i-1}, \ldots, \delta^n)$, i's expected utility from voting for j (the decision $\delta^i(j)$) is $W^i(\delta^i(j), \delta^{)i(}, e^i) \equiv \int V(\Theta, \delta^i(j) + \Sigma_{h+i} \delta^h(e^h), e^i)d \Psi^i(e^i) - (1 - \delta^i_o (j))C^i$.

The integral is i's expected utility of the outcome of the election and $(1 - \delta^i_o(j)) = C^i$ is the cost of his decision. That is, $(1 - \delta^i_o(j))C^i = C^i$ if $j = 1$, $\ldots, m$ and it is 0 if i abstains by choosing $j = 0$.

We can now state precisely the generalization of a voter equilibrium introduced in section II.

Definition. A voters' equilibrium for $<(\Theta_1, \ldots, \Theta_m), \Psi^1, \ldots, \Psi^{n+1}>$ is an $n + 1 -$ triple of strategies $(\bar{\delta}^1, \ldots, \bar{\delta}^{n+1})$ such that for all $i = 1, \ldots, n + 1$ and all $e^i \varepsilon E^i$, $\bar{\delta}^i(e^i)$ solves

$$\text{Maximize } W^i(\delta^i(j), \bar{\delta}^{)i(}, e^i)$$
$$j = 0, \ldots, m.$$

This concept of equilibrium is identical to that of a Bayes equilibrium.

For a variety of reasons, this model is extremely difficult to analyze without further assumptions on the structure of beliefs. Thus we introduce the following.

Assumption. (Independent–identical beliefs). For each voter i, $\Psi^i(e^i) = \mu x \ldots x \mu$ where $E^h \equiv E$ for all h and $\mu \varepsilon M(E)$.

Under this assumption, there is one voters' equilibrium which is of particular interest: the one in which all strategies are identical.

Definition. A symmetric voters' equilibrium is a voters' equilibrium such that $\delta^i(\cdot) = \delta^*(\cdot)$ for all $i = 1, \ldots, n + 1$.

We consider only symmetric equilibria throughout the rest of this paper and thus need only look at a common strategy, δ.

Given a strategy δ, the probability that a voter votes for candidate j is

$$q_j = \mu(\{e \mid \delta(e) = \delta(j)\}).$$

Thus, if all h use δ, the probability that the votes tally to $\underline{n} = (n_0, \ldots, n_m)$ when i is not considered can be computed to be

$$P(\underline{n}, q) = \frac{n!}{n_o! \ldots n_m!} (q_o)^{n_o} \ldots (q_m)^{n_m}. \tag{6}$$

Further, the probability of $\underline{n}$ if i votes for j is $P(\underline{n} - \delta^i(j), q)$. Therefore i's expected utility of voting for j given δ is

$$W_j(\Theta, e^i) = \Sigma_{n\varepsilon\Omega_{n+1}}V(\Theta, n, e^i) \, P(\underline{n} - \delta(j)) - (1 - \delta_o(j))C^i.$$

If we let $R_j(\Theta, p) = \{e \mid W_j(\Theta, e) > W_k(\Theta, e)$ for all $k = 0, \ldots, m$ and $k \neq j\}$, then the probability that a voter votes for j is (7) $q_j = \mu[R_j(\Theta, p)]$ for $j = 0, \ldots, m$.

Remark. δ^* is a symmetric voters' equilibrium for $<\Theta, \mu>$ if and only if (i) $\delta^*(e) = \delta(j)$ when $e \varepsilon R_j(\Theta, p^*(\cdot, q^*))$, and (ii) p^* and q^* simultaneously satisfy (6) and (7).

Remark. In applications, one need only calculate $p(n)$ for $n \ni h(\Theta, n) \neq h(\Theta, n - \delta^i(j))$ for some $j = 0, \ldots, m$. Further, one can "lump together" all $n,n,' \ni h(\Theta, n) = h(\Theta, n')$ and $h(\Theta, n - \delta^i(j)) = h(\Theta, n' - \delta^i(j))$ for all j. In section 1, $\alpha = p_3 + p_4$ and $\beta = p_2 + p_3$ did just that (see McKelvey and Ordeshook, 1972).

With one more definition, the continuity of μ, we can state an existence result for a symmetric voters equilibrium and some implications for turnout.

Definition. $\mu \varepsilon M(E)$ is "continuous" if $A^q \to A^o \Rightarrow \mu(A^q) \to \mu(A^o)$ where $A^q \to A^o$ iff (1) $a^q \varepsilon A^q$, $a^q \to a^o \Rightarrow a^o \varepsilon A^o$ and (2) $a^o \varepsilon A_o \Rightarrow \exists \, a^q \varepsilon A^q \ni a^q \to a^o$.

Proposition 7. A symmetric voters' equilibrium exists for $<\Theta, \mu>$ if (a) μ is continuous and (b) V is continuous in e^i.

Proof. Since $q \varepsilon [0,1]^{m+1}$ and $p \varepsilon [0,1]^{n!}$, if $\mu(R_j(\Theta, p))$ is continuous in p, then, since $p(n, q)$ is continuous in q, Brouwer's theorem applies and we are done. Thus it is sufficient to note that $R_j(\Theta, p)$ is a continuous correspondence in p since V is continuous in e and W_j is linear in p. QED.

Remark. Remember, $V(\Theta, n, e^i) = \int_H U(\gamma, d^i) \, dh(\Theta, n)$. Therefore, if U is continuous in d, so is V. Also, if $E \times [\delta, \infty) \le R^k$ and $\mu(D) = \int_D h(e,c) \, dc dc$ where h is continuous, then μ is "continuous."

Corollary 7.1. If the outcome function h has the property that $h(<n+1,0, \ldots, 0>, \Theta) = \Theta_j$ with probability $\frac{1}{m} \, \forall \, j$ and $h(<n,0, \ldots, 0> + \delta(j), \Theta) = \Theta_j$, then expected turnout is zero in a symmetric voters equilibrium if and only if $\mu(\{e \mid \frac{1}{m} \Sigma_{j=1}^m U(\Theta_j, d) \ge \max_j U(\Theta_j, d) - c\}) = 1$.

Corollary 7.2. (a) If $\Theta_1 = \ldots = \Theta_m$, then $q_o^* = 1$. (b) Let $\hat{U}(d) = \max_j U(\Theta_j, d)$ and $\underline{U}(e) = \min_j U(\Theta_j, d)$. Then (b.1) if $\mu(\{e \mid c > \frac{m-1}{m} (\hat{U}(d) - \underline{U}(d))\}) = 1$, then $q_o^* = 1$. (b.2) if $\mu(\{e \mid c < \frac{1}{m} (\hat{U}(d) - \underline{U}(d)\}) > 0$, then $q_o^* < 1$.

For type I preferences, if μ is represented by a continuous positive density on R^k and if $\Theta_j \neq \Theta_k$ for some $j, k = 1, \ldots, m$, then (b.2) obtains and expected turnout is positive.

One should not rush from corollary 7.2 to the conclusion that turnout increases as the number of candidates increases. To examine that issue, one must also consider candidate competition, given voters' behavior. Unfortunately, as the reader probably knows, M candidate competition ($M \geq 3$) is much more complex than what was analyzed in section II. Two new considerations enter. First, it is now conceivable, and likely, that voters may not vote for their most preferred candidate.[18] That is, candidate j may receive votes from voters who prefer candidate ℓ to j to k, if those voters view the probability of affecting the election of ℓ as much smaller than that of affecting the election of j. Second, if all m platforms are identical, any one candidate, j, need only ensure that $q^i > \dfrac{1}{m-1} q'$, where q' is the probability i votes for the others, to be better off. Thus as m increases, it is more probable that candidates can easily gain by shifting away from common platforms. However, if j does this and then k moves between Θ^j and Θ' (the platform of others), k may capture most of the votes for Θ' by the fact that they vote for their second highest alternative, and thus $\Theta^j \neq \Theta'$ is not an equilibrium. Under certainty, equilibria with $m \geq 3$ are rare. For the model in this paper, they are more likely to exist because of the uncertainty and the possibility of abstentions; however, it is probable that equilibria with $m > 2$ are less likely than those with $m = 2$. This remains an open question.

C. Some Thoughts on Testing

One issue which is constantly raised concerns the empirical validity of a model: "Is it consistent with facts?"

Let us first consider some facts which cannot be addressed. Since $<\Theta, \mu>$ are the only exogenous variables in the voters' model and μ is the only variable in the full model, such a question as "How is turnout affected by perceived closeness and/or party differences?" cannot be addressed, since turnout and closeness are simultaneously determined in the voters' model while turnout, closeness, and party difference are simultaneously determined in the full model. Thus regressions of the form used by Ferejohn and Fiorina (1975) are incorrectly specified in the context of this model. I must admit, it is possible that partial effects may be identifiable from some reduced form regressions; however, I suspect not. To see why, let us consider a variation on the two-candidate model in which we let a voter's characteristic be (e^i, b^i), where e^i parameterizes tastes and costs and b^i parameterizes beliefs. A strategy is now a function of (e, b). If we assume that when i is (e^i, b^i) he acts as if all other voters believe $\mu \; \varepsilon \; M(E)$ is $\mu(\cdot, b^i)$, we can partition $E \times B$ into four sets by choosing the values of two parameters (p, γ), as follows:
$$A_{11} = \{(e, b) \mid |U(\Theta_A, d) - U(\Theta_B, d)| \leq p, \alpha^* \leq \gamma\}$$
$$A_{12} = \{(e, b) \mid |U(\Theta_A, d) - U(\Theta_B, d)| \leq p, \alpha^* \geq \gamma\}$$
and so forth, where α^* is evaluated at the voters' equilibrium for b.

Thus, for example, A_{21} represents the tastes and beliefs which would yield a response that party differences are large, and the election will be close. $\mu(A_{ij})$ would be the probability that a randomly selected voter belongs in A_{ij}. Thus, by suitable choice of μ, p, and γ (and the class of preferences and beliefs, $E \times B$), one might be able to "explain" all response patterns.

This is an uncomfortable conclusion in that it seems to say the model has no predictive value with respect to voting behavior. I think, however, that is the wrong conclusion. In fact, the model predicts (in two-candidate elections) very precise outcomes. For example, if tastes are symmetrically and unimodally distributed, then both candidates' final platforms should be near the median and modal voters' choice and turnout should be light (or zero). Also, as we saw, asymmetrics and the composition of tastes (type I or type II preferences) significantly affected the predicted outcomes. Thus, in fact, the model is "testable." Further, since—in general equilibrium—both our model of voter behavior and the Ferejohn-Fiorina model predict identical outcomes, one must either await further refinements of each or use "disequilibrium phenomena" to differentiate between the two.

Needless to say, there is much more work to be done before we fully understand the complete implications of all the simultaneous interactions between voters and candidates.

APPENDIX

In this appendix we collect some results that deal with the comparative statics of a symmetric voters equilibrium for two-candidate elections.

Lemma A.1. If $G(r, \Theta_A, \Theta_B)$ has continuous second derivatives in (r, Θ) in a neighborhood of $(\frac{1}{\alpha^*}, \Theta^*)$ and $(-\frac{1}{\beta^*}, \Theta^*)$, where $(\alpha^*, \beta^*, \Theta^*)$ is a symmetric equilibrium for $<\Theta^*, \mu>$, then the solutions, $<\alpha(0), \beta(0)>$ of

$$f[q^A(\Theta, \alpha), q^B(\Theta, \beta)] - \alpha = 0$$
$$f[q^B(0, \beta), q^A(\Theta, \alpha)] - \beta = 0$$

have continuous first derivatives in Θ in those neighborhoods, if

$$D = \begin{vmatrix} f_1^1 q_\alpha^A - 1 & f_2^1 q_\beta^B \\ f_2^2 q_\alpha^A & f_1^2 q_\beta^B - 1 \end{vmatrix} \neq 0$$

where f_2^1 is $\dfrac{\partial f(q^A, q^B)}{\partial q^B}$

Proof. Implicit function theorem.

Lemma A.2. Under the conditions of lemma A.1,

$$\begin{pmatrix} \dfrac{d\,q^A}{dx} \\ \dfrac{d\,q^B}{dx} \end{pmatrix} = \begin{bmatrix} q_x^A + q_\alpha^A f_2^1 q_x^B - q_\beta^B f_1^2 q_x^A \\ q_x^B - q_\alpha^A f_1^1 q_x^B - q_\beta^B f_2^2 q_x^A \end{bmatrix}$$

where $x \in \{\Theta_A, \Theta_B\}$. Further, if $q^A = q^B$, then

$$\frac{d\,q^j}{dx} = q^j_x(1 - f_1 \cdot q^j_{\alpha j})$$

where $j = A, B$, $\alpha^A = \alpha$, $\beta^B = \beta$.

[*Note:* $f_1 < 0$ when $q^A = q^B$ from next lemma and $q^j_{\alpha j} \geq 0$ implies $\dfrac{d\,q^j}{dx} = 0$ *iff* $q^j_x = o$ whenever $q^A = q^B$.]

Lemma A.3. For

$$f(x,y) = \sum_{k=0}^{\left[\frac{n}{2}\right]} \frac{n!}{k!k!n-k!} x^k y^k (1 - x - y)^{n-2k}$$

$$+ \sum_{k=0}^{\left[\frac{n-1}{2}\right]} \frac{n!}{k!k+1!(n-2k-1)!} x^k y^{k+1} (1 - x - y)^{n-2k-1},$$

$$f_x = (y-x) \sum_{k=1}^{\left[\frac{n-1}{2}\right]} \frac{n!}{k+1!k-1!n-2k-1!} x^{k-1} y^k (1 - x - y)^{n-2k-1}$$

$$- x \sum_{k=1}^{\left[\frac{n-1}{2}\right]} \frac{n!}{k!k+1!n-2k!} x^{k-1} y^k (1 - x - y)^{n-2k-1}$$

$$- n(1 - x - y)^{n-1},$$

$$f_y = (x-y) \sum_{k=1}^{\left[\frac{n}{2}\right]} \frac{n!}{k!k-1!n-2k!} x^{k-1} y^{k-1} (1 - x - y)^{n-2k}.$$

Thus, for example, if $x = y$, then $f_y = 0$ and $f_x < 0$; if $x > y$, then $f_x < 0$, $f_y > 0$; and if $x < y$, then $f_y < 0$ and f_x is of indeterminate sign.

Lemma A.4. $(\alpha - \beta) = (q^B - q^A) \Gamma(q^A, q^B)$ where $\Gamma(q^A, q^B) \geq 0$.

Proof. $\alpha - \beta = f(q^A, q^B) - f(q^B, q^A) = (y - x)$

$$\sum_{k=0}^{\left[\frac{n-1}{2}\right]} \frac{n!}{k!k+1!n-2k-1!} x^k y^y (1 - x - y)^{n-2k-1}.$$

NOTES

I wish to thank both the Fairchild Foundation (as a Fairchild Scholar at Caltech) and the National Science Foundation (Grant #SOC 76-20953 to the Center for Mathematical Studies in Economics and Management Science, Northwestern University) for their support. My debt to John Ferejohn and Morris Fiorina, who tolerated my incursion into their domain with patience, help, and humor, will be obvious to any reader. A seminar at Caltech brought forth the expected boos, "What is that?" and help. I thank the participants. Finally, I alone am responsible for any errors and misrepresentations which may be left.

1. For a good summary of this literature, see Ferejohn and Fiorina (1974).

2. The exceptions include the model of Hinich, Ledyard, and Ordeshook (1972) in which voters choose probabilistically across voters. However, no model of individual decisions was given there to justify this behavior. Maybe none exists.

3. We use Kramer's (1977) terminology.

4. In their (1974) article (p. 527), they acknowledge the interactions of voters' decisions but suggest it is "a highly complex situation."

5. The basis for this claim is provided in section IIB(iii).

6. See the appendix for these facts.

7. See the article by Aranson, Hinich, and Ordeshook (1974) for these.

8. We later give an example of asymmetrically distributed tastes in which an electoral equilibrium does not exist.

9. The tail wags the dog?

10. For negative values of x, the proportion of voters with $d \leq x$ is $\dfrac{a}{a+1}\,e^x$; for positive values of x, the proportion of voters with $d \geq x$ is $\dfrac{1}{a+1}\,e^{-ax}$. For arbitrary $\bar{x} > 0$, $\dfrac{a}{a+1}\,e^{-\bar{x}} > \dfrac{1}{a+1}\,e^{-a\bar{x}}$ if $a > 1$.

11. See the appendix for the following fact.

12. See Hinich (1977) for a simliar result in a slightly different model.

13. Closeness may not count but it seems to be inevitable.

14. This approach must be well known to social-choice theorists. I welcome references on related work by others.

15. If voters' beliefs, and therefore their voting, are not independently and identically distributed, this approximation may be incorrect.

16. If $q^A > q^B$, then p_A is almost 1. If $q^A = q^B$, then p_A is almost $\dfrac{1}{2}$, and if $q^A < q^B$, then p_A is approximately 0.

17. See the appendix for this.

18. See Ferejohn and Fiorina (1974) for the case when $m = 3$.

REFERENCES

Aranson, P.; Hinich, M.; and Ordeshook, P. "Election Goals and Strategies: Equivalent and Nonequivalent Candidate Objectives," *American Political Science Review*, 68 (1974), 135–152.

Davis, O.; Hinich, M.; and Ordeshook, P. "An Expository Development of a Mathematical Model of the Electoral Process," *American Political Science Review*, 64 (1970), 426–448.

Downs, A. *An Economic Theory of Democracy*. New York: Harper and Row, 1957.

Ferejohn, J., and Fiorina, M. "The Paradox of Not Voting: A Decision Theoretic Analysis," *American Political Science Review*, 68 (1974), 525–536.

———. "Closeness Counts Only in Horseshoes and Dancing," *American Political Science Review*, 69 (1975), 920–925.

Hinich, M. "Equilibrium in Spatial Voting: The Median Voter Result Is an Artifact," *Journal of Economic Theory*, 16 (1977), 208–219.

Hinich, M.; Ledyard, J.; and Ordeshook, P. "Non-Voting and the Existence of Equilibrium under Majority Rule," *Journal of Economic Theory*, 4 (1972), 144–153.

Kramer, G. "A Dynamic Model of Political Equilibrium," *Journal of Economic Theory*, 16 (1977), 310–334.

McKelvey, R., and Ordeshook, P. "A General Theory of the Calculus of Voting," in *Mathematical Applications in Political Science VI*, Herudon and Bernd, eds. Charlottesville: University Press of Virginia, 1972.

Riker, W., and Ordeshook, P. "A Theory of the Calculus of Voting," *American Political Science Review*, vol. 62 (1968).

Tullock, G. *Toward a Mathematics of Politics*. Ann Arbor: University of Michigan Press, 1967.

Applied
Economics

An Empirical Study
of Decentralized Institutions
# of Monopoly Restraint

Vernon L. Smith

Several decades ago, Abba Lerner (1944) suggested the possibility that where markets are imperfectly competitive, due, for example, to there being too few sellers (or buyers), a central authority or marketing agency might by "counterspeculation" create the conditions whereby efficient resource allocation could be achieved. However, it remained for Vickrey (1961) to propose a scheme for operationalizing Lerner's concept of "counterspeculation"; this scheme has since been recognized as an example of an incentive compatible mechanism conceptually akin to the Clarke (1971) and Groves (1973) mechanism for demand revelation in public-good decision making. Vickrey's mechanism (pp. 9–14), using a marketing agency to process individual reported supply and demand curves, provided no direct incentives for misrepresentation of supply and demand, but because it was thought by Vickrey (perhaps correctly) to be impractical, he turned (pp. 14–29) to an analysis of various auctioning methods which represented realized or realizable institutions. His analysis showed that the English oral auction and the second-price sealed-bid auction (in which the high bidder wins, but pays a price equal to the second highest bid) were examples of decentralized price mechanisms which created incentives for efficient (Pareto-optimal) resource allocation even where numbers were few. In contrast, the Dutch descending bid and first-price sealed-bid auction (the high bidder wins and pays what he bids) were examples of decentralized mechanisms which created incentives for misrepresentation of demand and for Pareto-inefficient resource allocation.

Independently of Vickrey's work, Groves and Ledyard (1977) developed a quadratic cost allocation mechanism for solving the "free-rider" problem in public-good decisions that can be interpreted as a generalization of Vickrey's analysis of auctions. Both the Vickrey auctions and the Groves-Ledyard mechanism require agents to communicate points in ordinary Euclidean space, whereas the Vickrey-Clarke-Groves demand-revealing process requires agents to communicate functions (reported willingness to pay).

Contemporaneously with the work of Vickrey, Clarke, and Groves-Ledyard, but independently, experimental research in decentralized market mechanisms has studied the behavioral properties of several alternative pricing institutions. This research has documented, in numerous experimental replications (Smith, 1962, 1976b), the high efficiency and rapid convergence properties of the oral double-auction mechanism. Furthermore, this experimental research has identified alternative pricing institutions that differ behaviorally in terms of efficiency and convergence properties.

For example, Smith (1967) has compared discriminative with competitive sealed-bid auctions for multiple units of a commodity. Under the discriminative auction rules, all accepted bids are filled at their bid prices. Under the competitive auction rules, all accepted bids are filled at the lowest accepted bid price (as noted by Vickrey, the strictly correct procedure is to fill all bids at the first rejected bid price). The competitive rules provide an incentive for revealing demand, while the discriminative rules provide an incentive to understate demand. The experimental results are consistent with this and establish that the mean bid under discrimination is significantly less than the mean bid submitted under the competitive rules. Tsao and Vignola (1977) have shown that these results also hold in the primary market for U.S. Treasury bonds.

Smith (1964) compared the double oral auction with one-sided auctions—the oral offer and the oral-bid auction—and found that prices in the oral offer auction tended to be below those in the double auction, which in turn tended to be below those in the oral-bid auction. Williams (1973) compared the posted-bid and posted-offer institution, and found that posted-offer prices tended to be significantly above posted-bid prices. Plott and Smith (1978) compared the oral-bid auction with the posted-bid institution (similar to, but not the same as, the discriminative sealed-bid procedure) and found that posted-bid prices tended to be below the market clearing price (this replicated the results of Williams), while oral-bid contract prices tend to be above the competitive price.

Since the oral-offer auction and the posted-bid (discriminative) institution bias prices downward to the disadvantage of sellers by underrevealing demand, this raises the question of whether such institutions might function viably as decentralized mechanisms for monopoly control. Can the price advantage of monopoly be neutralized or countervailed by an institution that underreveals demand to the monopolist? Can the Pareto inefficiency of monopoly be improved by such an institution? This line of reasoning brings us back to the Lerner-Vickrey problem,[1] except that we ask not whether there is a centralized procedure for "counterspeculation" in the presence of monopoly, but is there a decentralized institution that can approximate the objectives of this "counterspeculation"? The "power" of a monopolist derives entirely from his ability to withhold production, and, in the absence of alternative sources of supply, obtain a higher price. But buyers have this same "power," that is, the ability to withhold purchase. Are some institutions more effective than others in enabling buyers to express this "power" against a single seller? The effectiveness of monopoly may be reduced or eliminated where the institution of contract promotes behavior that does not allow an increase in price sufficient to offset the reduction in sales. Recall that the monopoly price is inefficient; some gains from exchange are left unrealized. Are there institutions that allow fuller realization of these gains from trade?

This paper reports the results of eight monopoly experiments, using four contracting institutions for price determination. Two additional experiments, designed for the purpose of making certain comparisons discussed below, consisted of one "large group" competitive market experiment and one duopoly experiment.

EXPERIMENTAL DESIGN

The experimental design is standardized for all the monopoly experiments reported below. Each of five buyers has a capacity to buy a maximum of two units. The seller has a capacity to sell ten units. Table 1 lists the seller's

Table 1
Normalized Marginal Cost and Demand

Quantity	Seller (Subject No. 1) Marginal Cost (¢)	Resale Value (¢)	Buyer No.
0	0		
1	60	150	2
2	60	140	3
3	60	130	4
4	60	120	5
5	65	110	6
6	70	100	6
7	75	90	5
8	80	80	4
9	85	70	3
10	90	60	2

marginal cost for each of ten units, and each buyer's resale value (buyer marginal revenue) for each of two units. The corresponding monopoly marginal cost (competitive market supply), market demand, and monopoly marginal revenue are shown on the left of chart 1. These schedules represent flows per trading period, since all costs and values applied only to those units traded each period, as in a market where production is to order. The costs and values in table 1 and the vertical scales on all the charts to follow are normalized with a range of 60–90 for marginal cost and a range of 150–60 for demand. The actual experiments varied by an additive, constant from these normalized levels, in order to control the state of incomplete information more effectively. If the same marginal cost and demand had been used in all experiments, there was some slight possibility of this becoming known to a subject who had heard about an earlier experiment.

Chart 1
Double Auction 1
Monopoly

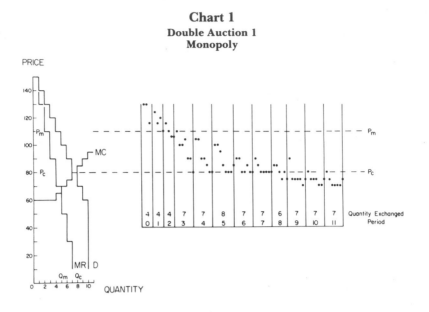

Since the ten experiments to be reported here were conducted at five dif-ferent universities over a four-year period, this possibility is indeed remote.

Appendices 1–4 contain the instructions and recordkeeping forms used in the monopoly and duopoly experiments. A total of 48 subjects partici-pated in the 8 monopoly experiments. The competitive market experiment used 10 subjects, the duopoly experiment used 12. The subjects were grad-uate or advanced undergraduate students in economics at Cal Tech, USC, UCLA, the University of Arizona, and Texas A. & M. The emphasis on relatively sophisticated subjects was intended to minimize the possibility of "uninformed" monopoly behavior. For the same reason, the seller position was not a random assignment among the subjects. In each experiment an effort was made to preselect a subject to be the seller—someone who was thought not likely to be "easy on the buyers." But in each experiment the remaining five subjects were assigned randomly to the five buyer valuation conditions shown in table 1. In all experiments the subjects were instructed, and were seated in a manner that would protect the privacy of individual cost or valuation assignments.

At the end of the experiment each buyer was paid in cash the difference between the assigned resale value and the purchase price, plus a 5-cent "commission" for every unit purchased from the seller. Similarly, the seller received a cash payment equal to the difference between the selling price and the assigned marginal cost, plus 5 cents for every unit sold to a buyer. The 5-cent "commission" was for the purpose of providing some minimum inducement to trade a unit at its cost or resale value, that is, to compensate for subjective transaction cost (Smith, 1976a). Consequently, there was some motivation to trade the marginal units.

The total number of trading periods varied among the experiments, but was always at least ten. In no case was this number known in advance by the subjects. If a seller were to achieve the monopoly price ($1.10) and quantity (5), his total earnings, including commission, in a ten-period experiment would be $27. If a seller were to achieve the competitive price ($.80) and quantity (8), total corresponding earnings would be $15. Hence the seller has a strong incentive to find and maintain the monopoly price-quantity exchange, if this is possible. Of course, the seller has no "true" demand information—only the bid, or offer, or contract information forthcoming in the market under the governing institution prescribed by the instructions of a particular experiment. Similarly, no seller in the economy can have "true" demand information—only the information generated by the pricing process that is the practice in a particular industry or market.

This experimental design allows an unambiguous measure of efficiency to be computed. If we omit the commissions, efficiency in any trading period is the ratio of total earnings by all subjects to the earnings that would result from the competitive price and quantity. If eight units trade at the competitive price ($.80), total earnings net of commission would be $3.90, which is just consumer plus producer surplus in the diagram on the left of chart 1. At the monopoly price and quantity, this total surplus would be $3.45. Hence, the theoretical monopoly equilibrium is 88.5 percent efficient. The actual efficiency of the experimental markets will be an important measure for comparing the different institutions.

DOUBLE-AUCTION EXPERIMENTS

Three monopoly experiments and one "large group" competitive experiment were conducted under the double-auction institution. Appendix 1 contains the instructions and recordkeeping forms for the monopoly experiments. The same procedures were used in the competitive market experiment. Each trading period in these experiments was timed to run four minutes, with an announced warning at the beginning of the final minute. Additional time was provided if there were delays, as sometimes occurred in recording bids, offers, and contracts, or if two buyers tied in the acceptance of an offer, and a coin toss was used to determine the winner. The institution was that of a relatively unstructured, double auction: any buyer could make a bid price for a single unit at any time without restriction; that is, it could be the same, higher, or lower than the last bid. The seller could make a price offer at any time, also without restriction. A bid or offer was outstanding (and binding) only for as long as it was not superseded by another bid or offer, or was accepted. A bid or offer that was accepted was a binding contract, and the seller and buyer recorded the contract price on his or her record sheet. At the end of each period the subjects were given a few minutes to compute and record their earnings for that period.

On the right of chart 1 is plotted the chronological sequence of contract prices for the first double-auction monopoly (DA1). Period 0 was a practice trial and was not counted in determining the cash payments. Price behavior in this market experiment does not inspire confidence in the proposition that a seller with imperfect information will achieve a monopoly equilibrium in double-auction trading. Buyers managed to lower prices progressively to an average level below the competitive price in the final three periods. The seller was able to sell at the monopoly price or higher only in trading period 1, but this was accomplished by not selling the fifth marginal monopoly unit. One measure of monopoly price effectiveness is to compare actual prices in each period with the quantity-conditional monopoly price. That is, since the seller does not know Q_m, the sales quantity required to support the monopoly price P_m, a different quantity, say $Q(t)$, may be, and normally is, supplied in any particular period. We ask what is the monopoly price, $P[Q(t)]$, conditional upon $Q(t)$ being the quantity actually supplied in period t. If the seller is monopoly price effective, but is not effective in determining the level at which to restrict output, we would expect actual prices in period t to be near $P[Q(t)]$.[2] Inspection of chart 1 reveals that only in periods 3, 4, and 5 did this seller's prices tend to be above $P[Q(t)]$. For example, in periods 10 and 11, $P[Q(10)] = P[Q(11)] = P[7] = \$0.90$, and in these periods every price was below \$0.80. Table 2 lists the difference

$$\delta(t) = \frac{1}{Q(t)} \sum_{q=1}^{Q(t)} P_q(t) - P[Q(t)]$$

for each period t, where $P_q(t)$ is the qth contract price in period t, and

$$\frac{1}{Q(t)} \sum_{q=1}^{Q(t)} P_q(t)$$

is the mean price in period t.

A second double-auction experiment (DA2) is exhibited in chart 2. Although the price pattern of contracts is much smoother than in DA1, the tendency of prices to erode to the benefit of buyers is strong. The number of trading periods (19) in this experiment was increased over DA1 to see if this declining price trend might be reversed through learning. In all periods, except the last, the mean price was below the conditional monopoly price (that is, $\delta < 0$ in table 2).

Similarly, experiment 3 (DA3) consisted of 16 trading periods (see chart 3). In this case, the pattern of steadily eroding prices up to period 7 was abruptly reversed in period 8. Note that sales were reduced from 7 units in period 7 to 4 units in period 8. Again, the pattern of price decline from period 8 to 16 was renewed, but much less strongly. Of the three experimental sellers, this one was the most effective (from periods 8–16) in holding prices nearer to the monopoly price than the competitive price.

One way of comparing the price effectiveness of the three sellers is to compute the mean difference between the quantity conditional monopoly

Price-Quantity Performance

Column groups: Double Auction, Monopoly (DA1, DA2, DA3); Posted-Offer Price (Monopoly, Duopoly); Offer Auction (Monopoly); Posted-Bid Pricing, Monopoly (PB1, PB2, PB3). Each reports Q and δ.

Trading Period, t	DA1 Q	DA1 δ	DA2 Q	DA2 δ	DA3 Q	DA3 δ	POP Mono Q	POP Mono δ	POP Duo Q	POP Duo δ	OA Mono Q	OA Mono δ	PB1 Q	PB1 δ	PB2 Q	PB2 δ	PB3 Q	PB3 δ
1	4	−.025	2	−.25	6	+.075	7	+.35	14	−.032	2	−.125	6	−.375	4	−.20	4	−.3
2	4	−.1125	4	−.125	7	+.0643	5	0	15	+.042	6	−.0083	1	−.0886	7	−.60	7	−.0329
3	7	+.0643	4	−.1375	6	−.1083	4	−.20	14	−.05	6	−.2517	0	−.0757	8	0	8	+.0675
4	7	+.007	4	−.15	6	−.15	6	0	14	−.061	5	−.398	6	−.0714	7	−.1	7	−.0829
5	8	+.08125	4	−.15	6	−.1143	5	0	14	−.066	6	−.3	4	−.0714	7	−.2875	7	−.0914
6	7	−.0643	4	−.15	5	−.33	5	0	14	−.076	7	−.1071	6	−.0771	7	−.1083	7	−.0194
7	7	−.0786	5	−.07	7	−.1357	5	0	14	−.032	7	−.0971	6	−.0871	7	−.1167	7	−.0929
8	6	−.2	5	−.1	4	−.1625	5	0	14	−.066	7	−.09	6	−.185	8	−.13	8	+.005
9	7	−.1357	5	−.1	5	−.07	5	0	14	−.05	7	−.08	6	−.0971	8	−.1184	8	+.0075
10	7	−.1571	5	−.1	6	+.0167	5	0	14	−.05	7	−.0486	7	−.1014	7	−.03	7	−.0871
11	7	−.1714	5	−.13	5	−.05			14	−.032	7	−.0114	7	−.1	7	−.0371	7	−.08
12			5	−.15	6	+.0333					7	−.0071		−.0971			7	−.07
13			5	−.15	6	0								−.0886			7	−.07
14			5	−.15	6	0											5	−.27
15			4	−.25	6	−.0083											7	−.07
16			5	−.05	6	−.025											7	−.06
17			5	−.05													7	−.06
18			6	−.05													7	−.06
19			7	+.02													7	−.06
Means, Periods 5–10																		
$\bar{Q}$	7		4.74		5.67		5		14		6.83		6.83		5.83		7.33	
δ		−.0924		−.1117		−.1326		0		−.0567		−.1205		−.1032		−.1318		−.0584
δ		−.0924		−.1117														
$\bar{Q}$, Pooled			5.78				5		14		6.83				6.66			
δ, Pooled				−.1122				0		−.0567		−.1205				−.0978		
Means, All Periods																		
$\bar{Q}$	6.45		7.47		5.9		5.18		14.09		6.17		6.69		4.64		7.00	
δ		−.0683		−.118		−.0553		+.0026		−.043		−.1174		−.1069		−.1345		−.0559
$\bar{Q}$, Pooled			5.54				5.18		14.09		6.17				6.12			
δ, Pooled				−.089				+.0026		−.043		−.1174				−.096		

price and actual prices across all (or a portion) of the trading periods for each experiment. Let this mean difference be

$$\delta = \frac{1}{T} \sum_{t=1}^{T} \delta(t)$$

for any experiment consisting of T trading periods. For the three DA monopoly experiments, these mean differences across all periods are $\delta_{DA1} = -.0683$, $\delta_{DA2} = -.1118$, and $\delta_{DA3} = -.0553$. Under this control over the

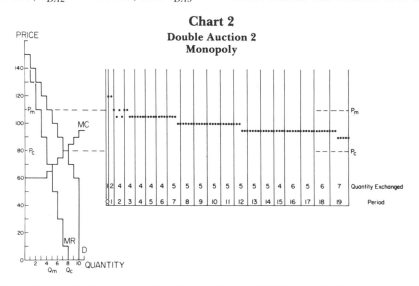

Chart 2
Double Auction 2
Monopoly

effect of supply, it is seen that the seller in DA3 was slightly more price effective than the seller in DA1, with the seller in DA2 being the least price effective. The seller in DA2 was the most effective in restricting supply ($\bar{Q} = 4.74$), but this did not lead to a corresponding increase in prices. It appears that in the double-auction institution, the more a monopoly seller restricts supply the stronger may be the bargaining resistance of buyers.

In comparison with previous experiments with the double-auction mechanism, where there are several sellers and several buyers, the most characteristic feature of these monopoly experiments is the remarkable bargaining resistance of the buyers. In double-auction trading with a single seller, buyers appear to have a capacity for tacit collusion against the seller that has not appeared before in nonmonopolistic experiments. To test this conjecture, it was decided to conduct a double-auction competitive market experiment with five buyers and five sellers, using the same demand (normalized resale values) as in the monopoly experiments. However, the assigned marginal costs (supply) only correspond to the normalized monopolist's MC function up to a quantity of five, then jump to the highest demand value. This configuration is shown on the left of chart 4. Hence, we "rig" the supply curve for five sellers so that it must effectively reproduce a monopolist's

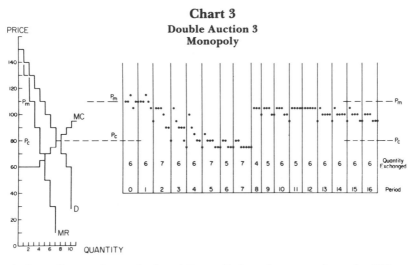

Chart 3
Double Auction 3
Monopoly

restriction of quantity to the level $Q_m = 5$. In substance, the only difference between this experiment and a monopoly experiment in which the seller is perfectly quantity effective is that we have five sellers instead of one. If our conjecture is true—namely, that buyers bargain more effectively against one seller than against several—then the five buyer–five seller experiment should produce prices near $P_m = \$1.10$.

On the right in chart 4 is shown the contract sequence for the "large group" experiment DA4. These results are typical of such experiments,

Chart 4
A Multi-Seller Auction

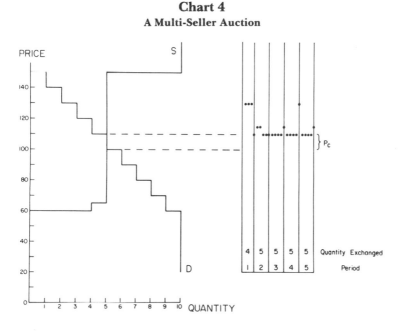

except that convergence is more commonly from below (Smith, 1976b) when producers' surplus is substantially in excess of consumers' surplus. Note the sharply higher level of prices in all periods of chart 4, compared with periods 7 to 14 in chart 2, in which the seller limited deliveries to five units per period. These results tend to support the hypothesis that in the double-auction institution, buyers bargain more effectively against a single seller than against several.

POSTED-OFFER EXPERIMENTS

Two posted-offer experiments will be reported in this section—one monopoly and one duopoly. The posted-offer institution operates as follows (see Plott and Smith, 1978, for a fuller discussion of the symmetrical posted-bid institution). Each seller independently selects a written offer price, with the understanding that each must be willing to sell at least one unit at the price quoted. These prices are collected and posted on the blackboard. The buyers are then ordered randomly in a sequence, and the first chooses one of the prices and states the quantity he is willing to buy at that price. The seller moves last by stating how much (but at least one unit) of this quantity will be accepted. If not all the buyer's bid for units is accepted, he may go to another seller to fill his unsatisfied demand. When the first buyer is finished, the second buyer in the random sequence states his quantity bid, and so on through the last buyer. Appendix 2 provides complete instructions for the monopoly and the duopoly experiments.

Based on the results reported in Plott and Smith (1978), we would expect this institution to work to the advantage of sellers. Of the four pricing mechanisms studied in this paper, this would be the one most likely to enable a single seller to achieve the monopoly price-quantity equilibrium. In this institution, a buyer's only recourse is to withhold purchase, denying himself short-run surplus, in the hope of getting more favorable subsequent price offers. Buyers are faced with a take-it-or-leave-it price offer, over which no bargaining is permitted under the rules of the experimental institution. This procedure approximates the pricing process in most large retail firms in which the separation of clerk and management functions makes it infeasible to permit price negotiations at the customer-clerk level.

The results of the posted-offer monopoly experiment are plotted on the right of chart 5. There was not a single instance of strategic behavior on thepart of a buyer. Each buyer in each period simple-maximized by buying the optimal short-run quantity at the monopolist's stated price (except that in period 1 buyer 3 purchased his second unit at a loss). In five periods the seller identified the profit maximizing price and proceeded to quote this price for the next seven periods. In postexperiment discussion, several buyers commented that they felt there was nothing else they effectively could do. In spite of the fact that strategic purchase behavior is possible, the buyers in this experiment perceived that they had no effective recourse but to

Chart 5
Posted Offer 1
Monopoly

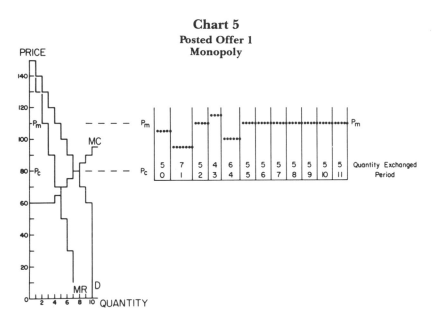

accept a take-it-or-leave-it price. Consequently, the experiment was behaviorally mechanical, even boring. This is in sharp contrast with the double-auction experiments in which buyers vigorously bargained under the procedures of that institution, and obviously perceived that they could influence the terms of trade.

Chart 6 exhibits the results of the posted-offer duopoly experiment. The procedures were identical to those in the previous monopoly experiment except that two sellers, each independently, selected a price which was then posted. Each seller had the same MC schedule as the single seller in the monopoly experiment, and there were two buyers with the same valuations as each single buyer in the monopoly experiment. Hence, the duopoly experiment exactly replicated the cost-value structure of the monopoly experiment, but doubled the size of the market (Shubik, 1975).

In chart 6, for each trading period the two posted offer prices are charted in increasing order and identified by seller number (1 or 2). The quantity exchanged at each price is represented by the length of the price bar. In every period, price was in the range $.80–$.90, determined by the competitive marginal demand unit and the next higher demand unit. Cooperative signals (price increases) by one or both duopolists occurred in periods 2, 3, 5, 7, 9, and 11; competitive signals occurred in periods 2, 3, 4, 5, 6, and 8. In every period, prices are above P_c but nearer to P_c than P_m. In no case did either of the two sellers strategically withhold sales to the buyers. In each case the low-priced seller sold his marginal unit at that price, while the sales of the high-priced seller were determined by the residual or contingent (Shubik, 1959, pp. 82–84) demand left by the low-priced seller. Table 3

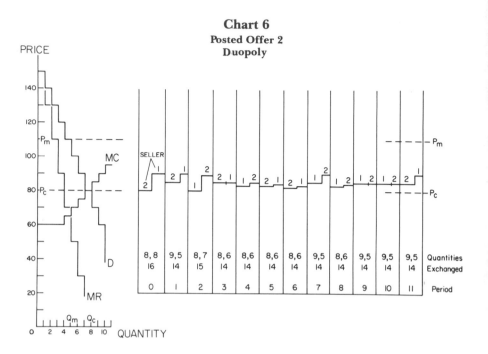

Chart 6
Posted Offer 2
Duopoly

Table 3
Efficiency

Trading Period, t	Double Auction			Posted Offer		Offer Auction	Posted Bid		
	1	2	3	Monopoly	Duopoly		1	2	3
1	76.9	41.0	96.2	97.4	97.4	41.0	46.2	66.7	100.0
2	76.9	66.7	91.0	88.5	100.0	96.2	82.1	23.1	100.0
3	97.4	74.4	83.3	76.9	100.0	80.8	100.0	0	100.0
4	100.0	74.4	96.2	96.2	100.0	93.6	100.0	82.1	100.0
5	98.7	74.4	84.6	88.5	100.0	83.3	100.0	57.7	100.0
6	95.0	74.4	74.4	88.5	100.0	100.0	100.0	75.7	100.0
7	97.4	83.3	100.0	88.5	97.4	100.0	100.0	89.7	100.0
8	96.2	83.3	69.2	88.5	100.0	100.0	80.8	85.9	100.0
9	95.0	83.3	88.5	88.5	97.4	100.0	100.0	84.7	100.0
10	100.0	83.3	96.2	88.5	97.4	100.0	82.1	100.0	100.0
11	95.0	83.3	88.5	88.5	97.4	100.0	82.1	90.3	100.0
12		83.3	96.2			100.0	82.1		100.0
13		83.3	96.2				100.0		83.3
14		83.3	96.2						100.0
15		66.7	97.4						100.0
16		96.2	96.2						100.0
17		78.2							100.0
18		96.2							100.0
19		89.7							
$\bar{E}$(Periods 5–10)	97.05	80.33	85.5	88.5	98.7	97.22	93.82	82.28	100.0
Pooled $\bar{E}$ (Periods 5–10)		87.63		88.5	98.7	97.22		92.03	

shows that the duopoly experiment was never less than 97.4 percent efficient in any period.

These results confirm the expectation that the posted-offer institution favors sellers. In the case of a single seller, it allows the monopoly price to be attained. The bias in favor of sellers persists with the introduction of a second seller, but the bias is not strong enough to significantly reduce efficiency below the competitive optimum.

AN OFFER-AUCTION EXPERIMENT

In the one-sided oral offer auction (Smith, 1964) any seller may freely make a price offer for a single unit, while buyers either accept or remain silent. This institution tends to operate to the advantage of buyers. Essentially, as sellers lower prices to attract buyer acceptances, buyers learn to wait for favorable prices. In experiments with many sellers, the offer competition of sellers, combined with waiting by buyers, tends to depress prices to a level below the competitive equilibrium. This section reports the results of one such experiment with a single seller. The instructional materials for the experiment are included in Appendix 3.

Chart 7 reports all of the seller's offers in sequence. The open circles represent unaccepted offers and the solid circles indicate contracts. The pattern of successive reductions in the offers, in response to buyers' waiting

Chart 7
Offer Auction 1
Monopoly

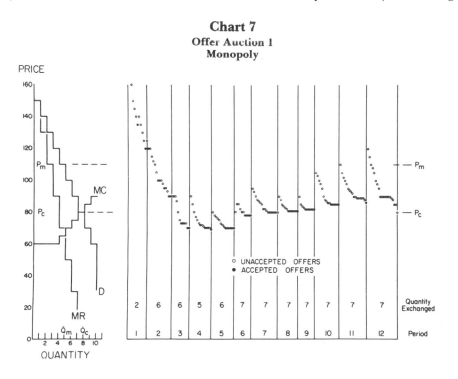

for more favorable terms, is typical of earlier reported experiments with
more than one seller. In periods 3, 4, and 5, for example, buyers strategically
wait for offers as low as \$.70. This appears to be a clear "counterspeculative"
form of restraint. The seller, perhaps realizing that the offer terms might
be too soft, changed the offer concession strategy in period 6 so as to begin
higher and concede less. Consequently, the seller succeeded in gradually
raising contract prices from periods 6 through 12. This trend suggests the
possibility that the seller might eventually have been able to approach the
monopoly price. The important test would come at a price of \$.90 and
above, and again at \$1 and above, where the corresponding marginal de-
mand units are excluded. Would buyer bargaining resistance have significantly stiffened? In period 12, it appears that this is what was happening as
the seller made several offer concessions in order (apparently) to pick up
the seventh contract. (Period 12 was not known to be the final period, so we
do not have a "doomsday" problem influencing behavior.)

POSTED-BID EXPERIMENTS

In the posted-bid institution, each buyer independently chooses a price with
the understanding that he or she must be willing to purchase at least one
unit at the price quoted. The bids are then posted publicly. The seller then
chooses a buyer and price and makes a quantity offer. The buyer moves last,
stating how much of the quantity offer he or she will purchase. The seller
then chooses another buyer and price, makes a quantity offer, and so on.
The seller may stop making quantity offers at any time and may refuse all
buyers. The instructions for the three posted-bid experiments are contained
in Appendix 4.

Since, in this institution, buyers have to pay what they bid, that is, buyers
know that the seller will discriminate down the posted-bid array of prices,
each has an incentive to avoid being among the highest bids accepted. The
ideal bid for each buyer is a bid just slightly above the highest rejected bid.
Hence, there are strong individual incentives that support the posting of
low bids with a small variance. If this is the case, the seller will be confronted
with a considerably underrevealed, relatively elastic, demand.

Charts 8, 9, and 10 plot the posted bids and corresponding sales at each
bid in decreasing order, from the highest bid to the lowest, for each trading
period. The circles represent bid prices that were rejected by the seller; that
is, no quantity was offered to buyers who posted these bids. All three experiments show a strong tendency for buyers to underreveal demand. In
experiments 1 and 3, the dispersion of bids narrows very sharply after the
first two or three trading periods. In each of these experiments the seller
stabilized early, with a delivery quantity of approximately seven units. In
each case the seller was faced with price bids very little above the competitive
price. In experiment 2 (chart 9), the seller aggressively rejected bids. After

selling six units in period 1, the seller rejected all but the highest bid in
period 2. This resulted in a very insignificant increase in the period 3 bids.
The seller then rejected all bids in period 3, resulting in a somewhat higher

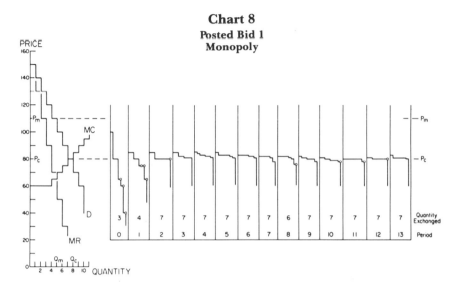

Chart 8
Posted Bid 1
Monopoly

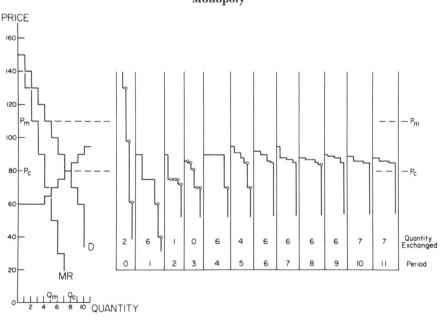

Chart 9
Posted Bid 2
Monopoly

Chart 10
Posted Bid 3
Monopoly

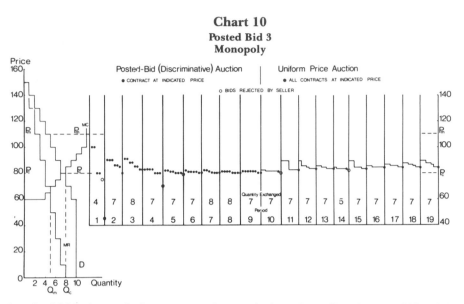

level of bids in period 4. Except for period 5, the seller then stabilized in the sale of 6 or 7 units in the remaining periods, with the result that the bids tended to drift lower and lower. These results suggest that the posted-bid institution operates very beneficially to the buyers. Even where the seller is particularly aggressive in restricting output, this action is not very effective, at least in the short run, in raising the bids. Hence, it is very costly to the seller to induce an increase in the bids by restricting sales.

In table 2 it will be noted that among the three sellers, across all periods, the seller in the second experiment (PB2) was the most effective in restricting output ($\overline{Q}$ = 4.64) but the least effective in obtaining the quantity conditional monopoly price, that is, δ_{PB1} = $-.1069$, δ_{PB2} = $-.1345$ and δ_{PB3} = $-.0559$. The seller in experiment 3 was the least effective in restricting output, but the most (quantity-conditional) price effective. As in the double auction, it seems that in the posted-bid institution the more a single seller restricts supply, the less is that seller's price effectiveness.

The theory that the discriminative feature of posted-bid pricing is a significant element in the underrevealing of demand was tested in the third posted-bid experiment (PB3). At the beginning of trial 10 it was announced that, henceforth, all bids accepted by the seller would be executed at the same price, and that the procedure would be as follows. After the bids are posted (as before), the seller will first announce the cutoff bid price, that is, the price below which all bids will be rejected by the seller. The seller then selects a buyer (as before), makes a quantity offer, the buyer responds with the amount he will buy, and so on, but with the understanding that all contracts will be at the cutoff bid price announced by the seller. The results are plotted in chart 10 in periods 10 through 19. Immediately with period

11, the effect was to increase the level of the posted bids, with the seller obtaining an increase in profit. The bids continued to rise (not monotonically) through the last period, with seller profit tending to rise, except for period 14, when the seller delivered only 5 units. Hence, buyers benefit by allowing bid-price discrimination, while the seller benefits from the uniform price auction rule. This result is largely attributable to the change in buyer bidding behavior resulting from the change in the price determining rule, since the seller continued to supply substantially the same quantity. However, the exception in period 14 is interesting. The posted bids in that period were not as high as in periods 11–13. The seller reduced deliveries from 7 units to 5 units, and an increase in the bids ensued which continued through the final trading period.

COMPARISON OF THE INSTITUTIONS

Since the posted-offer monopoly experiment resulted in the monopoly price-quantity equilibrium from periods 5 through 11, and since the posted-bid rules were used in PB3 for only the first 10 periods, it is natural to compare all experiments across the block of six periods from 5 through 10. This is done for price-quantity comparisons in table 2 and for efficiency comparisons in table 3.

From table 2, comparing the pooled means for periods 5–10, sellers in double-auction experiments were more effective in restricting output than sellers in the offer auction or in post-bid experiments. Mean quantity-conditional price effectiveness was slightly better in posted-bid pricing, and slightly worse in the offer auction by comparison with the double auction, but essentially, on average, the three institutions are comparably effective in restraining a seller relative to the posted-offer institution. The compatibility of the posted-offer institution with monopoly pricing is further evidenced by the fact that adding a second seller is less effective in monopoly restraint than changing the institution. In table 2, $\delta = -.0567$ for posted-offer duopoly, periods 5–10. The only experiment that is more price effective is posted-offer monopoly. All other pooled values of δ are nearly twice that of the duopoly experiment. Under all three institutional alternatives to posted-offer pricing, buyers countervail monopoly pricing better than does a second competing posted-offer seller.

But institutional restraint of monopoly does not imply an increase in efficiency. This is clear in table 3. Pooled average efficiency, $\overline{E}$, for periods 5–10, in the double-auction experiments is less $(\overline{E}_{DA} = 87.63)$ than for perfect monopoly $(E_m = 88.5)$. Average efficiency is better in the posted-bid experiments $(\overline{E}_{PB} = 92.03)$ and quite good in the offer auction $(\overline{E}_{QA} = 97.22)$, but highest under posted-offer duopoly. The efficiency of posted-offer monopoly, and duopoly, effectively bracket the range of efficiency for monopoly under the three other institutions. In substance, there is an efficiency cost to the institutional restraint of monopoly. If efficiency is the objective, then a second seller under posted-offer pricing is better than a change in the institution.

CONCLUSIONS

Our conclusions must be stated with considerable qualification:
1. The sample is very small. Ten experiments are few indeed for covering the study of four different price adjustment mechanisms.
2. Many of the experiments fail to exhibit evidence that an equilibrium state was reached in the number of periods that were allowed; longer sequences are definitely called for. Also, the effect of increasing the number of buyers confronting the seller needs exploration. Murnighan and Roth (1977), in a simplified game context, find that a monopolist's effectiveness increases with the number of players.

Subject to these qualifications, the following conclusions are supported by the data.

1. The posted-offer institution is the pricing mechanism most supportive of the monopoly price.
2. The double-auction, offer-auction, and posted-bid institutions are effective in constraining a single seller's attempt to obtain the monopoly price. In terms of the measure, δ, of monopoly price effectiveness, the four institutions are ordered as follows, from most to least effective:
$$\delta_{PO} > \delta_{PB} > \delta_{DA} > \delta_{OA}$$
3. Using the measure $\overline{Q}$ of quantity effectiveness, the institutions are ordered as follows, from most to least effective in output restriction:
$$\overline{Q}_{PO} < \overline{Q}_{DA} < \overline{Q}_{PB} < \overline{Q}_{OA}$$
4. In terms of average allocational efficiency, $\overline{E}$, the institutions are ordered from lowest to highest efficiency, as follows:
$$\overline{E}_{DA} < \overline{E}_{PO} < \overline{E}_{PB} < \overline{E}_{OA}$$
5. In terms of price advantage for buyers, posted-offer duopoly is inferior to monopoly under any of the other institutions.
6. In terms of efficiency, posted-offer duopoly is superior to monopoly that uses any of the four institutions.
7. A monopoly seller is more effective in increasing price and profits under the posted-bid uniform price rule than under the discriminative posted-bid pricing rule.

APPENDIX 1

Instructions (For Monopoly Double Auction)

This is an experiment in the economics of market decision making. Various research foundations have provided funds for this research. The instructions are simple, and if you follow them carefully and make good decisions you may earn a considerable amount of money which will be paid to you in cash.

In this experiment we are going to conduct a market in which some of you will be buyers and one of you will be a seller in a sequence of trading periods. Attached to the instructions you will find record and information sheets labeled "Buyer" # or "Seller" #. You are not to reveal this information to anyone. It is your own private information.

BUYER INSTRUCTIONS. A buyer can purchase from the seller at most two units of a fictitious good per trading period. For the first unit that you buy, you will be paid the amount listed in the row marked *1st Unit Resale Value*. If you buy your second unit, you will receive the amount in the column marked *2nd Unit Resale Value*. The profits (which are yours to keep) are computed by taking the difference between the resale value and the purchase price of the unit bought. In addition to this profit you will receive a 5-cent commission for each purchase. That is, (resale value) − (purchase price) + (5-cent commission) = PROFIT.

The three rows following the resale value are provided to allow you to compute your total profits at the end of each period. Please list the purchase price as soon as a contract is made in the row marked "Purchase Price." *Under no condition should you buy a unit for a price which exceeds the resale value.*

SELLER INSTRUCTIONS. Each seller can sell as many units as you wish to the buyers. For the first unit that you sell, you will be paid the amount listed in the row marked *Selling Price* for unit 1; for the second unit that you sell, you will receive the amount in the row marked *Selling Price* for unit 2; and so on for as many units as you sell. The profits for all units sold (which are yours to keep) are computed by taking the difference between selling price and the indicated cost of the unit sold. In addition to this profit you will receive a 5-cent commission for each sale. That is,

(selling price) − (cost of unit sold) + (5-cent commission) = amount earned

The three rows following the selling price are provided to allow you to compute your profit at the end of each period for all units. Please list the selling price as soon as a contract is made in the row for the unit selling price. *Under no condition should you sell a unit below the cost of that unit.*

MARKET ORGANIZATION. The market for this commodity is organized as follows. We open the market for a trading period (the length of a single period will be _____ minutes). The seller is free at any time to raise his hand and make an offer to sell one unit as long as the stated price is *not below* the cost on your sheet for that unit. Any buyer is free at any time to raise his hand and make a bid to buy one unit as long as the stated price is *not above* the resale price on your sheet for that unit. When a bid or offer is made, I will write the price on a data sheet and repeat it. At this point a new bid or offer may be made *which always supersedes the previous bid or offer* whether the new price is higher or lower than the previous price. Anyone wishing to accept a bid or offer may say "I'll take it" or "Sold." When a bid or offer is accepted it is a binding contract, and the buyer and seller will record the transaction price to be included in their profit calculation.

There are likely to be many bids and offers that are not accepted. You are free to keep trying, and make your profits as large as you can. Except in the bids and offers, you are not to speak to any other subject. Trading will take place over very many market periods. *Each column* in your table applies to *one* trading period. Trading period 0 will be a trial period to familiarize you with the procedure and will not count toward your cash earnings.

Are there any questions?

Record Sheet, Buyer

\# _____

Record of Purchases and Profits

Trading Period Number	0	1	2	3	4	5	6	7	8	9	10	11	12	13	14	15
1	1st unit resale value																
2	Purchase price																
3	Profit (row 1-row 2)																
4	Profit + 5¢ commission (row 3 + .05)																
5	2nd unit resale value																
6	Purchase price																
7	Profit (row 5-row 6)																
8	Profit + 5¢ commission (row 7 + .05)																
9	Total Profit (row 4 + row 8)																

Note: Record sheets are the same for all experiments.

Record Sheet, Buyer

\# _____

Record of Purchases and Profits

Trading Period Number	16	17	18	19	20	21	22	23	24	25	26	27	28	29	30	31
1	1st unit resale value																
2	Purchase price																
3	Profit (row 1-row 2)																
4	Profit + 5¢ commission (row 3 + .05)																
5	2nd unit resale value																
6	Purchase price																
7	Profit (row 5-row 6)																
8	Profit + 5¢ commission (row 7 + .05)																
9	Total Profit (row 4 + row 8																

Total profit, all trading periods _____

Name _____

Note: Record sheets are the same for all experiments.

Record of Sales and Profits, Seller #_____

Unit Sold	Trading Period Number		0	1	2	3	4	5	6	7	8	9	10
1	1	Selling Price											
	2	Cost of 1st Unit											
	3	Profit (row 1-row 2)											
	4	Profit + 5¢ Commission											
2	5	Selling Price											
	6	Cost of 2nd Unit											
	7	Profit (row 5-row 6)											
	8	Profit + 5¢ Commission											
3	9	Selling Price											
	10	Cost of 3rd Unit											
	11	Profit (row 9-row 10)											
	12	Profit + 5¢ Commission											
4	13	Selling Price											
	14	Cost of 4th Unit											
	15	Profit (row 13-row 14)											
	16	Profit + 5¢ Commission											

Note: Record sheets are the same for all experiments.

APPENDIX 2

Instructions (For Monopoly-Posted Offer)

Substitute the following in Appendix 1

MARKET ORGANIZATION. The market for this commodity is organized as follows. We open the market for a trading period. The seller decides on a selling price, which will be written on one of the cards provided. The seller will have two minutes to submit a price offer. The card will be collected and the price written on the blackboard. A buyer will be chosen at random, and if he wishes to make a purchase will offer the quantity (up to 2) he will buy. The seller may accept any number of the units offered by the buyer. However, when a seller posts a price it is with the understanding that you are willing to deliver *at least one unit* to a buyer at that price. When the seller accepts units offered by the buyer it is a binding contract, and the buyer and seller will record the transaction prices to be included in their profit calculation. After the first buyer has made his contract, a second buyer will be selected to offer a purchase quantity, and so on, until each buyer has had an opportunity to make a purchase. The market will then be closed, and reopened for a new trading period.

Except in the offers and their acceptance you are not to speak to any other subject. You are free to make your profits as large as you can. Trading will take place over very many market periods. *Each column* in your table applies to *one* trading period. Trading period 0 will be a trial period to familiarize you with the procedure and will not count toward your cash earnings.

Are there any questions?

Instructions (For Duopoly-Posted Offer)

Substitute the following in Appendix 1

MARKET ORGANIZATION. The market for this commodity is organized as follows. We open the market for a trading period. Each seller decides on a selling price which will be written on one of the cards provided. The sellers will have two minutes to submit a price offer. The cards will be collected and the prices written on the blackboard. A buyer will be chosen at random, and if he wishes to make a purchase will select a seller and offer the quantity (up to 2) he will buy. The seller may accept any number of the units offered by the buyer. However, when a seller posts a price it is with the understanding that you are willing to deliver *at least one unit* to *a* buyer at that price. When the seller accepts an offer of units by the buyer it is a binding contract, and the buyer and seller will record the transaction prices to be included in their profit calculation. If the buyer is unable to buy all he wishes from the first seller, he may make an offer to buy from the second seller any additional units that he wants. After the first buyer has made all his contracts, a second buyer is chosen at random who then chooses a seller, makes an offer to buy, and so on, until each buyer has had an opportunity to make a purchase. The market will then be closed, and reopened for a new trading period.

Except in the offers and their acceptance, you are not to speak to any other subject. You are free to make your profits as large as you can. Trading will take place over very many market periods. *Each column* in your table applies to *one* trading period. Trading period 0 will be a trial period to familiarize you with the procedure and will not count toward your cash earnings.

Are there any questions?

APPENDIX 3

Instructions (For Monopoly Offer Auction)

Substitute the following in Appendix 1

MARKET ORGANIZATION. The market for this commodity is organized as follows. We open the market for a trading period (the length of a single period will be _____ minutes). The seller is free at any time to make an offer to sell one unit by stating a price offer. When an offer is made I will write the price on a data sheet and repeat it. If any buyer wishes to accept the offer he may say "I'll take it" or "Sold." If no buyer accepts the offer, the seller may, if you wish, make a new price offer *which always supersedes the previous offer* whether the new price is higher or lower than the previous price. When an offer is accepted it is a binding contract, and the buyer and seller will record the transaction price to be included in their profit calculation.

There are likely to be many offers that are not accepted. The seller is free to keep trying, and as a buyer or a seller you are free to make your profits as large as you can. Except in the offers and their acceptance, you are not to speak to any other subject. Trading will take place over very many market periods. *Each column* in your table applies to *one* trading period. Trading period 0 will be a trial period to familiarize you with the procedure and will not count toward your cash earnings.

Are there any questions?

APPENDIX 4

Instructions (For Monopoly Posted Bid)

Substitute the following in Appendix 1

MARKET ORGANIZATION. The market for this commodity is organized as follows. We open the market for a trading period. Each buyer decides on a buying price which will be written on one of the cards provided. Buyers will have two minutes to submit a price bid. The cards will be collected and the prices written on the blackboard. The seller will then choose a buyer and state the quantity he is willing to sell to that buyer. The buyer may accept any number (up to 2) of the units offered by the seller. However, when a buyer posts a price it is with the understanding that you are willing to accept *at least one unit* from the seller at that price. When a buyer accepts units offered by the seller it is a binding contract, and the buyer and seller will record the transaction prices to be included in their profit calculation. After the first buyer has made his contract the seller will choose a second buyer, state the quantity he is willing to sell, and so on, until the seller has made all the sales he wishes to make. The market will then be closed, and reopened for a new trading period.

Except in the offers and their acceptance, you are not to speak to any other subject. You are free to make your profits as large as you can. Trading will take place over very many market periods. *Each column* in your table applies to *one* trading period. Trading period 0 will be a trial period to familiarize you with the procedure, and will not count toward your cash earnings.

Are there any questions?

NOTES

Support by the National Science Foundation is gratefully acknowledged. I wish to thank A. Williams, who conducted the experiment reported in chart 4, for permission to report these results, and M. Korody, who conducted a pilot monopoly experiment (not discussed here) in the Plott-Smith seminar in experimental economics at Cal Tech, spring quarter, 1974.

1. This monopoly study was motivated directly by the Plott-Smith (1978) study of the posted-bid and oral-bid auction institutions, and the author's earlier studies of one-sided auctions (Smith, 1964, 1967). The finding that certain institutions tended to favor buyers as against sellers led to the conjecture that if these performance characteristics were strong enough, they might provide a form of decentralized control over monopoly. Six of the experiments reported below had been conducted before I had read Vickrey's remarkable precursory contribution to the literature on incentive compatibility.

2. An alternative measure of the seller's monopoly effectiveness is to compare his actual profit in period t with the profit that would result from the quantity-conditional price, $p[Q(t)]$.

REFERENCES

Clarke, E. H. "Multipart Pricing of Public Goods," *Public Choice*, 2 (Fall 1971), pp. 17–33.

———. "A Market Solution to the Public Goods Problem," University of Chicago, Urban Economics Reports, 1968.

Groves, T. "Incentives in Teams," *Econometrica*, 41 (July 1973), pp. 617–633.

———. "The Allocation of Resources under Uncertainty: The Information and Intensive Roles of Prices and Demands in a Team," Technical Report 1, Center for Research in Management Science, U.C. Berkeley, 1969, pp. 71–73.

Groves, T., and Ledyard, J. "Optimal Allocation of Public Goods: A Solution to the Free-Rider Problem," *Econometrica*, 45 (May 1977), pp. 703–809.

Lerner, A. P. *Economics of Control*. London: Macmillan, 1944.

Murnighan, J. K., and Roth, A. E. "Results in Small and Large Group Characteristic Function Games Where One Player Is a Monopolist," Public Choice Society Meetings, New Orleans, Mar. 10–13, 1977.

Plott, C., and Smith, V. "An Experimental Examination of Two Exchange Institutions," *Review of Economic Studies*, 45 (Feb. 1978), pp. 133–153.

Shubik, M. *Strategy and Market Structure*. New York: John Wiley and Sons, 1959.

———. "On the Role of Numbers and Information in Competition," *Revue Economique*, 26 (1975), pp. 605–621.

Smith, V. L. "An Experimental Study of Competitive Market Behavior," *Journal of Political Economy*, 70 (Apr. 1962), pp. 111–137.

———. "Effect of Market Organization on Competitive Equilibrium," *Quarterly Journal of Economics*, 78 (May 1964), pp. 181–201.

———. "Experimental Studies of Discrimination versus Competition in Sealed-Bid Auction Markets," *Journal of Business*, 40 (Jan. 1967), pp. 56–84.

———. "Experimental Economics: Induced Value Theory," *American Economic Review*, 66 (May 1976a), pp. 274–279.

———. "Bidding and Auctioning Institutions: Experimental Results," chap. 6 in Y. Amihud, ed., *Bidding and Auctioning for Procurement and Allocation*. Studies in Game Theory and Mathematical Economics. New York: New York University Press, 1976b.

Tsao, C., and Vignola, A. "Price Discrimination and the Demand for Treasury's Long Term Securities," 1977. To appear in *Research in Experimental Economics*, vol. 2. Greenwich, Conn.: JAI Press.

Vickrey, W. "Counterspeculation, Auctions and Competitive Sealed Tenders," *Journal of Finance*, 16 (Mar. 1961), pp. 8–37.

Williams, F. "Effect of Market Organization on Competitive Equilibrium: The Multi-Unit Case," *Review of Economic Studies*, 40 (Jan. 1973), pp. 97–113.

The Theory of the Dam: An Application to the Colorado River

H. Stuart Burness and James P. Quirk

Certainly one of the major engineering achievements of the twentieth century is the system of dams, reservoirs, and aqueducts of the United States West, built mainly since the early 1930s. Most of the farming in the West relies upon this system for water, and the growth of population and industry in the arid Southwest (especially in Southern California and the Phoenix-Tucson area) rests upon this system as well. With only a few well-known exceptions, the water system of the West was built and is managed and maintained by two United States government agencies—the Corps of Engineers and the Bureau of Reclamation (Burec).

In this paper, we look at a vital part of the water system of the West, namely the Colorado River. We begin by reviewing the way in which the Colorado River system of dams, reservoirs, and aqueducts evolved, how it is managed, and what economic problems are associated with the system. The first part of this paper is concerned with the historical and institutional background of the river.[1] In the second part we look at management strategies with respect to the river as an application of the "theory of the dam." In particular, using a highly simplified analytical model, we derive an approximation to the steady-state probability distribution over storage of water on the Colorado.

The Colorado River and its tributaries are the only sources of surface water for much of the arid southwestern portion of the United States. The Colorado has a relatively small streamflow. To illustrate, while its drainage basin has more area than that of the Columbia River, the streamflow of the Columbia is an order of magnitude larger than that of the Colorado (180 million acre-feet [MAF] per year for the Columbia versus 13.5 MAF per year for the Colorado). Moreover, the Colorado is close to being a completely appropriated river, in the sense that water rights to the river have been spelled out in detail at the level of individual states (and Mexico).

107

The Colorado might well be the most closely controlled and monitored river in the world, and it has been subject to a host of lawsuits, treaties, compacts, agreements, and statutes. It has nine storage reservoirs, with two major aqueducts in operation and a third under construction. Currently, over 40 MAF of water are in surface storage on the river, and surface storage has reached as many as 48 MAF, or approximately four years' average flow of the river.

The story of the Colorado begins with the use of water by mines and small irrigated farms in Colorado in the 1850s and 1860s. Then, in 1870, the Palo Verde Irrigation District (near Needles, California) began diverting water from the river. In 1900, the Imperial Valley Irrigation District (in south-central California) began operations, diverting large amounts of water through a 40-mile gravity flow aqueduct, the Alamo Canal, that passed through Mexico. In 1905 there was a particularly heavy streamflow, the banks of the Alamo Canal collapsed, and the entire flow of the Colorado was diverted for two years into the Imperial Valley, forming the Salton Sea. This was the beginning of agitation by farmers in the Imperial Valley for federal government financing and construction of a high dam in Boulder Canyon for flood control and irrigation purposes, together with demands for an "all American" canal to replace the Alamo Canal.

The farmers of the Imperial Valley got support in their lobbying efforts from states in the upper basin of the Colorado, because of mutual self-interest. This derived from the western institution of water property rights (the so-called "appropriative" doctrine) under which water rights are established through use of water, with seniority based on the time at which water is first used: "First in time means first in right." The lower-basin farmers wanted a high dam and the upper-basin states wanted assurance that the fast-growing lower basin would not usurp an unreasonable share of the Colorado through prior appropriation. The grand compromise on these issues took place in 1922, when the Colorado River Compact was struck.

All seven states in the Colorado River Basin participated in the 1922 meetings in New Mexico at which the Colorado River Compact was written: Colorado, Wyoming, New Mexico, and Utah from the upper basin, and Nevada, Arizona, and California from the lower basin. The compact divided the river into two parts, the upper and lower basins, with the dividing line at Lee Ferry, Arizona, about 50 miles north of the Grand Canyon. Data were available on streamflows over the period 1896 to 1920, indicating that the average annual flow of the Colorado was approximately 16 MAF. In the compact, the upper-basin states were allocated 7.5 MAF, and the lower-basin states likewise got 7.5 MAF. The remaining 1 MAF of "surplus" water was unassigned, except that the lower basin was allowed first priority with respect to it. An added provision was that the upper-basin states would guarantee to deliver 75 MAF of water to the lower-basin states each ten-year period, thus essentially shifting the entire burden of shortfalls of water and variability of streamflows onto the upper-basin states. In effect, under the compact the upper basin obtained a maximum upper limit on the amount of claims to Colorado River water by the lower basin; and the lower basin obtained the agreement by the upper basin that was needed to obtain federal legislation and funds to build the high dam and all-American canal.

The Colorado River Compact did not attempt further to allocate water within basins among states; this was left for the future. Still, there was enough support for the compact that six state legislatures ratified the agreement; only Arizona resisted, on the grounds that no protection had been given to her interests vis-à-vis California. But in 1928 the Congress decided to treat the six-state agreement as a valid assignment of water rights and approved the Boulder Canyon Project Act, authorizing the building of Boulder (later Hoover) Dam. Under the 1928 act, Burec was directed to authorize contracts for delivery of water to the three states of the lower basin: 4.4 MAF annually to California, 2.8 MAF to Arizona, and .3 MAF to Nevada.

With the closing of Hoover Dam in 1936, the lower basin obtained the essential facilities for making use of a major share of its allotment of water under the compact. Shortly thereafter, the Colorado River aqueduct was completed by the Metropolitan Water District of Southern California, with capacity to deliver 1.2 MAF annually to the Los Angeles Basin and to San Diego. And in 1939 the All-American Canal opened, with capacity of delivering 3.5 MAF annually to the Imperial and Coachella Valley irrigation districts. So far as California was concerned, problems with the Colorado River were over.

However, what appeared to be the end of California's problems was only a respite, and a brief one at that. Technical problems had disappeared, but more problems would arise from a legal crusade on which Arizona was about to embark.

While California by 1939 was in a position to make full use (and more) of its water contracts under the 1928 act, Arizona lacked an aqueduct system to deliver Colorado River water where it was most wanted, namely, to the Phoenix-Tucson region. In the 1930s, Arizona was using roughly 1 MAF per year from the Gila River, a tributary of the Colorado, which had been dammed about the time of World War I to provide water primarily for irrigation in the Phoenix-Tucson area. Also, Arizona was using perhaps one-half to 1 MAF in irrigation districts along the Colorado, and wished to obtain a federally funded aqueduct to deliver an additional 1.2 MAF to Phoenix-Tucson.

Arizona found herself in a classic Catch-22 situation, which was exploited to the hilt for years by California congressmen. When Arizona asked for federal funds to build an aqueduct, California argued that the funds should not be provided until it could be established that Arizona had rights to the

1.2 MAF of water that would flow in the aqueduct. But when Arizona then went to the Supreme Court (six times between 1925 and 1958), to ask the court to rule on its claim that it held title to the water, the court refused (five times) to hear the case on the grounds that it would only look into rights conflicts which arise in connection with the use of water: it would not rule on what amounted to hypothetical claims. In essence, Arizona's desire was in fundamental conflict with the doctrine of prior appropriation: rights to water could not be obtained without first diverting the water and putting it to "beneficial consumptive use." Arizona could not get funding for an aqueduct unless it could show it had the rights to 1.2 MAF of water, and it could not show it had those rights until it actually used the water, and it couldn't use the water without the aqueduct.

This was the background in 1958, when the Supreme Court finally agreed to hear the sixth of Arizona's cases. After five years of testimony, disputes, and hearings, the Court ruled in favor of Arizona. The ruling in *Arizona v. California* (1963) established the allocation of water rights among the lower-basin states on the basis of the contracts that had been signed by Burec under the 1928 act: 4.4 MAF annually for California, 2.8 MAF for Arizona, and .3 MAF for Nevada. Moreover, the Court ruled that Arizona's use of 1 MAF annually from the Gila River was in addition to the 2.8 MAF awarded in *Arizona v. California*; the 2.8 MAF were to come from the mainstem of the Colorado.

Once Arizona had obtained legal confirmation of its water rights, the state again asked for federal funds to build an aqueduct to Phoenix-Tucson. The aqueduct was approved (as the Central Arizona Project) in the Colorado River Basin Project Act of 1968; but in order to obtain support from California, Arizona agreed to a provision which granted California an absolute priority for her 4.4 MAF, relative to Arizona's water claims. The Central Arizona Project has been under construction for the past ten years, and is scheduled for completion in the mid-1980s.

Assignment of water rights among the upper-basin states was accomplished by an agreement among the states rather than litigation. There were incentives to arrive at an agreement, since all the states were interested in obtaining federal funding for storage facilities and no such funding was available until water rights were established. In 1948 the Upper Colorado River Basin Compact was signed by Arizona, New Mexico, Colorado, Utah, and Wyoming, assigning a token amount of 50,000 acre-feet annually to Arizona, together with a percentage allocation to the major upper-basin states: Colorado, 51.75 percent; Utah, 23 percent; Wyoming, 14 percent; New Mexico, 11.25 percent.

In 1956 the Congress passed the Upper Colorado River Storage Project Act, authorizing the building of four storage facilities, at Curecanti, Flaming Gorge, Glen Canyon, and Navajo. The main facility is Glen Canyon Dam, with storage capacity in its Lake Powell reservoir (located 25 miles north of Lee Ferry) of 27 MAF. With the closing of Glen Canyon in 1964, the upper basin for the first time was in a position to control deliveries of water to the lower basin, since every upper-basin tributary to the Colorado enters the mainstem above Glen Canyon. In fact, there is no economic justification for the location of Glen Canyon, since none of the water in Lake Powell will be used in the upper basin; instead, Glen Canyon Dam was built where it was solely to enable the upper basin to control deliveries of water to the lower basin, according to the terms of the Colorado River Compact.

Thus the current status of the dam-reservoir-aqueduct system on the Colorado is the following. In the upper basin, there are six storage reservoirs: Lake Powell, Flaming Gorge, Navajo, Blue Mesa, Fontenelle, and Morrow Point; and in the lower basin, three storage reservoirs: Lake Mead, Lake Mohave, and Lake Havasu. There are two operating aqueducts in the lower basin; the Colorado River Aqueduct delivers water to the Los Angeles Basin and the All-American Canal delivers water to the Imperial Valley and the Coachella Valley in California. Another aqueduct is being built, the Central Arizona Project, to deliver water to Phoenix-Tucson.

The management problem on the river is to determine a release-storage policy involving the system of dams and reservoirs so as to satisfy the various claims to water incorporated in the structure of water rights, all in an efficient manner. But there are some major complications in such a task.

To begin with, the signers of the Colorado River Compact overestimated the amount of water in the river. The period 1896 to 1920, with its average annual flow of 16 MAF, turns out to have been one of the wettest periods in the history of the Colorado. Long-term studies, based on tree-ring data, indicate that the average streamflow is around 13.5 MAF (all streamflow estimates are estimates of virgin flow at Lee Ferry, that is, estimates of the amount of water that would flow through Lee Ferry if there were no reservoir evaporation losses or consumption of water in the upper basin). So the provision of the Colorado River Compact, requiring the upper-basin states to deliver 75 MAF each ten-year period to the lower basin, has the effect of dividing the river, such that the lower basin gets 7.5 MAF per year and the upper basin 6.0 MAF per year.

But beyond this, the Colorado is an international river, and Mexico has rights that must be satisfied. In the 1944 Mexican Treaty, the United States agreed to deliver 1.5 MAF per year to Mexico. Under the terms of the Colorado River Compact, the upper and lower basins are to share equally in deliveries to satisfy Mexican claims. Thus, effectively, the lower basin has 6.75 MAF per year, and the upper basin 5.25 MAF per year.

We should add that the dam-reservoir system itself is not without cost in terms of water availability, because of the arid climate of the region. In 1975, evaporation losses at reservoirs reached 1.5 MAF per year: .9 MAF in the lower basin and .6 MAF in the upper basin. Net of evaporation losses, the upper basin is left with 4.65 MAF per year and the lower basin with 6.75 MAF per year. (In the lower basin, reservoir evaporation losses of roughly .9 MAF per year are almost exactly offset on an average basis by tributary inflows entering the Colorado below Lee Ferry.)

Finally, to further complicate things, a number of recent court decisions have established the legal rule that when Indian reservations were set up by the federal government, there was an implicit grant of water rights sufficient to make the reservations economically viable. With only one or two exceptions, the reservations have operated without Colorado River water since they were established. Moreover, claims to water would be quite senior because the reservations were set up in the late nineteenth century, so that there is an unknown but substantial amount of water to be deducted from existing claimants, especially in the lower basin, to satisfy the claims of the reservations.

This summary history, while brief, gives a clear indication of the potentiality for conflicts among the various claimants and/or rights holders in the Colorado Basin. Actually, these conflicts are just now maturing as *uses* of the river begin to approach the amount of water available. In the upper basin, uses are still only 70 percent of the 4.65 MAF available; in the lower basin, uses currently run close to 95 percent of the 6.75 MAF available. But by 1985, upper-basin uses will crowd available supplies, and completion of the Central Arizona Project will boost Arizona's consumption to near 2.5 MAF from the mainstream and will eventually force a cutback in California consumption to 4.4 MAF or less (down from its present levels of around 5 MAF per year).

With this as background, we consider the historical pattern of releases and storage levels on the Colorado. The pattern is quite different between the periods 1935 to 1963 and 1964 to the present; the closing of Glen Canyon in 1964 changed the entire management strategy for the river. Table 1 summarizes data on virgin flow of the river and releases at Glen Canyon and at Hoover Dam for the period 1935 through 1974. Roughly, in the pre-1963 period, the difference between virgin flow and releases at Glen Canyon equals diversions in the upper basin less return flows (net diversions); after 1963, the difference includes evaporation losses and changes in storage levels at upper-basin reservoirs as well.

Table 1
Virgin Flow and Releases from Hoover Dam and Glen Canyon Dam for Water Years 1935–1974

Year	Virgin Flow (000 AF)	Releases (000 AF)	
		Glen Canyon*	Hoover Dam
1935	11,550	9,912	5,556
36	13,801	11,970	6,282
37	13,740	11,897	5,826
38	17,546	15,440	6,186
39	11,079	9,394	8,473
40	8,601	7,082	7,694
41	18,149	16,052	11,730
42	19,126	17,029	17,880
43	13,104	11,263	12,500
44	15,155	13,221	14,450
45	13,411	11,545	12,940
46	10,426	8,745	11,290
47	15,471	13,514	10,660
48	15,613	13,687	12,750
49	16,376	14,359	13,200
50	12,896	11,057	12,940
51	11,647	9,831	9,981
52	20,665	17,980	14,370
53	10,636	8,805	12,780
54	7,661	6,116	10,690
55	9,188	7,307	9,278
56	10,749	8,750	7,818
57	20,095	17,340	8,088
58	16,489	14,260	12,270
59	8,609	6,756	9,757
60	11,263	9,192	9,251
61	8,457	6,674	8,661
62	17,299	14,785	8,304
63	8,450	2,520	8,810
64	10,156	2,427	8,357
65	18,913	10,835	8,021
66	11,208	7,870	7,993
07	11,907	7,823	7,916

Continued next page

Table 1 continued

Year	Virgin Flow (000 AF)	Releases (000 AF)	
		Glen Canyon*	Hoover Dam
68	13,664	8,358	7,935
69	14,386	8,850	8,001
70	15,405	8,688	8,034
71	14,846	8,607	8,209
72	11,941	9,330	8,388
73	19,327	10,141	8,277
74	12,844	8,277	8,114
75	16,771		
76	11,451		
77	5,470		

*Releases from Glen Canyon are streamflows at Lee Ferry.

NOTE: Water years on the Colorado end on September 30; thus the 1959 water year begins on October 1, 1958 and ends September 30, 1959.

SOURCES: 1. Annual Reports, Colorado River Board of California, 1964–1975.
2. *Compilation of Records in Accordance with Article V of the Decree of the U.S. Supreme Court in Arizona v. California, March 9, 1964.* Annual issues, 1964–1975, U.S. Bureau of Reclamation.
3. Communication from Alden Briggs, U.S. Bureau of Reclamation.

Table 2 gives surface-storage levels at Lake Mead for the period 1935 through 1975 and at Lake Powell for the period 1964 through 1975. Surface-storage capacities at the two reservoirs currently are roughly 26 MAF each (but capacity falls over time with siltage buildup). Under the Flood Control Act of 1944, there must be excess capacity of at least 1.5 MAF in the fall of the year and at least 5.35 MAF of excess capacity on January 1 of each year. Originally, this requirement applied to Lake Mead only, but now excess capacity in Lake Powell also qualifies to meet this flood-control requirement.

Table 2
Surface-Storage Levels at Lake Mead and Lake Powell,
End of Water Years 1935–1975
(thousands of acre-feet)

Year	Lake Mead	Lake Powell
1935	4,270	
36	9,559	
37	15,225	
38	23,170	
39	23,800	
40	21,144	
41	26,150	
42	25,430	
43	24,070	
44	22,860	
45	21,620	
46	19,010	
47	21,625	
48	22,002	
49	22,827	
50	19,738	
51	19,118	
52	22,543	
53	18,384	
54	13,739	
55	12,090	
56	12,785	
57	21,522	
58	23,326	
59	20,036	
60	19,938	
61	17,919	
62	23,622	
63	17,373	
64	11,628	4,214
65	14,708	6,466
66	15,004	6,423
67	14,375	6,300

Continued next page

Table 2 continued

Year	Lake Mead	Lake Powell
68	15,018	7,514
69	16,131	9,708
70	16,769	12,039
71	16,886	13,609
72	17,543	12,488
73	20,176	17,284
74	19,358	18,011
75	20,154	20,202

SOURCES: 1. Annual Reports, Colorado River Board of California, 1964–1975.
2. *Compilation of Records in Accordance with Article V of the Decree of the U.S. Supreme Court in Arizona v. California, March 9, 1964.* Annual issues, 1964–1975, U.S. Bureau of Reclamation.
3. Communication from Alden Briggs, U.S. Bureau of Reclamation.

As indicated by tables 1 and 2, releases from Hoover Dam between 1935 and 1938 were held at low levels to permit the filling of Lake Mead. By 1939, storage had built up to 85 percent of capacity and releases over the next fifteen years were geared to maintaining storage in the 19 to 23 MAF range, levels which were acceptable from the point of view of maintaining a head for power generation and providing for recreational use of Lake Mead. Releases between 1941 and 1954 fell below 10 MAF only in one year, 1951, and were far in excess of demands for water by lower-basin users plus treaty commitments to Mexico. The main function of Hoover Dam was power generation; streamflows were more than adequate for all desired purposes, and reservoir evaporation losses were not true opportunity costs for the system, since such water would otherwise have simply flowed through to the Gulf of California.

In the early 1950s, streamflows fell to low levels, and releases were adjusted downward. However, the preeminence of power generation over recreational uses of the reservoir is reflected in the fall in storage at Lake Mead, from 22.5 MAF in 1952 to 12 to 13 MAF in 1954–56.[2] After 1955, releases from Hoover Dam exceeded 10 MAF only in 1958, when storage levels temporarily began to push against the flood-control margins required at Lake Mead.

The situation changed after Glen Canyon was closed, as releases from Hoover Dam after 1964 quite closely reflect the quantities required to fill contractual commitments to lower-basin users plus treaty commitments to Mexico. Thus releases between 1964 and 1974 are in the narrow range of 7.9 MAF to 8.4 MAF per year—1.5 MAF for Mexico plus demands by lower-basin users that range from 6.4 MAF to 6.9 MAF per year.

Releases from Glen Canyon are somewhat more variable. Low releases in 1963 and 1964, designed to aid in filling Lake Powell, led to lowering of Lake Mead and consequent problems with power generation. Since 1964, releases from Glen Canyon have ranged only between 7.8 MAF and 10.8 MAF. Under the terms of the compact and the treaty with Mexico, the upper basin has an obligation to deliver 82.5 MAF to the lower basin each ten-year period. Actual deliveries for ten-year periods beginning with 1953 and ending with 1975, are as shown in table 3.

Table 3
Releases from Glen Canyon
Ten-Year Periods, 1962–1975

Ten-Year Period	Releases from Glen Canyon (MAF)
1953–62	100.1
1954–63	93.8
1955–64	90.1
1956–65	93.6
1957–66	92.7
1958–67	83.2
1959–68	77.3
1960–69	79.4
1961–70	78.9
1962–71	80.8
1963–72	75.3
1964–73	82.9
1965–74	88.8
1966–75	89.7

SOURCES: 1. Annual Reports, Colorado River Board of California, 1964–1975.
2. *Compilation of Records in Accordance with Article V of the Decree of the U.S. Supreme Court in Arizona v. California, March 9, 1964.* Annual issues, 1964–1975, U.S. Bureau of Reclamation.
3. Communication from Alden Briggs, U.S. Bureau of Reclamation.

Note that required releases under the compact, 82.5 MAF per ten-year period, were not satisfied for any ten-year period ending between 1968 and 1972. This reflects in part a difference between the upper basin and the lower basin as to obligations under the Mexican treaty. (Roughly, the upper basin argues that streamflows from the Gila and other lower-basin tributaries should be used to satisfy such obligations, relieving it of the .75 MAF per year obligation; the lower basin disagrees.) It also reflects the temporary situation (1962–63) during which flows were restricted to permit filling of Lake Powell.

Rules governing the Burec management strategy for the Colorado are published in a memorandum titled *Criteria for Coordinated Long-Range Operation of Colorado River Reservoirs Pursuant to the Colorado River Basin Project Act of September 30, 1968 (P.L. 90–537)*. The basic provisions are roughly the following.

The secretary of the interior determines an amount of storage in Lake Powell considered necessary to satisfy the provisions of section 602(a) of PL 90–537, basing this on probabilities of streamflows, estimated future depletions in the upper basin, historic streamflows, and the necessity to ensure that upper-basin consumption uses not be impaired because of failure to store sufficient water to ensure deliveries to the lower basin.

Then, if the storage forecast for Lake Powell for the end of the water year is below this storage level, determined under PL 90–537 by the secretary, or if Lake Powell is forecast to have a lower storage than Lake Mead as of the end of the water year, the object is to provide a minimum release of 8.23 MAF for the water year. On the other hand, if the storage forecast for Lake Powell exceeds the storage level determined under PL 90–537 by the secretary, water can be released from Powell at a rate greater than 8.23 MAF per year, to the extent necessary to achieve any or all of the following objectives.

1. For use as surplus water by the lower-basin states, but only if storage in Lake Mead is less than in Lake Powell
2. For the purpose of bringing the storage level of Lake Mead up to equality with that of Lake Powell
3. To avoid anticipated spills from Lake Powell

Releases from Lake Mead are to meet obligations according to the following priorities: (a) meeting Mexican treaty obligations, (b) providing reasonable consumptive use requirements of mainstream users in the lower basin, (c) offsetting net river losses, (d) offsetting net reservoir losses, (e) offsetting regulatory wastes.

Furthermore, after the Central Arizona Project is completed, under "normal" conditions, 7.5 MAF (if demanded) will be released to satisfy the demands of lower-basin users according to the *Arizona v. California* assignment of rights (plus 1.5 MAF for Mexico). But the secretary of the interior can declare that a surplus exists, permitting a release in excess of 7.5 MAF, taking into account forecasted streamflows, storage levels, and requests for water by contract holders. Similarly, the secretary can reduce flows to below 7.5 MAF when a "shortage" exists, using the priorities set forth in *Arizona v. California* to determine allocation of releases.

Finally, reservoir evaporation losses on the river (1964–73) are summarized in table 4.

Table 4
Reservoir Evaporation Losses, 1964–1973
(thousands of acre-feet)

Year	Total	Upper Basin	Lower Basin
1964	853	144	709
65	840	237	603
66	987	307	680
67	931	288	643
68	941	307	634
69	1,043	360	683
70	1,122	410	712
71	1,246	476	770
72	1,253	494	759
73	1,414	548	866

SOURCES: 1. Annual Reports, Colorado River Board of California, 1964–1975.
2. *Compilation of Records in Accordance with Article V of the Decree of the U.S. Supreme Court in Arizona v. California, March 9, 1964.* Annual issues, 1964–1975, U.S. Bureau of Reclamation.
3. Communication from Alden Briggs, U.S. Bureau of Reclamation.

The problem with the historical data on the operation of the dam-reservoir system of the Colorado is that they reflect the short-term influences of (1) the closing of the two major dams, Hoover and Glen Canyon, and the filling of their reservoirs, and (2) the low level of net diversions in the upper basin. It would be of interest to see what the long-term pattern of releases, storage levels, and evaporation losses would be if the Burec rules are followed. We do not attempt such an ambitious task here; instead, we examine a highly simplified model that generates decision rules that are similar in some respects to the Burec rules.

We assume that the dam manager (Burec) operates the system so as to maximize the discounted present value of the sum of expected profits to downstream users.[3] Moreover, expected profits for any downstream user are taken to be linear in water use, which amounts to the assumption of constant returns to scale to water use.

Let x_t denote streamflow in year t, let X^c denote the storage capacity of the reservoir, and let X_t denote the volume of water in the reservoir at time t. We assume that evaporation losses in period t are simply kX_t, where k is a constant. Let y_t denote releases in period t chosen by the dam manager.

Following the usual dynamic programming approach of numbering periods in terms of time remaining to the end of the horizon, we have the following accounting identity:

$$X_t = \alpha X_{t+1} + x_t - y_t,$$

where $\alpha = 1 - k$ and x_t is a random variable with probability density function $f(x_t)$. We assume that before choosing releases, the dam manager is able to observe inflows (say, in terms of readings of upstream gauges). Thus, define $R_t \equiv \alpha X_{t+1} + x_t$ as the amount of water available for release at time t. Then

$$R_t = \alpha(R_{t+1} - y_{t+1}) + x_t.$$

Assume that there are t periods remaining to the end of the planning horizon and that the dam manager has R_t units of water available for release. The discounted present value of expected profits D^t is given by

$$D^t(R_t, y_t) = \pi^A(y_t) + \beta E\{G^{t-1}(\alpha(R_t - y_t) + x_{t-1})\},$$

where π^A is aggregate profits given the release y_t, β is a discount factor, $0 < \beta < 1$, E is the expectation operator relative to $f(x)$, and

$$G^T(R_T) = \underset{0 \leq R_T - y_T \leq X^c}{\text{Max}} D^T(R_T, y_T), \quad T = 1, \ldots, t - 1.$$

In particular, assume that each downstream user has an identical constant-return profit function so that

$$\pi^A = b \sum_{i=1}^{N} d_i - \sum_{i=1}^{N} C(a_i),$$

where N is the number of users, d_i is the amount of water diverted by user i, a_i is the diversion capacity of user i, C is the annualized cost of diversion capacity, and b is the revenue per unit of water use. Let $C^A = \sum_{i=1}^{N} C(a_i)$. Then expected profits are given by

$$E\pi^A = b \int_0^{A_N} xf(x)dx + bA_N[1 - F(A_N)] - C^A,$$

where $A_N = \sum_{i=1}^{N} a_i$ is the aggregate diversion capacity of downstream users.

The linear nature of $E\pi^A$ leads to a simple specification of the optimal release policy. Thus, with one period remaining and given the available stock of water R_1, y_1 is chosen to maximize $D^1(R_1,y_1) \equiv \pi^A(y_1)$, where

$$\pi^A(y_1) = \begin{cases} by_1 - C^A & 0 \leq y_1 \leq A_N \\ bA_N - C^A & y_1 \geq A_N. \end{cases}$$

Hence, the optimal release policy, y_1^*, is given by

$$y_1^* = \begin{cases} R_1 & \text{for } R_1 \leq A_N \\ A_N & \text{for } A_N \leq R_1 \leq A_N + X^c \\ R_1 - X^c & \text{for } R_1 \geq A_N + X^c. \end{cases}$$

With two periods remaining, and given R_2, y_2 is chosen to maximize

$$D^2(R_2,y_2) = \pi^A(y_2) + \beta EG^1(\alpha(R_2 - y_2) + x_1),$$

where

$$EG^1 = b \int_0^{A_N - \alpha(R_2 - y_2)} [\alpha(R_2 - y_2) + x_1]f(x_1)dx_1 + b \int_{A_N - \alpha(R_2 - y_2)}^{\infty} A_N f(x_1)dx_1 - C^A.$$

Thus,

$$\frac{\partial D^2}{\partial y_2} = \begin{cases} b - b\beta\alpha F(A_N - \alpha(R_2 - y_2)) \text{ for } 0 \leq y_2 < A_N \\ 0 - b\beta\alpha F(A_N - \alpha(R_2 - y_2)) \text{ for } y_2 > A_N. \end{cases}$$

Hence,

$$\frac{\partial D^2}{\partial y_2} > 0 \text{ for } 0 \leq y_2 < A_N, \frac{\partial D^2}{\partial y_2} < 0 \text{ for } y_2 > A_N.$$

The optimal release policy in period 2 is then

$$y_2^* = \begin{cases} R_2 & \text{for } 0 \leq R_2 \leq A_N \\ A_N & \text{for } A_N \leq R_2 \leq A_N + X^c \\ R_2 - X^c & \text{for } R_2 \geq A_N + X^c. \end{cases}$$

By induction, the same rule applies for every t. Under constant returns, the entire stock of available water is released up to the point where the diversion capacity of downstream users is reached. Beyond that point, A_N is released until the capacity of the reservoir comes into play. The reservoir is held at capacity if available water is greater than diversion capacity plus reservoir capacity.[4] That is,

$$y_t^* = \begin{cases} R_t & \text{for } 0 \leq R_t \leq A_N \\ A_N & \text{for } A_N \leq R_t \leq A_N + X^c \\ R_t - X^c & \text{for } R_t \geq A_N + X^c. \end{cases}$$

The piecewise linear nature of the optimal release rule permits a relatively straightforward derivation of the equations defining the probability distribution over stocks of water in the reservoir. Admittedly, some difficult problems remain if an analytic solution to the problem is to be achieved in the general case, but numerical methods can be employed to obtain approximate solutions.

Using the optimal release policy specified above, and given X_t, the stock of water with t periods remaining to the horizon, then recalling the definition of R_t, we have

$$X_{t-1} = \begin{cases} 0 & \text{if } x_{t-1} \leq A_N - \alpha X_t \\ x_{t-1} + \alpha X_t - A_N & \text{if } A_N - \alpha X_t \leq x_{t-1} \leq A_N + X^c - \alpha X_t \\ X^c & \text{if } x_{t-1} \geq X^c - \alpha X_t + A_N. \end{cases}$$

Let $g_t(X_t)$ denote the probability density function over X_t and let $g_{t-1}(X_{t-1})$ denote the p.d.f. over X_{t-1}. There are "mass points" at 0 and X^c, denoted by $\gamma_{t-1}(0)$ and $\gamma_{t-1}(X^c)$, respectively. Then $(\gamma_{t-1}(0), g_{t-1}(X_{t-1}), \gamma_{t-1}(X^c))$ is given by:

(1) $\gamma_{t-1}(0) = \gamma_t(0)F(A_N) + \int_0^{X^c} g_t(z)F(A_N - \alpha z)dz + \gamma_t(X^c)F(A_N - \alpha X^c).$

(2) $g_{t-1}(X_{t-1}) = \gamma_t(0)f(X_{t-1} + A_N) + \int_0^{X^c} g_t(z)f(X_{t-1} + A_N - \alpha z)dz$

$+ \gamma_t(X^c)f(X_{t-1} + A_N - \alpha X^c)$ for $0 < X_{t-1} < X^c.$

(3) $\gamma_{t-1}(X^c) = \gamma_t(0)[1 - F(A_N + X^c)] + \int_0^{X^c} g_t(z)[1 - F(A_N + X^c - \alpha z)]dz$

$+ \gamma_t(X_c)[1 - F(A_N + (1 - \alpha)X^c)].$

It is easy to verify that $(g_{t-1}(\cdot), \gamma_{t-1}(0), \gamma_{t-1}(X^c))$ is a p.d.f., if $f(\cdot)$ and $(g_t(\cdot), \gamma_t(0), \gamma_t(X^c))$ are p.d.f.s. We consider in more detail the special case where g_t, g_{t-1} converge to a stationary p.d.f., $g(\cdot)$. In this case we have:

(1') $\gamma(0) = \gamma(0)F(A_N) + \int_0^{X^c} g(z)F(A_N - \alpha z)dz + \gamma(X^c)F(A_N - \alpha X^c).$

$(2')\ g(X) = \gamma(0)f(X + A_N) + \int_0^{X^c} g(z)f(X + A_N - \alpha z)dz$

$\qquad + \gamma(X^c)f(X + A_N - \alpha X^c) \text{ for } 0 < X < X^c.$

$(3')\ \gamma(X^c) = \gamma(0)[1 - F(A_N + X^c)] + \int_0^{X^c} g(z)[1 - F(A_N + X^c - \alpha z)]dz$

$\qquad + \gamma(X^c)[1 - F(A_N + (1 - \alpha)X^c)].$

Here $g(X)$ is the steady-state probability density that the stock of water is X, $0 < X < X^c$, $\gamma(0)$ is the probability that $X = 0$, and $\gamma(X^c)$ is the probability that $X = X^c$, where X^c is maximum storage capacity.

Given the steady-state distribution $(g, \gamma(0), \gamma(X^c))$ over stocks X, then the steady-state distribution over evaporation losses $e = kX$ is given by:

$$
h(e) = \left\{
\begin{array}{l}
\gamma(0) \text{ for } e = 0 \\[2mm]
\dfrac{1}{k} g\left(\dfrac{e}{k}\right) \text{ for } 0 < e < kX^c \\[2mm]
\gamma(X^c) \text{ for } e = kX^c.
\end{array}
\right.
$$

Finally, the steady-state distribution over releases y^* is given by

$$w(y^*) = \gamma(0)f(y^*) + \gamma(X^c)f(y^* - \alpha X^c) + \int_0^{X^c} g(X)f(y^* - X)dX,$$

$$\text{for } 0 \le y^* < A_N$$

$$\Omega(A_N) = \gamma(0)\{F(A_N + X^c) - F(A_N)\} + \gamma(X^c)\{F(A_N + (1 - \alpha)X^c) -$$

$$F(A_N - \alpha X^c)\} + \int_0^{X^c} [F(A_N + X^c - \alpha X) - F(A_N - \alpha X)]g(X)dX,$$

$$\text{for } y^* = A_N$$

$$w(y^*) = \gamma(0)f(y^* + X^c) + \gamma(X^c)f(y^* + (1 - \alpha)X^c)$$

$$+ \int_0^{X^c} g(X)f(y^* - \alpha X + X^c)dX, \text{ for } y^* > A_N.$$

In this case, a mass point appears in the interior of the distribution.

In the general case, there are not techniques for obtaining closed form solutions to the above systems of integral equations; numerical methods must be employed to obtain approximate solutions. For illustrative purposes, however, consider a special case in which a closed form solution can be derived for the distribution of stocks, namely, the case of a uniform distribution over streamflows given by $f(x) = \dfrac{1}{\hat{x}}$, $0 \le x \le \hat{x}$, where $\hat{x}$ is the maximum flow of the river. Consider the case of a "small" dam, namely, where $X^c \leq \hat{x} - A_N$ (recall that $A_N < \hat{x}$).

In this special case, it is easy to verify that

$$g(X) = \frac{1}{\hat{x}} \quad 0 < X < X^c$$

$$\gamma(0) = \frac{1}{\hat{x} - \alpha X^c} \left\{ A_N - \alpha X^c + \frac{\alpha(X^c)^2}{2\hat{x}} \right\}$$

$$\gamma(X^c) = \frac{1}{\hat{x} - \alpha X^c} \left\{ \hat{x} - A_N - X^c + \frac{\alpha(X^c)^2}{2\hat{x}} \right\}.$$

Thus, given a "small" dam and a uniform distribution over streamflows, under an optimal release policy the stock of water in the reservoir is distributed uniformly with the same p.d.f. as x, except at the mass points 0 and X^c.

For the "small" dam, we also have

$$E(X) = \int_0^{X^c} Xg(X)dX + X^c\gamma(X^c) = \frac{(X^c)^2}{2\hat{x}} + \frac{X^c}{\hat{x} - \alpha X^c} \left\{ \hat{x} - A_N - X^c + \alpha\frac{(X^c)^2}{2\hat{x}} \right\}.$$

In particular, following a Burec strategy of limiting appropriations to the mean streamflow ($A_N = \hat{x}/2$), as is true in the case of the Lower Basin of the Colorado River, we have

$$E(X) = X^c \left[\frac{X^c}{2\hat{x}} + \frac{1}{\hat{x} - \alpha X^c} \left\{ \frac{\hat{x}}{2} - X^c + \frac{(X^c)^2}{2\hat{x}} \right\} \right].$$

For example, with $\hat{x} = 30$ MAF, $X^c = 10$ MAF, $\alpha = .97$, then $E(X) = 4.93$ MAF, with $\gamma(0) = .34$, $\gamma(X^c) = .326$.

We apply our simplified model to the Colorado River by considering the case where storage capacity $X^c = 60$ MAF, water rights equal the mean streamflow (13.5 MAF) of the Colorado, and evaporation losses are 3 percent of reservoir stocks. We take the probability distribution over streamflows of the Colorado to be normal, with mean of 13.513 MAF and standard deviation of 3.565 MAF, these parameter values being derived from the Lake Powell tree-ring studies covering 450 water years. The chi-square goodness-of-fit test yields a value of 9.581 with 14 degrees of freedom (significant at the 1% level), so that the empirical distribution offers a close fit to the normal.

Figure 1 plots the frequency distribution as observed in the Lake Powell study and for the normal distributions. Table 5 presents data on the steady-state probability distributions over stocks for various levels of water rights A_N. Table 6 summarizes steady-state probabilities of releases for various levels of water rights A_N.

Figure 1
Normal and Observed Frequencies of Streamflows
for the Colorado River*

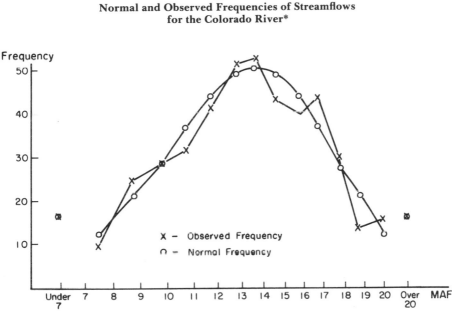

*Tail frequencies—under 7 MAF and over 20 MAF—are identical between the normal and observed frequencies.

From tables 5 and 6 we see that a strategy of limiting appropriations to mean streamflow (A_N = 13.5 MAF) leads to larger storage levels and a more reliable release policy than if appropriations beyond mean streamflow occur. With A_N = 14.0 (roughly what would happen if the Metropolitan Water District of Southern California were permitted rights to 1.2 MAF, with California's allocation raised to roughly 4.9 MAF), the probability of obtaining water sufficient to satisfy all rights holders falls to .815 from .911 when A_N = 13.5 MAF. In fact, only 90 percent of the time will more than 11 MAF be delivered; as contrasted to 97 percent chance of deliveries over 11 MAF when A_N = 13.5 MAF.

Because of the highly simplified nature of our model, it would be premature to argue too strongly the relevance of these theoretical results of the real-world problems of the Colorado. But it is interesting that whereas current storage levels are in the range of 40–50 MAF, with evaporation losses

Table 5
Steady-State Probabilities of Storage Levels
for the Colorado River
(Storage and Appropriations in MAF)

Probability of Storage X	$A_N = 13.5$	$A_N = 14.0$	$A_N = 15.0$	$A_N = 16.0$	$A_N = 17.0$	$A_N = 18.0$
$\gamma(0): p(X = 0)$	.125	.244	.481	.661	.787	.882
$p\{0 < X \leq 5\}$	.223	.318	.353	.271	.180	.101
$p\{5 < X \leq 10\}$	.216	.240	.121	.050	.017	.007
$p\{10 < X \leq 15\}$	.169	.118	.029	.006	.002	.001
$p\{15 < X \leq 20\}$	.120	.056	.005	.001	.001	0
$p\{20 < X \leq 25\}$	.077	.021	.001	0	0	0
$p\{25 < X \leq 30\}$	.041	.007	0	0	0	0
$p\{30 < X \leq 35\}$	.020	.002	0	0	0	0
$p\{35 < X \leq 40\}$	.008	0	0	0	0	0
$p\{40 < X \leq 45\}$	.003	0	0	0	0	0
$p\{45 < X \leq 60\}$	0	0	0	0	0	0
$\gamma(60): p(X = 60)$	0	0	0	0	0	0
$E(X)$	10.3	5.7	2.3	1.2	.8	.5
σ_X	8.8	5.9	3.8	3.8	3.7	3.3

near 1.5 MAF annually, the model (with $A_N = 13.5$) projects steady-state expected storage at around 10 MAF with storage losses near 300,000 acre-feet, a striking contrast.[5]

These steady-state estimates suggest questions as to how large a dam should be built. Clearly, if a dam is never filled to capacity, the dam is too large. Let $H(X^c)$ denote the cost of building a dam of capacity X^c and, as above, let $G^t(R_t)$ denote the discounted present value of expected profits with t periods remaining to the horizon, assuming an optimal release policy is followed. Then, given a T-period planning horizon, $X^c > 0$ is chosen in period T to satisfy $\dfrac{\partial G^T(R_T)}{\partial X^c} = H'(X^c)$.

Unfortunately, this simple statement of the marginal condition does not shed much light on the economic issues involved in the choice of dam capacity. We can, however, state a necessary condition that must be satisfied, derived directly from the expression for $\gamma(X^c)$, stated above.

Recall that under constant returns to scale,

$$\gamma(X^c) = \frac{1}{1 - F(A_N + X^c) + F(A_N + (1 - \alpha)X^c)} \left\{ [1 - F(A_N + X^c)] + \int_0^{X^c} g(z)[F(A_N + X^c) - F(A_N + X^c - \alpha z)]dz \right\}.$$

Table 6

**Steady-State Probabilities of Releases
for the Colorado River**

(Releases and Appropriations in MAF)

Probability of Releases y*	$A_N = 13.5$	$A_N = 14.0$	$A_N = 15.0$	$A_N = 16.0$	$A_N = 17.0$	$A_N = 18.0$
$p\{0 \leq y^* \leq 1\}$	0	0	0	0	0	0
$p\{1 < y^* \leq 2\}$	0	0	0	0	0	0
$p\{2 < y^* \leq 3\}$	0	0	.001	.001	.001	.001
$p\{3 < y^* \leq 4\}$	0	.001	.001	.002	.002	.002
$p\{4 < y^* \leq 5\}$	.001	.001	.003	.003	.004	.004
$p\{5 < y^* \leq 6\}$	.002	.003	.005	.007	.008	.008
$p\{6 < y^* \leq 7\}$	.003	.006	.010	.012	.014	.015
$p\{7 < y^* \leq 8\}$	.005	.010	.017	.021	.024	.025
$p\{8 < y^* \leq 9\}$	.009	.015	.026	.033	.037	.039
$p\{9 < y^* \leq 10\}$	.013	.023	.039	.048	.053	.056
$p\{10 < y^* \leq 11\}$	.019	.032	.053	.064	.071	.074
$p\{11 < y^* \leq 12\}$	.025	.042	.067	.080	.087	.091
$p\{12 < y^* \leq 13\}$	.031	.051	.080	.093	.100	.103
$p\{13 < y^* \leq 14\}$	.911	.815	.088	.101	.106	.109
$p\{14 < y^* \leq 15\}$	0	0	.610	.101	.105	.106
$p\{15 < y^* \leq 16\}$	0	0	0	.434	.096	.096
$p\{16 < y^* \leq 17\}$	0	0	0	0	.295	.080
$p\{17 < y^* \leq 18\}$	0	0	0	0	0	.191
$p\{18 < y^* \leq 19\}$	0	0	0	0	0	0
$E(y^*)$	13.2	13.3	13.4	13.5	13.5	13.5
σ_{y^*}	1.1	1.6	2.3	2.7	3.0	3.3

Hence, if $A_N + (1 - \alpha)X^c > \hat{x}$, then $\gamma(X^c) = 0$. That is, if X^c is an optimal capacity, then X^c must always satisfy $X^c < \dfrac{\hat{x} - A_N}{1 - \alpha}$, given constant returns to scale and risk neutrality.

Another way to derive this condition is to note that if, in every period, inflows were $\hat{x}$ and releases were A_N (so that dam capacity imposes no constraints on the release policy), then, over an infinite horizon, we would find that the stock of water in the reservoir, X_∞, would be given by

$$X_\infty = \lim_{t \to \infty} X_t = \sum_{t=1}^{\infty} \alpha^t(\hat{x} - A_N) = \frac{\hat{x} - A_N}{1 - \alpha}.$$

The optimal dam capacity must certainly be less than this magnitude.

Even in the special case of constant returns, obtaining a closed form solution for X^c creates important computational difficulties which have not yet been solved. Here we simply identify certain problems and present a solution only for the case of a dam with a very limited lifetime.

We are interested in calculating $\dfrac{\partial G^t(R_t)}{\partial X^c}$. Recall that $G^t(R_t)$ is given by

$$
G^t(R_t) = \begin{cases}
bR_t - C^A + \beta \displaystyle\int_0^{\hat{x}} G^{t-1}(x)dF, & 0 \le R_t \le A_N \\[2ex]
bA_N - C^A + \beta \displaystyle\int_0^{\hat{x}} G^{t-1}(\alpha(R_t - A_N) + x)dF, & A_N \le R_t \le A_N + X^c \\[2ex]
bA_N - C^A + \beta \displaystyle\int_0^{\hat{x}} G^{t-1}(\alpha X^c + x)dF, & R_t \ge A_N + X^c.
\end{cases}
$$

$G^t(R_t)$ depends on X^c, in that an increase in X^c can permit more water to be stored in period t (if $R_t \ge A_N + X^c$) or it can permit more water to be stored in future periods (if $R_T \ge A_N + X^c$ for some $T = 1, \ldots, t - 1$). At time t, R_t is given, but R_T, $T = 1, \ldots, t - 1$ are, of course, random variables. Hence,

$$
\frac{\partial G^t(R_t)}{\partial X^c} = \begin{cases}
\beta \displaystyle\int_0^{\hat{x}} \left\{ \dfrac{\partial G^{t-1}(x)}{\partial X^c} + \dfrac{\partial G^{t-1}(\cdot)}{\partial R_{t-1}} \cdot \dfrac{\partial R_{t-1}}{\partial X^c} \right\} dF, & 0 \le R_t < A_N \\[3ex]
\beta \displaystyle\int_0^{\hat{x}} \left\{ \dfrac{\partial G^{t-1}(\cdot)}{\partial X^c} + \dfrac{\partial G^{t-1}(\cdot)}{\partial R_{t-1}} \cdot \dfrac{\partial R_{t-1}}{\partial X^c} \right\} dF, & A_N < R_t < A_N + X^c \\[3ex]
\beta \displaystyle\int_0^{\hat{x}} \left\{ \dfrac{\partial G^{t-1}(\cdot)}{\partial X^c} + \dfrac{\partial G^{t-1}(\cdot)}{\partial R_{t-1}} \cdot \dfrac{\partial R_{t-1}}{\partial X^c} \right\} dF, & R_t > A_N + X^c.
\end{cases}
$$

Note that $\dfrac{\partial R_{t-1}}{\partial X^c} = 0$ for $0 \le R_t < A_N + X^c$, while $\dfrac{\partial R_{t-1}}{\partial X^c} = \alpha$ for $R_t > A_N + X^c$. Moreover, we have

$$
\frac{\partial G^t(R_t)}{\partial R_t} = \begin{cases}
b, & 0 \le R_t < A_N \\[2ex]
\beta \displaystyle\int_0^{\hat{x}} \alpha \dfrac{\partial G^{t-1}}{\partial R_{t-1}}(\alpha(R_t - A_N) + x)dF, & A_N < R_t < A_N + X^c. \\[2ex]
0, & R_t > A_N + X^c
\end{cases}
$$

Hence,

$$
\frac{\partial G^t(R_t)}{\partial X^c} =
\begin{cases}
\beta \displaystyle\int_0^{\hat x} \frac{\partial G^{t-1}(\cdot)}{\partial X^c} dF & 0 \le R_t < A_N \\[2ex]
\beta \displaystyle\int_0^{\hat x} \frac{\partial G^{t-1}(\cdot)}{\partial X^c} dF & A_N < R_t < A_N + X^c \\[2ex]
\beta \displaystyle\int_0^{\hat x} \left[\frac{\partial G^{t-1}(\cdot)}{\partial X^c} + \alpha \frac{\partial G^{t-1}(\cdot)}{\partial R_{t-1}} \right] dF, & R_t > A_N + X^c
\end{cases}
$$

In particular, for a dam with infinite life, the expression for $\dfrac{\partial G^t(R_t)}{\partial R_t}$ can be written

$$
\frac{\partial G(R)}{\partial R} =
\begin{cases}
b, & 0 \le R < A_N \\[1.5ex]
\beta \alpha b F(A_N - \alpha(R - A_N)) + \alpha \beta J & A_N < R < A_N + X^c \\[1.5ex]
0, & R > A_N + X^c,
\end{cases}
$$

where $J = \displaystyle\int_{A_N - \alpha(R - A_N)}^{A_N + X^c - \alpha(R - A_N)} \frac{\partial G}{\partial R}(\alpha(R - A_N) + x) dF.$

Evaluating the marginal benefits from a long-lived dam clearly involves solving the integral equations above for $\dfrac{\partial G}{\partial R}$, but thus far the problem appears intractable, at least in terms of obtaining closed form solutions. Instead, we indicate the form of the solution for horizons of 1 and 2 periods.

For $T = 1$, clearly $X^c = 0$ since $\dfrac{\partial G^1}{\partial X^c} = 0$ for all stocks R_1; for $T = 2$, note that

$$
\frac{\partial G^1(R_1)}{\partial R_1} =
\begin{cases}
b \text{ for } 0 \le R_1 < A_N \\
0 \text{ for } R_1 > A_N
\end{cases}
$$

while

$$
\frac{\partial G^2(R_2)}{\partial X^c} =
\begin{cases}
0 & 0 \le R_2 < A_N + X^c \\[1.5ex]
\alpha \beta \displaystyle\int_0^{\hat x} \frac{\partial G^1}{\partial R_1}(\alpha X^c + x) dF, & R_2 > A_N + X^c.
\end{cases}
$$

Hence, for $R_2 > A_N + X^c$, $\dfrac{\partial G^2(R_2)}{\partial X^c} = \alpha\beta b[F(A_N - \alpha X^c)]$.

Thus if a dam is to be planned before x_2 is observed, and if the criterion is to choose a dam capacity to maximize expected profits, the rule becomes: Chose X^c, such that

$$\alpha\beta b F(A_N - \alpha X^c) \cdot [1 - F(A_N + X^c)] = H'(X^c).$$

If f is uniform, with $f(x) = \dfrac{1}{\hat{x}}$, $0 \le x \le \hat{x}$, then X^c satisfies

$$\frac{A_n - \alpha X^c}{\hat{x}} \cdot \left(1 - \frac{A_N + X^c}{\hat{x}}\right) = \frac{H'(X^c)}{\alpha\beta b}.$$

NOTES

This research was conducted at the Environmental Quality Laboratory at Caltech, and was supported in part under a grant from the Department of Energy, No. EY-76-G-03-1305, Caltech Energy Research Program. We would also like to acknowledge the assistance of Joel Rubinstein and Albert Chang, and we want to thank Sheng Cheng Hu for his comments.

1. For a more detailed discussion of the institutional structure of the Colorado, see Burness and Quirk (1976); the economics of property rights in water is discussed in Burness and Quirk (1978).

2. Power generation and downstream water use are not independent, since from 20 to 40 percent of the power generated at Hoover is used to pump water through the MWD aqueduct to the Los Angeles Basin.

3. Thus the model of this paper ignores recreational uses and power generation, and conclusions derived from the model should perhaps be qualified to reflect these factors.

4. Thus the optimal release policy under our simple model of reservoir management has the same general linear characteristics of announced Burec policy, except that "shortages" and "surpluses" are not taken into account in our formulation.

5. It should be noted that the model is of a one-dam river rather than two, as in the case of the Colorado, and that we have not attempted to model the delivery requirements that were built into the compact.

REFERENCES

Burness, H. Stuart, and Quirk, James P. "The Colorado River: Water Rights, Institutions, Priorities and Allocations," Environmental Quality Laboratory, Caltech (Dec. 1976).
_____. "Appropriative Water Rights and the Efficient Allocation of Resources," *American Economic Review* (Dec. 1978).

Guidelines for a Responsible Natural Resources Policy

Charles W. Howe

Natural resource issues have become a prominent social concern during the past few years. Uncertainty about the adequacy of the resource base to sustain economic growth, continuation of technological change capable of mitigating the effects of increasing resource scarcity, and increasing concern over environmental problems have propelled natural resources from relative obscurity to prominence in the policy arena. Government, however, has failed clearly to state its perception of the problems from a national point of view and has developed no coherent set of policy guidelines. At best, national policy consists of a set of independently determined programs on a sector-by-sector basis, accompanied by a very large if somewhat arbitrary program for environmental protection.

This paper seeks to set current resource problems in a broader time perspective; to identify factors which will be important in determining future natural resource availability, and to suggest several guiding principles which might form part of an explicit natural resources policy statement. These guiding principles have been selected on the basis of consistency with historical trends and key technological and institutional factors, identified later in this paper.

DEFINING A RESPONSIBLE NATURAL RESOURCES POLICY

When we speak of "a responsible national natural resources policy," the underlying issue to which we implicitly make reference is the sustainability of aggregate production over time within an acceptable physical environment. This suggests the following definition:

A responsible natural resources policy on the part of the present generation of society consists of a set of rules, inducements, and actions relating to natural resource use which are sufficient to move the economy to an efficient, indefinitely sustainable, nondeclining pattern of aggregate consumption, with no irreversible deterioration of the physical environment, and without the imposition of significantly greater risk-bearing on future generations.

This long definition imposes some stringent conditions which will be qualified in later discussion, and it leaves several questions unanswered. Is it

131

possible to treat only a part of the world system, given the distribution of natural and environmental resources and the obvious importance of international trade and international pollution phenomena? What of population? Since equity and efficiency are both of concern, can we deal only with a part of the world's current population? Do policies, capable of achieving these goals, exist and are they unique, or is there likely to be a host of ways of achieving these ends?

A policy which is optimized from a national viewpoint can still contain constraints on external impacts, such as transboundary pollution or foreign resource dependence. While we resist any temptation to take a "save the world stance" in terms of providing for unlimited future population around the world, our concerns transcend narrowly defined national interests.

This definition draws heavily on the seminal writing of Rawls (1971), who proposed an egalitarian criterion for the distribution of material well-being and power under which inequalities are justified only when they provide the most effective avenue to improving the lot of the poorest members of society. Page (1977) has attempted to embody this Rawlsian criterion in his proposals for the maintenance over time of a "constant effective resource base," while Solow (1974) has used an interpretation of the Rawlsian criterion in his investigation of the possibility of unlimited production over time from limited natural resource inputs. Herman Daly (1973) has long been concerned with intergenerational equity and the primacy of guaranteeing the survival of human and other life systems as the criterion for public policymaking. Surprisingly little attention has been paid by policymakers and researchers to defining intergenerational equity and the mechanisms for effecting equity over the long-term future.

SOME HISTORICAL EPISODES
OF NATURAL RESOURCE SCARCITY

Concern with natural resources scarcity is, of course, not new, but the recital of a few colorful historical episodes will add zest to this Malthusian topic. These episodes are not meant to lull us into complacency but to exhibit some of the processes by which man and his economic systems have been able to adapt in the past to situations of increasing scarcity.

The concern in medieval England over timber supplies has been well documented. By Queen Elizabeth's time, the timber demands for shipbuilding, for charcoal in iron making, and the demands for open crop and pasture land had resulted in the devastation of English forests. As early as 1558, these heavy demands had led to prohibitions on the use of trees for fuel in proximity to the coast or navigable rivers. By the time of the English Civil War, timber prices were rising rapidly, adversely affecting the outputs of iron, other metals, and seasalt.

The high price of charcoal induced a large number of small entrepreneurs to experiment with coal as a substitute, seeking trial-and-error methods for producing usable iron products with various coals. Darby apparently achieved the major breakthrough in 1709 by converting coal to coke and thereby eliminating the problems of sulphur and other contaminants. Coal thus became the base of English industry, both for smelting and firing the boilers of the increasingly mechanized industries.

Should England have managed her forest resources differently? The denuding of land and the failure to replant the forests clearly reduced future timber potential and the esthetic qualities of the countryside, to say nothing of the environmental effects of the iron smelters, which poured their fumes into the environment. Yet England gained a head start over the Continent by being forced to experiment with coal. It isn't obvious that the sequence of events could have been changed to significant advantage.

Timber was, in principle, renewable, but coal was not. Jevons' 1865 publication, *The Coal Question: An Inquiry Concerning the Progress of the Nation and the Probable Exhaustion of Our Coal Mines,* brought this point to the public's attention.

> We are growing rich and numerous upon a source of wealth of which the fertility does not yet apparently decrease with our demands upon it. . . .
> But then I must point out the painful fact that such a rate of growth will before long render our consumption of coal comparable with the total supply. In the increasing depth and difficulty of mining we shall meet that vague but inevitable boundary that will stop our progress. [Quoted from "Keynes on Jevons" in Spiegel, 1959, p. 494]

Keynes, writing in the 1930s about Jevons' work, felt that Jevons' arguments were exaggerated and traceable to "a certain hoarding instinct, a readiness to be alarmed and excited by the idea of the exhaustion of resources." However, if we evaluate them in the light of the information available to Jevons, they seem wise and responsible.

An interesting case history of response to evolving resource scarcity was described by W. Philip Gramm (1973). In ninth-century France, whale oil came to be substituted for wood for internal lighting purposes because of its clean-burning properties. Under the pressure of the whalers, the whales apparently migrated toward the Arctic, making capture more difficult and costly. Innovation in shipbuilding helped overcome these difficulties. By the eighteenth century, the location of the whales plus the increasing shortage of shipbuilding timber combined to transfer the whaling industry to the northeastern United States. By 1800, however, it was becoming clear that whale stocks were being depleted and that catches were becoming more difficult. This was in part offset by further improvements in ship design and navigation techniques, which permitted ships to roam as far as the Indian Ocean in search of whales. In spite of these technological improvements, the price of whale oil increased 400 percent between 1820 and 1860.

The increased price induced various innovations, including the use of coal gasification for lighting in several European cities in the 1840s. The

American Civil War, with its destruction of whaling ships, caused prices to escalate even more, stimulating commercial interest in Drake's experiments with petroleum drilling. By 1863 there were approximately 300 experimental refineries in the United States, producing, among other products, kerosene. By 1867, kerosene had almost replaced whale oil, and in 1870 the price of whale oil struck a historical low.

While repetition of such a sequence of events should not be counted on in response to current shortages, the whale oil story poignantly illustrates the broad systems context within which natural resource scarcities must be considered. The range of technologies which proved directly relevant to alleviating the shortage of interior lighting fuels included not only those technologies directly associated with whaling but some which would never be picked as relevant to a "whale oil shortage": improved navigation techniques, a change in industry location to secure better inputs, coal gasification, and petroleum drilling and refining. It appeared that petroleum and its kerosene derivative had put the "whale oil crisis" to rest forever. But what of petroleum?

In 1874, Pennsylvania's state geologist (Pennsylvania being the site of nearly all producing wells) estimated that the United States had enough petroleum to keep its kerosene lamps burning for only four years. Before the turn of the twentieth century, adventuresome explorers had begun to look west of the Mississippi for oil, but the U.S. Geological Survey discouraged such exploration because of the unlikely geological conditions. Standard Oil's experts decided not to explore in the West. The Spindletop strike near Beaumont, Texas, in 1900 produced more petroleum than the rest of the United States! Again, threats of increasing scarcity seemed to have been overcome.

After World War II, there was concern about the adequacy of our natural resource base, stemming in part from the vast use of resources during the war. In January 1951, President Truman appointed the President's Materials Policy Commission under the chairmanship of William S. Paley to study "the broader and longer range aspects of the nation's materials problem." This landmark report concluded in a cautious, even somewhat pessimistic vein, recommending an important policy role for government and cautioning that the future would face materials-related difficulties. To paraphase from the report:

> . . . In this Commission's view, today's threat is that this downward trend in real costs may be stopped or reversed tomorrow, if indeed this has not already happened. . . .
> . . . Our strongest weapons for fighting the threat of rising real costs have been energy and technology, but this raises serious future problems. . . .
> How well supplied are we with energy and technology to support the burdens of the future? The simple answer is: not well enough. Petroleum and gas will experience strong upward pressures on costs. Coal is not the ideal fuel, and hydroelectric sites are limited. . . . Most Americans have been nurtured on the

romantic notion that technology will always come to the rescue whenever the need arises.

. . . There are formidable blocks to technological progress, including monopolistic restraints by industry and labor. Technological progress depends on scientifically trained personnel and basic knowledge, the development of which has been neglected. . . .

Less developed countries have resources but prefer to build industry than to develop these products of a "colonial" era. . . . Political instability and investor fear of expropriation hinder the flow of capital to these areas. At home, "buy American" legislation and tariffs further clog the channels of free world trade.

. . . Overcoming these barriers and offering positive spurs for developing and applying energy and technology . . . will never be achieved at random: only a consistent policy toward materials can hope to bring them about.[1]

It is difficult to imagine a more appropriate statement of today's concerns than these phrases from the Paley Commission report of twenty-five years ago. While it is possible to argue in retrospect that the popular lack of concern over the issues raised by the Paley Commission was appropriate and that the policy changes recommended in the report were unnecessary at the time, it is a bit frightening that a highly competent report on potentially crucial matters, issued by an eminent commission, stimulated no substantive policy change. Can we expect a response to any future reports in the absence of an immediate crisis?

In 1952, Resources for the Future, Inc., was established through the efforts of William Paley with Ford Foundation support. One of the most influential natural resource studies of history was the RfF study by Harold Barnett and Chandler Morse, *Scarcity and Growth: The Economics of Natural Resource Availability* (1963). Barnett and Morse gathered data on the labor and capital costs of the agricultural, forestry, fishery, minerals, and fuels sectors of the U.S. economy for the period 1870–1957. They also utilized the prices of natural resource commodities relative to the general price level, a measure reflecting scarcities not reflected in extraction costs. Two unit-cost hypotheses were tested: (1) the strong-scarcity hypothesis, that unit costs and relative prices of extractive outputs had been increasing, and (2) the weak-scarcity hypothesis, that unit costs of extractive outputs had been increasing relative to the unit costs of nonextractive outputs. Their conclusions are given in table 1 (with the exception of fisheries, for which they felt the data base too weak for definite conclusions).

Barnett has recently (in V. K. Smith, ed., forthcoming) updated the real unit-cost and relative price data to 1972 for the United States and several other countries. The new data offer no reasons for amending the earlier conclusions. Further analyses of the data to 1972 by V. K. Smith (May 1977) found a small but significant upward trend in the relative price of agricultural products and a strong but fluctuating upward movement in relative forestry prices for the period 1885–1972. Significant downward trends in the relative prices of fuels and metals were found for the same period. All these trends appeared to abate in the later part of the data period.

Table 1
Summary of Barnett and Morse's Results

	Strong Unit-Cost Hypothesis	Weak Unit-Cost Hypothesis
Late 1800s to 1920s		
Extractive sectors	rejected	rejected
Agriculture	rejected	rejected
Minerals	rejected	rejected
Forestry	not rejected	not rejected
1920s to 1957		
Extractive sectors	rejected	rejected
Agriculture	rejected	rejected
Minerals	rejected	rejected
Forestry	not rejected	not rejected

SOURCE: Table 1 in V. K. Smith, "A Re-Evaluation of the Natural Resource-Scarcity Hypotheses," Xerox, RfF (1975).

Ridker (1972) supervised a large-scale study for the Commission on Population Growth. Using an input-output model approach to estimate future natural resource demands and pollution loads in the United States, Ridker came to the following principal conclusions for the intermediate term to 2000.

1. The United States is not likely to experience truly serious shortages of raw materials during the next thirty to fifty years because of population and economic growth. (A "serious shortage" was defined as involving a relative price increase of more than 50 percent for a number of significant natural resources.)

2. The U.S. economy will become increasingly dependent on mineral, fuel, and other raw material imports.

3. Policies to clean up the environment will not be excessively expensive, constituting about 2 to 2½ percent of GNP through the year 2000.

These conclusions, drawn before OPEC raised petroleum prices, were based on the following assumptions (among others): that labor productivity would keep increasing as in the postwar period; that "best practice" in various industries today would become the average practice by the end of the century; that the trend toward services and away from goods would continue; that environmental constraints would not slow power plant development, nuclear or otherwise; and that the world trading and investing system would be maintained, including absence of OPEC "monopolistic control over a large fraction of the world's petroleum supplies." These conditions are fairly stringent, and some have obviously been breached.

Where do the foregoing episodes and studies leave us in our understanding of resources scarcity and in terms of forecasts for the intermediate-term future? The simple methodologies that were used in the studies certainly are not beyond criticism. As emphasized by the "whale oil crisis," the issue of scarcity must be understood in a broad systems context which encompasses technological change, substitution possibilities in production and consumption, exploration and discovery, and changes in taste and lifestyle. None of the large-scale studies to date has used this broad framework. Further, the data since 1973 have not been satisfactorily analyzed, partly because of the severity of the ensuing worldwide recession and the consequent difficulties of understanding what could be attributed to natural resource changes. These shortcomings notwithstanding, there seems to be no convincing evidence that the conditions of natural resource availability constrained U.S. economic growth through 1973, and there appear to be moderately convincing grounds for optimism in the intermediate term to the year 2000. That is, of course, a very short period. What, if anything, can be said about the very long term possibilities?

TECHNOLOGICAL FACTORS CONDITIONING LONG-TERM NATURAL RESOURCE AVAILABILITY

In this section we wish to identify five factors relating to technology, which will be crucial in determining future conditions of resource availability:

1. The physical conditions of resource availability in the earth's crust
2. The extent and nature of possibilities of substituting man-made systems (capital) for natural resource inputs
3. The continuation and nature of technological innovation, especially innovation *induced* by changing resource scarcities
4. The continued availability of economies of large-scale production in the natural resource industries
5. Long-term environmental constraints on natural resource use.

Conditions of Resource Availability

Economists and geologists alike have long thought in terms of the "resource triangle" for nonfossil minerals. That is to say, there should be a smoothly increasing supply of the minerals, with decreasing quality of deposits, until practically infinite resource plateaus—such as the oceans or average crustal concentrations—are reached. This concept was reassuring as long as energy was plentiful, in a time when "energy too cheap to meter" was thought likely. Now Brobst (in V. K. Smith, forthcoming) and others are arguing that, aside from a few of the most plentiful minerals (such as iron and aluminum), many minerals appear to have a bimodal distribution by quality or concentration: relatively rare mineralized deposits, followed by different types of deposits of lesser concentration which, while containing vast quantities, are in a different chemical form, no longer mineralized or existing as a separate element in a matrix of rock but now atomically bound to the matrix. For those deposits, separation of the mineral requires 10^3 to 10^4 times more energy. If these conditions prove to dominate the minerals scene, the implications for cost and energy use are profound.

Substituting Man-Made Inputs for Natural Resources

Solow, in his well-known Ely Lecture (May 1974), posed the importance of the substitutability of other inputs for natural resources: "If it is very easy to substitute other factors for natural resources, then there is in principle no 'problem.' The world can, in effect, get along without natural resources, so exhaustion is just an event, not a catastrophe." (p. 11).

Common sense tells us that capital and labor can be substituted for natural resources in many production processes. Rosenberg (1973) showed that American woodworking technology, while quite advanced, was very wasteful of wood compared with contemporary nineteenth-century English technology. English saws were made of better steel and were thinner, producing less sawdust. The fuel efficiency of steam engines increased as insulation, higher pressures, higher temperatures, and more complex controls came into use. In agriculture, intensity of cultivation can be substituted for land, although one of the principal inputs of intensive cultivation is fertilizer, another natural resource commodity input. Water input can be saved in agriculture, home, and industry through increased labor inputs in controlling applications and through more capital in the forms of better transport systems, sprinkling systems, and recycling systems. In the aggregate, such opportunities may represent the potential for very large savings of natural resource inputs.

At the theoretical level, the work of Dasgupta, Heal, and Solow (1974) indicated the importance of substitution possibilities to the long-term sustainability of aggregate output in the face of limited resources. Thus, while measures of substitutability do not constitute measures of resource scarcity per se, they do reflect one of our major capabilities for adapting to resource scarcity. Since economics uses the production function to represent the efficient production technologies available to an economy or a sector within an economy, it is natural that some characteristic of the production function be used to summarize available substitution possibilities. The elasticity of substitution, designated σ, is the most commonly used measure:

$$\sigma \equiv \frac{d\left(\frac{L}{R}\right) \Big/ \left(\frac{L}{R}\right)}{d\left(\frac{\partial f/\partial R}{\partial f/\partial L}\right) \Big/ \left(\frac{\partial f/\partial R}{\partial f/\partial L}\right)}$$

that is, the ratio of the percentage change in the factor ratio to the percentage change in the marginal rate of substitution. A production function that has three inputs, such as $f(K, L, R)$, can be described in terms of three partial elasticities of substitution, σ_{12}, σ_{13}, σ_{23}, which characterize the ease of substitution between two inputs, given the value of the third. In this case, however, inputs can be *complements* as well as *substitutes*; that is, some pairs of inputs may increase together along an isoquant as the third input is reduced. σ_{ij} takes on negative values if inputs i and j are complements.

Several mathematical forms of production functions are used in empirical studies, but the most common are the Cobb-Douglas, the constant-elasticity of substitution function, and the very general translog function. The Cobb-Douglas is characterized by $\sigma = 1$ and the *CES* by a constant elasticity, while the translog function has an elasticity which can change with the parameters and arguments of the function.

Experience and intuition indicate that partial elasticities can be expected to change sign (that is, factors shift from a substitute to complementary relationship) if relative factor prices change radically. An example is found in various capital-energy-labor applications. Historically, when energy was cheap, capital and energy were substituted for increasingly costly labor. More recently, as energy prices have escalated, capital has increasingly been applied to the saving of energy. One would obviously observe different partial elasticities of substitution during these two periods.

Humphrey and Moroney (1975) examined the partial elasticities of substitution between labor, capital, and natural resource commodities for two-digit manufacturing industries. The natural resource commodity input in their production-function and cost-function approaches was the sum of values of twelve renewable natural resource commodities (for example, farm dairy products, meat, cotton, vegetables, forestry and fishery products, etc.) and seven nonrenewable natural resource commodities (iron and ferroalloy ores, copper ore, nonferrous metal ores, coal, crude petroleum and gas, stone and clay, chemical and fertilizer mineral mining). Data for 1963 for 235 four-digit industries were grouped into twelve two-digit industries, but six industries, exhibiting a very low level of natural resource commodity inputs, did not yield meaningful results. The results are presented in table

Table 2
Partial Elasticities of Substitution, 1963

	σ_{KR}	σ_{LR}
Food and beverages	0.64*	0.64*
Textiles and apparel	0.17	0.47
Lumber and products	1.12*	0.61
Pulp and paper	−0.68*	4.49*
Stone, clay, and glass	−0.58	0.06
Primary metals	1.84	5.92*

*Indicates statistical significance.
SOURCE: Humphrey and Moroney (1975), table 6.

2. With the exceptions of primary metals and lumber, substitution possibilities appear limited. It is interesting that the exceptions occur with the use of *in situ* resources or, at least, resources farther down the production chain.

Brown and Field (forthcoming) estimated partial elasticities for the steel, aluminum, copper, and pulp paper industries for 1967, with the results shown in table 3. The results on primary metals agree with the Humphrey-Moroney results, including the extraordinarily high values for σ_{LR}. The pulp and paper sector results are not consistent between the studies.

Table 3
Partial Elasticities of Substitution, 1967

	σ_{KR}	σ_{LR}
Steel	3.0	4.5
Aluminum	3.4	3.0
Copper	9.4	15.1
Pulp and paper	6.0	1.9

SOURCE: Brown and Field (1976), table 4.

Substitution possibilities against energy are of great contemporary interest and importance. In a sharply focused study of thermal-electric power generation using cross-sections of data from firms, Christensen and Greene (1976), found very limited substitution possibilities, as indicated in table 4.

Table 4
Partial Elasticities in Electric Power Generation

	Capital-Fuel	Labor-Fuel
1955 I*	0.22	0.65
1955 II	0.20	0.57
1970	0.22	0.17

*1955 II groups various firms into holding companies.
SOURCE: Christensen and Greene (1976), table 6.

A recent study by Griffin and Gregory (1976) utilized intercountry data to study energy substitution possibilities in manufacturing. Their contention was that the range of relative price variation would be much greater than in time series of one country and that the data would represent a more complete degree of adaptation to these persistent price differences. Their data were collected on the manufacturing sectors of nine industrialized countries for the years 1955, 1960, 1965, and 1969. Their results were $\sigma_{KE} = 1.05$ and $\sigma_{LE} = 0.85$. Thus it seems that when significant and persistent energy price differentials exist, very significant substitution possibilities between capital and labor exist and are exploited.

The Continuation and Nature of Technological Innovation

History has clearly demonstrated the importance of technological innovation to economic growth and the dramatic rise in per capita income in the industrialized world. A substantial body of recent research emphasizes the endogenous nature of technological change itself and presents impressive evidence of the responsiveness of technological change to input prices.

In Hayami and Ruttan's study of international agricultural development (1971), the enormous differences observed in land/labor ratios could not be explained by the ordinary process of factor substitution. As noted in a later paper:

> In the early 1960's, the U.S. had a land/labor ratio of 141 hectares per worker while Japan's ratio was 1.74 hectares per worker. The U.S. ratio exceeded the Japanese ratio by a factor of 81. However, Japan's land/labor price ratio exceeded the U.S. ratio by a factor of less than 30 during the same period. To explain the difference in factor ratios by factor price effects, the elasticity of substitution between the two factors would have to be 3 or more. [Ruttan, Binswanger, and Hayami, August 1977, p. 7]

They concluded that the large differences in factor ratios over time and among countries had to result from a process of dynamic factor substitution in response to changing relative prices.

The demonstration of a dynamic, induced innovation process is certainly an optimistic factor in the natural resources outlook. It also has important implications for the role of markets and prices.

The process of discovery, invention, and innovation is very poorly understood. Much of past technological change has come in thousands of small steps, none startling in itself. The improvements in electric power generation from 1900 to 1970 provide an excellent example of this gradual but significant type of progress, as do the improvements in metallurgy over the centuries. Thousands of interested artisans or firms were able to experiment through trial and error, ensuring a broad advance in these technologies, even though many individuals must have failed to design viable changes. Are the types of future technological change, needed to mitigate natural resource constraints, subject to the same type of broad, frontal attack, or have we advanced to a need for such esoteric technologies that only a few collectivities can pursue them, and with a much higher risk of failure?

The evidence on this point is mixed. If we think of fusion power or other nuclear technologies, the research costs are so great that only the largest corporations or governments can afford the costs and the risks of failure. On the other hand, energy alternatives to fusion, such as solar or self-sufficient micro utility units, seem to be subject to the traditional research and development approach. Optimism is suggested, too, by the incredible and widely dispersed progress in computers and micro circuitry of all types.

Scale Economies

Ruttan has characterized scale economies as a disequilibrium state resulting from technological change. In a dynamic setting, technological change is a continuing process across numerous sectors; so one might expect always to find some unexploited scale economies. Several factors might act to change this state of affairs. Technological change might cease in a particular sector, or it might take forms that do not involve scale economies. Christensen and Greene (1976) convincingly demonstrated that scale economies in thermal-electric generation have been exhausted. In civil works (dams, tunnels, highways, buildings, and so forth), pure construction scale economies appear to have been exhausted, but technological change continues to improve the quality of the product (for example, the strength of concrete and dams) and the capability of difficult tasks (for example, construction in remote canyons).[2] While the evidence is slim, it suggests that the probability of successful technological change, leading to further scale economies, has fallen across a broad front, implying loss of a historically important source of increased efficiency.

Long-Term Role of the Environment as Amenity and Constraint

The maintenance of environmental quality has become a major national objective (for example, as manifested in the *Principles and Standards* of the U.S. Water Resources Council). This environmental objective can be thought of as having three dimensions: (1) maintenance of a high-quality ambient environment; (2) prevention of further change in the more remote parts of the global system, such as the upper atmosphere or the ocean depths; (3) provision of socially appropriate quantities of natural environmental systems for recreational and scientific purposes.

It now appears that adequate ambient environmental quality levels are attainable (though expensive), even in the face of continuing economic and population growth. Evidence is found in the reports of the Council on Environmental Quality (for example, 1976). Pollution abatement technology is relatively young, and it seems likely that significant advances will continue in those technologies. This is not to assert that ambient environmental quality will not constrain economic activity, for its costs have risen to a significant fraction of the gross national product and have caused a slowing in the growth of output available for consumption and investment. Nonetheless, these costs are predictable and will rise smoothly with the standards we impose and with levels of output, rather than standing as an absolute barrier to further growth.

It is not clear that some of the larger-scale environmental changes can be prevented through technological change or even reversed as a result of future decisions. The buildup of carbon dioxide and fluorocarbons in the upper atmosphere, the accumulation of radioactive wastes in the earth's crust and oceans, and other forms of oceanic pollution are examples. While the implications of these conditions are not clearly known at present, it is conceivable that future generations may face the need to restrict economic activity severely to avoid catastrophic global consequences, such as the flooding of coastal areas or severe genetic damage. It is not clear that the common property nature of the global environment will make globally concerted actions possible, even if needed. What is clear is that the risks faced by future generations are substantially increased as a result of our past and current resource use patterns.

Regarding environment as amenity, the demand for outdoor recreation and esthetics continues to increase rapidly as incomes rise. As Krutilla (1967) argued in his classic article, "Conservation Reconsidered," natural environment is one good which cannot be produced by technology. Through improved transportation, we gain access to more remote areas, while reclamation techniques permit us partially to restore lands which have been committed to development. However, we already are realizing the limits to these solutions as energy costs increase. Thus Krutilla's basic argument remains intact, that there is a basic asymmetry in technology's ability to permit expansion of the usual goods and services and expansion of natural environment amenities. This is a significant constraint on our production possibilities.

A final facet of the relationship between environmental conditions and future production possibilities is found in the uncertainty of our understanding of the factors to which our past growth can be attributed. Smith and Krutilla (1977) have suggested that omission of use of the environment as a factor of production for waste disposal may have biased our estimates of the causes of economic growth. Since the waste-assimilative capacities of the environment have been common property resources, they have been freely used, and one would expect that technological innovation would have been strongly biased toward the use of that factor. If this has been true, Smith and Krutilla argue, much of the growth of output which has been imputed to technological change, education, and other qualitative factors should have been attributed to increasing use of the environment. Increased use of this factor may not be available in the future. Furthermore, if technological change has in fact been less productive than we have thought, future technological change must be more heavily discounted as a partial solution to our resource problems.

INSTITUTIONAL AND EQUITY FACTORS CONDITIONING LONG-TERM NATURAL RESOURCE AVAILABILITY

In this section, we point to four factors relating to institutions and equity which will condition the long-term availability of natural resources:

1. The role of the market and induced innovation
2. Problems of likely biases in market processes
3. The issue of intergenerational risk-bearing
4. The conditions of world trade.

The Market and Induced Innovation

Ruttan, Binswanger, and Hayami (Aug. 1977, p. 23) conclude their survey of the literature on the induced innovation hypothesis with the following:

> The single most important conclusion that emerges out of the several tests of the induced technical change hypothesis is the powerful role of economic forces in inducing technical change. In view of the great differences in the physical, cultural and economic environments in the historical cases against which the tests were conducted and the different methodologies employed in the test, this conclusion must be regarded as remarkably robust.
>
>   . . . The effectiveness with which research resources have been allocated to release the constraints on growth imposed by resource endowments has been strongly influenced by the efficiency of market mechanisms in interpreting the factor price implications of relative resource endowments.
>
>   The pervasive role of economic forces in research resource allocation places a major burden on the efficiency of the pricing system. Our analysis suggests that if price relationships are distorted through either market imperfections or public intervention in market processes, the innovative behavior will be biased.

This again emphasizes the important historical role played by markets. It points out that distortions of market prices and incentives affect not only the short-run efficiency of natural resource allocation but the long-term potential for invention and innovation.

Biases in the Market Process

The efficiency of the market in allocating nonrenewable resources over time has been analyzed by Stiglitz (1974 and 1979) and, at a more elementary but still comprehensive level, Nichols (1974). While it is certainly *not* clear that markets have performed in a grossly inefficient manner in the past, nor that they would perform in a socially less satisfactory manner than the public-sector agencies that might assume their responsibilities, it is clear that some major sources of bias of increasing relevance exist within the market process. To provide a framework for discussing these biases, let us formulate the problem of optimum utilization of nonrenewable resources over time as follows: the output of natural resource commodities from *in situ* resources is given by the production function

$$R_o(t) = g[L(t), S(t), t] \qquad (1)$$

where $L(t)$ represents combined capital-labor and $S(t)$ is the stock of *in situ* resources. The demand function for natural resource commodities is simply $p(t) = D[R_o(t), t]$, and $A[S(t)]$ is the value (rate) of environmental services as a function of the remaining stock. The optimum path of natural resource utilization is then obtained:

$$\text{maximize} \int_0^\infty \left[\int_0^{R_o(t)} D(\eta, t) d\eta + A[S(t)] - wL(t) \right] e^{-\rho t} \, dt \qquad (2)$$

$$\text{subject to } S(t) = S(0) - {_0\int^t} R_0(\eta)d\eta$$

$$\dot{S}(t) = -R_o(t)$$

$$R_o(t) = g[L(t), S(t),t]$$

$$S(t) \geq 0.$$

The following necessary conditions help in characterizing the optimum resource use path:

$$\text{basic condition } 1: p(t) = \frac{dA[S(t)]}{dS(t)} + \frac{w}{\frac{\partial g}{\partial L(t)}} + q(t) \qquad (3)$$

$$= \frac{d\Lambda}{dS(t)} + MC(t) + q(t)$$

where $q(t)$ is the scarcity rent or user cost associated with the marginal unit extracted at time t. This simply says that marginal social value (price) should be equated to the marginal loss of environmental services plus marginal extraction costs plus marginal user cost.

A second condition is

$$\text{basic condition } 2: \dot{q}(t) = pq(t) - \frac{dA(t)}{dS(t)} - MC(t) \cdot \frac{\partial y}{\partial S(t)}. \qquad (4)$$

Society receives three rewards from holding *in situ* resources and carrying them forward: a change in their value, $\dot{q}$, greater environmental services, and lower future extraction costs. If one transposes the last two terms to the left-hand side, basic condition 2 simply says that at the margin of resource use, the sum of these rewards should equal the social opportunity cost of the value of the unit carried forward.

We can identify sources of bias in the competitive market process by asking the extent to which the above conditions would hold under perfect competition. In brief, the following points stand out:

1. The costs from loss of environmental services are likely to be ignored or understated.

2. A smoothly functioning market for *in situ* resources to establish the appropriate value $q(t)$ is essential (or producing firms holding *in situ* reserves must be fully cognizant of their own intertemporal opportunity costs). *Common property* characteristics of *in situ* resources can preclude such markets or recognition of such costs.

3. The rewards in the form of reduced future extraction costs will be ignored by firms in common pool situations (see the term $MC(t) \cdot \frac{\partial g}{\partial S}$ in 4).

4. Private discount rates are likely to differ substantially from the social rate of discount (see ρ in 4).

5. The absence of futures markets limits the role of speculation and increases the risk to producers of carrying *in situ* resources.

6. Price regulations can further seriously distort the time path of resource utilization.

Naturally, monopoly or other market structures will result in other patterns.

Intergenerational Risk Bearing

The need to face uncertainties is a burden on society. While one can speculate about the potentially beneficial roles of uncertainty (so that we don't know our ultimate fates, so that optimistic expectations are not suppressed, and so forth), people generally desire to escape uncertainty in the economic dimensions of their lives. This is manifested in the many forms of insurance, in the cartelization of markets to avoid price wars, and in the higher expected rates of return which are necessary to induce investment in risky enterprise.

Some types of risks can be pooled and ensured against through the law of large numbers or by taking advantage of negative correlations among the streams of returns from different investments. Arrow and Lind (1967) have also shown that spreading the returns and costs of a single investment project over a large number of persons reduces the cost of risk bearing toward zero. However, some types of risk cannot be totally prevented or guarded against. The risks of irreversible change in the global environment are of this type; for example, the buildup of carbon dioxide, the accumulation of nuclear wastes and oceanic pollution, and the extinction of ecological diversity.

The ultimate effects of these changes simply are not known at present, but they could be disastrous. The risks are of a greater order of magnitude than the risks which were involved in the earlier evolution of technology. At the same time, the common property nature of the environmental media makes worldwide control almost impossible. The point is that current and projected natural resource uses and related technologies imply growing uncertainties for future generations. If, in the past, it proved impossible to repair Appalachia after the rape of strip mining or to resettle the Dust Bowl, at least there were other regions to absorb migration and support life; but the greenhouse effect of CO_2, or the killing effects of oxygen-generating zooplankton in the oceans through pollution, cannot be escaped.

A similar type of risk is created for future generations if we increase future dependence on the successful evolution of particular technologies. As noted earlier, the nature of some of the technological improvements needed for massive substitution of capital for natural resources, which are frequently mentioned as panaceas for natural resource shortages (for example, fusion), are quite different from the technological improvements which have served us so well in the past. Reliance on such breakthroughs imposes risks on the future.

World Trade

The future of world trade in natural resource commodities is uncertain. While vast stocks of minerals, fuels, and timber are known to exist on the less-developed continents and while the prospect of future discoveries there is promising, the conditions of future availability to the currently industrialized nations are quite uncertain. OPEC-like blocs might proliferate, international organizations might press for improved terms of trade for primary commodities, and individual countries might establish higher levels of processing or manufacture.

Such changes would redistribute income in favor of the resource-supplying areas and would induce changes in the composition and growth of economic output in the importing countries. Overall natural resource consumption would be slowed. Exploration activities in the supplying areas would depend on capital availabilities and the ability to buy advanced technical services, but, overall, would probably increase. Innovation toward greater efficiencies and the use of substitutes would be stimulated in the importing areas.

GUIDELINES FOR A RESPONSIBLE NATURAL RESOURCES POLICY

The preceding technological and institutional factors which will condition future natural resource availability might be classified, in terms of our current state of knowledge, into two sets: those which clearly lend optimism to the future outlook and those which raise major uncertainties. An attempt to do this would likely result in a larger number of pessimistic than optimistic factors. This strongly suggests that the United States needs to adopt explicit policies which will help to reduce the uncertainties noted above and which will motivate both public and private actions aimed at mitigating natural resource scarcity. The following general principles are suggested as guidelines for more detailed action programs. As with the several objectives recognized in multiple-objective planning (economic efficiency, environment, etc.), there may be conflicts or trade-offs among these principles and between this set and the level of economic activity.

1. *Avoidance of irreversibilities in all renewable resource systems.* This represents Professor Wantrup's (1952) call for observance of "safe minimum standards" for all renewable systems; that is, avoidance of those physical conditions which would make it impossible to halt and reverse depletion. Maintenance of a safe minimum standard costs very little in relation to the

losses which might follow from extinction of the resource system. The safe minimum standard thus acts as a base level of preservation, above which economic optimization is free to determine practices. By this practice, the narrowing of potential genetic and physical development over time is avoided.

The concept of the safe minimum standard has already been embodied in significant national legislation: the Wild and Endangered Species Act, the Wilderness Act, and the Wild and Scenic Rivers Act. Other relevant programs would include international treaties on whaling and fishing, regulations on fishing technologies to minimize porpoise kills, and air and water quality legislation. Still, these constraints are continually under attack and require continuing public education and explanation.

2. *Avoidance of irreversibilities in local, ambient environmental conditions*; for example, the buildup of nitrates in groundwater, pesticides in soils, or persistent chemicals in lakes.

3. *Avoidance of irreversibilities in the condition of global environmental systems.* Further changes in these systems cannot be totally avoided. Even if the high-income nations decided to take the necessary steps, the common property nature of the global environmetal systems would result in some continued change. Yet, these changes are the major source of the increasing risk that is being imposed on future generations. These issues should be debated in the national and international policy arenas with the objective of international consensus on the assignment of specific national goals for protecting these systems. Federal concern is expressed in the air and water quality programs, as well as through support of international programs such as the United Nations Environment Programme and the International Biological Programme.

4. *A clear determination of the role of free markets and prices.* Current practice consists of a bad mixture of attempts at public control and partial reliance on private markets. The market can be much more effectively enlisted as a part of resources policy, while undesired side effects from market processes can be mitigated through appropriate taxation and redistribution. The demonstrated responsiveness of technical change to changes in factor prices emphasizes the importance of letting prices reflect the actual conditions of scarcity.

5. *Undertaking an integrated data base and forecasting program for natural resources at the federal level, supplemented by federal actions aimed at the perpetuation of a "constant effective natural resource base."* The natural resource information base in the United States is very poor in comparison with, say, agricultural, transportation, or health statistics. The absence of futures markets leaves little opportunity for consensus on future supply and demand conditions. This indicates a more active data and forecasting role for appropriate agencies of the federal government. Once these objectives have been achieved, other activities should be considered which would be aimed at maintaining

a "constant effective natural resource base." This concept was proposed by Page (1977), and implies not an unchanging resource base but a set of resource reserves, technologies, and policy controls which maintain or expand the production possibilities of future generations.

6. *Increased long-term support of social and technological research and development.* The past importance of technological improvement and human adaptation in the mitigation of resource scarcity has been elaborately demonstrated. Recent years have seen a slackening in private-sector research and a decrease in the level of national government support. Given the nature of emerging problems and the "public good" nature of knowledge generated through research, higher levels of research and development support, some directed at specific technologies and social changes, are called for.

Calling for research and development support nevertheless fails to define an efficient strategy for allocating that support. How government agencies are to decide on efficient extramural allocations of funds and efficient in-house research programs is not totally clear. The history of success of agricultural research within public-sector laboratories and experiment stations should be studied in this regard. The decentralized nature of that program made it responsive to regional problems and the needs of the user of applied research results. The effectiveness of other research and development support programs, such as those supported by the Office of Water Research and Technology, might also provide valuable insights.

NOTES

The author thanks K. William Easter, Lee R. Martin, and Vernon W. Ruttan for very helpful comments on an earlier draft.

1. *Resources for Freedom*, President's Materials Policy Commission, 1952, chapters 4 and 5.

2. R. Kraynick (1975) has documented the exhaustion of scale economies in earthmoving, tunneling, and cement pouring.

REFERENCES

Ames, Edward, and Rosenberg, Nathan. "The Enfield Arsenal in Theory and History," *Economic Journal*, vol. 78 (Dec. 1968).

Arrow, Kenneth J., and Lind, Robert C. "Uncertainty and the Evaluation of Public Investment Decisions," *American Economic Revolution*, vol. LX, no. 3.

Barnett, Harold J. "Scarcity and Growth Revisited," in V. K. Smith, ed., *Scarcity and Growth Reconsidered* (Baltimore: Johns Hopkins Press, 1979).

———— and Chandler Morse. *Scarcity and Growth: The Economics of Natural Resource Availability* (Baltimore: Johns Hopkins Press, 1963).

Brobst, D. A. "Fundamental Concepts for the Analysis of Resource Availability," in Smith, ed., *Scarcity and Growth Reconsidered.*

Brown, Gardner M., Jr.; and Field, Barry. "The Adequacy of Measures for Signalling the Scarcity of Natural Resources," in Smith, ed., *Scarcity and Growth Reconsidered* (Baltimore: Johns Hopkins Press, 1979).

Christensen, Laurits R., and Greene, William H. "Economies of Scale in U.S. Electric Power Generation," *Journal of Political Economy*, vol. 84 (Aug. 1976).

Ciriacy-Wantrup, S. V. *Resource Conservation: Economics and Policies* (Berkeley: University of California Division of Agricultural Sciences, Agricultural Experiment Station, 1976).

Daly, Herman E. *Toward a Steady State Economy* (San Francisco: W. H. Freeman and Co., 1973).

d'Arge, R. C., and Kogiku, K. C. "Economic Growth and the Environment," *Review of Economic Studies*, vol. 40 (Jan. 1973).

Dasgupta, P., and Heal, G. M. "The Optimal Depletion of Exhaustible Resources," *Review of Economic Studies: Symposium Issue* (1974), pp. 3–28.

Gramm, W. Philip. "The Energy Crisis in Perspective," *Wall Street Journal*, Nov. 30, 1973.

Griffin, James M., and Gregory, Paul R. "An Intercountry Translog Model of Energy Substitution Responses," *American Economic Review*, 66, no. 5 (Dec. 1976), 845–857.

Hayami, Yujiro, and Ruttan, Vernon W. *Agricultural Development: An International Perspective* (Baltimore: John Hopkins Press, 1971).

Houthakker, H. S. "The Pareto Distribution and the Cobb-Douglas Production Function in Activity Analysis," *Review of Economic Studies*, vol. 23 (1955–56).

Humphrey, David B., and Moroney, J. R. "Substitution among Capital, Labor and Natural Resource Products in American Manufacturing," *Journal of Political Economy* (Feb. 1975), pp. 57–82.

Kneese, Allen V., and Ayres, Robert. *A Materials Balance Approach to Residuals Management* (Baltimore: Johns Hopkins Press, 1968).

Kraynick, Roger G. "Studies on the Relevance of Technological Change in the Planning of Public Projects in the Civil Works Category" (Ph.D. dissertation, University of Colorado, 1975).

Krutilla, John V. "Conservation Reconsidered," *American Economic Review*, 57, no. 4 (Sept. 1967), 777–786.

Marsden, J.; Pingry, D.; and Whinston, A. "Engineering Foundations of Production Functions," *Journal of Economic Theory*, vol. 9 (1974).

Nichols, Donald A. *The Economical Use of Exhaustible Resources* (module 50) (New York: MSS Modular Publications, 1974).

Page, Talbot. *Conservation and Economic Efficiency: An Approach to Materials Policy* (Baltimore: Johns Hopkins Press, 1977).

Quirk, James P., and Smith, Vernon L. "Dynamic Economic Models of Fishing," in *Economics of Fisheries Management: A Symposium* (Vancouver: University of British Columbia Press, 1969).

Rawls, John. *A Theory of Justice* (Cambridge, Mass.: Belknap Press, 1971).

Ridker, Ronald G. *Population, Resources and Environment*, vol. 3 of Report of the Commission on Population Growth and the American Future (Washington, D.C.: USGPO, 1972).

Rosenberg, Nathan. *Technology and American Economic Growth* (New York: Harper Torchbooks, 1972).

————. "Innovation Responses to Materials Shortages," *American Economic Association Proceedings* (May 1973).

Ruttan, Vernon W.; Binswanger, Hans P.; and Hayami, Yujiro. "Induced Innovation in Agriculture," paper presented at 5th World Congress of the International Economic Association, Tokyo, Aug. 1977.

Smith, V. K. "The Ames-Rosenberg Hypothesis and the Role of Natural Resources in the Production Technology," Discussion Paper D-13, Resources of the Future, Inc., Aug. 1977

———. "A Re-Evaluation of the Natural Resource Scarcity Hypothesis," Xerox, Resources for the Future, Inc., May 1977.

——— and John V. Krutilla. "Resource and Environmental Constraints to Growth," Discussion Paper D-17, Resources for the Future, Inc., Nov. 1977.

———, ed. *Scarcity and Growth Reconsidered* (Baltimore: Johns Hopkins Press, forthcoming).

Smith, Vernon L. "On Models of Commercial Fishing," *Journal of Political Economy*, vol. 77, no. 2 (Mar./Apr. 1969).

———. "The Primitive Hunter Culture, Pleistocene Extinction, and the Rise of Agriculture," *Journal of Political Economy*, vol. 82, no. 4 (Aug. 1975).

Solow, R. M. "Intergenerational Equity and Exhaustible Resources," *Review of Economic Studies: Symposium Issue* (1974), pp. 29–46.

———. "The Economics of Resources or the Resources of Economics," *American Economic Review, Papers and Proceedings*, vol. 64 (May 1974).

Spiegel, Henry William, ed. *The Development of Economic Thought* (New York: John Wiley and Sons, 1952).

Stiglitz, J. "Growth with Exhaustible Natural Resources: Efficient and Optimal Growth Paths" (pp. 123–138) and "Growth with Exhaustible Natural Resources: The Competitive Economy" (pp. 139–151), *Review of Economic Studies: Symposium Issue* (1974).

———. "A Neoclassical Analysis of the Economics of Natural Resources," in Smith, ed., *Scarcity and Growth Reconsidered* (Baltimore: Johns Hopkins Press, 1979).

Uselding, P. J. "Technical Progress at the Springfield Armory, 1820–1850," *Explorations in Economic History*, vol. 9 (Spring 1972).

(U.S.) President's Materials Policy Commission, *Resources for Freedom* (5 vols.; Washington, D.C.: USGPO, June 1952).

Wantrup, S. V. *Resource Conservation: Economics and Policies* (3d ed.; Berkeley: University of California Press, 1976).

In Search of the Historical Imperialist

Lance E. Davis and Robert A. Huttenback

Because the world is complex and outcomes often depend crucially on some unpredictable aspect of human behavior and because he can never replicate an "experiment," the traditional historian must meld the skills of the social or physical scientist (classification, description, formal modeling, counterfactual exploration, measurement, and prediction) with the novelist's ability to develop characters in a way that makes his interpretation of their behavior appear more "reasonable" than any alternative.

Given the examples set by writers, scientists, and traditional historians, it is a bit surprising that historians, working in the area of political economy, have often chosen to ply a quite different trade. Take, for example, the question of Western imperialism in general and of British imperialism in the nineteenth century in particular. In his classic statement, Hobson argues that "although the new imperialism has been bad business for the nation it has been good business for certain classes and certain trades."[1] Aside, however, from owners and workers in the armament industry, he identifies neither the imperialist parasites nor the sectors of the nation that bore the costs. Fieldhouse, in his excellent and critical survey of the imperialist literature, talks of "financial interest and other imperialists," but does not greatly narrow the "other" category or even specify what part of the financial community profited from colonial ventures.[2] On what appears on the surface to be a quite different tack, Schumpeter asserted that capitalists tend to be anti-imperialists and the imperial classes are the aristocracy and warriors.[3]

If we are to understand the nature of the imperialist venture, talk of class behavior (imperialist or anti-imperialist) is not particularly helpful unless we can define these classes in some precise way. The definitions implied by Hobson *et al.* are not precise, nor do they lead to a specification that is amenable to careful analysis. After all, the crux of both the Hobsonian–neo-Marxist and the Schumpeterian analysis lies in the ability of the imperialist to turn government power to his personal profit while transferring at least some of the costs of that enterprise to other citizens. In the Hobson–Marx case, the imperialist's motivation was money; in the Schumpeterian scenario it was honor; but both arguments rest on fairly strong assumptions about the behavior of a particular group of individuals. In neither case, however, is the composition of that group clearly defined.

Although final resolution of the "imperialist controversy" will not likely be seen in our lifetime, we should at least be able to move the discussion from the area of political rhetoric to the domain of pre- (if not pure) science. The questions are the same as those posed by the Continental Op, Nero Wolf, or Lou Archer: "What was the crime?" "How was it carried out?" "What was the motive?" and, finally, "Who did it?"* Fictional detectives are presented with a corpse; the historian's task is more difficult, since it is never so clear exactly what crime has been committed. But still it is alleged that imperialism was a crime, and if we are to prove it, it is necessary to ascertain the identity of the shadowy and diabolical imperialist who has apparently done something to somebody.

This paper attempts to provide some preliminary answers to the imperialist mystery. The investigation is based on a series of new data sets, but the analysis of those sets is not yet complete. The reader, then, should view the case presented as analogous to the fictional detective's having taken his evidence to a preliminary hearing or a coroner's jury (adequate for indictment but insufficient for conviction). For the argument presented in this paper, the data sets are (1) complete budgets for each relevant year from 1860 through 1912 for the United Kingdom, the eighty-eight colonies and dominions, India, and a number of independent countries at a variety of stages of economic development; (2) stock ownership lists containing names, addresses, occupations, and number and value of shares held, along with published balance sheets and profit and loss statements for a randomly selected list of 364 corporations whose shares traded on the London Stock Exchange; the sample of firms has been stratified by industry, location of primary business activity (colonial, foreign, and domestic), and, roughly, by size (big and small); and (3) the records of a second group of 372 firms (included on the basis of availability, not random selection), encompassing both corporate and noncorporate members and also classified by industry, location, and size. Those latter records include more complete financial information, company directors' minutes, internal memoranda, and correspondence.

For the moment, let us put aside the Schumpeterian thesis, since rewards derived from power and honor are difficult to measure, and let us instead make the usual economic assumption that imperialists were interested in maximizing money profits.[4] If we are to identify the gainers, the first order of business is to isolate the source of profits from investment in empire. As a working hypothesis, let us assume that all the profits did not accrue to

---

*For those who have spent their entire lives between the pages of *Wealth of Nations,* the Op, Nero, and Lou are fictional detectives.

colonial residents. Imperialism was expensive to the home country, and if it were only the colonial residents who received the benefits, it is difficult to argue that imperialism was the result of a rational economic decision.

Logically, we could assume that both the rewards and the costs of imperial activity might have been broadly distributed and the average citizen of the imperial power was a net gainer from his "investment" in the political structure. Alternatively, it is possible that both revenues and costs were unequally distributed, but returns were high enough that, if appropriate bribes had been paid, there would have been an increase in the welfare (in the Paretian sense) of the average citizen of the imperialist nation. Finally, costs and revenues might have been localized, with net benefits negative overall, but positive for some individuals and groups. We exclude the fourth logical category, losses for everyone, since that appears more appropriate for an explanation of the Schumpeter variety than one based on an economic calculus.

If the true explanation is the first—widespread net benefits—or the second—localized costs and revenues with revenues sufficient for bribes and those bribes paid—Hobson was wrong and Britain did (at least in some sense) benefit from its investment in empire. Imperialism, then, should be amenable to relatively simple political analysis in terms of the British ability to exercise control over other economies for its own benefit.

If, however, those explanations are incorrect and, instead, either bribes were not paid or losses exceeded profits for some but not all, Hobson will have been proved right. It would still be necessary to explain how such a situation arose and what forces prevented its modification. That analysis, however, involves identification of citizens who profited and those who paid, as well as enumeration of the sources of the profits, since "imperial profits" would not usually exist in a free-enterprise competitive economy. When critics speak of the level of "imperial profits," they clearly are not referring merely to normal profits but to some additional monopoly rent. They are, however, less clear in their explanation of the source of those rents. The first questions, then, are the source of those rents and how were they allocated.

In an earlier period, monopolies, enforced by the military power of an autocratic state, might have provided the institutional explanation of the existence and accrual of certain rents. Later, similar transfers might have been effected by the agent of an imperial power that was able to assert ownership over some valuable resource in relatively fixed supply and thus claim ownership of a stream of rents that otherwise would have gone to local residents.

By 1860 Britain was committed to free trade. As a consequence, the empire was open to all British subjects, whether natives in the colonies or residents of the home islands, and to almost any foreigner interested in plying his trade. The migration of Indians into South Africa and later into the West Indies, where they joined the "league of the merchants of empire," are cases in point. The possibilities of direct monopoly power were small and the same competitive forces must have made it almost equally difficult to hold a long-run monopsonistic rent. Britons may have had a head start and been able to acquire ownership of some valuable resources before the rest of the world awoke to their potential profitability. Then, unless property rights are redefined, those assets could have become the source of long-run profits to the initial holders. Still, there are questions. While by the 1860s or 1870s the United Kingdom may not have been a democracy, it was certainly moving in that direction. Since it is unlikely that the losers were all among the politically unrepresented poor, the question remains: how, if Hobson was correct, did the imperialists "pull it off"?

Given the economic environment of late nineteenth-century Britain, any exploitation must rest on a set of government policies that either thwarted competition or gave the "imperialist" an edge over his colonial, foreign, and domestic rivals. However, one fact should be borne in mind. Rents make it possible to earn incomes in excess of competitive profits, but once the rights to those rents have been transferred, the question of exactly who is exploiting whom becomes very fuzzy.

The problem is the same as that facing the owners of a professional sports franchise. In the late 1950s, Bill Veeck discovered the "cattle" loophole in the IRS regulations (that is, the right to pay only capital-gains taxes on the profits on the sale of culls), and that discovery, coupled with the "reserve clause," gave the wealthy a chance to extract substantial monopoly rents from the ownership of sports franchises. The rents, of course, were quickly capitalized into the franchise price. Once ownership had changed, the costs of alterations in the tax ruling or the weakening of the reserve clause fell not on those who had become sports millionaires, but on those who had purchased franchises at the "inflated" prices (prices that reflected both elements of the existing institutional structure) and who would be earning only normal, not monopoly, profits. A similar problem is faced by Rhodesian farmers today and by the "imperialists" in the late nineteenth century. Both groups, as well as the sports franchise owners, have found themselves fighting to maintain not exploitative but only normal profits.

What were the rates of return on imperial investment? This question has occupied economic historians at least since the turn of the century. In 1913, Lehfeldt found that colonial bonds yielded more than domestic, but that foreign bond yields were higher than colonial during the first decade of the twentieth century.[5] Forty years later, Cairncross' work indicated that, for the 1870s, colonial investment paid better than foreign, but colonial investment paled in comparison with American returns.[6] Moreover, he concluded that the colonial figures were biased upward because of returns from the colonies of white settlement. More recently, Michael Edelstein has examined returns on a sample of first- and second-class securities (including bonds and preferred and common stock) over the period 1870–1914.[7] His data indicate that after adjustment for risk, British foreign investment paid better than domestic, but the overall average reflected the results of the years 1875 to 1885 and 1895 to 1910, when foreign earnings dominated returns at home.[8]

Edelstein is aware of the problems inherent in using any stock market data: to the extent the market works, capital values adjust to earning differentials and, in equilibrium, the rate of return on all equally risky activities is the same. In fact, he attributes the higher observed returns in foreign activities to unanticipated profits and to the lag in the market's recognition of those gains. Putting aside the theoretical questions raised by this explanation, Edelstein's data—even taken at face value—do not provide a complete answer to the question of the relative profitability of imperial adventures, since his totals are not easily disaggregated into colonial and foreign components. A crude disaggregation along those lines, however, indicates that colonial investment yielded only slightly more than domestic and that most of the foreign-domestic differential can be traced to overseas noncolonial activities. Robinson and Gallagher might conclude that those returns reflect "free trade imperialism," but a substantial part was earned in areas like the United States, and to call these investments "imperial" involves substantial restructuring of the argument.

Even if one is prepared to ignore the basic theoretic problems raised by the use of stock exchange data, the conclusions are again called into question by certain features of the British economy in the late nineteenth century. At the time there were very rapid changes in the firm and industrial composition of securities listed on the London Exchange.[9] Any sample that reflects the composition of firms in one period would contain different firms in different periods. If the rate and source of entry were similar across industrial and geographic categories, the distortion might not be too great, but, unfortunately, there were substantial intertemporal differences.

Britain had a long history of tightly controlled (frequently individual or family) firms in the domestic sector. The colonial sector also had a substantial number of such firms, but they were a smaller proportion of the total. Finally, the foreign noncolonial sector had the smallest proportion of closely held firms. Firms most often enter the stock exchange list either at birth (the promoters list the firm because it is the easiest way to sell shares) or on obtaining maturity (the owner of an established enterprise decides to "go public," either to obtain more capital or to make it easier to withdraw his investment), and the proportions of new to mature firms entering each locational category in a typical year were different: highest for foreign, lowest for domestic. While it may take buyers some time to adjust to the profit stream of a newborn firm, there is likely to be less uncertainty about a mature firm just going public. Since the original owners are most aware of the profit potential, they value their holdings in light of a discounted stream of "insider's knowledge" of expected future earnings, and when the public's expectations fall below theirs, they do not go public. Thus, for that category of firms, if capital markets are less than perfect, market-induced deviations would tend in the direction of overpricing shares and, *ceteris paribus*, result in the lower rates of return. (As an aside, almost certainly a part of the relative decline in U.K. domestic earnings after 1885 can be traced to this phenomenon. It was, after all, a period of very rapid movement from private to public ownership in domestic industry.)

Given these problems inherent in the use of stock exchange data, we feel it is reasonable to complement these studies with an examination of the rates of return on "book value of assets," admitting, of course, to the problem raised by those measures. (Not the least, of course, is that numbers on a balance sheet or a ledger page are at best only shadows of the real assets held by the firms.)

No matter whose series you prefer, it is difficult to argue that those who purchased symbolic capital made great fortunes from their investments in empire. Our study of company histories suggests that the original entrepreneurs did better than those who purchased public issues, and some in fact acquired large fortunes. However, a preliminary comparison of rates of return on original book value of assets (as opposed to the "watered" basis that obtained after public sale) suggests that their returns were only marginally higher than those of entrepreneurs who employed their talents domestically—and (though the evidence is sparse and perhaps biased) probably lower than those who looked to parts of the world that were not colored red.

Taken together, it appears that while "blue water" imperialists may have benefited from their investments in the empire, those who bought into "public imperialism" were struggling to earn competitive returns. Moreover, it is almost certain that if the full costs of the imperialist experience had been assessed against the returns from that activity, the average return would have fallen well below that available at home—to say nothing of those available elsewhere in the world.[10]

A study of British and Colonial budgets suggests that—stylized facts and historiographic rhetoric to the contrary—transfers from Britain to the empire were substantial. Direct subsidies were not large, but they were made, and payments of governors' salaries and the telegraph and mail subsidies added to that total. Special access to the London capital markets was almost certainly an even more important source of transfer—a conclusion borne out by a comparison of foreign and colonial borrowing rates. The value of this item in the transfer had always been substantial, but it must have increased significantly in the latter part of the period when Parliament granted trustee status to colonial issues. The most important source of resource transfer, however, was the subsidization of the colonial defense budget. Not only did Britain *not* draw on the colonies for her defense, but, in fact, the transfers were large and in the other direction.

Examination of the expenditure patterns, both within and without the empire, suggests that in the late nineteenth and early twentieth centuries, the United Kingdom had one of the world's highest—if not the highest—level of military expenditure and, concomitantly, taxes. At the same time, residents of the empire provided very low levels of military support—levels that made it possible for them either to levy few taxes or to support much higher levels of investment in "productive" sectors, with levels of aggregate taxes no higher than those prevailing elsewhere in the world. As table 1 suggests, over the period 1860–1912 Britain's annual spending on its military establishment (in constant pounds per capita) was £1.32, foreign developed countries' was £.36, and underdeveloped countries' was £.20. India spent only £.08, and the self-governing colonies only slightly more, £.11. Even more surprising, the "true" colonies, types 2 and 3, spent only £.03 and £.05 respectively. With the exception of India, the same story emerges from the study of the fraction of government expenditures directed toward defense (a partial measure of "effort").

Nor are these numbers the statistical artifacts produced by the onset of World War I, or even the South African adventure. The data show a similar story whether the focus is placed on the years 1860–1900 or 1906–1912. It is clear that Britain provided the defense umbrella and that the empire took advantage of it. Even India, long singled out as the most "exploited" of the colonies, seems to have gotten off relatively lightly when the standard of comparison is not the rest of the empire but the rest of the world. India *did* supply troops for imperial adventures in Ethiopia, the Sudan, and West Africa (the Ashanti war), but the average per capita level of expenditure, while high by colonial standards, was still quite low compared with the defense spending of politically independent poor countries.

This point can be brought out in a different way if one looks at the "UK Home 1 and 2" estimates. These figures allocate British military and naval expenditures between home and imperial defense.[11] The "home" estimates indicate levels of expenditure slightly higher than the average of all developed countries, but about equal to those in France and Germany. England, therefore, appears to have maintained two defense establishments: one for the British Isles and a second for the empire.

Table 2 tells the same story from the point of view of the British taxpayer. Shifting the defense burden to the non-Indian empire would have eased the tax load of the average Briton, but a policy that would have produced Indian expenditures, equivalent to those of the underdeveloped countries included in the survey, would have made that taxpayer much "better off" than his peers in the rest of the developed world. Nor were the British becoming more efficient as the operation of empire became more routin-

Imperial Defense Expenditures, per Capita and as a Percentage of the Government Budget for U.K., Colonies, and Selected Foreign Countries, 1860–1912

Panel A — Average per Capita Expenditure on Defense (Constant £'s)

Period	UK Total	UK¹ Home 1	UK² Home 2	France & Germany 2	Foreign Developed	Colonies Type 1[5]	UK¹ Imperial 1	UK² Imperial 2	Foreign Undeveloped	India	Colonies Type 2[4]	Colonies Type 3[5]	Colonies Type 2 (Including Police)	Colonies Type 3 (Including Police)
1860–69	.94	.38	.45	.39	.27	.05	.56	.49	.17	.09	.01	.04	.12	.10
1870–79	.80	.39	.44	.52	.24	.07	.41	.36	.18	.08	.04	.04	.16	.11
1880–89	.98	.46	.53	.58	.41	.11	.52	.45	.18	.08	.06	.04	.18	.12
1890–99	1.28	.56	.70	.80	.40	.13	.72	.58	.27	.07	.03	.06	.24	.13
1900–12	2.31	.97	1.20	.77	.43	.19	1.33	1.11	.20	.07	.01	.05	.20	.09
1900–05	2.96	1.20	1.42	.79	.49	.17	1.74	1.52	.18	.07	.01	.07	.21	.11
1906–12	1.75	.78	1.00	.76	.39	.20	.97	.76	.22	.07	.01	.04	.20	.08
1860–1912	1.32	.58	.69	.62	.36	.11	.74	.63	.20	.08	.03	.05	.18	.11

Panel B — Average Proportion of Government Budget Spent on Defense (Percent)

Period	UK Total	UK¹ Home 1	UK² Home 2	France & Germany 2	Foreign Developed	Colonies Type 1[5]	UK¹ Imperial 1	UK² Imperial 2	Foreign Undeveloped	India	Colonies Type 2[4]	Colonies Type 3[5]	Colonies Type 2 (Including Police)	Colonies Type 3 (Including Police)
1860–69	38.2	15.3	18.5	16.8	31.4	2.7	22.8	20.3	28.0	35.9	1.4	6.9	12.9	16.0
1870–79	34.9	17.0	19.1	29.5	25.3	3.3	18.0	15.9	20.9	21.4	4.3	6.3	16.8	16.6
1880–89	34.9	16.3	18.9	23.1	24.2	1.8	18.6	16.1	15.3	24.2	4.0	4.3	12.8	14.4
1890–99	38.2	16.7	20.9	27.4	22.2	2.2	21.5	17.4	16.8	27.7	1.2	7.4	12.4	15.6
1900–12	47.2	20.2	24.9	24.0	21.9	3.1	27.0	22.3	14.4	22.3	.6	10.0	12.4	17.2
1900–05	55.2	22.7	27.0	24.1	23.7	2.5	32.6	28.2	14.0	21.6	.6	11.5	12.4	18.1
1906–12	40.3	18.0	23.0	24.0	20.2	3.6	22.2	17.3	14.9	22.8	.7	8.7	12.4	16.4
1860–1912	39.1	17.3	20.7	24.2	24.9	2.7	21.9	18.6	18.8	26.1	2.2	7.1	13.3	16.1

[1] Mediterranean fleet included in Imperial expenditures.
[2] Mediterranean fleet included in Home expenditures.
[3] Colonies with responsible Government. (Elected parliamentary and executive bodies)
[4] Colonies with partial responsible Government. (Appointed Executive, some elected legislative or consultative body)
[5] Colonies without responsible Government. (India excluded)

ized. The data indicate that the "subsidy" to the non-Indian empire was increasing, particularly during the latter part of the period. In the last decade of the period, the per capita British "subsidy" to the colonies with responsible self-government was £.09, and the subsidies to those with no self-government at all had risen to £.12.

The important question, however, remains: Why did the British allow themselves to be exploited in this fashion? Quantitative evidence provides few clues, but the qualitative evidence suggests that even the Victorians worried about that question. The Treasury, in particular, expressed continual concern. As early as 1860, Sir Charles Adderley asked in Parliament, "Why should Great Britain contribute £4,000,000 to the cost of security while the colonies paid less than £40,000?" "Why," he asked, "should the colonies be exempted from paying for their own defense?" He argued: "It was absolutely unparalleled in the history of the world that any portion of an empire—colonial, provincial, or otherwise—should be exempted in purse and person from the costs of its own defenses as was a British colony."[12]

In the case of the self-governing colonies, one part of the answer is relatively simple: they refused to pay and the British could do very little about it. With the advent of responsible government, the British subsidies were withdrawn, but in return constitutional autonomy allowed those colonies to refuse aid on matters of general imperial concern. The British must have remembered 1775 when an attempt to collect some fraction of defense costs led to a costly war and the loss of a large and very British part of the empire.

In the case of Canada, for example, the British tried for years (without success) to collect some payment for the funds they had spent to put down Louis Real's revolution on the Red River—a matter almost purely of Canadian concern. Almost every attempt to increase the Canadian contribution to imperial defense was met with such arguments as "the best defense for Canada is no defense at all"—and that statement was made in 1863, when U.S. armies posed a serious threat to Canadian security.[13] Nor did those attitudes change.

The British should have had more control over the dependent empire, and the figures suggest they were probably more successful—but only marginally so. Regardless of their state of consitutional development, all colonies were in an advantageous position vis-à-vis the British government when it came to paying for the cost of actual hostilities. Wars were not infrequent along the imperial borders and the initial expenses were almost always paid by the governors from the treasury chest, a fund of £1 million spread throughout the empire, to cover emergencies. Once the imperial monies had been expended and the hostilities concluded, the British Treasury usually enjoyed but small success in recouping its monetary advances. Thus, for example, the British taxpayer bore the entire £900,000 cost of the Ashanti war of 1873–1874 and almost all the cost of the Zulu war.

Table 2
Hypothetical UK Defense Expenditures
(Assuming that Colonies Spent Amounts Equal to Those Spent by Similar Non-Empire Political Units)

Period	(1) Type 1 as a Foreign Undeveloped	(2) Type 2 as a Foreign Undeveloped	(3) Type 3 as a Foreign Undeveloped	(4) India as a Foreign Undeveloped	(5) (1) + (2) + (3)	(6) (1) + (2) + (3) + (4)	(7) Foreign Developed	(8) Actual UK
			Panel A					
		Reductions in UK Annual Average Per Capita Expenditures (Constant £s)						
1860–69	−.05	−.01	−.02	−.48	−.08	−.56		
1870–79	−.04	−.01	−.01	−.63	−.06	−.73		
1880–89	−.08	−.01	−.02	−.77	−.11	−.88		
1890–99	−.09	−.01	−.05	−1.68	−.15	−1.83		
1900–12	−.09	−.01	−.12	−1.01	−.22	−1.23		
			Panel B					
		New Levels of UK Annual Average Per Capita Expenditures (Constant £s)						
1860–69	.89	.93	.92	.46	.86	.39	.27	.94
1870–79	.76	.79	.79	.17	.74	.11	.24	.80
1880–89	.90	.97	.96	.22	.87	.10	.41	.98
1890–99	1.19	1.27	1.23	−.40	1.13	−.55	.40	1.28
1900–12	2.22	2.30	2.19	1.30	2.09	.79	.43	2.31

Even a colony as insignificant as Bermuda successfully refused a Treasury request for a military contribution. And when, as in the case of Mauritius, the government achieved a temporary success, there was usually a compromise settlement that reduced the total charge.

India, however, was the Treasury's ideal. It conducted its affairs as a British dependency should. Having no self-government, it was "at the mercy" of whatever plans its governors and the authorities in Whitehall might devise. The expenses of the Indian army and the British regiments stationed in India were paid from Indian revenues. India provided a military reserve for the whole of the British empire, and this reserve was paid for almost exclusively by Indians. Still, as examination of the budgets suggests, Indian payments were almost certainly less than they would have been had the country *not* been under British rule—the umbrella worked even there. The charges would have been higher had the Treasury (or even the India Office) had its way, but the Treasury was continually faced with the opposition of the British governors, who were almost always sympathetic either to the plight of the Indians (the governors saw the need for expenditure on famine prevention and relief) or to the British resident in India, who, like the colonists in the remainder of the empire, had no desire to pay taxes.

As table 2 indicates, if the colonies (and particularly India) had assumed levels of defense expenditure about the same as those borne by countries at similar states of development, the tax load on the British taxpayer could have been reduced or government resources would have been freed for other "more productive" purposes with no reduction in consumption income. The magnitudes involved amount to about 10 percent of savings. It is impossible to determine the correct counterfactual, and perhaps it is unreasonable to think that resources could have been diverted to education or research and development. However, even some social welfare scheme might have altered the direction of British growth. As for the colonies, they certainly received substantial benefits, but those benefits were not evenly distributed. The colonies of white settlement did very well, but the benefits to the remainder of the empire are less clear. Clearly, they received a subsidized market basket of government services, but it was a basket they might well have chosen not to buy, even at these sale prices.

So much for the costs. What can we say about the revenues from the empire? Our data allow us to make some tentative hypothetical calculations. If we subtract from the British defense budget an amount equal to that spent in a typical developed country, then divide that difference by an estimate of British investment in the empire (take, for example, the £471.6 million estimate of Segal and Simon for portfolio investment and double it to take account of short-term credit), the result is a minimum estimate of the social costs of imperial investment.[14] This calculation indicates that the "rate of return" on empire investment should be reduced between ½ and 1½ percentage points to take account of the defense costs alone. If, for example, defense cost accounted for one-half the total imperial subsidy, the reduction is between 1 and 3 percent. So perhaps Hobson was correct: imperialism was certainly not good for the many, but it may have been good for the few who earned competitive (or slightly greater) returns in empire investment and did not carry the full burden of the subsidy. If, however, that group benefited, consider the benefits that accrued to colonial investors—usually white men in the colonies of white settlement, but at times natives, like the migrant Indians in South Africa, who bore none of the social costs.

If the crime was robbery, it appears that Britons were the victims. But who were the criminals? Most likely those who earned competitive returns on empire investment, at the expense of those who subsidized the level of colonial government expenditure that offset some of the private costs of business in colonial areas. They certainly had the motive, but did they have the means and opportunity? Although we can as yet give no final answer, we have begun to identify the "imperial winners." To that end, we have studied (in a preliminary manner) the composition of stockholders of a sample of corporations operating in the United Kingdom, the empire, and the rest of the world in the late nineteenth century.[15] Ignoring, for the moment, the original owners, who may have acquired some monopoly rents from their association with the enterprise, let us focus on those "public imperialists" who held stock in the firm three to five years after it had gone public. While problems of nominee stockholders and unidentified owners remain, even these preliminary figures appear to reveal some major differences between the "public imperialists" and those who invested their assets at home or in the foreign sector.

Chart 1 (a histogram) divides stockholders of empire, foreign and domestic firms, into five rough categories, but makes no allowance for inter-industry differences. The first stockholder category, loosely labeled the "Elite," includes military officers and persons who identified themselves as gentlemen (esquire), members of the aristocracy, and justices of the peace. The second category, the "Middle Class," includes persons who identified themselves with trade, manufacturing, and the professions. "Women" is a special class, since it is not clear what motivated them to acquire shares, nor can they easily be linked to a husband or father about whom we might have more information. The fourth group, "Possible Nominees," could have been included in "Middle Class" since the category includes solicitors, clerks, secretaries, accountants, and stockbrokers. Subsidiary studies have indicated that, with "Women," these occupational groups account for most of the nominee holders. Including them in "Middle Class" makes the results less impressive, but it does not alter the thrust of the argument. Finally, the fifth

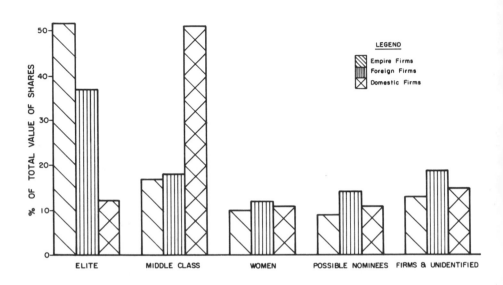

Chart 1
Equity Holdings of Twenty-Five British Firms
by Location and Occupation of Stockholder

category, "Firms and Unidentified," includes shareholders who did not list their occupations and shares that were held by other firms.

The standard tests for independence indicate that divisions into colonial, foreign, and domestic make sense, while division by individual firm tends not to (that is, there is evidence of independence between categories but not between firms). Casual observation suggests that the "elitists" dominated ownership in colonial and, to a lesser extent, foreign business (the military class was important only in colonial enterprises). The middle class, on the other hand, held the major portion of the shares of domestic industry. Perhaps in this sense Schumpeter was correct: the imperialists were warriors and aristocrats while the capitalists tended to concentrate their investments in domestic activities.

The same records provide a locational breakdown of the shareholders, but there the data are less "clean." Not only does locational distribution correlate quite closely with the occupational breakdowns, but many addresses appear to have been those of the owners' stockbrokers ("London E.," for example, is a frequent entry). With these caveats (if Scottish owners are excluded), there was a heavier concentration of rural stockholders in colonial and foreign than in domestic firms. At the same time, ownership of the overseas firms was more concentrated in London and in the south than that of the domestic businesses, and the proportions of domestic stockholders who lived in the Midlands and the north were much higher than the fraction of foreign and colonial owners.

These conclusions are partly confirmed by examination of other aspects of firm ownership. With the reminder that there are substantial industry-to-industry variations and that railroads have been excluded because of problems with the domestic data, it appears that (1) the distribution of ownership by size of investment displays substantially more variance for colonial (the coefficient of variation is 6.0) than for foreign (3.8) and more for foreign than domestic (1.6); (2) the distribution of shareholders in colonial firms is more skewed toward the upper end than either of the other two classifications; (3) the average stockholder in a colonial firm held a larger proportion of the total shares than a similar shareholder in a foreign or domestic firm (the numbers are .087 percent for a domestic firm, .078 percent for a foreign firm, and .27 percent for colonial firms). Taken together, the analysis suggests that ownership in colonial enterprises was concentrated in a relatively small group of stockholders, drawn from quite different occupational backgrounds than the owners of domestic and foreign firms.

We are currently examining a second group of firms. For these firms, we are not limited to the official Stock Exchange list or even to the corporate sector; and more important, we have some measures in the changes of ownership over time. Even the preliminary analysis has not begun in a systematic fashion, but we have attempted an examination of some "typical firms." This casual survey indicates that colonial firms were not so different from domestic firms if they began as small enterprises, but were very different if they were launched as large-scale enterprises. It will be interesting to compare the profits withdrawn when the small colonial firms were first "listed," with the profits earned by similar firms in the domestic sector (a cursory check seems to indicate no appreciable differences, though there are significant questions of length of ownership). The data seem to indicate that "small" colonial firms had more owners drawn from the gentry and military officers than did domestic firms, but they also had a much larger middle-class representation than the "full blown" colonial firms. In the "small" foreign firms, there appears to have been little upper-class and no military participation. Again, it appears that the imperialist was a Schumpeterian warrior and aristocrat rather than a Hobsonian capitalist businessman.

When we put the major parts of the study together and speculate in terms of the general hypothesis, it appears that the empire was not profitable for the average Briton, but definitely was profitable for some, and relatively profitable for others (many of the "public imperialists" managed to earn normal profits). The British world was largely competitive, and supernormal and normal earnings could be maintained only by the imposition of an imperial system that, while profitable for some investors and colonists, and perhaps for the natives, was not costless to citizens of the United Kingdom who had not direct stake in the empire.

At this stage, the investigation moves from economics to politics. If the preliminary findings hold up under more complete analysis, the suspect has been identified, but it is necessary to prove he had the means and opportunity. In short, how was it possible for the imperialist to manipulate the political mechanism to produce a transfer of rents from middle to upper class (with some leakage to the colonies)? The data exist, and positive political theory provides a methodological tool that should let us complete our investigation.

NOTES

The research on which this paper is based was supported by National Endowment for the Humanities Grant RO–27612–77–1415 and by National Science Foundation Grant SOC 7809080.

1. J. A. Hobson, *Imperialism, a Study* (3d ed.; London: Allen & Unwin, 1938).

2. D. K. Fieldhouse, *The Theory of Capitalist Imperialism* (London: Longmans, 1967).

3. Joseph Schumpeter, "Imperialism," in *Imperialism, Social Classes: Two Essays by Joseph Schumpeter* (New York: Meridian Books, 1955).

4. We may, of course, come back to the question of psychic income if the more traditional analysis leads us nowhere.

5. R. A. Lehfeldt, "The Rate of Interest on British and Foreign Investment," *Journal of the Royal Statistical Society,* 76 (Jan. 1913), pp. 196–203; 77 (May 1914), 432–435; 78 (May 1915), 452–453.

6. A. K. Cairncross, *Home and Foreign Investment, 1870–1913: Studies in Capital Accumulation* (Cambridge: Cambridge University Press, 1953).

7. Michael Edelstein, "Realized Rates of Return on U.K. Home and Overseas Portfolio Investment in the Age of High Imperialism," mimeograph, July 11, 1975.

8. His risk adjustment is based on a mean-variance model that assumes the utility function is quadratic in wealth (an acknowledged unlikely event) or that the distribution of returns is normal. Like the U.S. data, the British distributions appear to have fat tails.

9. H. A. Shannon, "The First Five Thousand Limited Companies and Their Duration," *Economic History,* vol. 2 (1932), and "The Limited Companies of 1866–1883," *Economic History Review,* vol. 4 (1932–33); James B. Jefferys, *Business Organization in Great Britain, 1865–1914* (New York: Arno Press 1978), and "The Denomination and Character of Shares, 1855–1885," *Economic History Review,* vol. 16 (1946).

10. There is, of course, a question of what would happen to the marginal rate on domestic investment if the transfer from empire to home were large. However, the third margin (i.e., the rest of the world) could well have absorbed a substantial part of the excess investment without too drastic declines in rate, particularly since the colonies would still have represented some market for business services. The experience of the Crown Agents in the Empire after independence appears relevant on this latter point.

11. The allocations are made on the basis of the location of manpower. The two estimates differ because of the allocation of the Mediterranean fleet. In *1* it is

included in the empire, in 2 in home defense. The naval allocation for the period 1893–1921 is made on the basis of the distribution in 1893.

12. Sir Charles Adderley, quoted in *Hansard* (May 31, 1860).

13. The quote in the Canadian Parliament is from Mr. Desmond in a letter to Sir Charles Monk, June 20, 1863 (Newcastle Papers, Nottingham University Library).

14. H. Segal and M. Simon, "British Foreign Capital Issues, 1865–1894," *Journal of Economic History* (Dec. 1961). This argument ignores the alleged benefits of "assured markets." However, since the vast bulk of British trade and investment was in North and South America (where markets were unassured) and since the colonies with responsible government were never hesitant to levy tariffs against British goods, those revenue adjustments appear to be small.

15. The data reported here are from a subset of 25 of the 367 firms alluded to earlier.

Professor Hobsbawm
on the Evolution
of Modern Capitalism

Jonathan Hughes

Adonis was of an extraordinary beauty. At his birth Aphrodite put him in a coffer which she confided to the goddess of the underworld, Persephone. When later she came to reclaim the coffer she found that Persephone had already opened it, beheld the great beauty of the child and refused to give him up. The dispute between the two goddesses was brought before Zeus, who decided that Adonis should spend half the year on earth and half in the underworld.
(*Larousse Encyclopedia of Mythology*, p. 81)

In this paper I examine the work of Prof. Eric Hobsbawm, primarily as it concerns economic development and its supposed relationship to the ultimate appearance of socialism from the ruins of historical capitalism. This is an exercise in critical approaches to historical evidence. I am one of those who has derived pleasure and knowledge from Hobsbawm's books and papers. However, he also infuriates me a good deal of the time, since his prejudices and my own tend to be in opposite corners.

I want to begin by setting certain clear intellectual boundaries regarding economic history. I will then try to place Dr. Hobsbawm's work within those boundaries.

First, I will concentrate on Hobsbawm's work on the British economy, since it is there, primarily, that our work overlaps and my opinion is most informed. Hobsbawm's work covers a lot of territory and I don't pretend to be able to follow all his journeys.

Work in what is known as economic history tends to be of two kinds: (1) that which depends for its choice of subject matter and explanatory power on the received body of economic theory, and (2) descriptions and explanations of economic events, where the explanations are based upon other systems of thought. The differences between the two kinds of historical work are marked. Economic theory is quantitative and precise. Explanations of historical evidence according to theory, either by econometric techniques or, more loosely, where data are inappropriate for econometrics, are capable of falsification. The explanations hold only in well-understood sets of initial and background conditions. What is known in this kind of work is precisely specified (or can be), and it is pretty clear what is not known, where the limits of the explanatory models are. As my old colleague, Lance Davis, once put it, "You may not know much, but at least you understand what it is you know." This kind of economic history is very efficient in explaining quantitative phenomena such as the rise and fall of prices, interest rates, exchange rates, and even such economic magnitudes as fluctuations in national income.

But there is no causal link, no mechanism, which connects this sort of work with the great issues that tend to interest general historians—for example, the rise and fall of governments, nations, or even empires. Also, it is important to note that economic theory tends to be perfectly agnostic regarding social institutions, and apart from some simple rules of thumb, theory has little to say about income distribution, social classes, and what have you. For these reasons, economic historians tend to lose their distinctive claims to authority when their work moves away from quantitative phenomena which can be understood by invoking the logic of economic analysis. Even so, many economic historians have ventured into these dangerous waters. Partly, I think, they are legitimately concerned to help in understanding the "big issues." Partly their hunches, based upon a firm knowledge of subsidiary components, lead them to suppose that they cannot do worse than noneconomic historians in these areas. And partly, they carry other explanatory paradigms, for example, Marxism, nineteenth-century liberalism, or even less reputable systems of thought in their bags of tools, and hope to utilize these systems to create convincing explanations of sequences of historical events which are, at least partly, "economic" in origin. Marx was not the first economist, after all, to try the smorgasbord of economic, historical, and "philosophical" explanations to account for historical developments. Down through Veblen, the Muckrakers, Galbraith, and even Keynes, and now Sir John Hicks, Marx's intellectual descendants have not lacked company in the attempt to understand the great events of history which have involved developments in the sphere of economic activity. Professor Kindleberger complained that economic historians tend to "overgeneralize,"[1] and it is not difficult to find examples.

Economic theory is a tool, like a wrench or a power saw, and what it produces can depend a great deal upon who uses it (though not entirely, of course). An ax cannot produce the same finishing results as a fine sandpaper. Hobsbawm has done a lot of work within ranges narrow enough that the tools of theory can be of decisive importance. In addition, of course, he had much to say of problems about which economic theory cannot aid understanding. In the narrower problems, Hobsbawm uses the tools of economic thought as he pleases, to achieve his ends, and one should know what the ends are in order to comprehend the sometimes astounding uses of the tools.

This is part of the fun, as well as exasperation, of reading Hobsbawm. He is, or seems to be, a rather old-fashioned kind of determinist, a holdover from the 1940s or perhaps even earlier. The sort of chap who might still genuflect dutifully to "the late J.V." (Stalin),[2] or cluck approvingly over some similarity between wartime British and Soviet agricultural organization,[3] oblivious to the possibility that, had British agriculture been as incompetent as Soviet agriculture, the British would have starved.[4]

Hobsbawm has a dislike for the capitalist form of economic organization, similar to a hard-core vegetarian's view of rare beef. He finds the production of profit, divided into unequal shares, repulsive—at least where the instruments of production are privately owned. Given that taste, he has elevated it into a moral position. Capitalism is not only distasteful, it is wicked. Since it is wicked, it cannot last, and history is filled with tantalizing glimpses of the terrible, forthcoming justice. Thus Hobsbawm's work is mostly of rebels and crises. Now one can hold such views, and work on such materials, without ever having heard of Karl Marx. It is these views, and not Marx, which, it seems to me, motivate Hobsbawm's work. Where he does get on with specifically Marxist conclusions, insisting on both falling profits and falling real wages up to the 1840s in British industrial history, for example,[5] the result is historiographical parody and a logical disaster area. Usually, though, it is Hobsbawm's sympathies, and not Marx, that determine what is going to be studied and why. I have found very little of Hobsbawm's major work which hangs upon any explicit class-struggle mechanism to bring about major changes in history. Mostly, the Marxist analytical pieces hang about the pages of Hobsbawm like baubles on a Christmas tree. I haven't measured the ground here, but it seems to me that a complete excising of straight Marxist gospels from the mass of Hobsbawm's work on economic history (which I have read) would shorten it very little indeed. However, such editing would eliminate a lot of Marxist and quasi-Marxist conclusions which, in my opinion, mar Hobsbawm's straight economic history, and which are not supported by evidence anyway. I will return to this in a moment.

In my opinion, Hobsbawm is a romantic, with deep sympathies for certain kinds of poor and oppressed peoples, a taste for strong central governments, which deal decisively with enemies of the people, and purple prose to describe these events.

These sympathies sometimes lead him and his readers into fairly exotic territories where economic history would not normally lead anyone. The bias produces the interpretation as well as the interest. For example, when he celebrates Robespierre and the "terrible and glorious"[6] events of Year II of the French Revolution, one's eyes just glaze over. These are events, after all, which led mankind directly down the road to Auschwitz—assembly-line murder. Take the guillotine, that mechanical horror, slicing away in Paris; it cut off more than 1,300 heads in the six weeks from June 10 to July 24, 1794.[7] Taking a six-day week and an eight-hour day, I make the output about four an hour. Here a mechanical device was used to mass-produce the deaths of innocent people, many of them tried in batches, which produced a steady flow of people waiting to be processed. Things were worse, of course, at places like Nantes and Lyons.

Hobsbawm's celebration of this grisly stuff is simply beyond my comprehension. Just a matter of taste, presumably. It is certainly no requirement of Marxian economics to hold any normative views at all about Year II of the Revolution. These events were merely historically necessary, so to speak. The economic process—an assembly line of public murder, running from the Revolutionary Tribunal to the place of execution—is not better understood by the use of words like "glorious." "Terrible," perhaps, but that isn't economics either. In Hobsbawm's work one is never far from such diversions, which makes his writing maddening to a reader like me, and interesting as well. All sorts of things get mixed up with Hobsbawm's biases. Glued together in a book like *Industry and Empire*,[8] they arouse real curiosity, to which I shall return in a moment.

Hobsbawm's old-fashioned determinism compounds his sympathies in ways that produce statements that seem at first glance to be really firm, even "scientific." It is like magic. Consider this rather complex, complex sentence:

> Over Germany, Italy, and Spain the three monarchies of the "Holy Alliance" and France agreed, though the latter exercising the job of international police with gusto in Spain (1823), was less interested in European stability than in widening the scope of her diplomatic and military activities, particularly in Spain, Belgium, and Italy, where the bulk of her foreign investments lay.[9]

The last part of the sentence is supposedly the Marxist twist; the government of France seems to be mucking about in the affairs of a neighboring state in the interests of private French citizens who have invested there. It is only an inference, but seems to be the point of the sentence. What direct evidence is there that the government's willingness to support Ferdinand, with the blessings of the other members of the Holy Alliance, had anything to do with the wishes of French investors? The Russians apparently were willing to take the action as early as 1820.[10] Were they investors too? There is a wide inference here, but does it represent *any* history at all? Correlation is not cause; the historical parallelism of political and economic links does not imply a causal link between them. It is the Marxist twist that the opposite is true. So far as I know, economics does not start wars. They are started by men, against men, all of whom have far broader interests than economics alone.

Given that Professor Hobsbawm usually seems to be headed in the same direction in his work, what sorts of historical themes does he choose to develop? No doubt he is best known among economic historians over here for the exchange he had with R. M. Hartwell concerning the "standard of living" (or whatever) from 1790 to 1850.[11] This is economic history in the narrower sense, and simple economic theory can be a great help in sorting out the issues. In this case Hobsbawm undertook a really heroic endeavor. He tried to show that the most unlikely event happened, while Hartwell countered by demonstrating that what was nearly bound to be true, was. What Professor Hobsbawm had to show was that somehow, in industry after industry, over a long period of time, the increased productivity brought about by the Industrial Revolution did not result in a rise in the real wages of labor, and/or real income, or if it did, it was not much, and/or it was not passed on to most of the population. The impression is easily gained that Professor Hobsbawm was trying to show that, up to the time Marx and Engels wrote, industrialization had made the English worse off than they were back at some "Sweet Auburn" in 1790 or thereabouts.[12]

In terms of the relevant economic theory, the way to get no rise in wages (or the standard of life), or a fall, would have been for the industrial labor force to increase more rapidly than productivity in industry, or for population to increase more rapidly than total output. In spite of Professor Hobsbawm's notions about the theory of economic growth, it exists, and what it suggests as the most likely historical outcome is the "optimist" position (Hartwell's) on the British Industrial Revolution and the common experience of industrialization in the Western nations since.[13] Given the facts of British population growth, Hobsbawm was trying to set fire to water. The case where productivity rises and wages fall, if the increase in labor supply is not as great as the rise in productivity, is not possible unless the market for the finished good collapses and the resulting decline in the marginal revenue offsets the increase in the marginal physical product.[14] That is hardly a long-run phenomenon at all. The Marxist case, where investment rises, productivity rises, total output rises, profits fall and wages fall, is the case for mass emigration of both the capitalists and the proletarians.

Since the controversy was not conducted along any explicit theoretical lines, evidence on both sides was piled on. Professor Hobsbawm rejected aggregate data,[15] which was against the "pessimist" case, and fell back to individual counterexamples, and finally settled for a sociological position.[16] People were less happy in industrial cities, since they had to forego life in "Sweet Auburn" and go live in Rotherham, or wherever. Who could disagree? Incidentally, if industrial growth begins from a long-term Ricardian-Malthusian equilibrium position, and the labor force starts out from subsistence levels, and then per capita income rises, say, for five or six decades, the gap between rich and poor might easily widen;[17] but how do the poor get poorer while the rich are getting richer?

The aggregate data are compelling. I will be brief here, since after Hartwell's 1963 riposte no further data are really needed if one can be convinced by data and logic.[18] Agricultural income grew, but relatively slowly in this period.[19] Income returns to manufacturing inputs tripled.[20] The cost of borrowing—"on the average"—measured by interest rates, moved along a declining trend from 1790 to the early 1850s.[21] With rising productivity and falling prices,[22] coupled with rapid growth of capital facilities,[23] it is clear that production costs were falling rapidly. The steady growth of the business sector and wealth aggregates show that profits were sufficient to maintain the overall rate of growth.[24] Estimated national income, including the agricultural sector, grew from £225 million to £523 million,[25] or by more than 130 percent, from 1801 to 1851. The apparent rate of growth of income to *occupied* population grew in a range of 1.4 to 1.5 percent per annum,[26] with most rapid rates of growth in manufacturing, mining, and building. Hoffman's production index, the infirmities of which I well appreciate, rose from 6.64 (1913 = 100) in 1801 to 25.0 in 1850,[27] more than a factor of three. That this represented the output of investment that embodied great technical improvement there is no doubt. The total gains from international trade ran in Britain's favor.[28]

If this enormous growth in the material resources of the United Kingdom did not, in fact, fall partly upon real wages, where did it go—into thin air? It went to support a working population which just about doubled, rising from 4.8 million in 1801 to 9.7 million in 1851,[29] and a total population that had grown somewhat slower, from just over 14.5 million in Scotland, Ireland, England, and Wales in 1790 to 27.4 million[30] in the same countries at the end of the 1840s, using the new factories, railways, machines, steamship fleets, cities, and social overheads. No conceivable historical British economy could have maintained the sort of growth we know about, if the workers did not share to some extent in this increased output. There was some slippage about where "the period" in question really ended, Hobsbawm preferring 1842, a trough year in the business cycle when conditions were particularly poor. There is no solution here except by appeals to authority. If there is to be a coherent "end of an era" on this debate, the two years 1849 and 1850 have a lot to be said for them, as a new set of circumstances was forming. However, even though in the 1850s the economy expanded rapidly, with a sense of exhilaration, the *real* expansion was not all that much more rapid than in earlier periods.[31]

There is no doubt that the poor were very poor indeed in 1848. Henry Mayhew paints an appalling picture of this.[32] But the great increase in the labor force obviously disposed of much larger real resources per head by the end of the 1840s than in 1790. It could hardly have been otherwise. But why was the record so spotty? The growth rates I mentioned are not high, compared to several other countries during similar periods in their growth histories.[33] Had Hobsbawm asked simply why the British did no better for their working people (a question that vexed Mayhew), he would have started a really interesting debate. Instead, he seemed determined to show that by the time Marx and Engels wrote (in 1848—or even Engels in 1844), British capitalism was "immizerizing"[34] its workers, grinding them into an industrial reserve army. Moreover, he argued, this was necessary to raise the investment level[35]—an anti-Keynesian view, but one which accorded well with those who claimed the same concrete necessity to cover up for the brutality of Soviet industrialization in the 1930s—a poor and illegitimate use of British economic history, in my opinion.

I do not think the Hobsbawm-Hartwell debate added significantly to our historical knowledge, and I think it may have distracted attention from far more interesting questions. For had Hobsbawm granted *all* the claims of Clapham, Ashton, and Hartwell out of hand, he could then have asked why the British apparently did so much less well for their people by industrialization than did other countries similarly placed, for example, Germany, the United States, or Japan later in the century. We would now consider the British economy of 1850 only partly industrialized, and it leaves open the very interesting questions of what world Britain could so long have served as a "workshop," and in view of the mass emigration of people out of Britain together with its lagging growth, whether there was *enough* industry in Britain, even with free trade, to support those burgeoning population growth rates. Was the world Mayhew described limited to London? He suggests otherwise, and one wonders what it was in the Victorian economy that produced such a vigorous economy of poverty "below" the industrial and commercial economy that has been so celebrated. I think the really interesting questions regarding the "standard of life debate" up to 1850 remain to be asked. Unfortunately, the Hobsbawm-Hartwell exchange was based upon theoretical questions framed a century ago, before demand theory had developed, before modern cost and production theory. One advantage of coming along a century after Marx is that one knows how it actually came out.

In his overall view of British industrial history, as exemplified mainly by *Industry and Empire* and chapter 2 of *The Age of Revolution*, Hobsbawm is still inflammable, but this time his history is an exotic mixture indeed. The main analytical components are (1) Schumpeter, (2) Rostow, (3) early-start thesis, (4) mercantilism, or neo-mercantilism, and (5) determinism.

1. Schumpeter's entrepreneur,[36] creating by destroying, has held a fascination for many economic historians. The whole direction of economic change in the nineteenth-century capitalist society rested upon the man who mobilized the capital, hired the labor, directed production. Insofar as the product of his factories and mills found a market, and his actions were not constrained by society at large, the entrepreneur was the architect of economic change, for good or ill. Schumpeter saw the entrepreneur as the titan of economic development, a hero figure.

But there are other possibilities. After all, the whole point of Marxist historiography is the division of humanity into bad guys and good guys. The successful entrepreneur gobbled up the businesses of the unsuccessful, his very success swelling the impoverished mass of the industrial reserve army. Marx "predicted" this,[37] after all. When the entrepreneur closed his mills, or put them on short-time, his actions produced misery for his work people. He introduced the machinery that displaced the working man, and left him destitute. He reduced wages when he felt the need and he brought in the strikebreakers, preferred charges against labor agitators, and manipulated the law and government when he could. His conspicuously luxurious style of life was morally an affront to the privations of the honest workman. So the innovating entrepreneur can play as creative a role for Hobsbawm as he did for Schumpeter. For Hobsbawm, the entrepreneur creates the conditions for the rise of socialism.

2. Just why Rostow should fit importantly into this story is clear enough, since the idea of a sudden change to self-sustained growth when investment, ground out of consumption, reaches a critical level, is a congenial notion to the "breakthrough" historians, and to Hobsbawm. The critical beating the takeoff theory has sustained makes no difference to Hobsbawm.[38] The slow rise of the level of investment found by Deane and Cole (taking half a century to reach Rostow's takeoff level)[39] makes no impact on Hobsbawm. Nor, apparently, does Simon Kuznets' evaluation: "Unless I have completely misunderstood Professor Rostow's definition of take-off and its statistical characteristics, I can only conclude the available evidence lends no support to Professor Rostow's suggestion."[40]

If there is no such thing as a takeoff in the history of industrial societies, if sustained industrial development is a cultural phenomenon, involving long decades of social change, then there is no easy route, no quick political route, to successful industrialization that is known, or at least warranted, by history. The necessary background conditions in Britain and all other presently industrialized countries took a long time to develop.

Here, it turns out, there is no help from Schumpeter, either. One of his legacies, once extensively developed by Rostow in the context of cyclical growth, was the "leading sector" notion. Somehow, critical innovations, powerfully pursued, could pull the whole economy along.[41] The great nineteenth-century breakthrough was, of course, the railroad. Historians grasped at this idea like a straw. "Railroadization" (Schumpeter's word) was the key to an otherwise mysterious process. It was Robert Fogel,[42] in this country, who cut this one down to size, finding that in the 1840s the iron in railroads weighed less than the tons of iron consumed in the manufacture of nails.[43] Could it have been different in Britain? Hobsbawm lays enormous store on the railroad.[44] It not only solved the problems of excess accumulation by fat-cat English investors (who, paradoxically, gain profits from the industrial economy but cannot find an appropriate place to invest it, except in railroads), but provided that "massive demand"[45] for capital goods in other industries. He cites data for coal and iron in the first two decades of railway construction, 1830–1850, and says "That dramatic rise was due primarily to the railway, for on average each mile of line required 300 tons of iron merely for track."[46]

Gary Hawke[47] denies that the weight of nails was as great as that of railways in Britain. Just how important to the iron industry was the railway? Hawke finds that from 1835 to 1843 the weight of iron used for permanent ways equaled 6.0 percent of iron output, from 1844 to 1851, 12.6 percent.[48] Hobsbawm could not have known of Hawke's calculations but he could easily have made similar calculations from his own evidence and readily available data for the years 1830–1850, the years when he argued that the railway was "primarily" responsible for the rise of the iron industry. By 1850 Britain had 6,084 miles of railroad.[49] At 300 tons a mile, that would have consumed 1,825,000 tons of rail iron—not even one year's output at the end of the period (2,249,000 tons in 1850).[50]

I pieced together all estimates of British iron output in 1830–1850 and I estimate, by most conservative methods, that about 27,400,000 tons of pig iron were produced.[51] Construction of railways, at 300 tons of rail per mile, appear to have consumed less than 7 percent of the output for rails alone. Adding all other possible railway uses—perhaps doubling total tonnage, just to be safe—one probably must still account for the use of over 80 percent of Britain's pig iron output. Hawke's data indicate that I am far too generous with this, but generosity is cheap, as my point is so simple. The British railway in 1830–1850 simply cannot carry the Schumpeter-Rostow load that Hobsbawm tries to heap on it. A growing, iron-using British economy *can* carry such a weight, but that is not what Hobsbawm is after, if the mass of the people are to be made no better off, or not significantly better off materially, by British industrialization up to 1850. Per capita output of pig iron (if we use the population of England and Wales only, the most conservative denominator)[52] more than doubled in 1830–1850, from about 98 pounds per head in 1830 to 252 pounds in 1850. A more complex notion of economic development, based on a host of new iron products, could account for the increase in per capita output, but hardly if the mass of the population is impoverished.

3. The early-start thesis is extra congenial to Hobsbawm for obvious reasons. The old capitalist economies are doomed to fall behind the surging, dynamic, thrusting, "new" socialist economies. The trouble with the early-start thesis is that it is illogical.[53] There is no way to refute it by any appeal to the facts, unless you can show that Britain was as technically up to date as anyone else by the end of the nineteenth century, and in major areas it apparently was not.[54] Britain was falling behind the other industrializing economies in terms of growth rates. An abundant literature, stretching back to the 1950s, refutes the logical props of the early-start thesis, but Hobsbawm either has not read it or prefers to ignore it. It is precisely the most advanced ("mature") economies that should be best placed, by virtue of past

accretions of technical infrastructures and supporting institutions, to carry forward new productivity-raising innovations. Hence, one looks to the United States, Japan, Sweden, Germany, etc., rather than, say, India, Bulgaria, or Algeria, for sustained industrial advance. Whatever the source of Britain's troubles in the late nineteenth century, they were not inexorably due to her pioneer position, and that, oddly enough, is precisely what the early-start thesis says.

4. Hobsbawm's mercantilism[55] is, to my mind, the most bizarre thing in all of his vast output. In my opinion, his notions of international trade and payments, theory and fact, are exotic indeed. I think he lets his biases carry him away. He appears to wish a self-sufficient economy upon Britain, criticizing her for increasingly trading commodities with her empire in the late nineteenth century,[56] for shifting from grain to dairy production,[57] for investing abroad.[58] To Hobsbawm, the pursuit of comparative advantage in trade is weakness, *evasion*,[59] not competition. He seems to see the desire to trade as, *ipso facto*, a sign of national weakness. Just as he refers to the ability of Eastern Europe to supply the West with food as the sign of a "dependent economy,"[60] so he pokes fun at Britain for developing a "parasitic"[61] economy. Here he is on Britain in the late nineteenth century: "To retreat into her satellite world of formal or informal colonies, to rely on her growing power as the hub of international lending, trade and settlements, seemed all the more obvious a solution because, as it were, it presented itself."[62]

Quite. We are speaking here of nineteenth-century capitalism. That the British adjustment to overseas competition in heavy industry moved her into the provision of financial and communications services was a rational act may be seen by comparing the rate of growth of invisibles in the British balance of international payments with data for the growth of heavy industry.[63] If wheat, iron, meat, and raw materials can be acquired more cheaply by concentrating upon the production and sale of services than by home production, such a solution does indeed "present itself." Moreover, this kind of interdependence is what specialization in the world economy is all about. Making all the world "dependent" upon all the world not only maximizes world output, but led J. S. Mill to foresee (wrongly, as it turned out) that world economic interdependence would produce world peace.[64]

Every rational man, including Professor Hobsbawm, finds his comparative advantage, and concentrates his efforts there. We all "hide behind" our comparative advantage if we can. Moreover, the British, late in the nineteenth century, were only doing what all non-Communist industrial societies have done since: shifting labor resources away from direct production of food and goods into more sophisticated and productive uses of human labor as improvements in agricultural and industrial productivity make such shifts possible.[65] Successful industrialization limits the growth of the industrial proletariat and feeds the growth of science, finance, communications, and the arts. Britain was the first country to launch itself on this path, just as she had been the first to industrialize. Her opportunities were international, and she took them. What British people did not foresee (and who did?) was the terrible twentieth century, in which a primitive military dictatorship, ruling a command economy at near barter levels, would create a better chance of national survival than did the methods of nineteenth-century liberalism and laissez-faire economics. In retrospect, the British of the late nineteenth and early twentieth centuries seemed short-sighted, but only if we suppose that post-1914 events were known to them. They were not.

5. Hobsbawm is no crude determinist in most of his writing. In his essays on bandits and primitive rebels he allows the full range of human motivation to come into play. There is no "economic determination of everything." Freud lived, and so did primitive notions of honor and justice—Robin Hood. Yet when he turns to economic history, we tend to get the wooden scarecrows of Marxist Leninism. Nations think, and they think that overseas military adventures are good business. (In the example of modern Germany, he would have a case. What the Germans wanted to steal in Europe from their neighbors was worth having, as Lenin observed.)[66] He credits economic historians, at one point, with supporting him in this.[67] I think the support is very thin, not only because of the work of people like David Fieldhouse and other political historians, but because of Feis, Schumpeter, and the late Matt Simon.[68] Very little foreign investment in the age of the New Imperialism went to the deserts and jungles of the newly acquired overseas empires. Mostly, foreign investment went where it paid to send it: to Europe and its overseas offshoots.[69] The tragedy for the determinists on "economic imperialism" is that Hobson wrote before Paish, and Lenin read Hobson.[70] Otherwise, the need to tie up the imperialism of Russia, Britain, France, Germany, Belgium, the United States, and Japan in the last half of the nineteenth century with "economic necessity" might never have arisen, and we could view military aggression for what it is, instead of through a smokescreen of metaeconomics. The language Hobsbawm uses, the stock phrases—the masses, labor cadres, the proletariat, overseas *outlets* for capital, parasitic economy, and so forth—give his writing a vigorous and aggressive determinist flavor. Yet his subtlety, skill, wit, and stretches of fine writing and sympathetic understanding immediately disarm the hostile critic, who might hope that in Hobsbawm one would merely be dealing with the conventional Marxist hack. This critic who finds himself hostile to much of Hobsbawm's economics and historical interpretation also finds himself fascinated by the great learning and ability in Hobsbawm's work.

I will forbear going into further detail regarding my objections to Hobsbawm's economic history of the narrower sort. It should be clear that I find his uses of the materials imperfect. What is good in his economic history—

and there is a lot that is good—I find to be overwhelmed by the consequences of his extraneous interests and commitments.

What of the larger view? After all, anyone who has read extensively of Hobsbawm's work will be aware that economics is just one piece of a brilliant mosaic. Hobsbawm is like the late Garrett Mattingly: he disposes of vast erudition and culture and utilizes his real comparative advantage—to write fascinating, rich history. Hobsbawm's commitment to a romantic view of social revolution leads him to look after the history of such phenomena as farm laborers' revolts, bandits—the mythology behind the phenomenon of primitive rebellion. It is perfectly clear that we are greatly in his debt for this, and I, for one, would not trade what he has done for work on more conventional subjects, based upon axioms I agree with. His different point of view is a great stimulus to me, and ought to be to any open-minded reader.

Social revolution and premature appearances of it are the basic raw materials of Hobsbawm's work. Crises and rebels. One's head is filled with them after a few months' immersion in Hobsbawm's books and papers. One is sometimes disappointed if, after a few tantalizing glimpses, the revolution disappears under the surface of normal life.[71] But one doubts not that the revolution will reappear when conditions are right, and sometimes, hopefully, under the leadership of "modern politics."[72] According to legend, the god Adonis came back to the sacred sites of his cult, only to be slain again and again, his blood making the grass green and the crops abundant. Half in the underworld and half in the world of men, Adonis is there, if unseen. The revolution—or a poor second, socialist reformism—is inevitable.

The latter is, in my opinion, the key to all of Hobsbawm's work. He has an overall view, not only about how history went in the past but how it will go in the future. The patterns are there, for him, and the object of historical inquiry is to elucidate those patterns. To have such a metaphysical intellectual framework is a considerable advantage to a broad-gauge historian; it gives guidance and motivation to the work. Essentially, the process is similar to the role played by economic theory for the economic historian who works, usually, in much narrower spheres. The main difference is that one hardly ever expects to find things in history just as theory might suggest. The difference between the reality and the theory is what the theory is supposed to illuminate. There is no reason, in principle, why larger systems—for example, the system of Karl Marx—could not play the same role, except that, unlike the economic historian who is "guided" by theory, the Marxist historian too often devotes himself to showing why it was that Marx really predicted what happened, no matter what the condition of the historical evidence.

Now Karl Marx is a very useful author for anyone to read. I think he was probably the greatest contemporary observer of the Victorian British economy, and I think, against *his evidence*,[73] his explanatory paradigm was reasonable in general terms. But it is now more than a century since volume 1 of *Capital* was published, and longer yet since the *Communist Manifesto*. The Communist dictatorships of this world either came to power in economically backward areas of the world or were imposed in advanced areas like East Germany and Czechoslovakia by the Red Army. So far, the industrial nations have not generated the Communist revolution. Bomb throwing by intellectuals is not what Marx had in mind. The greatest revolutionary force today is outside the industrial world altogether; it is the impoverished and desperate pre-industrial proletariat (as Professor Hicks calls them)[74] of the economically underdeveloped two-thirds of mankind. The industrial workers, the 500 million inside the industrial economies, non-Communist and Communist alike, are the mainstays of the political systems in power there. Hobsbawm's search for rebels in the remote fields and mountains of the West is perhaps necessitated by the spectacular nonrevolutionary character of the affluent hardhats in the industrial nations.

The future? I will not venture to prophesy here, but presumably Hobsbawm will keep watch for the reappearance of Adonis.

NOTES

1. Charles P. Kindleberger, *Economic Growth in France and Britain, 1815–1950* (Cambridge, Mass.: Harvard University Press, 1964), p. 324.
2. E. J. Hobsbawm, *Industry and Empire. The Making of Modern English Society, 1750 to the Present Day* (New York: Pantheon Books, 1968), p. 45.
3. Ibid., p. 172.
4. By 1939 the British had less than 6 percent of the "occupied population" in agriculture, forestry, and fishing. To raise this figure to Soviet levels would involve a massive transfer of labor to proportions existing in the first decades of the nineteenth century, or even earlier. The U.S.S.R. could easily have had 50 percent of its labor force working in agriculture in 1939. See Edward Ames, *Soviet Economic Processes* (Homewood, Ill.: Irwin, 1965), p. 124. British data are in Phyllis Deane and W. A. Cole, *British Economic Growth, 1688–1959* (Cambridge: Cambridge University Press, 1962), table 30, p. 142.
5. For example, E. J. Hobsbawm, *The Age of Revolution, 1789–1848* (New York: Mentor Books, 1964), pp. 58–60. He illustrates falling profits with the cotton industry, but in an astonishing way. "As the total sales soared upwards, so did the total of profits even at their diminishing rate. All that was needed was continued and astronomic expansion. Nevertheless, it seemed that the shrinking of profit margins had to be arrested or at least slowed down" (p. 60). Profits are maximized when the *total* is the largest. But for Hobsbawm it is profit per unit of output that matters. What, then, does he think mass production is—a capitalist philanthropy? No falling share of profits over time in the distribution of national income was found by Deane and Cole (op. cit., table 80, p. 301). The problem regarding real wages is taken up below.
6. *The Age of Revolution*, p. 94.

7. Leo Gershoy, *The French Revolution and Napoleon* (New York: Crofts, 1947), p. 289. Gershoy puts the figure at more than 1,300. In an older account, Louis Adolphe Thiers, *History of the French Revolution, 1789–1800* (London: Richard Bentley and Son, 1895 [3: 451]), the figure is 1,862 between June 10 and July 17, 1794. Precision is irrelevant, of course, except to indicate that killing such a number one at a time, even by machine, would involve considerable effort. At Nantes, ships were filled with victims and sunk in the Loire to solve the problems of human and mechanical bottlenecks. Revolutions are murderous affairs, and the French Revolution was one such.

8. This book will doubtless be a classic of its kind, if for no other reason than the extent to which it must outrage English readers by its patronizing attitude, and Hobsbawm's posture as the expert on such matters as the suitability of English social institutions for the English. Common-room masochists must love it. See, for example, p. 3 for a display of Hobsbawm's profundities on the English constitution. Also, virtually all of chapter 14.

9. *The Age of Revolution*, p. 131. In E. J. Hobsbawm and George Rudé, *Captain Swing* (London: Lawrence and Wishart, 1969), there is another fine example of this aspect of Hobsbawm's writing. Perhaps it might be called the "Hobsbawm twist"—the conclusions assumed, almost subliminally. The implications of the writing, in context, convey far more of the "message" than does the actual argument or the evidence. In discussing farm area disturbances, in which there were 1,876 cases heard (and 800 outright acquitals) out of an agricultural labor force of about 1.8 million, the atmosphere that the writing tries to produce is the drama of great and ubiquitous events. "The Weald did not move until the Battle area in Sussex had given the signal" (p. 90). So far as I can tell from their table (p. 308), fewer than 200 men were involved in this episode.

10. Harold Nicolson, *The Congress of Vienna* (London: University Paperbacks, 1961), pp. 269–270.

11. This academic dispute, conducted with no little amount of invective, began with E. J. Hobsbawm, "The British Standard of Living, 1790–1850," *Economic History Review* (Aug. 1957). Hartwell replied with two papers: "Interpretations of the Industrial Revolution in England: A Methodological Survey," *Journal of Economic History* (June 1959), and "The Rising Standard of Living in England: 1800–1850" *Economic History Review* (Apr. 1961). Both authors had a further direct exchange in the *Economic History Review* (Aug. 1963), "The Standard of Living during the Industrial Revolution: A Discussion."

12. One of the frustrating aspects of the Hobsbawm–Hartwell exchange is what is meant by "standard of living" and when the discussion is supposed to be germane to that issue. To some extent, the whole discussion was framed by the nature of the evidence available, and that, possibly as much as willful "disputemanship," underlies the problem. At the beginning of "The British Standard of Living, 1790–1850," Professor Hobsbawm says: "Among academic historians, in Britain at any rate, the pendulum has swung away from the classical view. . . . It is today heterodox to believe that early industrialization was a catastrophe for the labouring poor of this or other countries, let alone that their standard of living declined. This article proposes to show that the currently accepted view is based upon insufficient evidence, and there is some weighty evidence in favour of the old view." If to one contestant the "labouring poor" includes employed factory workers and to the other it includes Irish paupers and displaced handloom weavers, how is the problem to be resolved? In Hobsbawm's part of the 1963 discussion, the pessimist side is weakened to ". . . some deterioration is plausible for the middle of the 1790's to the early or middle 1840's" (p. 120). Since virtually all of Hobsbawm's efforts are devoted to establishing this plausibility, I take it he wanted

to make "plausible" into "evident." He spends little effort examining the evidence supporting the opposite case. The purple prose of chapter 4 of *Industry and Empire* is hardly designed to present a carefully weighed judgment of the evidence on both sides.

13. A most informative roundup of the theoretical issues from the classical economists forward, together with the main empirical findings to the late 1960s, is found in P. A. Samuelson, *Economics* (8th ed.; New York: McGraw-Hill, 1970), chapter 37.

14. Of course, wages could be kept down by force (e.g., secret police, etc.), and the added product of labor expropriated. In a competitive factor market, only the two examples that are given could keep additional wages from accruing to labor if capitalists were employing labor in order to maximize profit. The marginal revenue product is a downward-sloping function whose values are determined by the marginal revenue times the marginal physical product. Marginal revenue is determined by the demand function for the product in the market, and the marginal physical product is determined by the production function. Hence an upward shift in the production function could be offset by a collapse of market demand, so far as the marginal revenue product is concerned, and wages fall, or men be thrown out of work, or both. But the trend is what I am discussing (six decades or so are at issue) and I am assuming that it is a rising trend so far as the marginal revenue product is concerned. Basically, the long-term shift of distributive shares of income toward labor and away from capital is due to the change in factor proportions, with capital increasing so much more rapidly than labor.

15. Hobsbawm (1963), pp. 121–123. See Hartwell (1963), pp. 137–138, on this.

16. Hobsbawm (1963), pp. 128–131, and chapter 4 of *Industry and Empire*.

17. That this is a clear possibility does not mean that it happened. In fact, the evidence is that long-term growth in the Western countries tended to narrow the distribution. See Simon Kuznets, *Six Lectures on Economic Growth* (New York: Free Press, 1961), pp. 66–67 and table 7. See also Richard Easterlin, "Economic Growth: Overview," in *International Encyclopedia of the Social Sciences* (New York: Macmillan and Free Press, 1968), 4: 399.

18. Especially impressive was Hartwell's part of the 1963 discussion (cited above). His earlier papers were convincing enough, in my opinion. Professor Hobsbawm obviously disagrees.

19. Deane and Cole, op. cit., table 37, pp. 166–167; table 38, pp. 170–171.

20. Ibid., table 37, pp. 166–167. Income, in current prices, to manufacturing, mining and building was £54.3 million in 1801, £179.5 million in 1851. The increase is more than triple, and since prices were far higher in 1801 than in 1851, real income was even more rapidly increased in these sectors. Proportionately, agriculture's share, 32.5 percent in 1801, fell to 20.3 percent in 1851. Manufacturing, mining, and building received 23.4 percent of income in 1801 and 34.3 percent in 1851.

21. Interest rates may be found in B. R. Mitchell and Phyllis Deane, *Abstract of British Historical Statistics* (Cambridge: Cambridge University Press, 1962), pp. 455 (consol yields and bank Rate). See also Sir John Hicks, *Critical Essays in Monetary Theory* (Oxford: Clarendon Press, 1967), chapter 5, "The Yield on Consols" (yields are charted on p. 84).

22. Productivity of labor, measured as output per man-hour, would be the most unambiguous single measure of productivity, if such data were available. A most *conservative proxy* would be the proportion of total income paid in wages, assuming that competitive conditions held, and that the wage was equal to the marginal

revenue product of employed labor over time. Wages paid in mining, manufacturing, and building were 22.1 percent of total wages and salaries in 1801, 37.3 percent in 1851 (Deane and Cole, table 34, p. 152). The proportion of the labor force in manufacturing, mining, and industry rose from 29.7 percent in 1801 to 42.9 percent in 1851. The shift of distributive shares indicated by these data was *half again* as rapid as the shift of labor supply. But then, Dr. Hobsbawm does not claim that *productivity* in industry fell, only that the increase was not captured by wage earners, or not significantly. These data hardly support him. Unfortunately for the "optimist" case, the data are not completely comparable in the two series, judging from the description of the coverage given by Deane and Cole. Prices may be found in Mitchell and Deane, *Abstract of British Historical Statistics*, pp. 470–472. The fall in prices between 1800 and 1850, of course, was great. The indicated decrease for 1790–1850 is about one-third.

23. According to Deane and Cole (op. cit., pp. 261–266), net capital formation was 5 to 6 percent of national income in annual rates in the early 1780s, rising slowly to a rate in excess of 10 percent per annum in the 1850s.

24. Had such not been true, then, tautologically, the Victorian British economy could never have come into existence, under competitive conditions. Even Hobsbawm agrees, apart from the question of the rate of profit (in his case, per unit of output, as noted in footnote 5, above), that Victorian Britain was a monument to capitalist accumulation. Or as he puts it, so much more dramatically: "There is, of course, no dispute about the fact that *relatively*, the poor grew poorer, simply because the country, and its rich and middle class, so obviously grew wealthier. The very moment when the poor were at their tether—in the early and middle forties—was the moment when the middle class dripped with excess capital, to be wildly invested in railways and spent on the bulging, opulent household furnishings displayed at the Great Exhibition of 1851" (*Industry and Empire*, p 72).

25. Deane and Cole, op. cit., table 37, p. 166.

26. Ibid., table 39, p. 172. The rates of growth here are *compound*.

27. Mitchell and Deane, op. cit., p. 271. Hoffman's index contains a large number of relatives of output by industry, which are not given by Mitchell and Deane. See W. G. Hoffman, *British Industry, 1770–1950* (Oxford: Oxford University Press, 1955).

28. Albert Imlah, *Economic Elements in the Pax Britannica* (Cambridge, Mass.: Harvard University Press, 1958), pp. 94–95.

29. Deane and Cole, op. cit., table 31, p. 143.

30. Ibid., table 3, p. 8.

31. My preference for the 1849–50 break was a matter of judgment concerning all the available data: J. R. T. Hughes, *Fluctuations in Trade, Industry and Finance* (Oxford: Clarendon Press, 1960), pp. 28–29. Deane and Cole found the *real growth rates* by their measures *maximized* during Hobsbawm's bleak age: ibid., table 73, p. 283 (a compound rate), and table 77, p. 297. In other words, by these measures the 1850s actually represented a *slowing down*, compared to 1801–1851. I have dealt with these findings elsewhere: "Measuring British Economic Growth," *Journal of Economic History* (Mar. 1964). Dr. Hobsbawm should find their results most distressing and in need of comment by him. Worse still was W. W. Rostow's opinion of 1815–45: "The period emerges as one of extraordinary development, perhaps the most rapid rate of development of domestic resources throughout the whole of Britain's economic history"—Strong stuff (*British Economy of the Nineteenth Century* [Oxford: Clarendon Press, 1948], p. 19). He does say, somewhat incredulously, considering his findings, that the period has a "bad name."

32. Henry Mayhew, *London Labour and the London Poor* (New York: Augustus Kelly, 1967), 4 vols. A beautifully reproduced version.

33. Easterlin, op. cit., p. 403, and references to the relevant works of Simon Kuznets, p. 408.

34. The word is Schumpeter's rendering. In the *Communist Manifesto,* part I, the historical development of the revolutionary proletariat is outlined; indeed, the relevant chapters of *Capital* (e.g., vol. I, chapter X, "The Working Day," and the great chapter XV, "Machinery and Modern Industry") might have served as models for Hobsbawm's own work on early British industrialization. But for that matter, they might still usefully serve as models of their kind for all historians.

35. "The British Standard of Living, 1790–1850," op. cit., p. 47. In the 1963 paper (op. cit., p. 122, n. 4), Hobsbawm returns to this point. It is not only anti-Keynesian, in the sense that consumption and savings (investment) cannot increase simultaneously, but the "paradox of thrift" seems not to apply, and he seems to have in mind that there was some problem about savings financing investment because given pounds (the same physical ones) must be found by borrowers to invest. At any rate, how could it make any difference if there were no shortage of loanable funds anyway? Was there? Do we know of investment being retarded by lack of money during 1790–1850? When and where? See *Industry and Empire*, p. 72. Apparently not.

36. Joseph A. Schumpeter, *The Theory of Economic Development* (New York: Oxford University Press, 1961), is the best single statement of the role of the entrepreneur in Schumpeter's scheme.

37. In chapter 3 of *Industry and Empire,* Hobsbawm uses the Schumpeterian model skillfully (e.g., pp. 46–47 on Robert Peel); also, in chapter 9 (p. 106) the socialist revival of the Great Depression coincides with the troubles of capitalists and the troubles of the growing masses of the laboring classes. "The era of the Great Depression was also the era of the emergence of mass socialist (that is, mainly Marxist) working-class parties all over Europe, organized in a Marxist International." As noted above, Marx and Engels "foresaw" the development of a revolutionary proletariat out of the crises of industrial capitalism.

38. *The Age of Revolution*, p. 45. Here we find the Industrial Revolution virtually defined as Rostow's takeoff, which supposedly "is now technically known to the economists as the 'take-off' into self-sustained growth." Also, pp. 46, 52. In *The Age of Revolution*, in the 1760s, "all the relevant statistical indices took that sudden, sharp, almost vertical turn upwards which marks the 'take-off.' The economy became, as it were, airborne" (p. 46). In *Industry and Empire*, the takeoff appears on p. 32 and through chapters 2 and 3 as the great breakthrough, especially on pp. 26–27 and 47, and on p. 273 as that "ruthless plunge into industrial capitalism." The idea of a fast change from one structure of society to another is crucial to Hobsbawm's notion of the British Industrial Revolution. A central issue for Hobsbawm in rapid development is the conquest of empire for the benefit of manufacturers by a willing government, anxious to comply with their needs (*ibid.,* p. 33), which acquires a market for cottons "without which . . . the Industrial Revolution cannot be explained" (p. 41). There is another tradition, of course, that of the gradualist, described by Maurice Dobb's *Studies in the Development of Capitalism* (New York: International Publishers, 1947 [p. 260]) as that of the "worshipper of continuity." It is very extensive, and persuasive. With that tradition in mind, the takeoff and drama disappear together, to a large extent.

39. Deane and Cole (op. cit., pp. 261–268) could not find Rostow's "takeoff" level of net investment (10 percent of national income) until the 1850s. To make matters worse, they insist that the period 1745–60 is really when the upward inflection point of British growth occurs (pp. 82–97). Stretched out a century

from when their period starts—to the 1850s, when Rostow's 10 percent appears—the sudden breakthrough of the Industrial Revolution is hard to believe. But that is nothing compared to those who are willing to stretch it back to the thirteenth century and beyond.

40. Simon Kuznets, quoted in Douglass North, *Growth and Welfare in the American Past* (Englewood Cliffs, N. J.: Prentice-Hall, 1966), pp. 87–88, as part of North's criticism of the Rostowian timing in American economic history. In Robert Fogel's *Railroads and American Economic Growth* (Baltimore: Johns Hopkins University Press, 1964), chapter IV, the takeoff thesis is simply dismembered so far as the United States is concerned.

41. The idea, which played an important role in the evolution of Rostow's later work, appears at least as early as 1948 in connection with recoveries from cyclical downswings. *British Economy of the Nineteenth Century,* pp. 54–57.

42. *Railroads and American Economic Growth: Essays in Econometric History.*

43. Ibid. The famous nails appear on pp. 135 and 233.

44. *The Age of Revolution,* pp. 63–67. Here Hobsbawm is simply carried away. Railway expansion was so fast it was "an irrational passion" (p. 65). The "comfortable and rich classes accumulated income so fast and in such vast quantities as to exceed all possibilities of spending and investment" (p. 65). The railways "could not conceivably have been built as rapidly and on as large a scale without this torrent of capital flooding into them, especially in the middle 1840s. It was a lucky conjuncture for the railways happened to solve virtually all the problems of the economy's growth at once" (p. 67). Very un-Marxian. Since when does luck play any role in the concrete determination of the play of inexorable historical forces?

45. Ibid., p. 64. See also *Industry and Empire*, pp. 88–95, for similar comment.

46. *The Age of Revolution,* p. 64.

47. G. R. Hawke, *Railways and Economic Growth in England and Wales, 1840–1870* (Oxford: Clarendon Press, 1970), p. 244.

48. Ibid., table IX, 11, p. 240. Hawke concludes: "Although contemporaries made extravagant statements about the effect of railways on the iron industry, it is clear that the existence of railways was not necessary for the development of an iron industry" (p. 244).

49. Mitchell and Deane, op. cit., p. 255.

50. Iron output before the regular mineral returns began in 1854 are estimates made at various intervals. This figure is reported by Mitchell and Deane, op. cit., p. 131, and is close to I. L. Bell's 2.5-million-ton estimate. Isaac Lowthian Bell, *The Iron Trade of the United Kingdom* (London, 1886), pp. 6–7.

51. From the data in Mitchell and Deane, op. cit. (p. 131), and A. D. Gayer, W. W. Rostow, and A. J. Schwartz, *The Growth and Fluctuation of the British Economy, 1790–1850* (Oxford: Clarendon Press, 1953, [vol. 1]), estimates for all but four years are available. I filled in the missing years by using the previous year's output where only one year is missing in a sequence, or by a linear expansion in 1837–38 when only 1836 and 1839 are available in estimates. It would appear from this that total 1830–50 output was in the neighborhood of 27,483,000 tons.

52. That is, since Ireland's population was falling, United Kingdom output per capita would rise faster, including Ireland. I want to be conservative on all such estimates.

53. There have been three good discussions of the early-start thesis from a logical viewpoint in the last two decades: Marvin Frankel, "Obsolescence and Technological Change," *American Economic Review* (June 1955); Donald F. Gordon, "Obsolescence and Technological Change: Comment," ibid. (Sept. 1956); and a reply by Frankel. This was followed by Edward Ames and Nathan Rosenberg,

"Changing Technological Leadership and Industrial Growth," *Economic Journal* (Mar. 1963).

54. Not in all industries, but apparently in the "traditional" ones (Derek Aldcroft, ed., *The Development of British Industry and Foreign Competition* [London: G. Allen, 1968]). The theme of the backwardness of British technology after 1875 is undergoing extensive revisionist investigation now, and may not survive in a form usable by "general" historians.

55. I define mercantilism here as the notion that the object of industrialization and foreign trade is the aggrandizement of power in the form of economic self-sufficiency. This is a very odd notion for anyone, educated in modern economics, to hold up as an ideal of economic development, but it has had some vogue in "development economics" since 1950. A country which manufactures or grows commodities which it could buy cheaper by concentrating its own efforts on more efficient output, and then trading, is voluntarily lowering its own income. Why do it? Protectionism, desire for "balanced growth," fear of war, etc. For a bald statement of the early-start thesis in such a context, see *Industry and Empire*, pp. 158–159.

56. This theme runs throughout *Industry and Empire*. See especially pp. 2–3, all of chapter 7, and pp. 161, 168–169.

57. Ibid., p. 168.

58. Ibid., pp. 88–92, 96–97, 121–122.

59. Ibid., p. 2.

60. *The Age of Revolution*, p. 31.

61. *Industry and Empire*, p. 161.

62. Ibid., p. 160.

63. Imlah, op. cit., table 4, pp. 172–175. This is not news to Hobsbawm, by the way (see *Industry and Empire*, p. 161)—just as he knows all about the lack of support for Rostow that Deane and Cole report upon (*Industry and Empire*, pp. 56–57). The point is interpretation of such information, and Professor Hobsbawm "goeth where he listeth."

64. J. S. Mill, *The Principles of Political Economy* (London: Longmans, 1911), p. 352.

65. Alfred Maizels, *Industrial Growth and World Trade* (Cambridge: Cambridge University Press, 1963), pp. 26–37; J. R. T. Hughes, "Industrialization: Economic Aspects," *International Encyclopedia of the Social Sciences*, op. cit., 7: 255–258.

66. V. I. Lenin, *Imperialism: The Highest Stage of Capitalism*, published in English in Emile Burns, *A Handbook of Marxism* (London: Left Book Club, Victor Gollancz, 1937), pp. 692–700, on Germany's options in Europe.

67. *Industry and Empire*, p. 107.

68. Herbert Feis, *Europe, the World's Banker* (New York: Norton, 1965); Joseph Schumpeter, *Imperialism and Social Classes* (New York: Meridian Books, 1955); this book is two long essays, one of them on imperialism. Schumpeter argued that imperialisms, all the way back to antiquity, represented almost everything except "economic necessity." Matthew Simon's work on the direction of British portfolio investment sharpened our knowledge very considerably. Harvey Segal and Matthew Simon, "British Foreign Capital Issues, 1865–1894," *Journal of Economic History* (Dec. 1961); Matthew Simon, "The Pattern of New British Portfolio Foreign Investment: 1865–1914," International Economic Association Round Table Conference on Capital Movements and Economic Development, 1965.

69. Feis, op. cit., pp. 23, 51, 74, for the geographical distribution of foreign investment by Britain, France, and Germany.

70. See Feis, op. cit., pp. 14–15, n. 11, on Paish's papers in 1909, 1911, and 1914. C. K. Hobson's *Export of Capital* (London, 1914) was not the Hobson re-

ferred to by Lenin (op. cit., pp. 701, 703, 704, 705, 707, 710, 712, 716, etc.); that was J. A. Hobson, whose book *Imperialism* was first published in 1902 (my copy is London: George Allen & Unwin, 1954, 5th impression). Hobson's investment data were not disaggregated by country sufficiently for him to know where the foreign investment was going, and he thought a lot more of it was going to the newly acquired empire than in fact was. Hobson's notion of imperialism, growing out of capitalist development and the trade cycle, was one of Lenin's main inspirations regarding foreign investment as "economic necessity."

71. For example, *Industry and Empire*, p. 6, and *Captain Swing*, op. cit.: "The labourer in the 1820's was desperately poor, unemployed, oppressed, helpless and hopeless. Nothing was more natural than that he should rebel, as the table overleaf demonstrates" (p. 81). For Professor Hobsbawm, a little rebellion is better than none. One cannot but admire Hobsbawm's sheer skill in research and writing on such matters. In *Bandits* (New York: Delacorte Press, 1969), chapter 8, concerning the life of Francisco Sabaté Llopart, is an artistic masterpiece.

72. E. J. Hobsbawm, *Primitive Rebels* (New York: Norton Library, 1959). Speaking of the Monarchist vote in Naples: "In 1956 it polled almost three times as many votes there as the Communists. However, this lack of interest in modern politics among the big-city poor—which expresses itself as some sort of conservatism, when they do vote . . . may be due simply to the absence of anything—such as large factories, craft or village solidarity—which helps to crystallize their political opinions" (p. 117). Preference for a monarchy is not "crystallized"? Hobsbawm's work is filled with judgments about other people's institutional behavior. Here the Italian urban poor are considered backward for preferring a lifetime leader, who is born to power, to one who comes to power by "other means." In the Communist party regimes, the leadership tends to extreme longevity, hardly ever changing as a result of popular elections. Perhaps the urban mobs of Naples knew that much and preferred an evil with which they were familiar.

73. Like any historian, Marx found the evidence to which his theory guided him. He was hardly looking for data that would support the "optimist" view.

74. Sir John Hicks, *A Theory of Economic History* (New York: Oxford University Press, 1969), final chapter.

Macroeconomics

The Economics of Professor Friedman

John H. Wood

Milton Friedman's name is closely associated with the policy recommendation that a rule should be adopted whereby the monetary authorities are required to cause the stock of money to change at some (any?) constant rate. He has argued that such a rule is more conducive than discretionary policies to the moderation of fluctuations in prices, employment, and output. In support of this position, Friedman and his collaborators have amassed a great deal of historical evidence that, they say, suggests a close relation between variations in the quantity of money and variations in economic activity. But his critics have charged that Friedman, unlike Keynes, for example, has advanced no model, no theory from which his policy rule may be derived. They point out that Friedman has not shown us *how* money influences economic activity and that, without such an explicit statement, the correlations between money and income upon which he places so much emphasis tell us nothing of causation.

There is considerable merit in this criticism. Friedman is a respected economic theorist. But he has yet to set forth systematically his theory of how money affects prices and output.[1] He has done useful theoretical work on (1) the demand for money, (2) the effects of money on the demands for and prices of real and financial assets and other goods and services his "transmission mechanism"—and (3) the influence of income on consumption. But he has not explicitly completed his model. We have so far seen only half a model. It is one thing to develop the implications of variations in the quantity of money for the demands for goods and services, and quite another to show how these variations in demand induce corresponding variations in supply. Until this connection is made, we have no theory of the relations among money, prices, and output.

The controversy that has long surrounded Friedman's model, aggravated by his own often conflicting accounts of that model and its implications for policy, suggests that we can expect no more than a modest degree of success in penetrating its mysteries. One is reminded of Churchill's characterization of Russian foreign policy.[2] Yet, an understanding of Friedman's theory is important in view of his influence on policy discussions and, perhaps, even on policy, although we can never be sure of the motives of central bankers. Furthermore, just in case Friedman's impact on monetary theory eventually

191

turns out to be commensurate with the publicity that he has attracted, it may be worthwhile, if only as an academic exercise, to make the effort to achieve a better understanding of the theoretical advances from which we will have benefited.

My objective is to determine whether, by an examination of Friedman's writings, particularly his discussions of monetary history, we can gain a better understanding of the theory underlying his predictions of economic phenomena and his policy proposals. This is not an easy task, and the conclusions will be highly tentative, for reading the historical discussions of Friedman and his associates, including Friedman and Schwartz's *Monetary History of the United States,* is a frustrating experience. On the one hand, we are presented with a wealth of highly suggestive and expertly handled data. But on the other hand, just as Friedman and Schwartz seem on the verge of explaining causal relationships—of giving an explicit statement of the processes through which, in their view, money influences output—they retreat into an orgy of economically meaningless algebraic manipulations of M, V, P, and T.[3] But if we carefully examine the way in which Friedman and his collaborators handle historical data, perhaps we can get an inkling of how, in this theory, money matters. Section I describes how Friedman has attempted to construct a consistent theory from another's historical descriptions in his analysis of the work of W. C. Mitchell.

No attempt will be made here to lay out a complete version of Friedman's monetary theory, even as such a theory may be implicit in any one of his writings, much less to profess a statement of the framework underlying all of his (as we shall see) irreconcilable positions. But it is hoped to fill in one or two of the gaps that have long existed in Friedman's accounts of his theory and, by so doing, achieve a somewhat better understanding of the bases of his historical analyses and policy recommendations.

The plan of the paper, which is separated into eight sections, may be described as follows. My approach will be two-pronged. First, as indicated above and illustrated in section I by Friedman's analysis of Mitchell, I hope to achieve a systematic understanding of Friedman's view of the connections between money and output based on his treatment of historical episodes. Second, Friedman is only one of a long line of economists who have (1) emphasized the importance of money and (2) advocated monetary rules. Many of those economists were more explicit than Friedman concerning the channels through which money influences economic activity. If Friedman's policy proposals and discussions of history are consistent with those prevalent among an identifiable group of economists, is it possible that the explicit aspects of their theories that, apparently, are shared by these economists may give us some insight into parts of Friedman's theoretical framework? At the very least, I maintain that Friedman cannot be understood independently of his predecessors. In support of this view, the development of the quantity theory and some of the better-known arguments for mon-

etary rules prior to Friedman are summarized in sections II and III. An
important part of the argument in favor of rules limiting the discretionary
powers of governments is that the behavior of nongovernmental units, if
not surprised by the authorities, tends to be conducive to economic stability.
Friedman has, with one exception, supported this line of argument and has
tried to give it some empirical foundation. For example, it is shown in section
IV that, contrary to Friedman's work with David Meiselman (discussed in
section VI) but consistent with most of Friedman's other work, especially his
Theory of the Consumption Function, the stability of the multiplier is as essential
as is the stability of the demand for money to Friedman's theory and rule.

It is then argued, in section V, that the causal relationships implicit in the
descriptions of historical events by Friedman and his collaborators, most
notably Anna Schwartz, are fully consistent with the more explicit theories
of their predecessors. The theme that will be emphasized is *surprise*. It will
be argued that, explicit in the theories of many of Friedman's predecessors
and implicit in Friedman's historical discussions, the influence of money on
economic activity depends upon the relation between anticipated and realized monetary events. In particular, if money is to exert a significant influence on anything but prices, the public must be surprised. Mill, Marshall,
and others have contended that perfectly anticipated monetary changes are
neutral. It is easy to see how this view, when combined with other classical
assumptions, led nineteenth-century economists to search for rules and institutional arrangements designed to limit variations in money, one of the
principal benefits of which would be the reduction of uncertainty.

There is nothing new in this. This paper makes no claim either to any
advance in theory or to greater insight into any aspect of the history of
thought before Friedman. The argument is simply that there has been remarkable continuity in the development of theories of money and output
and that a close look at the course of this development will increase our
understanding of the connections between the theories of earlier writers
and Friedman's theory—with the important, sometimes dominant, exception that forms the subject of section VI. This exception is the 1963 study
by Friedman and Meiselman.

It is not commonly realized how far the Friedman-Meiselman paper sig-
nified a departure from Friedman's earlier work. Before that paper, Friedman held a position, as evidenced in his work as an economic historian, very
much like that attributed above to Mill and Marshall. This meant that it was
impossible, in the absence of knowledge of anticipations (which in practice
means explicit hypotheses concerning the formulation of expectations), to
predict the influences of monetary changes on economic activity. Monetary
expansions were equally consistent with expansions and contractions in output; and so were monetary contractions. But some of the estimated equations in FM asserted a very close, stable, contemporaneous relation between
money and output. If this is believed, all that was said above goes by the

board. It becomes possible, through monetary fine-tuning, to make output anything we like, whenever we like.

Of course, Friedman has not accepted the policy implications of FM. Sometimes, as in his presidential address (1968), he has even expressed views wholly consistent with those that he held so unflinchingly before FM. But more and more, especially in the late 1960s and early 1970s, he and his followers have emphasized the potency and predictability of monetary impacts and, therefore, by implication, have supported discretionary monetary policy. Nevertheless, Friedman continues to advocate a money supply rule. The objectives of the concluding sections of this paper, VII and VIII, are to show that (1) a rule similar to, but not precisely the same as, Friedman's rule is consistent with Friedman and Schwartz and, in general, with Friedman before FM, but (2) no such rule is consistent with FM or with much of the work by Friedman and his followers after 1963.

I. FRIEDMAN'S APPROACH TO THE HISTORY OF THOUGHT: W. C. MITCHELL AS ECONOMIC THEORIST

> There is of course no sharp line between the empirical scientist and the theorist. (Friedman, 1950, p. 465)

Wesley Mitchell is best remembered for his empirical approach to the analysis of business cycles—"measurement without theory," as it was characterized by Koopmans. Many economists think of Mitchell as nontheoretical and associate him with the view that if we collect sufficient data, tabulate enough leading and lagging indicators, and go to church on Sunday, we will somehow, through the sheer weight of the numbers, be able to understand, or at least to forecast, economic phenomena.

But Friedman, in a paper titled "Wesley C. Mitchell as an Economic Theorist" (1950), argued that this picture of Mitchell as "primarily an empirical scientist rather than a theorist," although valid, "can easily be misunderstood." Friedman saw Mitchell's "preoccupation [with the] faithful observation and summarizing of the cyclical characteristics of a large number of economic series" (to quote Koopmans again) as a way to the development of a theoretical framework. In Friedman's words,

> the ultimate goal of science in any field is a theory—an integrated "explanation" of observed phenomena that can be used to make valid predictions about phenomena that have not yet been observed. Many kinds of work can contribute to the ultimate goal and are essential for its attainment: the collection of observations about the phenomena in question; the organization and arrangement of observations and the extraction of empirical generalizations from them; the development of improved methods of measuring or analyzing observations; the formulation of partial or complete theories to integrate existing evidence.

In this sense, Wesley Mitchell's empirical work is itself a contribution to economic theory—and a contribution of the first magnitude. (p. 465)

Specifically, "Mitchell's work was consistently and almost exclusively devoted to the development of a theory of economic change."

Mitchell's emphasis on "process," on economic change, is already clearly evident in his *A History of the Greenbacks,* and more explicitly in a 1904 article on "The Real Issues in the Quantity-Theory Controversy," in which he listed as one of the real issues: "How does the quantity of money exert its effect on prices?" and went on to say, "Adherents of the quantity theory. . .have usually neglected to trace the process by which a change in the supply of money affects prices with the care required by the subject." (p. 467)

Friedman's objective was to set forth an explicit business-cycle theory based on the causal relationships implicit in Mitchell's descriptive empirical work. But he did not find this task without its difficulties.

Careful study of Part III of Mitchell's 1913 *Business Cycles* induces in me both exasperation and admiration. It induces exasperation, because numerous significant theoretical insights are so carefully hidden under the smooth, casual-sounding exposition of descriptive material. Time and again, Mitchell seems on the verge of making explicit abstract statements about an essential element in the cyclical process, only to withdraw into a summary of empirical regularities or a listing of special cases or an elaboration of qualification. (p. 478)

However, despite these problems Friedman believed that by a "free-rendering" of Mitchell's work and by casting that work in modern terminology, it should be possible "to show that an integrated business-cycle theory can be constructed from—or read into—Mitchell's work and to express it in terms that bring out its similarities and dissimilarities to other existing theories."[4] The present paper attempts to perform a similar service for Friedman's theory of the connections between money and output. The success of this effort will be limited by many of the same difficulties that Mitchell's work placed in Friedman's way. The *caveat* issued by Friedman when he wrote that his statement of Mitchell's theory takes the form of "a synthesis that I cannot confidently say he would have accepted as his own" applies with equal force to my rendition of Friedman's framework.

II. QUANTITY THEORIES BEFORE FRIEDMAN

Mr. Locke lays it down as a fundamental maxim that the quantity of produce and merchandise in proportion to the quantity of money serves as the regulator of market prices . . . he has clearly seen that the abundance of money makes everything dear, but he has not considered how it does so. The great difficulty of this question consists in knowing in what way and in what proportion the increase of money raises prices. (Cantillon, 1730, part II, ch. 6)

I will argue that Friedman's theory of employment has more in common with the classical economists and, to an even greater extent, pre-classical writers than is generally recognized. But to make headway along these lines it is necessary to disregard another of Friedman's self-caricatures: that the quantity theory is essentially a theory of the demand for money.[5] The nature of the demand for money is certainly an important component of the theory underlying Friedman and Schwartz. But the conclusions drawn by FS and Friedman's policy rule require a more complete theoretical foundation than merely the specification of one blade of the scissors in one market.[6]

The quantity theory—Friedman's and other versions—is also more than the equation of exchange. Before conclusions can be drawn about either short-run or long-run responses of prices to money, we must first specify not only the money market but also the supplies and demands for, at least, commodities and labor, including income, wealth, and price effects, as well as the influence of expectations and adjustment costs on the system's responses to monetary disturbances. Easier said than done. Many economists have recognized this need and have strived, never with complete success, to supply the necessary specifications. Not least among these were Adam Smith's predecessors.

In the late seventeenth and early eighteenth centuries, a period of fluctuating prices about a slight downward trend and recurrent episodes of unemployment and depressed trade, there grew up a substantial body of thought regarding the connections between money and output. The view set forth by Locke, Law, and others was that increases in the quantity of money caused not only price rises but also expansions in output and employment. They proposed a variety of measures designed to increase the supply and velocity of money in the belief that rising prices encouraged trade.

Richard Cantillon agreed that increases in M usually cause both P and T to rise. But he was critical of the static nature of the analyses of his predecessors. They had tended to look at only two points in time and to compare the state of prices and trade before the change in M with that state existing after the impact of a monetary disturbance had worked its way through the system and the economy had arrived at some new position of rest or equilibrium. Or perhaps they were comparing the original position of the economy with some intermediate or transitory state preliminary to the new equilibrium. They had not made this clear. In the passage quoted at the beginning of this section, Cantillon criticized Locke, as others have more recently found fault with Friedman,[7] for not clearly specifying his model.

Cantillon's discussions of the processes by which changes in the quantity of money lead to changes in prices and production may have been the most sophisticated analyses of dynamic monetary processes before the appearance of Keynes' *Treatise on Money* 200 years later. Cantillon was careful to point out that the effects of money on prices and output depend upon how money is injected into the economy—upon who gets the money. He considered a variety of ways in which an increase in the quantity of money may come about: domestic gold discoveries, a favorable balance of trade, or borrowing from foreigners. An important consequence of monetary expansions was a decline in interest rates so that "entrepreneurs in the state find it possible to borrow more cheaply to set people to work and to establish factories in the hope of profit" (part II, ch. 8).

But further output and employment effects result from increases in commodity prices that in turn give rise to expectations of further price changes. Price uncertainty played a central role in Cantillon's analysis, largely through the activities of entrepreneurs such as the farmer. This was made clear in the chapter titled "The Circulation and Exchange of Goods and Merchandise, as Well as Their Production, Are Carried On in Europe by Entrepreneurs, and at a Risk":

> The farmer is an entrepreneur who promises to pay to the Landowner, for his Farm or Land, a fixed sum of money (generally supposed to be equal in value to a third of the produce) without assurance of the profit he will derive from this enterprise. He employs part of the land to feed flocks, produce corn, wine, hay, etc., according to his judgment without being able to foresee which of these will pay best. The price of these products will depend partly on the weather, partly on the demand; if corn is abundant relatively to consumption it will be dirt cheap, if there is scarcity it will be dear. Who can foresee the number of births and deaths of the people in a State in the course of the year? Who can foresee the increase or reduction of expense which may come about in the families? And yet the price of the Farmer's produce depends naturally upon these unforeseen circumstances, and consequently he conducts the enterprise of his farm at an uncertainty. (part I, ch. 13)

Cantillon then went on to give illustrations of how unforeseen events (that is, disappointed expectations), affected the profits and subsequent activities of entrepreneurs. Neither he nor his comtemporaries were explicit about the ways in which expectations regarding future prices might have been formulated. But their discussions of the favorable short-term effects of inflation on economic activity suggest that they assumed expectations to be highly elastic. As a result, monetary expansions that led to increased prices, and expectations of further price rises, induced profit-seeking entrepreneurs to employ more inputs in order to be able to increase their sales at the higher prices that would, hopefully, prevail in the future.

Alternatively, Cantillon's results might be rationalized along the lines of recent incomplete-information quantity-adjustment models.[8] But in either case, the non-neutrality of money depended upon uncertainty and surprise.

Cantillon distinguished between the initial and long-run effects of monetary disturbances. He recognized what many were later to point out: first, that the increased quantity of money is beneficial to trade only during the period in which it is actually increasing, and, second, that the inflationary process cannot go on indefinitely because the increase in prices and incomes leads to an adverse balance of payments and an outflow of money. The trick is to keep the inflationary process going in order to gain the attendant

benefits to output and employment and, at the same time, to keep it sufficiently under control to prevent domestic prices from getting out of line
with foreign prices. "But . . . it is not easy to discover the time opportune
for this, nor to know when money has become more abundant than it ought
to be for the good and preservation of the advantages of the State" (part II,
ch. 8).

David Hume's (1752) analysis was less detailed than Cantillon's, but the
short-run dynamic (money affects output) and long-run comparative-statics
(money is neutral) conclusions of the two writers were identical.[9] Henry
Thornton (1802) agreed that an increased quantity of money at first induces
increases in output and was explicit about the role played by unanticipated
price changes.

> Probably no small part of that industry which is excited by new paper is pro-
> duced through the very means of the enhancement of the cost of commodities.
> While paper is encreasing, and articles continue rising, mercantile speculations
> appear more than ordinarily profitable. The trader, for example, who sells his
> commodity in three months after he purchased it, obtains an extra gain, which
> is equal to such advance in the general price of things as the new paper has
> caused during the three months in question:—he confounds this gain with the
> other profits of his commerce, and is induced, by the apparent success of his
> undertakings, to pursue them with more than usual spirit. The manufacturer
> feels the same kind of encouragement to extend his operations; and the en-
> larged issue of paper supplies both him and the merchant with the means of
> carrying their plans into effect. As soon, however, as the circulating medium
> ceases to encrease, the extra profit is at an end; and, if we assume the augmented
> paper to be brought back to its ordinary quantity, we must suppose industry to
> languish for a time, through the ill success which will appear to attend mercan-
> tile transactions. (pp. 237–238)

But Thornton, even more than Cantillon and Hume, emphasized the
transient nature of the effects of monetary changes.[10] In Thornton's view,
the price increases following an increase in money would come about very
rapidly and be large relative to any increases in output that might ensue.
This increasing emphasis on the rapidity of economic adjustments and a
progression toward the view that money does not matter—in the sense that
interest rates, employment, and output are independent of variations in the
stock of money—had already been stated in perhaps its most extreme form
by Adam Smith,[11] was soon to be given a systematic theoretical basis by
Ricardo,[12] and eventually was given its most lucid and popular expression
by John Stuart Mill. Mill carried on the Smith-Ricardo tradition of disdain
for disequilibria. He denied that changes in the quantity of money upset
equilibrium relationships (that is, affect output, employment, or relative
prices) even during the transition from one level of prices to another. He
criticized as unrealistic the policy of a continuing increase in money and
prices suggested by Cantillon and Hume. He pointed out that people learn.
They observe increases in money, foresee the effect on prices, and make

their plans and draw up their contracts accordingly. A price rise that is
expected by all parties exerts no influence on employment or output. Those
who propose an increase in the currency in order to stimulate "every producer to his utmost exertions" and bring "all the capital and labour of the
country into complete employment"

> could only succeed in winning people on to those unwonted exertions by a
> prolongation of what would in fact be a delusion; contriving matters so, that by
> a progressive rise of money prices, every producer shall always seem to be in
> the very act of obtaining an increased remuneration which he never, in reality,
> does obtain. It is unnecessary to advert to any other of the objections to this
> plan than that of its total impracticability. It calculates on finding the whole
> world persisting for ever in the belief that more pieces of paper are more riches,
> and never discovering that, with all their paper, they cannot buy more of any-
> thing than they could before. (book III, ch. 13)

Knut Wicksell similarly dismissed the possibility of achieving real effects
through systematic monetary changes.

> If a gradual rise in prices, in accordance with an approximately known sched-
> ule, could be reckoned on with certainty, it would be taken into account in all
> current business contracts; with the result that its supposed beneficial influence
> would necessarily be reduced to a minimum. Those people who prefer a con-
> tinually upward moving to a stationary price level forcibly remind one of those
> who purposely keep their watches a little fast so as to be certain of catching
> their trains. But to achieve their purpose they must not be conscious or remain
> conscious of the fact that their watches are fast; otherwise they become accus-
> tomed to take the extra few minutes into account and so after all, in spite of
> their artfulness, arrive too late. (1898, ch. 1)

The upshot of these criticisms of "surprise" theories of economic growth
through continuous monetary expansion is that

> there cannot, in short, be intrinsically a more insignificant thing in the economy
> of society than money; except in the character of a contrivance for sparing time
> and labour. It is a machine for doing quickly and commodiously what would be
> done, though less quickly and commodiously, without it; and like many other
> kinds of machinery, it only exerts a distinct and independent influence of its
> own when it gets out of order. (Mill, 1848, book III, ch. 7)

But this is no mean exception, as the classical economists came increasingly to realize, and as Keynes, Friedman, and others were to argue in the
twentieth century. Such discussions beg the whole question of panics and
cycles brought about by monetary upheavals. It is not possible to have rapid
changes in the quantity of money without the "machinery getting out of
order."

Mill's position came to be less and less representative of economists as the
assurance of Smith and Ricardo was supplanted by the qualifications of
Marshall and Pigou. Marshall, who to his great credit was quite incapable
of making an apparently decisive statement without at once qualifying it by
"other things being equal" and then proceeding to a long list of things that

would not be equal, kept to this practice in his treatment of money. He responded as follows to a question put to him by the chairman of the Indian Currency Committee about "the relation between the volume of currency and the general level of prices in the country."

> I hold that prices vary directly with the volume of currency, if other things are equal; but other things are constantly changing. This so-called "quantity theory of the value of money" is true in just the same way as it is true that the day's temperature varies with the length of the day, other things being equal; but other things are seldom equal. This theory has been the cause of much controversy; but it has never been seriously denied by anyone who has taken it as a whole, and has not stopped short, omitting the words "other things being equal." (1899, question 11, 759)

Marshall considered both permanent and temporary changes in the relation between the quantity of money and the price level. Of the temporary or short-run changes in this relation, one of the most important was due to variations in production caused by price fluctuations. In his paper "Remedies for Fluctuations of General Prices" (1887), Marshall's objective was the development of a scheme whereby the gold standard might be replaced by a system more conducive to a stable currency and therefore to stable prices. He argued that instability in economic activity was promoted by price instability because of the added uncertainty to which businessmen and workers were exposed and, related to this, the tendency of wages to be less flexible than prices. These problems arise in a monetary economy because, in addition to serving as a medium of exchange,

> the second function of money is to act as a *standard of value,* or *standard for deferred payments*—that is, to indicate the amount of general purchasing power, the payment of which is sufficient to discharge a contract, or other commerical obligation that extends over a considerable period of time. For this purpose stability of value is the one essential condition.
> . . . a great deal of our modern business life is made up of such contracts. Much of the income of the nation goes to its ultimate recipients in the form of fixed money payments on Government bonds, on the debentures of private companies, on mortgages and on long leases. Another large part consists of salaries and wages, any change in the nominal value of which involves great friction. . . .
> And, lastly, the complex nature of modern trade and industry puts the management of business into the hands of a comparatively small number of men with special ability for it, and most people lend the greater part of their wealth to others instead of using it themselves. It is therefore a great evil that whenever a man borrows money to be invested in his business he speculates doubly. In the first place he runs the risk that the things which he handles will fall in value relatively to others—this risk is inevitable, it must be endured. But in addition he runs the risk that the standard in which he has to pay back what he has borrowed will be a different one from that by which his borrowing was measured. (pp, 189–190)

Marshall then described the relationship between the real rate of interest (ρ), the contract or nominal rate (r), and the rate of inflation (p) that Irving

Fisher (1896) later stated algebraically: $\rho = (r-p)/(1+p)$. Since, in an uncertain environment, nominal interest rates often do not fully reflect expected price changes,

> the consequence of this uncertainty is that, when prices are likely to rise, people rush to borrow money and buy goods, and thus help prices to rise; business is inflated, it is managed recklessly and wastefully; those working on borrowed capital pay back less real value than they borrowed, and enrich themselves at the expense of the community.
>
> Salaries and wages, unless when governed by a sliding scale, generally retain their nominal value more or less fixed in spite of trade fluctuations; they can seldom be changed without much friction, worry and loss of time . . . so that the employer pays smaller real salaries and wages than usual, at the very time when his profits are largest in other ways, and is thus prompted to over-estimate his strength, and engage in ventures which he will not be able to pull through after the tide begins to turn.
>
> When afterwards credit is shaken and prices begin to fall, everyone wants to get rid of commodities and get hold of money which is rapidly rising in value; this makes prices fall all the faster, and the further fall makes credit shrink even more, and thus for a long time prices fall because prices have fallen. At such a time employers cease their production because they fear that when they come to sell their finished product general prices will be even lower than when they buy their materials. . . . [They] may not happen to remember that every stoppage of work in any one trade diminishes the demand for the work of others; and that, if all trades tried to improve the market by stopping their work together, the only result would be that every one would have less of everything to consume. (Marshall, 1887, pp. 190–191)

The short-run non-neutrality of money in Fisher's analyses (1911, ch. 4; 1928, ch. 5) of transition periods also depended upon unanticipated price changes—especially, as with Marshall, on the inability of parties to loan contracts to forecast future rates of inflation correctly.

This section will conclude with the argument that Keynes, of all people, is one of the truest of Friedman's intellectual forebears. For Keynes, one of the essential features of our economic system—a feature that, when combined with instability of prices, is the main source of "risk . . . one of the heaviest, and perhaps the most avoidable burden on production" (1923, preface)—was that decisions to save were largely independent of decisions to invest.

> We leave savings to the private investor, and we encourage him to place his savings mainly in titles to money. We leave the responsibility for setting production in motion to the businessman, who is mainly influenced by the profits, which he expects to accrue to himself in terms of money. Those who are not in favour of drastic changes in the existing organisation of society believe that these arrangements, being in accord with human nature, have great advantages. (1923, preface)

Keynes' objective in *Tract on Monetary Reform* was to persuade the authorities of the need for currency reforms that "would diminish the wastes of *risk*, which consume at present too much of our estate" (1923, preface), for he was writing in a time of extraordinary upheaval. Prices had more than trebled between 1914 and 1920, including a 40 percent rise between 1919 and 1920, followed by a 50 percent fall during the next three years. Keynes, as Marshall had done in 1887, argued that existing arrangements

> cannot work properly if the money, which they assume as a stable measuring rod, is undependable. Unemployment, the precarious life of the worker, the disappointment of expectation, the sudden loss of savings, the excessive wind-falls to individuals, the speculator, the profiteer—all proceed, in large measure, from the instability of the standard of value. (preface)

The overriding influence on investment is price expectations. Expectations of price increases encourage investment; expected deflation discourages investment. Worst of all is uncertainty. If rapid monetary changes have occurred in the past and are expected to be repeated in the future—in which direction no one knows—businessmen will not bear the risk of investment. If they are to develop their productive capacity, if the savings of households are to be converted into investment projects, businessmen must be able to foresee with a reasonable degree of assurance the prices of the products coming out of their new plants and the costs of the inputs from which those products will be made.

Without underrating the important advances in methods and results in *The General Theory,* we can say that the central theme running through all of Keynes' work was the importance of stability to the efficient functioning of the economy—in particular, to the smooth transmission of resources from savers to investors. Without stable prices, we cannot take for granted with Adam Smith that "what is saved is immediately employed as capital," because

> Thrift may be the handmaid and nurse of Enterprise. But equally she may not. And, perhaps, even usually she is not. For Enterprise is connected with thrift not directly but at one remove, and the link which should join them is frequently missing. For the engine which drives Enterprise is not Thrift but Profit.
> Now, for Enterprise to be active, two conditions must be fulfilled. There must be an expectation of Profit; and it must be possible for enterprisers to obtain command of sufficient resources to put their projects into execution. . . . Their power to put their projects into execution on terms which they deem attractive, almost entirely depends on the behaviour of the banking and monetary system. (1930, II, ch. 30)

In particular, the banking system ought to behave in a manner conducive to price stability. Keynes is often thought of as an inflationist, but this is because deflation and unemployment were the dominant problems of the interwar period. The policy recommendations of economists of the day were advanced with these problems in mind. Their objective was economic stability, which meant inflationary policies during periods of deflation. Their consistency in the pursuit of this objective is illustrated by the tight-money advice given to the Treasury by Keynes, Hawtrey, and Pigou during the postwar inflation.[13]

Keynes felt that the blame for the violent price fluctuations of the early postwar period belonged to "careless adherents of the quantity theory." After a summary of that theory in its unqualified form, according to which V and T are independent of M, so that the only influence of a change in M is a change in P in the same proportion, he continued:

> Now in "the long run" this is probably true. If, after the American Civil War, the dollar had been stabilised and defined by law at 10 percent below its present value, it would be safe to assume that M and P would now be just 10 per cent greater than they actually are and that the present values of V and T would be entirely unaffected. But this *long run* is a misleading guide to current affairs. *In the long run* we are all dead. Economists set themselves too easy, too useless a task if in tempestuous seasons they can only tell us that when the storm is long past the ocean is flat again.[14] (1923, ch. 3)

The concern that Keynes showed for the short run in his attack on the naive quantity theory in the *Tract* was maintained in the *Treatise* and *The General Theory*. Furthermore, the processes by which monetary disturbances lead in the first instance to variations in output are the same in all three works and depend principally upon their influence on expectations. For example, in his discussions of "the marginal efficiency of capital" and "the state of long-term expectation," he argued that by far the most important determinant of investment decisions is the relation between "the *supply price* of the capital asset" and the "series of prospective returns" which the businessman "expects to obtain from selling its output . . . during the life of the asset," that is, the relation between current and expected prices.[15] (1936, ch. 11–12)

I hope that it will become apparent below that Friedman shares with a long line of economists—at least from Cantillon to Keynes—a common view of the conditions necessary to the non-neutrality of money, a view in which uncertainty and disappointed expectations play the leading part, as well as the somewhat less common view (Keynes is the most important exception) that the best way to avoid those conditions is by the substitution of rules for the discretionary powers of central bankers and governments.

III. RULES VS. AUTHORITIES

> It may even be said that for the Rule of Law to be effective it is more important that there should be a rule applied always without exceptions, than what this rule is. Often the content of the rule is indeed of minor importance, provided the same rule is universally enforced. To revert to a former example: it does not matter whether we all drive on the left- or the right-hand side of the road so long as we all do the same. The important thing is that the rule enables us to predict other people's behaviour correctly, and this requires that it should apply to all cases—even if in a particular instance we feel it to be unjust. (Hayek, 1944, Ch. 6)

The pedestal upon which nineteenth-century monetary arrangements were placed by Westminster and the City of London after 1918 has tended to

obscure the intense dislike of the gold standard shared almost universally
by economists before the war. The lack of affection for the gold standard
in the 1920s by scholars and businessmen, who thought gold might not be
a bad thing sometime in the future, under favorable conditions, was mild
compared with the abhorrence of that system by their nineteenth-century
counterparts.

Marshall began his discussions of monetary reform with the premise that
the "evils of our present monetary system are great." He, Fisher, and others
agreed with Wicksell that the "excellence of our present monetary system
is . . . largely an illusion, and the danger of basing the whole of our economic
system on something so capricious as the occurrence of a certain precious
metal must sooner or later come to light."[16] The gold standard was seen as
deficient because of its inherent tendency, aggravated by the conduct of the
Bank of England, toward unwanted fluctuations in the quantity of money
and, as a consequence, instability of prices. The goal of students of monetary
affairs, respectable and otherwise, was to reform the monetary system in
such a way as to cause the quantity of money to vary in line with output.

In the United States, where before 1914 peculiarly inflexible banking laws
exacerbated the effects of the gold standard, this objective was expressed as
the need for an "elastic currency."[17] Fisher meant by this something very
different from the perfectly elastic money supply implied by the real bills
doctrine. The deficiencies of that doctrine are the opposite of those of a
rigid metallic standard. Hicks has stated the problem succinctly:

> In order for a credit system to work smoothly, it needs an institutional frame-
> work which shall restrain it on the one hand, and shall support it on the other.
> To find a framework which can be relied on to give support when it is needed,
> and to impose restraint just when it is needed, is very difficult; I do not think
> it has ever been perfectly solved. Even in this day we do not really know the
> answer. (1967b, pp. 158–159)

The concluding chapters of Wicksell (1898) and Fisher (1911) contain
excellent critical surveys of alternative schemes that had been put forward
with these objectives in mind, followed by their own proposals. Wicksell
maintained that the bank rate should respond to movements in the price
level, while Fisher preferred a variant of the gold exchange standard.

But even the carefully hedged schemes of Wicksell and Fisher left too
much scope for discretionary behavior to suit Englishmen, already painfully
aware of the dangerous possibilities that the existing system left for miscon-
duct by the central bank. The search for an optimal rule to govern the
monetary authority's actions had been the principal source of controversy
among English monetary economists during the first half of the nineteenth-
century, and the debate was resumed as soon as it became clear that the
Bank of England was mismanaging even the supposedly foolproof Bank
Charter Act of 1844. Marshall was one of those who proposed a version of
bimetallism in an attempt to reduce the variability of the reserve, since

fluctuations in the production of gold and silver might be less than perfectly correlated.[18] He also followed Mill (1848, p. 674) in advocating an increase in the reserve and a further reduction in the Bank's discretionary powers.

But Marshall was not sufficiently optimistic to believe that instability of the price level would be eliminated even if the proposed arrangements were adopted. Further measures were needed to reduce the uncertainty that is inevitable in a monetary economy. This brings us to the second part of his program, which was a form of indexation called the "tabular standard." The intention was to render "our standard of value . . . altogether independent of our currency." A government department "would publish from time to time the amount of money required to give the same general purchasing power as, say, £1 had at the beginning of 1887. . . . This standard unit of purchasing power might be called for shortness simply THE UNIT." No legislation, except of a permissive kind, would be required, but the courts would be instructed to "give every facility to contracts, wills and other documents made in terms of the unit. . . ." This new standard of deferred payments would enable industry to "avoid those heavy risks which are caused by a rise or fall in general prices."

Those who have learned classical economics from Keynes, from post-1936 textbooks, or even from many accounts by the classical economists themselves, might reasonably be surprised by these proposals for currency reform. After all, if there is no more insignificant thing than money, if variations in M lead only to proportional changes in P, with no real side effects, what does it matter how the central bank behaves or in what way the financial system is organized? Is it not inconsistent to argue that there is no more insignificant thing than money and, at the same time, take considerable pains to achieve monetary stability?[19]

One approach to the resolution of this apparent inconsistency is that the classical economists very much *wanted* money not to matter and felt that it *ought* not matter. If only monetary stability, and therefore the insignificance of money, could be achieved, then employers, workers, and consumers could go about their business, free of the distorting effects of unanticipated fluctuations in the value of money. Only under these conditions might all of the potential benefits of free exchange be realized. For under these conditions, quoting the passage immediately following Mill's "insignificance of money" statement,

the introduction of money does not interfere with the operation of any of the Laws of Value laid down in the preceding chapters. The reasons which make the temporary or market value of things depend on the demand and supply, and their average and permanent values upon their cost of production, are as applicable to a money system as to a system of barter. Things which by barter would exchange for one another, will, if sold for money, sell for an equal amount of it, and so will exchange for one another still, though the process of exchanging them will consist of two operations instead of only one. The relations of commodities to one another remain unaltered by money: the only new relation introduced is their relation to money itself; how much or how little money they will exchange for; in other words, how the Exchange Value of money itself is determined and this is not a question of any difficulty. . . . I shall therefore treat of the Value of Money in a chapter apart. (Mill, 1848, book III, ch. 7)

This passage is as much a value judgment by Mill of how the world *ought to be* as it is descriptive of how the world *will be* under certain conditions, that is, monetary stability. Currency reform was needed in order to bring those conditions about.

But this does not explain why the classical economists often failed to qualify their insignificance-of-money statements nor why many of their theoretical analyses and policy recommendations were based on the assumption that money did not matter under *any* conditions. In view of their familiarity with short-run monetary problems, their frequent espousals of this position look like a deliberate effort to mislead. Before judging them too harshly, however, we must try to understand their motives.

A large body of public and "unorthodox" economic opinion argued for discretionary monetary policy as a means of promoting a variety of goals. Much of this opinion favored monetary and price stability. But much tended to be more opposed to deflation than inflation and some of it can even be classified as inflationary. The classical economists felt—"felt" is the appropriate word, because they had not "proved" this result within any rigorous theoretical short-term disequilibrium framework—that discretionary policies would have more bad effects than good. The long history of ill-conceived and badly managed currency schemes, in Britain and elsewhere, was very much in their minds. The *practical* case against a managed currency appeared overwhelming. But no equally compelling *theoretical* refutation of the beneficial inflation argument of the preclassical economists and nineteenth-century popular opinion had been developed. In fact, Mill had earlier admitted the possibility of achieving increased production through monetary expansion. He believed with Thornton that the mischief arising from monetary stimuli would dwarf any conceivable short-term benefits.[20] Still, if some benefits, however short-lived, are realized, is it not possible that the electorate, or the government, may place a higher weight on the immediate advantages of inflation than on the more distant costs?[21] Moreover, might not enlightened and intelligent governments succeed in substantially reducing those costs? Since the classical economists were unable to make a convincing theoretical case for negative answers to these questions, they chose either to ignore or to deny the problem. Hicks describes the change in the way that Mill approached this dilemma as follows.

There is no doubt at all that when Mill wrote that essay ["Of the Influence of Consumption upon Production"] he was on what we have been calling Hume's side. But it is a remarkable thing that when we turn to Mill's *Principles*. . .Mill appears . . . to be just a hard-boiled "classic." The argument of the essay is not withdrawn, but it is just not there. I feel sure that we can best explain Mill's position by supposing that he always held to what he had said in the essay, but he did not want to emphasize it, for he held that it was *dangerous*. (1967b, p. 163)

We have already seen that Mill's capacity for ignoring the real effects of monetary upheavals was not fully communicated to his successors. And by the 1920s and 1930s, whatever one's attitude toward the effectiveness of monetary policy as a means of increasing employment, it was not possible for any monetary economist seriously to deny that significant fluctuations in money meant trouble. Pigou, Robertson, Hawtrey, and Keynes were deeply involved in discussions about the appropriate conduct of monetary policy. But the area of agreement was much larger than that of conflict. In particular, all deplored the prevailing policy of subordinating domestic stability to the exigencies of the gold standard. Keynes, despite his fondness of the maverick's role, was representative of the academic view when he argued that the money supply should be governed by the objective of "stability of trade, prices, and employment" (1923, p. 153). But the policy prescriptions of English economists were seldom much more detailed than this. Even Hayek, in his 1931 lectures at the LSE, was reluctant to propose a hard-and-fast rule in light "of the enormous difficulties of the problem of the elimination of disturbing monetary influences, difficulties which monetary reformers are always so inclined to underrate."[22] (1931, pp. 117–118)

The vigorous advocacy of inflexible rules, taking all discretionary powers away from the monetary authorities, was left to Chicago. Their focus on the short-run effects of monetary disturbances distinguishes Simons, Mints, and Friedman from the classical economists, who were concerned first of all with the problems of distribution and resource allocation under conditions of what we call long-run equilibrium. But I believe there is a strong link between the two schools of thought. I believe that we will achieve a better understanding of the Chicago economists, and perhaps become more sympathetic to them, if we see their policy prescriptions, like the prescriptions of Marshall and Fisher, as attempts to secure the kind of world that Mill assumed.

Friedman has on more than one occasion stressed his affinity with Mill. For example:

The quantity of money in general appears not to be an important factor affecting secular changes in real magnitudes. They are determined primarily by such basic phenomena as the kind of economic system, the qualities of the people, the state of technology, the availability of natural resources, and so on. These, not monetary institutions or policy, are the critical factors that ultimately determine the "wealth of nations" and of their citizens. In general, the major long-run impact of the quantity of money is on nominal magnitudes, and especially on the absolute level of prices. Our conclusions are in no way inconsistent with that celebrated—and much misunderstood—statement of John Stuart Mill [that is, the insignificance of money except when the machinery gets out of order].

> What we can now add to this is a much more explicit specification of what it
> means for the machinery of money to "get out of order." (1964, p. 278)

The explicit specification to which Friedman referred was not a statement
of his theory[23] but rather a summary of cyclical movements in money and
output, with emphasis on the variability of leads and lags. On the basis of
these empirical observations, Friedman "tentatively concluded" that "money
matters," that is, that the machinery "gets out of order . . . when the quantity
of money behaves erratically, when either its rate of increase is sharply
stepped up—which will mean price inflation—or sharply contracted—which
will mean economic depression—and especially when such erratic movements succeed one another" (1964, p. 278).

In his presidential address (1968), Friedman drew some lessons from
these observations for the conduct of the central bank. First, because the
"monetary machine has gotten out of order even when there has been no
central authority with anything like the power now possessed by the Fed"
(for example, "the 1907 episode and earlier banking panics"), "There is
. . . a positive and important task for the monetary authority—to suggest
improvements in the machine that will reduce the chances that it will get
out of order, and to use its own powers so as to keep the machine in good
working order" (1968, p. 106).

In addition, the Federal Reserve ought to behave in a steadier, more
predictable manner. "The Great Contraction might not have occurred at
all" and the "past few years . . . would have been steadier and more productive of economic well-being if the Federal Reserve had avoided drastic
and erratic changes of directions." That is, "a second thing monetary policy
can do is provide a stable background for the economy—keep the machine
well oiled, to continue Mill's analogy. Accomplishing the first task will contribute to this objective, but there is more to it than that" (1968, p. 106).

Friedman continues in a manner strikingly similar to the quotations from
Marshall and Keynes given above:

> Our economic system will work best when producers and consumers, employers
> and employees, can proceed with full confidence that the average level of prices
> will behave in a known way in the future—preferably that it will be highly stable.
> Under any conceivable institutional arrangements, and certainly under those
> that now prevail in the United States, there is only a limited amount of flexibility
> in prices and wages. We need to conserve this flexibility to achieve changes in
> relative prices and wages that are required to adjust to dynamic changes in
> tastes and technology. We should not dissipate it simply to achieve changes in
> the absolute level of prices that will serve no economic function. (1968, p. 106)

In short, Friedman's ultimate objective, like that of Marshall and Keynes,
is less to show that money matters under some conditions than to produce
conditions such that money does not matter. Friedman is a faithful follower
of his teachers in this respect. Henry Simons, for example, wrote that "the
liberal creed demands the organization of our economic life through indi-

vidual participation in a game *with definite rules*. It calls upon the state to provide a stable framework of rules within which enterprise and competition may effectively control and direct the production and distribution of goods" (1936, p. 160).

Administrative discretion may be desirable or necessary in some areas, but "it is utterly inappropriate in the money field. An enterprise system cannot function effectively in the face of extreme uncertainty as to the action of monetary authorities or, for that matter, as to monetary legislation. We must avoid a situation where every business venture becomes largely a speculation on the future of monetary policy" (p. 161).

As the best means of attaining a monetary framework in which uncertainty would be minimized (i.e., in which "a neutral money" [p. 163] would be achieved), Simons looked to the "ultimate establishment of a simple, mechanical rule of monetary policy" (p. 170), preferably "the fixing of the quantity of circulating media" (p. 163). But the time was not yet ripe for adoption of such a rule, which to be effective required competition in labor and product markets and substantial alterations in the financial structure. Discretionary policies, designed to achieve stable prices, would be necessary for some time, because prevailing financial arrangements contributed both to "sharp changes" in velocity and "the abundance of what we may call 'near-moneys'—with the difficulty of defining money in such a manner as to give practical significance to the conception of quantity" (p. 171).

We know that Friedman's advocacy of a money supply rule has been stronger than Simons was willing to make. The last section of this paper is devoted to an examination of the consistency, or lack thereof, of Friedman's rule with his monetary theory. The intervening sections present the results of my efforts to understand that theory.

IV. THE STABILITY OF A FREE-MARKET ECONOMY

There is a current tendency to look upon a competitive economy as highly unstable. On the contrary, Western industrial economies have shown an impressive degree of stability and resistance to shock in the light of the unstable monetary conditions under which they have been forced to operate. (Mints, 1950, p. 197)

The case for rules, begun in the preceding section, is not yet complete. Constraints on the authorities to behave in a predictable (that is, non-destabilizing) manner are not by themselves sufficient to guarantee economic stability. Also required is stability in the behavior of the private sector.

Friedman's claim that the demand for money is stable is well known.[24] Also well known (although occasionally forgotten), and equally important for his theoretical framework, and especially for his policy prescription, is his argument that the consumption function is stable.[25] Certainly, the opposition to discretionary policies, designed to counterbalance potentially

destabilizing shifts in the behavior of the private sector is most convincing
in a world in which such shifts are nonexistent or weak.[26] Friedman argued
that the results reported in *A Theory of the Consumption Function* suggested
that even the Keynesian system—properly understood—is more stable than
is commonly supposed. His position on this point was that he rejected the
income-expenditure theory on other grounds, but if one were inclined to
accept that theory, the permanent income hypothesis lent a stability to it
that Keynesians had not recognized. The following quotation is taken from
the next-to-last paragraph of Friedman's book.

> In its short-run aspect, as an interpretation of cyclical fluctuations, the central
> role in the income-expenditure theory is played by the relation between con-
> sumption and current income. The permanent income hypothesis has, so far
> as I can see, no implications for the empirical validity or acceptability of this
> interpretation of cyclical fluctuations; that must be decided by comparing its
> predictions with the predictions of alternative theories. But it does have
> important implications for the form of the consumption function and, in
> consequence, for the cyclical characteristics of an economy for which the
> income-expenditure explanation of fluctuations holds. The permanent income
> hypothesis leads to an aggregate consumption function . . . in which current
> consumption is largely determined by past incomes. . . . The effect is almost
> certain to be a much smaller estimate of the marginal propensity to consume
> out of current income than would be obtained from a function that makes
> consumption dependent on current income alone. . . . The result is a smaller
> investment multiplier, and an inherently cyclically more stable system. . . . To
> avoid misunderstanding, I hasten to repeat that these are not intended to be
> assertions about the actual empirical characteristics of our economy; they are
> conditional assertions and dependent for their validity on the prior acceptance
> of the income-expenditure theory as an explanation of economic fluctuations.
> (1957, P. 238)

I would have thought the last thing suggested by these views is that the
empirical validity of income-expenditure theories must be judged by the
stability of the multiplier, as measured by the relationship between current
income and current consumption, or, alternatively, current autonomous
expenditures, with no allowance whatever for past or expected income
streams.[27] Yet this was the approach taken by Friedman and Meiselman.

V. FRIEDMAN AND SCHWARTZ

> Perhaps the most puzzling feature of postwar monetary developments is the
> coincidence of a relatively slow rate of rise in the stock of money with a fairly
> rapid rate of growth of money income. . . . Of the various explanations that
> have been offered, we are inclined to believe that the most fundamental is that
> it reflects changes in the public's expectations about the degree of future eco-
> nomic stability. (FS, 1963a, p. 14)

The following stories are, I believe, typical of those told by Friedman and
Schwartz.[28] Following their lead, let us begin with the post-Civil War period.
The wartime inflation had forced the suspension of convertibility of green-

backs. It was decided, following the war, to return to the gold standard at the prewar exchange rate. Because foreign prices fell, this required a 50 percent reduction in prices between 1865 and 1879. After some fluctuations immediately following the war, the stock of money remained remarkably stable from 1872 to 1879 and wholesale prices fell continuously at a fairly even rate—about 6.5 percent per year. During this period, output grew steadily at annual rates between 5 and 7 percent.

The years following the return to the gold standard in 1879, on the other hand, were years of extreme monetary uncertainty. The return to a system of fixed exchange rates meant that the domestic money supply and price level were subject to the vagaries of the balance of payments—to foreign prices and to the size of American harvests relative to those in Europe. For example, because of good weather in the United States, combined with bad weather in Europe in 1879 and 1880 (presumably a heavenly reward for the seven preceding years of monetary responsibility), agricultural exports led to an increase in the money supply at an average rate of 16 percent per year during the three years 1879 to 1882. Prices and output also rose rapidly. However, due to the worldwide deflation, the next fifteen years were years of price decline in the United States, except after particularly good harvests.[29]

The deflation gave rise to the Populist movement, which hoped to halt the decline in prices by increasing the money supply through the free coinage of silver. The Populists became an important political force, and the fear that they would succeed in bringing about a monetary expansion and a rise in prices placed the gold standard in jeopardy and induced a series of bank panics and flights from the dollar in the 1890s. Finally, the export of gold from South Africa reversed the decline in prices and ended the agitation for silver. But the intervening period was one of great instability of money, prices, and output—although the *average* rate of growth of output was as large as in the period 1865–1879.

In comparing these two periods, 1865–1879 and 1879–1897, as well as other intervals, Friedman and Schwartz concluded that, over long periods,

> generally declining or generally rising prices had little impact on the rate of growth [of output], but the period of great monetary uncertainty in the early nineties produced sharp deviations from the long-term trend. (p. 93)
> Apparently the steadiness of the price movement is more important than the direction. (p. 242)

They make this point again and again, writing as follows toward the end of their book: "Apparently the forces determining the long-run rate of growth of real income are largely independent of the long-run rate of growth of the stock of money, so long as both proceed fairly smoothly. But marked instability of money is accompanied by instability of economic growth" (p. 678).

To the extent that changes in money and prices proceed smoothly and are foreseen, money does not influence economic activity. But sudden and unforeseen monetary disturbances produce fluctuations in output. We see a close connection here and elsewhere between FS's descriptions of historical periods and Mill's argument that changes in the money supply that people expect and upon which they can plan allow employment, output, and other economic variables to be determined by nonmonetary forces.

FS also argued that the intensity of the Great Depression was due to the destabilizing behavior of the monetary authorities. They accepted that the stock-market crash was partly a symptom of underlying forces making for a contraction. But more important, it changed the atmosphere within which businessmen and others made their plans. It spread uncertainty and, possibly, reduced the willingness of consumers and firms to spend—which had as its counterpart an increased desire for money balances. The decrease in velocity during 1929 and 1930 was consistent with other periods of recession.

However, the decline in economic activity during this period was mild— it looked like just another contraction. There was no distrust of banks, and banks did not attempt to build up reserves. The fall in the money supply was entirely due to a reduction in Federal Reserve credit. The restrictive policy of the Fed, combined with crop failures, led to the first banking crisis in October 1930. (Federal Reserve credit fell 30 percent between October 1929 and October 1930.)

This banking crisis did not have a significant impact on economic activity. In fact, industrial production revived somewhat between January and April 1931.

But the restriction of Federal Reserve credit and the decline in the money supply continued, leading to the second banking crisis in March 1931. From then on, it was all downhill. Bank failures induced increases in both the public's demand for currency and the demand by banks for reserves—a scramble for liquidity.

Finally, the Federal Reserve began large-scale open-market purchases in April 1932, which, combined with gold inflows, served first to moderate the decline in money and then to bring about its increase. The money supply began to increase in October 1932 and the recovery in economic activity began shortly thereafter.

FS argue that postwar fluctuations in economic activity, like those in the past, continue to be susceptible to explanation in terms of rates of change in money and prices. They do not accept the view that is frequently advanced (and has been a recurring theme since the 1880s in both Britain and America): that because of the growth of monopolistic price- and wage-fixing powers of large corporations and unions, economic models that assume flexibility in actual and expected prices are no longer relevant to the world as it actually exists. Deviations of actual from expected price movements play as large a role as ever in their analysis. Consider, for example, FS's discussion of the 1948–1949 contraction in the United States. Typically in American history, declines in output and employment have been associated not with decreases in the money stock but with slowdowns in the rate of increase of M. Recessions that have been accompanied by even mild absolute declines in money, such as 1929–1933 and 1937–1938, have with one exception been severe. The exception was 1948–1949, when the money supply fell but the recession was mild and short-lived. For FS, "the reason is not far to seek. . . . In the immediate postwar years, the public . . . anticipated a substantial decline in prices at some future date" (p. 597). But, in fact, prices fell only slightly, much less than had been expected. The failure of the feared postwar deflation to develop resulted in an upward revision of price expectations, and those businessmen and other potential spenders who had been holding back on their purchases of durable goods now began to spend.

Recent events in Britain, America, and some other countries have been a traumatic experience for many economists. For years we have been told and the textbook Keynesian model has implied that inflation and unemployment are tradeoffs; we must have either one or the other. But now we have both. However, while this is a paradox when considered within the framework of what has become the orthodox macroeconomic model, it is not inconsistent with Friedman's view of economic processes, in which it is not inflation or deflation that is relevant to the determination of output and employment but, rather, price movements relative to anticipated prices. Within this framework, unemployment may coexist with either inflation or deflation.

VI. FRIEDMAN, MEISELMAN, AND ST. LOUIS

The crucial questions are (a) whether investment or the stock of money can better be regarded as subject to independent change, and to changes that have major effects on other variables, and (b) whether the multiplier . . . or velocity . . . is the more stable. (FM, 1963, p. 169)

So far, we have seen that (1) Friedman's view of the appropriate role of government depends upon stable forms of behavior by nongovernmental units, where this requirement is satisfied at least in the cases of the public's demands for consumption goods and money (sections III and IV), and (2) the effects of money on economic activity depend upon surprise and are highly unpredictable (sections II and V). Pursuant to the last point, consider the following statements by Friedman in a Joint Economic Committee document (1958), reprinted in *The Optimum Quantity of Money and Other Essays*:

One proposition about the effect of changes in the stock of money and prices that is widely accepted and hardly controversial is that large and unexpected changes in prices are adverse to the growth of output—whether these changes are up or down. . . .

So much is agreed. The more controversial issue is the effect of moderate change in prices. (p. 182)

Then, after summarizing opposing positions—that rising prices may be favorable to, adverse to, or without effect on growth—Friedman writes that "historical evidence on the relation between price changes and output changes is mixed and gives no clear support to any one of these positions." (p. 183)

He then recounted historical episodes in which output grew rapidly during periods of (1) sharply falling prices, (2) moderately falling prices, (3) stable prices, and (4) rising prices. He also referred to evidence that falling prices may be associated with either rising or falling output.

All in all, perhaps the only conclusion that is justified is that either rising prices or falling prices are consistent with rapid economic growth, provided that the price changes are fairly steady, moderate in size, and reasonably predictable. The mainsprings of growth are presumably to be sought elsewhere. But unpredictable and erratic changes of direction in prices are apparently as disturbing to economic growth as to economic stability. (p. 184)

After these statements, one might reasonably suppose that if Friedman had been asked to guess the correlation between money and output in the United States between 1867 and 1960, he would have said "not significantly different from zero." Certainly, he would not have based the defense of his framework of analysis on such a correlation. But he and Meiselman in fact took quite the opposite position in their paper for the Commission on Money and Credit. They pointed to the higher correlation between money and consumption (in both nominal and real terms) than between autonomous expenditure and consumption as evidence that (1) monetary policy is superior to fiscal policy as a means of controlling output and (2) the demand for money is more stable than the consumption function; that is, velocity is more stable than the multiplier.

The entire approach by FM was contrary to all of Friedman's early work. This exercise in the comparison of correlations between the two simplest fine-tuning models imaginable could not possibly have had any implications for the validity of Friedman's approach to the explanation of the relations between money and output—nor of the validity of the approaches of any of Friedman's predecessors considered in section II above, including Keynes.[30] Yet it was followed by Andersen and Jordan (1968) and others, especially at the Federal Reserve Bank of St. Louis,[31] and formed the first of a series of steps that led to an attitude among monetarists that is reminiscent of the early Keynesians. Their claims regarding the certainty of the influence of money grew more confident, although Friedman himself was ambivalent. Consider, for example, his "Dialogue" with Walter Heller (1969); after quoting from his 1958 Joint Economic Committee paper (pp. 48–49) and emphasizing the impossibility of making precise predictions about economic activity on the basis of monetary changes, he later (p. 60) argued that "one thing that came out of that controversy [over FM] is that everyone agreed that the monetary magnitudes did have an important and systematic influence."

The schizophrenia in this exchange with Heller is also apparent in Friedman's other writings of the late 1960s and early 1970s. His position varied from one that is highly consistent with Friedman and Schwartz, as expressed in his presidential address, to statements that are closely akin to the fine-tuning implications of Friedman and Meiselman.[32] But the latter personality increasingly showed signs of dominance as Friedman seemed to come more and more under the influence of FM and the monetarists.

VII. FRIEDMAN'S MODEL?

To understand is to forgive. A cynic might retort that to be intelligible is to be found out. (Hawtrey, 1928, p. 65)[33]

We have seen two Professor Friedmans: one represented by the uncompleted suggestion of a model in which the influence of money on output may be highly variable and cannot be predicted without detailed knowledge of the state of expectations and the nature of adjustment processes, the other by the single-equation model, in which, quite simply, current output is determined by the current level of M. I believe the first is consistent with Friedman's historical discussions and his opposition to discretionary monetary policy—with Friedman and Schwartz, Friedman's *Program for Monetary Stability*, and his presidential address. The second, the model of Friedman and Meiselman, is inconsistent with all of these. Nevertheless, the latter statement was for several years widely accepted, by friends and foes, as *the* empirical representation of Friedman's theory, and occasionally, with modifications such as the introduction of lags, came to be synonymous with "monetarism."

Criticisms of Friedman's theory focused on the Friedman-Meiselman–St. Louis (that is, monetarist) model. But Friedman accepted none of these criticisms, and confusion, instead of enlightenment, was the main product of the controversy. A large part of the confusion was due to Friedman's ambivalence, discussed at the end of the preceding section—by his attempted simultaneous attachment to FS and FM. Although his stated positions seemed to grow closer to FM, when he was attacked on those grounds he tended to deny the validity of criticisms in terms reminiscent of FS.

An example of the frustration of Friedman's critics was shown by James Tobin during the exchange that followed publication of his "Money and Income: Post Hoc Ergo Propter Hoc?" (1970a). Tobin's criticism was directed at that version of monetarism in which the tendency of cyclical turning points in M to lead turning points in money income, Y, is adduced as convincing evidence that changes in M *cause* changes in Y.[34] He presented two models: (1) an "ultra-Keynesian model," in which money exerts no influence on income but still leads income, and (2) a "Friedman model," in which M lags Y, even though the direction of causation runs strongly from the former to the latter. In short, Tobin's paper presented an interesting illustration of the often repeated view that observed timing relationships between M and Y imply nothing about causation.

Friedman fended off this apparently telling blow to monetarism by denying that he had ever held the monetarist views attributed to him by Tobin, and then summarizing his *real* position in moderate, unexceptional Friedman and Schwartz terms. Constructive response in the face of these tactics was impossible, and Tobin could only give vent to his frustration as follows: "I am continually perplexed by Friedman's propensity in professional debate to evade by verbal quibbling the responsibility and the credit for the characteristic propositions of 'monetarism' associated with his name" (1970b, p. 329).

I think we are now in a position to understand the behavior that has perplexed Tobin and so many others. This understanding comes with the realization that *Friedman has never been a monetarist*—if we understand monetarism in its most popular Friedman-Meiselman–St. Louis form as the assertion that money determines output in a systematic, predictable manner[35]—and that he has never, deep down, abandoned the views that Friedman and Schwartz shared with Mill, Marshall, and Keynes. The remainder of this section is devoted to the outlines of a model consistent with these latter views. All traces of FM are expunged. I believe such an approach is necessary to the development of a model consistent with Friedman's monetary rule and FS's monetary history. Furthermore, this approach has recently received support both from a decided shift in the economics profession's understanding of Friedman and from Friedman's own writings, most notably his Nobel lecture (1977), which consists essentially of a restatement of his presidential address and its application to events of the 1970s. Academic writers nowadays seldom refer, as did Tobin in the article cited above, to FM and monetarism. Instead, attention is paid increasingly to the presidential address—to the "natural rate of unemployment" and its independence of monetary phenomena.[36]

Now let us state Friedman's model—or as much of it as he has told us. The demand sides of the money and commodity markets present few problems. His specification of the demand for money as a function of income, wealth, the opportunity cost of holding money, and expected interest rates is pure Keynes;[37] and his representation of the demand for consumption goods as dependent principally on expected future income, suitably discounted by interest rates and risk, is unalloyed Fisher (1907, 1930).[38] Friedman has devoted less attention to the determination of aggregate investment. However, he has indicated acceptance of the widely held theory that firms undertake productive activities up to the point at which their marginal yields equal the cost of capital.[39] This is contrary to FM's assumption that aggregate investment is completely autonomous. But we cannot infer from Friedman's non-FM discussions that investment, any more than consumption or the demand for money, has no autonomous components, that is, that it is entirely determined within his system. He is usually careful to point out that all of these behavioral relations are subject to unpredictable and imperfectly understood shifts due to changes in tastes, technology, anticipations, and other factors. (However, these shifts are apparently of little practical importance, for they seldom account for more than 5 percent of the variation of the dependent variable in Friedman's empirical work.)

On the supply side, the nominal money stock has been unpredictable and extremely volatile, both under the pre-World War I gold standard and since the formation of the Federal Reserve. The correction of this important source of instability is Friedman's chief goal and will be considered in detail in the next section.

The supply of commodities is a more difficult question and is that part of Friedman's system which has received the most attention in recent years. Discussion has focused on Friedman's (1966, 1968) rediscovery, with Phelps (1967), of "the natural rate of unemployment." In the introduction to "The Role of Monetary Policy" (1968), in what now appears to have been a reaction to FM and other monetary fine-tuning models, Friedman argued that "we are in danger of assigning to monetary policy a larger role than it can perform, in danger of asking it to accomplish tasks that it cannot achieve, and, as a result, in danger of preventing it from making the contribution that it is capable of making" (p. 99).

In particular, we cannot reasonably expect the monetary authority to be able, with any consistency, to achieve a target level of unemployment different from the natural rate. This is because,

> at any moment of time, there is some level of unemployment which has the property that it is consistent with equilibrium in the structure of *real* wage rates. At that level of unemployment, real wage rates are tending on the average to rise at a "normal" secular rate, i.e., at a rate that can be indefinitely maintained so long as capital formation, technological improvements, etc., remain on their long-run trends. A lower level of unemployment is an indication that there is an excess demand for labor that will produce upward pressure on real wage rates. A higher level of unemployment is an indication that there is an excess supply of labor that will produce downward pressure on real wage rates. The "natural rate of unemployment," in other words, is the level that would be ground out by the Walrasian system of general equilibrium equations, provided there is imbedded in them the actual structural characteristics of the labor and commodity markets, including market imperfections, stochastic variability in demands and supplies, the cost of gathering information about job vacancies and labor availabilities, the costs of mobility, and so on. (p. 102)

Attempts to reduce unemployment below the natural rate by means of monetary expansion (that is, the achievement of a Phillips curve trade-off) can only be temporarily successful. However, these temporary effects may be substantial and long-lived. Suppose, for example, that we start from a situation characterized by price stability and a rate of unemployment equal to the natural rate, which exceeds 3 percent. Now suppose, in an effort to reduce the rate of unemployment to 3 percent,

> the authority increases the rate of monetary growth. This will be expansionary. By making cash balances higher than people desire, it will tend initially to lower interest rates and in this and other ways to stimulate spending. . . .
>
> To begin with, much or most of the rise in income will take the form of an increase in output and employment rather than in prices. People have been expecting prices to be stable, and prices and wages have been set for some time in the future on that basis. It takes time for people to adjust to a new state of demand. Producers will tend to react to the initial expansion in aggregate demand by increasing output, employees by working longer hours, and the unemployed, by taking jobs now offered at former nominal wages. This much is pretty standard doctrine.
>
> But it describes only the initial effects. Because selling prices of products typically respond to an unanticipated rise in nominal demand faster than prices of factors of production, real wages received have gone down—though real wages anticipated by employees went up, since employees implicitly evaluated the wages offered at the earlier price level. Indeed, the simultaneous fall *ex post* in real wages to employers and rise *ex ante* in real wages to employees is what enabled employment to increase. But the decline in *ex post* real wages will soon come to affect anticipations. Employees will start to reckon on rising prices on the things they buy and to demand higher nominal wages for the future. "Market" unemployment is below the "natural" level. There is an excess demand for labor so real wages will tend to rise toward their initial level.
>
> Even though the higher rate of monetary growth continues, the rise in real wages will reverse the decline in unemployment, and then lead to a rise, which will tend to return unemployment to its former level. (pp. 103–104)

Friedman concluded that "there is always a temporary trade-off between inflation and unemployment; there is no permanent trade-off. The temporary trade-off comes not from inflation per se, but from unanticipated inflation, which generally means, from a rising rate of inflation" (p. 104).

Friedman repeated these arguments in his Nobel lecture (1977) and further argued that, in addition to the temporary effects of discrepancies between anticipated and realized monetary growth, employment may be permanently affected by monetary instability via the impact of the variability of inflation on the natural rate of unemployment. This is so, Friedman wrote, for two reasons. First, an increased variance of the rate of inflation induces expensive and, in an uncertain environment, imperfect arrangements by the public in their attempts to accomplish what (so Mill, Marshall, and Friedman have contended) the government should have achieved on their behalf: the neutrality of money. These arrangements include indexing and the frequent renegotiation of contracts. In addition, "a second related effect of increased volatility of inflation is to render market prices a less efficient system for coordinating economic activity"[40] (p. 467).

The relevant information transmitted by the price system is about *relative* prices.

> But the information in practice is transmitted in the form of *absolute* prices. . . . The more volatile the rate of general inflation, the harder it becomes to extract the signal about relative prices from the absolute prices. . . . At the extreme, the system of absolute prices becomes nearly useless, and economic agents resort either to an alternative currency or to barter, with disastrous effects on productivity. (p. 467)

As a consequence, Friedman argued, an increased volatility of inflation clearly reduces economic efficiency and output. The effect on "recorded unemployment" is less clear. The increase in uncertainty and the necessity for more frequent adjustments may mean either labor hoarding or a reluctance on the part of employers to take on workers in response to possibly ephemeral shifts in demand or relative prices. However, it "seems plausible" to Friedman that (1) "the slow adjustment of commitments and the imperfections of indexing" and (2) "the increased amount of noise in market signals" will raise "the average level of unemployment . . . , at least during the period when institutional arrangements are not yet adapted to the new situation."

The ways in which money matters in these discussions may be summarized under three headings: (1) direct quantity effects of unanticipated shifts in demand, (2) further quantity effects as these demand shifts cause actual prices to deviate from expected prices, and (3) reductions in economic efficiency as resources are diverted to the development and policing of arrangements made necessary by the *possibility* of unanticipated price changes, whether realized or not. Friedman has not presented even the beginnings of a formal framework within which these effects may be explained. Nor, as far as I am aware, has anyone else attempted to achieve all of Friedman's results within the confines of one model. Nor do I know of a formal model of the aggregate output and employment effects of item (3) alone, the costs associated with the public's attempts to defend themselves against the Federal Reserve System.

However, substantial formal work has been done in areas (1) and (2). Furthermore, most writers have explicitly drawn parallels between their results and Friedman's. Work in these two areas has not overlapped a great deal, and in most cases, we do not know which of the various rationalizations of his results that Friedman accepts. Nevertheless, it may be useful, in the absence of other formal evidence, to review the sources of what *might* be systematic statements of parts of Friedman's theory of aggregate supply.

The first set of effects, (1), in which quantity responses precede price changes, is commonly associated with Hume (1750)[11] and, more recently, Clower (1965) and Barro and Grossman (1971, 1976). To those who accept Leijonhufvud's (1968) interpretation of Keynes, in which the distinguishing feature of *The General Theory* was the analysis of disequilibrium quantity adjustments in markets that fail to clear by means of equilibrating price adjustments, this is another example of the similarities between the theories of Keynes and Friedman.

However, most writers who have connected their theories with Friedman's have focused on area (2), that is, on unanticipated price movements. Specifically, they have presented equilibrium-trading models (that is, where flexible prices clear markets) in which (a) deviations from the natural rate of unemployment (or the natural rate of output) depend upon random shocks and unanticipated price changes and (b) expectations are rational (that is, are calculated by using all available information). The essential parts of the supply sides of these models can be summarized in terms of notation similar to that used by Gordon (1976). Let

$$U_t = U_t^n - \beta(p_t - p_t^e) + \gamma_t \tag{1}$$

where U_t and U_t^n are the actual and natural rates of unemployment in period t, p_t is the actual rate of inflation, p_t^e is the rate "generally anticipated at the beginning of the period," β is a constant, and γ_t is "an exogenous 'supply shock' (with mean zero) outside of the control of the policy makers."[42] The "expectation of inflation is 'rational' in the sense of Muth (1961), i.e., an unbiased predictor of actual inflation (p_t) given all the information available just before the period begins, say I_{t-1}" (Gordon, 1976). The available information is usually assumed to consist of observations on current and past values of all endogenous and exogenous variables through period $t-1$. This conditional expectation of inflation may be written

$$p_t^e = E(p_t|I_{t-1}) \tag{2}$$

"This implies that p_t and p_t^e differ only by a random forecast error ε_t,

$$p_t - p_t^e = p_t - E(p_t|I_{t-1}) = \varepsilon_t \tag{3}$$

where ε_t is uncorrelated with everything known before the beginning of the period" (Gordon, 1976). Substituting (3) into (1), we see that the actual rate of unemployment differs only randomly from the natural rate. This means that the authorities cannot systematically influence employment or, therefore, output. But they may be able to achieve ephemeral effects by surprising the public—i.e., by policies that cause prices to differ from those anticipated by the public.

The specification of aggregate commodity demand in these models varies considerably. But most specifications are similar to the supply side in making provision for exogenous random shocks and unanticipated price changes.[43]

These models are all consistent with Friedman (1968)[44] in their main conclusions: (1) short-term unemployment-inflation (Phillips curve) tradeoffs are possible, but (2) long-run classical conclusions regarding the neutrality of money continue to hold, and (3) inflation is consistent with both high or low, rising or falling, employment. This last relation—or set of relations—is the principal subject of Friedman's Nobel lecture (1977).

In that lecture, Friedman restated "the natural-rate hypothesis" and illustrated its long-run properties by supposing a shift from monetary conditions conducive to a constant price level to conditions producing a steady 20 percent inflation. The neutrality of money requires correct anticipations along with prices and contracts that reflect those anticipations.

> Ultimately, if inflation at an average rate of 20 percent per year were to prevail for many decades, these requirements could come fairly close to being met, which is why I am inclined to retain the long-long-run vertical Phillips curve. But when a country initially moves to higher rates of inflation, these requirements will be systematically departed from. And such a transitional period may well extend over decades. (p. 465)

We can almost hear the echo: *But in the long-long-run we are all dead.* And, like Keynes, Friedman has been vitally interested in the short run, during which money is not neutral. Specifically, either negatively sloped or positively sloped Phillips curves may exist in the short run. The apparent paradoxes of stagflation are easily explained. In a highly concentrated dose of the kind of empirical analysis contained in Friedman and Schwartz, the Nobel lecture presents a summary of five-year averages of rates of inflation and unemployment in seven developed countries from 1956 through 1975.

> According to the 5-year averages in table 1, the rate of inflation and the level of unemployment moved in opposite directions—the expected simple Phillips curve outcome—in five out of seven countries between the first two quinquennia (1956–60, 1961–65); in only four out of seven countries between the second and third quinquennia (1961–65 and 1966–70); and in only one out of seven countries between the final two quinquennia (1966–70 and 1970–75). (pp. 460, 463)

Again, consistent with FS and the natural rate hypothesis but contrary to FM, over long periods, "the rate of unemployment will be largely independent of the average rate of inflation" (p. 464).

Furthermore, short-term positive and negative correlations between unemployment and inflation are also consistent with the natural rate hypothesis, depending on the relation between anticipated and realized rates of inflation. In short, everything is explained.

But perhaps Friedman has explained too much. For not only has he explained all of history, but every conceivable future occurrence is subject to explanation by the natural rate hypothesis as he has specified it. One is reminded of Karl Popper's comparison of the theories of Marx, Freud, and

Adler to astrology, "with its stupendous mass of empirical evidence based on observation—on horoscopes and on biographies" (1962, p. 34):

> I began to feel more and more dissatisfied with these three theories—the Marxist theory of history, psychoanalysis, and individual psychology; and I began to feel dubious about their claims to scientific status. . . .
>
> . . . what worried me was neither the problem of truth, at that stage at least, nor the problem of exactness or measurability. It was rather that I felt that these . . . theories, though posing as sciences, had in fact more in common with primitive myths than with science; that they resembled astrology rather than astronomy.
>
> I found that those of my friends who were admirers of Marx, Freud, and Adler, were impressed by a number of points common to these theories, and especially by their apparent *explanatory power*. These theories appeared to be able to explain practically everything that happened within the fields to which they referred. The study of any of them seemed to have the effect of an intellectual conversion or revelation, opening your eyes to a new truth hidden from those not yet initiated. Once your eyes were thus opened you saw confirming instances everywhere: the world was full of *verifications* of the theory. Whatever happened always confirmed it. (pp. 34–35)

But what, asked Popper, was actually confirmed by these observations?

> No more than that a case could be interpreted in the light of the theory. But this meant very little, . . . since every conceivable case could be interpreted in the light of Adler's theory, or equally of Freud's. I may illustrate this by two very different examples of human behavior: that of a man who pushes a child into the water with the intention of drowning it; and that of a man who sacrifices his life in an attempt to save the child. Each of these two cases can be explained with equal ease in Freudian and in Adlerian terms. According to Freud the first man suffered from repression . . . , while the second man had achieved sublimation. According to Adler the first man suffered from feelings of inferiority (producing perhaps the need to prove to himself that he dared to commit some crime), and so did the second man (whose need was to prove to himself that he dared to rescue the child). I could not think of any human behaviour which could not be interpreted in terms of either theory. It was precisely this fact—that they always fitted, that they were always confirmed—which in the eyes of their admirers constituted the strongest argument in favour of these theories. It began to dawn on me that this apparent strength was in fact their weakness. (p. 35)

This weakness is, of course, incomplete specification, resulting in the impossibility of refutation. As with Marx, Freud, and Adler, the missing parts of Friedman's theory can be supplied, tailor-made, in response to each new observation. The missing part is usually the state of expectations, although other examples are given below. Popper would admit Friedman's theory of the relation between money and employment to scientific status only if its specification is completed such that it becomes "incompatible with certain possible results of observation"; only if, by the "risky predictions" implicit in the theory, it becomes "falsifiable, refutable, or testable" (Popper, 1962, pp. 36–37).[45]

This is an admission, of course, that the principal objective of this paper has not been achieved. I have failed to specify Friedman's model and the reader may justifiably feel cheated. But I have done all I can. I have told you everything of Friedman's model, if such it may be called, that I have been able to discover—and, I believe, all that he has revealed in print. And readers were warned at the outset not to expect too much. It should have been clear, from the beginning, that disappointment inevitably lies at the end of the only path left to us by Friedman and Mitchell. We may learn something of their theories, but not everything, for it is logically impossible to infer refutable theories from descriptions of observed phenomena in which everything is explained. There are no degrees of freedom in this approach to economic history; there are as many independent variables as observations. It seems that some new factor always crops up to account for each observation of any sign of inconsistency with previous explanations—such as the Boer War as a reason for the "puzzling" U.S. capital exports around the turn of this century, "the explicit measures to raise prices and wages undertaken with government encouragement and assistance" as a factor contributing to the surprisingly large rise in wholesale prices in 1933–37, or "changes in the public's expectations about the degree of future economic stability" in explanation of the increase in velocity between 1948 and 1960 (FS, 1963a, pp. 14, 140–146, 498–499).

But we should not be too hard on Friedman. He is not alone among economists in making excessive claims for an unverified and unverifiable theory. Moreover, I believe that he has provided valuable insights into the workings of a monetary economy under uncertainty. Probably more important in the long run (even if we are all dead), he has simultaneously stimulated (1) an increased awareness and understanding of the work of his predecessors and (2) attempts to build upon that work. If such a thing as a "Friedmanian revolution" does come about, at least we shall have reason to be thankful that, unlike the last revolution, it will not be accompanied by a sweeping rejection of earlier views.[46]

He has not yet given us a testable theory. But he has brought us closer to one.

VIII. FRIEDMAN'S RULE

Of all these schemes [not including money-supply rules], those which contemplate stabilization of price indexes are least illiberal; but they, too, are unsatisfying. They define programs in terms of ends, with little discussion of appropriate means; they call for an authority with a considerable range for discretionary action and would require much intelligence and judgment in their administration; and they would leave us exposed to continuous legislative (if not administrative) tinkering, since no particular price index has much greater inherent reasonableness than many others. (Simons, 1934, p. 169)

We saw at the end of section III that Henry Simons favored the eventual adoption of a monetary rule, but only if substantial reforms of the financial sector were first carried out. Lloyd Mints (1950), also of the University of Chicago, shared Simons' position. Milton Friedman's support of a money-supply rule has been less tentative than that of his teachers. Friedman would also like to see changes in the financial structure (1959a, pp. 100–101), but the importance of the rule far outweighs that of other reforms: "But, though important, these further [banking and fiscal] reforms are far less basic than the adoption of a rule to limit the discretion of the monetary authorities with respect to the stock of money" (1962a, p. 54).

Friedman's rule is described and supported at length in the last chapter of *A Program for Monetary Stability* and is stated succinctly as follows in *Capitalism and Freedom:*

> My choice at the moment would be a legislated rule instructing the monetary authority to achieve a specified rate of growth in the stock of money. For this purpose, I would define the stock of money as including currency outside commercial banks plus all deposits of commercial banks. I would specify that the Reserve System shall see to it that the total stock of money so defined rises month by month, and indeed, so far as possible, day by day, at an annual rate of X per cent, where X is some number between 3 and 5. The precise definition of money adopted, or the precise rate of growth chosen, makes far less difference than the choice of a particular definition and a particular rate of growth. (1962a, p. 54)

I believe Friedman's insistence on a money-supply rule is consistent with neither Friedman-Meiselman nor Friedman-Schwartz. The empirical work of FM, St. Louis, and the monetarists, which shows a close correspondence between money and output, clearly supports discretionary monetary policy. The model of FS, the presidential address, and the Nobel lecture, on the other hand, implies a rule but not a money-supply rule. A defense of the last assertion is the main objective of this section. But first let us consider the conditions under which rules, money-supply or not, are desirable.

Arguments for discretionary policies (that is, against rules) are most compelling in a world that is highly volatile and unpredictable even in the presence of steady and predictable behavior on the part of the government. In such a world, the apparent need for discretionary stabilization policies is combined with the strong possibility of success, at least in the short term, of those policies. We saw in section VII that the neutrality of money depends on the ability of economic agents to form unbiased estimates of future occurrences based on all of the past and current information that is available. This is no easy task, even with government cooperation. Furthermore, the more volatile the world, the greater the incentives for the government to withhold its cooperation, especially if the present is weighted much more heavily than the future.[47] Monetary policy can influence *real* events only if the private sector is surprised, only if the central bank succeeds in tricking the public. And a strategy of trickery is most likely to succeed in a volatile world. The conditions existing in such a system make it difficult for the public to understand and predict the pattern of central bank behavior, that is, to disentangle the responses and effects of central bank actions from the noise generated by the rest of the system.

This is why I cannot understand the eagerness of Friedman and Meiselman to demonstrate the "instability" of consumer behavior. If FM are right, that is, if the Friedman of *A Theory of the Consumption Function* is wrong, the case for discretionary policies is strengthened.

This does not mean that the acceptance of FM—or the belief that the public's behavior in other spheres causes unstable macroeconomic conditions—completely does away with the case for rules. After all, no matter how bad things are, an unrestrained central bank can always make them worse. I believe that Friedman would, if necessary, make this case and that, if he did so, he would be consistent with his own reading of the history of economic policy.[48] This contrasts with the inconsistency of Keynes. Friedman and Keynes are very much alike in their assessment of the history of economic policy: it is a history of almost unrelieved disaster.[49] But they have drawn very different lessons from this experience. For Friedman, the lesson is to take away the discretionary powers of policymakers. But Keynes recommended both an increase in those powers and the more vigorous use of existing powers.[50]

Now let us suppose the case for rules is made—because of the inherent stability of the economy in the absence of discretionary monetary policies and/or the inevitable incompetence of central banks. What is/are the appropriate rule or rules? Or to put the question only slightly differently: What rule of action should we require of the monetary authority? Without doubt, the set of possible answers, the set of candidates for policy rules that satisfies Friedman's objective of eliminating uncertainty in central bank behavior, is limited to possible central bank instruments. At the present time, these include security purchases, reserve requirements, direct lending to banks, regulations A to Z, and a host of other controls sought by and granted to the Federal Reserve—but not the money supply, however defined. The set of instruments that might be granted to the Federal Reserve in the future is, of course, quite large. But not large enough to achieve complete control over the money supply—unless we arbitrarily define M in some way (but necessarily with an economically ambiguous meaning) and supply the central bank with a police force approximately equal to that required for an effective incomes policy. The definition and enforcement of a specific level of wages is no more difficult than the definition and enforcement of some quantity of M.

Under present arrangements, the monetary base (high-powered money), H, is the sum of Federal Reserve security purchases and loans to banks, float, the monetary gold stock, credits to Special Drawing Rights accounts, and Treasury currency outstanding less Treasury cash holdings. Thus, not even the monetary base is an instrument of monetary policy. A large portion of what Roosa (1956) has called the Federal Reserve's "defensive responsibilities" is devoted to activities intended to offset fluctuations in the noncontrolled factors that affect the monetary base. As Federal Reserve personnel have often stressed, this is not an easy task.[51]

Predicting the impact of changes in H on M is even more difficult than controlling H. The connection between H and M may be written $M = mH$, where m is the money-multiplier and is defined differently for different specifications of M. Under most definitions, m depends on commercial bank reserve ratios (desired or required) and the distribution of total bank deposits between time and demand deposits and among banks with different preferences or subject to different reserve requirements. The total and the distribution of bank deposits in turn depend on the public's preferences with respect to holding currency and the time and demand deposits of the various banks. These preferences cannot be predicted with certainty. They depend upon current and expected income, wealth, interest rates, and service charges. They also depend upon expectations concerning future actions of the Federal Reserve. Current loans and loan commitments are influenced not only by current credit conditions, but also by expectations regarding the future course of monetary policy. Reserve adjustments by banks and portfolio adjustments by firms and households are not costless even within the sophisticated financial structure existing in the United States. The allocation of bank resources between reserves and earning assets and the allocation of the public's liquid assets among currency, time deposits, demand deposits, and other financial instruments depend upon expected flows of funds, which are in turn affected by current and future Federal Reserve actions.

In summary, to paraphrase Friedman's description of the link between M and the price level (1959a, p. 87), "the link [between central bank actions and M] is not direct and rigid, nor is it fully understood." Both H and m are imperfectly predictable. Furthermore, their unpredictability and volatility are very likely directly related to the degree of uncertainty about future monetary policy. I agree with Simons and Friedman that the difficulties in the way of the precise control of M are probably less than those that obstruct the direct control of the price level through monetary policy. But I believe that Friedman underestimates the problems involved in attempts to control M when he writes that

> even under present circumstances, the links between Reserve action and the money supply are sufficiently close, the effects occur sufficiently rapidly, and the connections are sufficiently well understood, so that reasonably close control over the money supply is feasible, given the will. I do not mean to say that the process would not involve much trial and some error, but only that the errors need not be cumulative and could be corrected fairly promptly. The process involves technical problems of considerable complexity, but they are of a kind

with which the System has much experience and for which the System has trained personnel. (Friedman, 1959a, p. 89)

Federal Reserve personnel have consistently declined the flattery offered by Friedman, and not entirely because they lack "the will" to control M. As I have indicated, the problems are more than "technical." They also include all the problems normally associated with attempts to explain and forecast the behavior of economic agents. Furthermore, these problems might be worsened by the adoption of a feedback or other adjustment mechanism that seems implicit in the above quotation—unless that mechanism is understood by all concerned. If it were not well understood, we would have a situation in which the Fed would be trying to achieve a particular level of M by using the instruments at its disposal to offset or accentuate (its predictions of) the public's actions; the public (banks and others) would be arranging their affairs partly on the basis of their guesses of what the Fed is going to do; and the Fed would be attempting to guess what the public is guessing what the Fed will do, etc., etc., etc. It is not difficult to envisage conditions under which the adoption of a money-supply rule might even lead to an increase in the volatility of M.

Some of these difficulties would be eliminated by the application of a 100 percent reserve requirement to commercial banks. Next to the money supply rule (and certainly consistent with that rule), this is the financial reform most often advocated by Friedman.[52] Under this proposal, it is argued, variations in the kinds of bank and nonbank preferences discussed above will not affect the money supply, defined as currency in the hands of the nonbank public plus adjusted deposits in commercial banks. This is not quite true. For example, suppose I repay my bank loan with currency earlier than the bank expects or, for whatever reason, before the bank is prepared to relend the funds received from me. My ownership of bank deposits is unchanged, my currency holdings have declined, and no other nonbank individual or organization has increased its deposit or currency holdings; that is, the money supply has fallen. Or suppose that in the normal course of business the nondepository part of the bank (see Friedman, 1959a, pp. 69–70) chooses to hold currency for transactions or portfolio diversification reasons. In each of these cases, the bank holds high-powered money in amounts that are imperfectly predictable and which affect the money supply.

This particular problem can be avoided merely by redefining money to include currency in the "investment" (nondepository) departments of banks. But this would not be the end of the story. It would only be the first of a series of arbitrary, economically meaningless definitions, supported by equally arbitrary regulations, made necessary by any program of absolute control of the money supply. For example, the definition of money to include commercial bank deposits requires that we define a "commercial bank." Up to now, Friedman appears satisfied to accept that commercial banks are whatever the comptroller of the currency and state banking officials say they are. But this is most unsatisfactory from the standpoint of Friedman's rule, especially at the present time, when other financial institutions are, for all practical purposes, able to create demand deposits, that is, money. Does Friedman really want licensing agencies to set the goals for monetary policy? I am sure he does not. But the definitional problem would, if anything, be worsened by freeing the financial system of regulation. For then we would have no comptroller to tell us what a bank is. We would have to decide for ourselves. And we might be faced with a myriad of different types of demand and other short-term financial assets that, from time to time and under various conditions, serve as means of payment. What would be the meaning of a money-supply rule then?

Simons recognized these problems and wanted to deal with them vigorously. He argued that "a liberal program of monetary reform should seek to effect an increasingly sharp differentiation between money and private obligations and, especially, to minimize the opportunities for the creation of effective money-substitutes . . . by private corporations" (1936, p. 182).

Earlier in his article he had gone into detail concerning the reforms made necessary by these objectives:

> This would mean, above all, the abolition of banking, i.e., of all special institutional arrangements for large-scale financing at short-term. Demand-deposit banking would be confined . . . to the warehousing and tranferring of actual currency. Savings banks would be transformed into strictly mutual institutions or investment trusts. Narrow limitation of the formal borrowing powers of other corporations would obviously be necessary, to prevent their effectively taking over the prerogatives of which banking corporations as such had been deprived. Further limitations might also be necessary with respect to financing via the open account (book credit) and instalment sales. (p. 171)

Simons saw clearly that these measures were only as the tip of the iceberg to the steps required to achieve complete control of the money supply:

> Banking is a pervasive phenomenon, not something to be dealt with merely by legislation directed at what we call banks. The experience with the control of note issue is likely to be repeated in the future; many expedients for controlling similar practices may prove ineffective . . . because of the reappearance of prohibited practices in new and unprohibited forms. It seems impossible to predict what forms the evasion might take or to see how particular prohibitions might be designed in order that they might be more than nominally effective. (p. 172)

Friedman has tended to ignore or underrate these problems and the costly measures required for their solution. My guess is that he prefers not to think about the problems because the solutions would be inconsistent not only with his economic goals of efficiency, stability, and the reduction of uncertainty, but also—and more importantly—with the larger goal of personal freedom. I think it is noteworthy that none of the problems of controlling the money supply, not even the 100 percent reserve requirement, was mentioned in *Capitalism and Freedom*.[53] The reason may have been a desire to be brief and nontechnical in a popular exposition. But the omission of any detailed discussion of the regulatory and other government activities that would be made necessary by a money-supply rule may at least partly have been due to a realization that such a discussion would have been out of place. It would not have been consistent with the rest of the book. The 100 percent reserve requirement and other actions implied by Friedman's rule would have startled those readers who had been persuaded in the early chapters that "the scope of government must be limited. Its major function must be to protect our freedom both from the enemies outside our gates and from our fellow citizens" (p. 2).

Friedman summarized the themes of the book as follows: "Its major theme is the role of competitive capitalism . . . as a system of economic freedom and a necessary condition for political freedom. Its minor theme is the role that government should play in a society dedicated to freedom and relying primarily on the market to organize economic activity" (p. 4).

For Friedman, narrow economic goals, such as material living standards, are not the most important objectives (although he believes that desirable economic consequences will best be attained in a political system that emphasizes personal freedom). His overriding objective is the extension of personal freedom. Economic policies should be judged mainly in terms of their contribution to this goal:

> Economic arrangements play a dual role in the promotion of a free society. On the one hand, freedom in economic arrangements is itself a component of freedom broadly understood, so economic freedom is an end in itself. In the second place, economic freedom is also an indispensable means toward the achievement of political freedom. (p. 8)

By avoiding discussion of the financial reforms that he and Simons had described elsewhere, Friedman escaped the necessity of explaining that remarkable anomaly in his system of political economy, of explaining why a system that emphasizes freedom in other areas requires such extensive central control and such severe limitations on private arrangements in the financial sphere.[54] After all, should not even bankers be free? (The answer to this question might be the ultimate test of one's commitment to personal freedom.)

The contradictions in which Friedman has involved himself by his attachment to a money-supply rule are completely unnecessary. Other rules, not inconsistent with his political and economic goals, are readily available within the existing financial structure. The most obvious candidate, and one requiring the least disruption of existing practices, is a rule for the conduct of open market operations. Such a rule might require the Federal Reserve to increase its holdings of some class of government (or private) securities by X percent per period. Once the class of securities is defined and the time pattern of purchases is specified, nothing further needs to be said. These purchases are an instrument of policy. They are completely under the control of the monetary authority. No definitional problems arise and no further regulations with regard to private actions need be imposed.

However, severe limitations would have to be placed on the activities of the monetary authority. Any rules imposed by Congress must not only be requirements for action, they must be understood to define *all* that the central bank is allowed to do. At the present time, the Federal Reserve System is able to exercise discretion in unpredictable ways in many areas. Even if the above open market operations rule were imposed, the Fed would still possess a capability for generating instability through arbitrary or otherwise unforeseen changes in regulation Q, reserve requirements, lending to banks, and other instruments now under their control. The elimination of the Fed's capacity for surprise requires either the elimination of these instruments or their strict governance by legislated rules.[55]

In addition to eliminating uncertainty regarding the behavior of the authorities and promoting personal freedom, the principle of choosing rules that can actually be implemented because they are direct instruments of policy is also conducive to economic stability—subject to the validity of Friedman's theoretical framework as I understand it. That framework depends crucially on the assumption of stability of private behavior in all areas—including the demands and supplies of all financial instruments—not just in the demand for money and the supplies and demands of commodities and labor discussed above. For example: "Aside from extreme liquidity crises, [the deposit-currency and deposit-reserve] ratios are relatively stable and change fairly gradually" (Friedman, 1959a, p. 68).

We saw above, in the summary of FS in section V, that Friedman has attributed liquidity crises to perverse actions of central banks, the destabilizing properties of the gold standard, or a combination of the two. The gold standard and other fixed-exchange-rate systems must be eliminated from consideration if one of our goals is economic stability. Then, in Friedman's framework, predictable behavior on the part of the central bank, as would follow from an open market operations rule, would be conducive to stability in financial markets, including the stability of both the money supply and velocity, no matter how defined—and it would no longer matter how M (or the corresponding V) is defined because of the stability of the relative quantities of financial assets that would result from the combination of steady central bank behavior with stability of private behavior. These consequences of a realistic rule would in turn contribute to price stability and, under the natural-rate hypothesis, steady growth in output and employment.

NOTES

The author is indebted to William Breen, Soumen De, George Horwich, Richard Rendleman, and Robert Taggart for comments on an earlier draft. Discussions with Terence Hutchison and Douglas Vickers were helpful at the beginning of the research that led to this paper. Dale Osborne has been a continuous source of good advice.

1. I think it is possible to say, without arrogance, because the same view is so widely held, that the IS-LM model presented in Friedman's "Theoretical Framework" papers in the *JPE* in 1970–71 bears little relation to his earlier work and cannot seriously claim to be representative of the kind of model that might have given rise either to the historical analysis of Friedman and Schwartz or to Friedman's policy rule. For example, see Brunner and Meltzer (1974, p. 72), Tobin (1974, p. 77), Teigen (1972), and Carleton (1976). Friedman himself disclaimed the "Theoretical Framework" in a reply to the critics of that model (1974a, p. 135).

2. "I cannot forecast to you the action of Russia. It is a riddle wrapped in a mystery inside an enigma." Broadcast, Oct. 1, 1939.

3. An example of Friedman and Schwartz's tendency to put forth mechanistic statements as explanations of economic phenomena occurs on page 561 during their discussion of World War II inflation: "The decline in velocity and of course also the accompanying rise in output explain why prices rose so much more slowly than the stock of money during the period of wartime deficits."

4. Perhaps algebraic summaries of complex theories that have required hundreds of pages of verbal presentation are bound to omit key elements and, at times, even be misleading. In any case, Friedman's mathematical rendering of Mitchell's business-cycle theory neglected several aspects of that theory which in his preceding disucssion Friedman had claimed to be essential. An example is Mitchell's emphasis on differential price movements, particularly wages and product prices. What Friedman presented, as in 1970, was in effect an IS-LM model that took no account of the labor market (or, therefore, aggregate supply) or disappointed expectations. There were some differences, however, from his 1970–71 model, differences that caused Friedman's statement of Mitchell's theory to be less unlike Friedman's theory than the later "Theoretical Framework." Friedman made Mitchell's consumption and investment depend on lagged income and interest so that the resulting model was identical to what would be obtained if a Samuelson (1939) multiplier-accelerator model were combined with interest-elastic investment, a Keynesian liquidity-preference function, and a money supply made endogenous by the separation of money into its deposit and currency components and the inclusion of endogenous currency and bank reserve demands.

5. "The quantity theory is in the first instance a theory of the *demand* for money. It is not a theory of output, or of income, or of the price level" (Friedman's emphasis). (1956, p. 4)

6. Friedman indicates an awareness of this in the sentence immediately following those quoted in the preceding footnote: "Any statement about these variables requires combining the quantity theory with some specifications about the conditions of supply of money and perhaps other variables as well." But his frequent identification of the quantity theory with the demand for money—see, for example, Friedman (1970a, pp. 194–202)—combined with his reluctance to supply the specifications to which he refers, has greatly hindered the profession's understanding of Friedman's model. Witness the debate over Friedman-Meiselman,

as if the validity of Friedman's model somehow rested solely on the stability of the demand for money compared to the stability of other behavioral relations.

7. See Culbertson (1964), Meltzer (1965), and Tobin (1965).

8. For example, Alchian (1970), Barro and Grossman (1976), Clower (1965), Leijonhufvud (1968), Lucas and Rapping (1969), Mortenson (1970), and Phelps (1970b).

9. The relevant passages from *Of Money* are too well-known to need repeating here. This important contribution to the development of monetary thought has been reprinted many times, including Rotwein (1970) and Walters (1973).

10. For discussions of Thornton's ideas, see chapter 10 of Hicks (1967a) and Hayek's *Introduction to Thornton (1802)*. Perhaps the finest critiques of eighteenth- and nineteenth-century monetary thought available are chapter 9 of Hicks (1967a) and Lecture I of Hayek (1931).

11. "Immediate" was Smith's favorite characterization of macroeconomic adjustments. The following quotation is from his discussion of the accumulation of capital (1776, book II, ch. 3): "Parsimony, and not industry, is the immediate cause of the increase of capital. . . . What is annually saved is as regularly consumed as what is annually spent, and nearly in the same time too. . . . That portion of his revenue which a rich man . . . annually saves . . . is immediately employed . . . by labourers, manufacturers, and artificers . . . ." Smith had earlier ridiculed the position that monetary disturbances might even temporarily have real effects and contended that the arguments by Locke and Hume along these lines constituted evidence of their guilt of the "absurd" opinion that "riches consist in money" (1763, part II, div. 2.9). See Schumpeter (1954, part II, ch. 7), Hutchison (1958), and Corry (1962) for useful discussions of Smith's role in the development of classical macroeconomics.

12. For the clearest statement by Ricardo that (1) variations in the quantity of money induce equiproportional variations in the price level, (2) the Bank of England has, if it chooses, effective control over the money supply, and (3) the cause of the contemporary inflation was the Bank's misapprehension that it was merely the instrument by which the community was supplied with the quantity of money requisite for trade, see *The High Price of Bullion* (Sraffa, III, pp. 88–93). Later, in Parliament, he gave his estimate of the length of the long-run: "If the Bank had doubled its circulation, it still would have no permanent effect upon the value of money. If such a thing had taken place, the general level of interest would be restored in less than six months" (Sraffa, V, p. 222).

13. Discussed in Howson (1973; 1975, ch. 2).

14. Keynes' symbols have been converted to the more familiar M, V, P, and T. All emphasis in quotations in this paper is unchanged from the original sources.

15. See Keynes (1937) for a development of the argument that the principal difference between short-run and long-run analysis (i.e., in his view, between *The General Theory* and classical economics) lies in the greater emphasis given by the former to uncertainty. See Shackle (1967) for the argument that Keynes' 1937 article contains his "ultimate meaning"; also see Kregel (1976) for a discussion of the role of uncertainty and expectations in the theories of Keynes and his contemporaries.

16. Marshall (1887), Wicksell (1906, part III, ch. 6).

17. For example, see Fisher (1911, ch. 13).

18. The disadvantages of bimetallism were to be avoided by letting the reserve consist of stamped bars, as in Ricardo's Ingot Plan, except that the bars should consist of both gold and silver. (Marshall, 1887)

19. In the words of Professor Sayers, "What I find more shattering [than the

assumption that the effect of increased money in forcing prices upwards is almost instantaneous] is the inconsistency between on the one hand this view that long-run effects come quickly and easily, and on the other hand Ricardo's continual complaints of the distributional evils of a variation in the value of money." (1953, p. 94)

20. ". . . periods of 'brisk demand' are also the periods of greatest production. . . . This, however, is no reason for desiring such times; it is not desirable that the whole capital of the country should be in full employment. For, the calculations of producers and traders being of necessity imperfect, there are always some commodities which are more or less in excess, as there are always some which are in deficiency. If, therefore, the whole truth were known, there would always be some classes of producers contracting, not extending, their operations. If *all* are endeavoring to extend them, it is a certain proof that some general delusion is afloat. The commonest cause of such delusion is some general, or very extensive, rise of prices (whether caused by speculation or by the currency) which persuades all dealers that they are growing rich. And hence, an increase of production really takes place during the progress of depreciation, as long as the existence of depreciation is not suspected; and it is this which gives to the fallacies of the currency school, principally represented by Mr. Attwood, all the little plausibility they possess. But when the delusion vanishes and the truth is disclosed, then those whose commodities are relatively in excess must diminish their production or be ruined: and if during the high prices they have built mills and erected machinery, they will be likely to repent at leisure." (1844, pp. 67–68)

21. See Phelps (1972).

22. Hayek feared the consequences of "a more or less arbitrarily managed currency" and indicated a slight preference for an invariant money supply. But he recognized several conditions under which such a rule ought to be relaxed.

23. ". . . we are still a long way from having a detailed and tested theory of the mechanism that links money with other economic magnitudes" (Friedman, 1961, p. 280).

24. See, especially, Friedman (1956). Friedman's position on this point differs from that of Simons, as indicated by the discussion at the end of section III.

25. It may be useful at this point to define stability. *Webster's New Collegiate Dictionary* gives three definitions, all applicable in greater or lesser degree to the present discussion: (a) "Steadiness or firmness of character, resolution, or purpose; constancy"; (b) "(Mech. & Aeronautics) That property of a body which causes it, when disturbed from a condition of equilibrium or steady motion, to develop forces or moments which tend to restore the body to its original condition"; (c) "(R. C. Ch.) A vow binding a monk for life to one monastery." The first definition is the layman's, which is the opposite of "volatility," the second corresponds to the economist's definition of "stability of equilibrium," and the third applies, more or less equally, to monetarists, Keynesians, and other "religious" groups. Friedman's use of "stability" in connection with, especially, the demand for money is the econometrician's definition, which is closely related to (a). That is, in Friedman's words, a stable demand for money or consumption goods is a stable function of a small number of significant variables (1956). An econometric theorist might similarly describe a stable function as one in which structural shifts do not occur over time, that is, in which observations "may be considered to come from the same population" (Johnston, 1972, p. 207). Also see Chow (1960). I think, taking all of Friedman's writings into account, he believes all of the above forms of stability to hold in the absence of arbitrary government behavior. Sometimes, as in the case of his "permanent" consumption function in the face of

volatile private investment of government spending, or in the case of his money-demand function when combined with a money-supply rule, one kind of stability (a) contributes to another (b).

26. Of course, such opposition could (and no doubt would) still be mounted even if private sector behavior were highly volatile if it were believed that government action might exacerbate rather than moderate the effects of such behavior. But this is a second line of defense, upon which Friedman has not found it necessary to rely.

27. Also see Friedman and Becker: "The accuracy with which a consumption function enables consumption to be predicted from current *income* is a poor criterion of the usefulness of this consumption function in predicting income from investment via a Keynesian model. In general, for a given accuracy in predicting consumption from income, a consumption function gives better results in predicting income, the lower the implicit multiplier, that is, the larger the fraction of consumption regarded as autonomous of investment" (1957, pp. 74–75).

28. Chapter 1 of Friedman (1959a) contains an excellent summary of the historical discussions published later in FS.

29. It is important to note that the question of whether the supply of money is exogenously or endogenously determined is irrelevant to FS's discussions of the impact of M on other economic variables. M was clearly endogenous under the gold standard and it might have had a large exogenous component during some episodes after the founding of the Federal Reserve. But none of the impacts attributed by FS to M are conditional upon its origins. For a concise statement of this position, see Friedman (1959b, pp. 116–117).

30. FM's "test" was incapable even of distinguishing between the two simple models in question. Write $Y = VM$, where Y is nominal income. But FM do not regress Y on M as a test of the stability of V. Rather, they regress consumption, C, on M—for comparability with their regression of C on autonomous expenditure, A, which is their test of the stability of the multiplier. But a stable and significant relation between Y and M implies a stable and significant relation between C and M only if there is a stable and significant relation between C and Y. Let the inverse of the consumption function be $Y = C^{-1}(C)$, so that $Y = C^{-1}(C) = VM$, or, in the linear case assumed by FM, $C = a + (bV)M$. A stable and significant relation between C and M requires a relation between C and Y with the same characteristics, including a stable multiplier, $1/(1 - b)$.

Ando and Modigliani (1965) complained that "there is no justification for FM's posing the problem as one of choosing between a Keynesian multiplier mechanism and a monetary mechanism of income determination," because "if broadly understood as a theory of the demand for money, the quantity theory, far from being inconsistent, is actually an important part of the mechanism in the Keynesian framework." The dependence works both ways, for a stable multiplier (as defined contemporaneously by FM) is equally necessary to the stability of monetary velocity (as tested by FM).

31. For example, see Andersen and Carlson (1970) and Keran (1969).

32. See, for example, Friedman (1972, 1974b).

33. In a sympathetic yet critical essay on Thomas Attwood and the Birmingham currency school.

34. In support of this interpretation, Tobin quoted from a Friedman *Newsweek* (1967b) column: "This monetary expansion explains the long-continued economic expansion. And it is the turnabout in monetary policy since April 1966 that explains the growing signs of recession."

35. This is, of course, not the only sense in which "monetarism" is used. "Monetarists" are nearly as diverse a group as "Keynesians." For example, the mone-

tarism of Karl Brunner (1970) has much in common with FS and, like FS, is inconsistent with FM.

36. See, for example, Lucas and Rapping (1969), Phelps (1970b), Mortenson (1970), Lucas (1972, 1973), Barro (1976), Barro and Fischer (1976), and Gordon (1976).

37. Patinkin (1969) has discussed this point at length. Certainly, an algebraic representation of chapters 13 and 15 of *The General Theory* would include a money-demand function very much like equation (7) in Friedman's "Restatement" (1956).

38. For example, compare the figures in Fisher (1930, p. 254) and Friedman (1957, p. 8).

39. See, for example, Friedman (1969b, p. 35). For a lengthy discussion of the "tendency" of the demand for investment goods to be inversely related to interest rates, see Friedman (1951).

40. Friedman here expresses his indebtedness to Hayek (1945) in the development of this point and later cites supporting work by Lucas (1973, 1975) and Harberger (1967).

41. Friedman (1975) has expressed his indebtedness to Hume.

42. The process by which discrepancies between anticipated and realized prices affect U is seldom specified in these models any more rigorously than in the quotations from Friedman (1968) above. Exceptions are Alchian (1970), Mortenson (1970), and Lucas and Rapping (1970). Mortenson's and Alchian's papers were early contributions to the imperfect-information, cost-of-search models of employment. An important part of the Lucas-Rapping paper is the distinction between the labor supply effects of permanent and transitory changes in real wages suggested by Friedman (1962b, pp. 205–207).

43. Sargent and Wallace (1975) have perhaps the most complete specification, with an extensive dynamic IS-LM statement. Barro (1976) and Barro and Fischer (1976) made commodity demand dependent on an expected real balance effect. Lucas (1973, 1975), on the other hand, lets demand be a function of current price.

44. Although, as indicated above, not capturing the full complexity of Friedman's discussion.

45. Of course, Friedman knows all of this. He has stressed it in many places, including the introduction of his Nobel lecture and the widely discussed "Methodology of Positive Economics," in which he argued that theories should be judged not by the realism of their assumptions but, rather, by their "predictions about phenomena not yet observed" (1953b, p. 7). Friedman has learned the first lesson (as indicated by his refusal to specify his model, including his assumptions, in detail) but not the second.

46. This rejection (of earlier work on the problems of uncertainty and variations in aggregate demand and supply caused by price fluctuations) was less "Keynes" than "Keynesian," to use these words in Leijonhufvud's sense. But Keynes contributed to this rejection on the part of his disciples by ridiculing and misrepresenting his predecessors (while, as we have seen, relying extensively upon their work).

47. See Phelps (1967, 1972) for discussions of optimal government policies under these conditions.

48. This still does not explain why Friedman (in collaboration with Meiselman) gratuitously weakened his case for rules by placing another weapon in the hands of those already convinced of the need for discretionary policies because of a belief in the inherent instability of the economy.

49. Keynes' condemnation of policymakers and their actions was actually much more severe than Friedman's. Keynes' attacks (including personal attacks of a

kind eschewed by Friedman) are strewn through *The Tract, The General Theory,* and *Essays in Persuasion.*

50. Friedman's line of reasoning is consistent with that of the classical economists; see section III above and Corry (1962, pp. 172–173). The explanation of Keynes' defection in this respect—whether due to a difference in political philosophy such as that which in Friedman's view (1967a) partially explained the different policy recommendations of Keynes and Simons, to a belief that he (Keynes) would be successful in educating policymakers, or to a belief that the world had become so unstable that *any* government action would be an improvement—is beyond the scope of this paper.

51. For example, "Financing the Federal Government's operations involves large and irregular transfers of funds between the Treasury and the general public" (Bloch, 1958). Also, from the Federal Reserve Board's *Banking and Monetary Statistics, 1941–1970* (Washington: Government Printing Office, 1976, p. 515): "Float characteristically shows wide seasonal and week-to-week variations, depending on the volume of checks handled. From one week to another, the daily-average amount outstanding may vary by as much as $600 million or more, and within a year it may vary by as much as $2 billion." The difficulty of controlling M is widely recognized by economists both inside and outside the Federal Reserve System, and the literature on ways of improving monetary control is large and growing rapidly. For example, see Poole and Lieberman (1972), Starleaf (1975), and Kaminow (1977), and the references contained therein.

52. For discussions of 100 percent reserves and its academic history, see Friedman (1959a, pp. 65–76) and Hart (1935).

53. See chapter 3, "The Control of Money."

54. See Klein (1974) for a criticism of arguments by Friedman and others supporting government control of the money supply.

55. Of course, none of these steps will be of any avail if Congress frequently changes its mind regarding the rules.

REFERENCES

Alchian, Armen A. "Information Costs, Pricing and Resource Unemployment" (1970), in Phelps (1970a).

Andersen, Leonall, and Carlson, Keith M."A Monetarist Model for Economic Stabilization," Federal Reserve Bank of St. Louis *Review,* 52 (Apr. 1970), 7–25.

——, and Jordon, Jerry L. "Monetary and Fiscal Actions: A Test of Their Relative Importance in Economic Stabilization," Federal Reserve Bank of St. Louis *Review,* 50 (Nov. 1968), 11–23.

Ando, Albert, and Modigliani, Franco. "The Relative Stability of Monetary Velocity and the Investment Multiplier," *American Economic Review,* 55 (Sept. 1965), 693–728.

Barro, Robert J. "Rational Expectations and the Role of Monetary Policy," *Journal of Monetary Economics,* 2 (Jan. 1976), 1–32.

——, and Fischer, Stanley. "Recent Developments in Monetary Theory," *Journal of Monetary Economics,* 2 (Apr. 1976), 133–168.

——, and Grossman, Herschel I. "A General Disequilibrium Model of Income and Employment," *American Economic Review,* 61 (Mar. 1971), 82–93.

——. *Money, Employment and Inflation.* Cambridge: Cambridge University Press, 1976.

Bloch, Ernest. "The Treasury's Deposit Balances and the Banking System," Federal Reserve Bank of New York *Monthly Review,* 40 (Apr. 1958), 51–56.

Brunner, Karl. "The Monetarist View of Keynesian Ideas," *Lloyds Bank Review* (Oct. 1970), pp. 35–49.

———, and Meltzer, Allan H. "Friedman's Monetary Theory," in Gordon (1974), pp. 63–76.

Cantillon, Richard. *Essay on the Nature of Trade in General* (probably written between 1730 and 1734). Trans. from the French text of 1755 by Henry Higgs, with essays by Higgs and W. S. Jevons. London: Macmillan, 1931. Rep. by Augustus M. Kelley (New York).

Carleton, Willard T. "Review of Milton Friedman's Monetary Framework: A Debate with His Critics," *Journal of Finance*, 31 (Sept. 1976), 1263–1264.

Clower, Robert. "The Keynesian Counterrevolution: A Theoretical Appraisal," in F. H. Hahn and F. P. R. Brechling, eds., *The Theory of Interest Rates*. London, Macmillan.

Chow, G. C. "Tests of Equality between Sets of Coefficients in Two Linear Regressions," *Econometrica*, 28 (July 1960), 591–605.

Corry, B. A. *Money, Saving and Investment in English Economics, 1800–1850*. London: Macmillan, 1962.

Culbertson, J. M. "United States Monetary History: Its Implications for Monetary Theory," *National Banking Review* (Mar. 1964), pp. 359–379.

Fisher, Irving. *Appreciation and Interest*. New York: Macmillan, 1896.

———. *The Rate of Interest*. New York: Macmillan, 1907.

———. *The Purchasing Power of Money*. New York: Macmillan, 1911.

———. *The Money Illusion*. New York: Adelphi, 1928.

———. *The Theory of Interest*. New York: Macmillan, 1930.

Friedman, Milton. "Wesley C. Mitchell as an Economic Theorist," *Journal of Political Economy*, 58 (Dec. 1950), 465–493.

———. "Comments on Monetary Policy," *The Review of Economics and Statistics*, 33 (Aug. 1956), 186–191. Rep. in Friedman (1953a).

———. *Essays in Positive Economics*. Chicago: University of Chicago Press, 1953a.

———(1953b). "The Methodology of Positive Economics," in Friedman (1953a), pp. 3–43.

———. "The Quantity Theory of Money—A Restatement," in Friedman, ed., *Studies in the Quantity Theory of Money*. Chicago: University of Chicago Press, 1956.

———. *A Theory of the Consumption Function*. Princeton: Princeton University Press, 1957.

———(1958). "The Supply of Money and Changes in Prices and Output," in Friedman (1969a). Rep. from *The Relationship of Prices to Economic Stability and Growth*, 85th Congress, 2d session, Joint Economic Committee, Washington, U.S.G.P.O.

———. *A Program for Monetary Stability*. New York: Fordham University Press, 1959a.

———. "The Demand for Money: Some Theoretical and Empirical Results," *Journal of Political Economy*, 67 (Aug. 1959b), 327–351.

———. *Capitalism and Freedom*. Chicago: University of Chicago Press, 1962a.

———. *Price Theory: A Provisional Text*. Chicago: University of Chicago Press, 1962b.

———(1964). "The Monetary Studies of the National Bureau." Rep. in Friedman (1969a) from *The National Bureau Enters Its 45th Year*, 44th Annual Report, National Bureau of Economic Research, pp. 7–25.

———. "Comments," in George P. Shultz and Robert Z. Aliber, eds., *Guidelines, Informal Controls, and the Market Place*. Chicago: University of Chicago Press, 1966.

————. "The Monetary Theory and Policy of Henry Simons," *Journal of Law and Economics* (Oct. 1967a), pp. 1–13. Rep. in Friedman (1969a).

————. "Higher Taxes? No," *Newsweek,* Jan. 30, 1967b.

————(1968). "The Role of Monetary Policy," *American Economic Review,* 58 (Mar. 1968), 1–17. Rep. in Friedman (1969a).

————. *The Optimum Quantity of Money and Other Essays.* Chicago: Aldine, 1969a.

————(1969b). "The Optimum Quantity of Money." Rep. in Friedman (1969a).

————. "A Theoretical Framework for Monetary Analysis," *Journal of Political Economy,* 78 (Mar./Apr. 1970a), 193–238. Combined with Friedman (1971) and reprinted with alterations in Gordon (1974).

————. "Comment on Tobin," *The Quarterly Journal of Economics,* 84 (May 1970b), 318–327.

————. "A Monetary Theory of Nominal Income," *Journal of Political Economy,* 79 (Mar./Apr. 1971), 323–337. Combined with Friedman (1970a) and reprinted with alterations in Gordon (1974).

————. "Have Monetary Policies Failed?" *American Economic Review,* 62 (May 1972), 11–18.

————(1974a). "Comments on the Critics," in Gordon (1974), pp. 132–177.

————. "Letter on Monetary Policy," Federal Reserve Bank of St. Louis *Review,* 56 (Mar. 1974b), 20–23.

————. "Rediscovery of Money-Discussion," *American Economic Review,* 65 (May 1975), 176–179.

————. "Nobel Lecture: Inflation and Unemployment," *Journal of Political Economy,* 85 (June 1977), 451–472.

————, and Becker, Gary S. "A Statistical Illusion in Judging Keynesian Models," *Journal of Political Economy,* 65 (Feb. 1957), 64–75.

————, and Heller, Walter W. *Monetary vs. Fiscal Policy: A Dialogue,* New York: Norton, 1969.

————, and Meiselman, David. "The Relative Stability of Monetary Velocity and the Investment Multiplier in the United States, 1897–1958," in *Stabilization Policies.* Englewood Cliffs, N.J.: Prentice-Hall, 1963.

————, and Schwartz, Anna J. *A Monetary History of the United States, 1867–1960.* Princeton: Princeton University Press, 1963a.

———— (1963b). "Money and Business Cycles," *The Review of Economics and Statistics,* 45 (Feb., supplement), 32–64. Rep. in Friedman (1969a).

Gordon, Robert J., ed. *Milton Friedman's Monetary Framework: A Debate with His Critics.* Chicago, University of Chicago Press, 1974.

————. "Recent Developments in the Theory of Inflation and Unemployment," *Journal of Monetary Economics,* 2 (Apr. 1976), 185–220.

Harberger, Arnold C. "The Inflation Problem in Latin America," in Economic Development Institute, *Trabajos sobre desarrollo económico.* Washington: IBRD, 1967.

Hart, Albert G. "The 'Chicago Plan' of Banking Reform," *Review of Economic Studies,* 2 (Feb. 1935), 104–116.

Hawtrey, R. G. *Trade and Credit.* London: Longman's, Green, 1928.

Hayek, F. A. *Prices and Production.* London: Routledge, 1931.

————. *The Road to Serfdom.* London: Routledge & Kegan Paul, 1944.

————. "The Use of Knowledge in Society," *American Economics Review,* 35 (Sept. 1945), 519–530.

Hicks, J. R. *Critical Essays in Monetary Theory.* Oxford, Clarendon Press, 1967a.

————(1967b). "Monetary Theory and History—An Attempt at Perspective," in Hicks (1967a).

Howson, Susan. " 'A Dear Money Man'? Keynes on Monetary Policy, 1920," *Economic Journal*, 83 (June 1973), 456–464.

———. *Domestic Monetary Management in Britain, 1919–38*. Cambridge: Cambridge University Press, 1975.

Hume, David. (1752). "Of Money," in Rotwein (1970) and Walters (1973).

Hutchison, T. W. "Keynes and the History of 'Classical' Economics," trans. of "Keynes und die Geschichte der Klassischer Nationalokonomie," *Zeitschrift fur Nationalokonomie* (1958), pp. 393–410.

Johnston, J. *Econometric Methods*. 2d ed.; New York: McGraw-Hill, 1970.

Kaminow, Ira. "Required Reserve Ratios, Policy Instruments, and Money Stock Control," *Journal of Monetary Economics*, 3 (Oct. 1977), 389–408.

Keran, Michael W. "Monetary and Fiscal Influences on Economic Activity—The Historical Evidence," Federal Reserve Bank of St. Louis *Review*, 51 (Nov. 1969), 5–24.

Keynes, J. M. *A Tract on Monetary Reform*. London: Macmillan, 1923.

———. *A Treatise on Money*. 2 vols. London: Macmillan, 1930.

———. *Essays in Persuasion*. London: Macmillan, 1931.

———. *The General Theory of Employment, Interest and Money*. London: Macmillan, 1936.

———. "The General Theory of Employment," *The Quarterly Journal of Economics*, 51 (Feb. 1937), 209–223.

Klein, Benjamin. "The Competitive Supply of Money," *Journal of Money, Credit, and Banking*, 6 (Nov. 1974), 423–453.

Koopmans, Tjalling C. "Measurement without Theory," *The Review of Economics and Statistics*, 29 (Aug. 1947), 161–172.

Kregel, J. A. "Economic Methodology in the Face of Uncertainty," *Economic Journal*, 86 (June 1976), 209–225.

Law, John. *Money and Trade Considered: With a Proposal for Supplying the Nation with Money*. Edinburgh: Andrew Anderson, 1705. Rep. by Augustus M. Kelley (New York).

Leijonhufvud, Axel. *On Keynesian Economics and the Economics of Keynes*. New York: Oxford University Press, 1968.

Locke, John. *Several Papers Relating to Money, Interest and Trade*. London: Awnsham and John Churchill, 1696. Rep. by Augustus M. Kelley (New York).

Lucas, Robert E. "Expectations and the Neutrality of Money," *Journal of Economic Theory*, 4 (July 1972), 103–124.

———. "Some International Evidence on Output-Inflation Tradeoffs," *American Economic Review*, 63 (June 1973), 326–334.

———. "An Equilibrium Model of the Business Cycle," *Journal of Political Economy*, 83 (Dec. 1975), 1113–1144.

———, and Rapping, Leonard A. "Real Wages, Employment, and Inflation," *Journal of Political Economy*, 77 (Sept./Oct. 1969), 721–754. Rep. in Phelps (1970a).

Marshall, Alfred. "Remedies for Fluctuations of General Prices," *Contemporary Review* (Mar. 1887). Rep. in A. C. Pigou, ed., *Memorials of Alfred Marshall*. London: Macmillan, 1925.

———(1899). "Evidence Offered to the Indian Currency Committee," pub. in J. M. Keynes, ed., *Official Papers by Alfred Marshall*. London: Macmillan, 1926.

Meltzer, Allan H. "Monetary Theory and Monetary History," *Schweizerische Zeitschrift Volkswirtschaft und Statis*, 4 (Spring 1965), 409–422.

Mill, J. S. "Of the Influence of Consumption upon Production," in *Essays on Some Unsettled Questions of Political Economy*. London: Longmans, Green, Reader and Dryer, 1844.

_____. *Principles of Political Economy*. 1st ed. London: Parker, 1848. References are to the edition edited by W. J. Ashley (London: Longmans, Green, 1909).

Mints, Lloyd W. *Monetary Policy for a Competitive Society*. New York: McGraw-Hill, 1950.

Mitchell, W. C. *A History of the Greenbacks*. Chicago: University of Chicago Press, 1903.

_____. "The Real Issues in the Quantity-Theory Controversy," *Journal of Political Economy*, 12 (June 1904), 403–408.

_____. *Business Cycles*. Berkeley: University of California Press, 1913. Part III was published separately, also by the University of California Press, in 1941.

Mortenson, Dale T. (1970). "A Theory of Wage and Employment Dynamics," in Phelps (1970a).

Muth, John F. "Rational Expectations and the Theory of Price Movements," *Econometrica*, 29 (July 1961), 315–335.

Patinkin, Don. "The Chicago Tradition, the Quantity Theory, and Friedman," *Journal of Money, Credit, and Banking*, 1 (Feb. 1969), 46–70.

Phelps, Edmund S. "Phillips Curves, Expectations of Inflation, and Optimal Unemployment over Time," *Economica*, 34 (Aug. 1967), 254–281.

_____, ed. *Microeconomic Foundations of Employment and Inflation Theory*. New York: Norton, 1970a.

_____(1970b). "The New Microeconomics in Employment and Inflation Theory," introductory chapter in Phelps (1970a).

_____. *Inflation Policy and Unemployment Theory*. New York: Norton, 1972.

Poole, William, and Lieberman, Charles. "Improving Monetary Control," *Brookings Papers on Economic Activity*, 2 (1972), 293–335.

Popper, Karl R. *Conjectures and Refutations: The Growth of Scientific Knowledge*. New York: Basic Books, 1962 (page references are to the Harper Torchbook edition).

Ricardo, David. *The High Price of Bullion, a Proof of the Depreciation of Bank Notes*. London: John Murray, 1810. Rep. in Sraffa, vol. III.

_____. "Speech on the Budget in the House of Commons," as reported in *Hansard* (1822). Rep. in Sraffa, vol. V.

Roosa, Robert V. *Federal Reserve Operations in the Money and Government Securities Markets*. New York: Federal Reserve Bank of New York, 1956.

Rotwein, Eugene, ed. *David Hume: Writings on Economics*. Madison: University of Wisconsin Press, 1970.

Samuelson, Paul A. "Interactions between the Multiplier Analysis and the Principle of Acceleration," *The Review of Economics and Statistics*, 21 (May 1939), 75–78.

Sargent, Thomas J., and Wallace, Neil. " 'Rational' Expectations, the Optimal Monetary Instrument, and the Optimal Money Supply Rule," *Journal of Political Economy*, 83 (Apr. 1975), 241–254.

Sayers, R. S. "Ricardo's Views on Monetary Questions," *The Quarterly Journal of Economics*, 67 (Feb. 1953), 30–49. Rep. in T. S. Ashton and R. S. Sayers, eds., *Papers in English Monetary History* (Oxford, Clarendon Press).

Schumpeter, Joseph A. *History of Economic Analysis*. London: Allen & Unwin, 1954.

Shackle, G. L. S. *The Years of High Theory*. Cambridge: Cambridge University Press, 1967.

Simons, Henry C. "Rules versus Authorities in Monetary Policy," *Journal of Political Economy*, 44 (Feb. 1936), 1–30. Rep. in Simons (1948).

_____. *Economic Policy for a Free Society* . Chicago: University of Chicago Press, 1948.

Smith, Adam (1763). *Lectures on Justice, Police, Revenue and Arms.* Edited with an introduction and notes by Edwin Cannan in 1896 by the Clarendon Press, Oxford. Rep. by Augustus M. Kelley (New York).

———. *An Inquiry into the Nature and Causes of the Wealth of Nations* (1776).

Sraffa, Piero. *The Works and Correspondence of David Ricardo.* 10 vols. Cambridge: Cambridge University Press, 1951–55.

Starleaf, Dennis. "Nonmember Banks and Monetary Control," *Journal of Finance,* 30 (Sept. 1975), 955–976.

Teigen, Ronald L. "A Critical Look at Monetarist Economics," Federal Reserve Bank of St. Louis *Review,* 54 (Jan. 1972), 10–25.

Thornton, Henry. *An Enquiry into the Nature and Effects of the Paper Credit of Great Britain* (1802). Rep. in 1939 with an introduction by F. A. Hayek, by George Allen and Unwin (London).

Tobin, James. "The Monetary Interpretation of History," *American Economic Review,* 55 (June 1965), 464–485.

———. "Money and Income: Post Hoc Ergo Propter Hoc?" *The Quarterly Journal of Economics,* 84 (May 1970a), 301–317.

———. "Rejoinder," *The Quarterly Journal of Economics,* 84 (May 1970b) 328–329.

——— (1974). "Friedman's Theoretical Framework," in Gordon (1974), pp. 77–89.

Walters, A. A., ed. *Money and Banking.* Harmondsworth, Middlesex: Penguin, 1973.

Wicksell, Knut (1898). *Interest and Prices.* Trans. by R. F. Kahn with an introduction by Bertil Ohlin. London: Macmillan, 1936.

———(1906). *Lectures on Political Economy.* Vol. II. Trans. by E. Classen with an introduction by Lionel Robbins. London: Routledge & Kegan Paul, 1934.

The Stability of Macro Models

George Horwich and Sheng Cheng Hu

This study offers a systematic analysis of the stability of macro-economic models of *IS-LM* genre in which the price level and supply of output are active variables. This class of models was first introduced by Jacob Marschak in his lectures on income, employment, and the price level in the mid-to-late 1940s (Marschak, 1951). The simultaneous analysis of prices and output was facilitated by the use of aggregate supply and demand schedules on a two-dimensional graph of the price level and total output. The obvious parallel of this diagram to its single-product micro-counterpart gave it considerable appeal, but apart from a lone paper by O. H. Brownlee (1950) and the pioneering text of J. P. McKenna (1955), the diagram received scant attention in the economics literature until the early 1970s, when it surfaced as a major tool of macro textbooks.[1]

Our purpose here is to analyze the stability of the aggregate supply and demand framework. This will enable us to generalize the stability properties of the underlying *IS-LM* model beyond the routine admonition that *IS* must not have a greater slope than *LM* (Modigliani, 1944, p. 64; Dernburg and McDougall, 1976, p. 446; Chang and Smyth, 1972), or even that *IS* must not be upward sloped (Bailey, 1971, pp. 58–59, 89). Indeed, we will show that *IS* may have any slope whatever, without sacrificing the system's stability, provided there is a proper combination of dynamic adjustment process and structure elsewhere in the economy.

Our dynamics is a pairing of alternate Marshallian and then Walrasian adjustment in the output market with a nontâtonnement adjustment based on the stock-flow (loanable funds) security-market adjustment process developed in the 1950s by Horwich (1954), Rose (1957), and others,[2] and developed further within a variable-output framework by Hendershott and Horwich (1974). This security-market adjustment is an improvement, in our opinion, over the nontâtonnement dynamic processes that appear increasingly in the macro-disequilibrium literature. Most of such recent stability analyses either ignore the financial markets or do not allow for a complete stock and flow adjustment. For example, Solow and Stiglitz (1968) do not have a money market and are concerned exclusively with adjustment in the goods and labor markets. Barro and Grossman (1971) do not have an investment function, although they do introduce money. Korliras (1975) allows only for flow, but not stock disequilibrium, thus precluding the interaction between both stocks and flows.

We begin in section I by describing the essential features of our model, including its dynamics. Section II analyzes the stability of the aggregate supply and demand equilibrium, assuming that the securities market is always equilibrating and that there is, alternately, Marshallian and Walrasian adjustment in the output market. A useful by-product of this section is the derivation of effective demand and effective demand-price paths that can be combined with aggregate supply to determine directly a given model's stability. While the aggregate supply schedule is assumed to be the *de facto* path of output, aggregate demand, derived from *IS-LM* intersection points, is a market-equilibrium curve that provides no direct information on the course of effective demand or demand price in disequilibrium situations.

Section III generalizes the analysis by assuming finite intraperiod speed of adjustment in the securities market. Section IV introduces the real balance effect on saving. Section V is a summary.

I. THE MODEL

The Static Framework

The underlying *IS* and *LM* equations are

$$I(y,r) = S\left(y,r,\frac{M(r)}{P}\right) \tag{1.1}$$

$$L(y,r) = \frac{M(r)}{P} \tag{1.2}$$

where our variables are: S, real saving; y, real output; r, the rate of interest; M, the nominal stock of money; P, the general price level; I, real investment; and L, the demand for real balances. S, I, and y are flows, M and L are stocks. The partial derivatives have the following signs: $S_y > 0$, $S_r > 0$, $S_{\frac{M}{P}} \leq 0$, $I_y > 0$, $I_r < 0$, $L_y > 0$, $L_r < 0$, and $M_r \geq 0$.

Aggregate demand (AD) is the relationship between P and y, implied simultaneously by (1.1) and (1.2):

$$y = AD(P). \tag{1.3}$$

In terms of *IS-LM*, *AD* is derived by simply allowing the price-level parameter of *LM* and *IS* to assume different values, shifting both curves and altering the equilibrium income. The slope of AD is found by differentiating (1.3):

$$\frac{dy}{dP} = -\frac{S_M\left(\frac{M_r}{P} - L_r\right) + \left(I_r - S_r - S_M\frac{M_r}{P}\right)}{\left(I_y - S_y\right)\left(\frac{M_r}{P} - L_r\right) + \left(I_r - S_r - S_M\frac{M_r}{P}\right)L_y}\frac{M}{P^2}$$

(1.4)

$$= -\frac{\dfrac{1}{\dfrac{M_r}{P} - L_r} - \dfrac{1}{\dfrac{M_r}{P} - \dfrac{I_r - S_r}{S_M}}}{\left(\dfrac{dr}{dy}\right)_{LM} - \left(\dfrac{dr}{dy}\right)_{IS}}\frac{M}{P^2}$$

which is $\{\lessgtr\}\, 0$ if

$$\left(\frac{dr}{dy}\right)_{LM} \{\gtrless\} \left(\frac{dr}{dy}\right)_{IS} \quad \text{and} \quad 0 \geq S_{\frac{M}{P}} > \frac{I_r - S_r}{\frac{M_r}{P}}$$

(1.4a)[3]

or

$$\left(\frac{dr}{dy}\right)_{LM} \{\lessgtr\} \left(\frac{dr}{dy}\right)_{IS} \quad \text{and} \quad 0 > \frac{I_r - S_r}{\frac{M_r}{P}} > S_{\frac{M}{P}}.$$

(1.4b)[4]

In our general analysis in this section and in sections II and III we assume:
(1) $S_{M/P}$, the real balance effect on saving, is zero; its influence on the system, when negative, is summarized in section IV.
(2) $M_r = 0$. The impact of $0 < M_r < +\infty$ can be seen by simply replacing $L_r < 0$ by $L_r - M_r < 0$ wherever L_r appears.
Given these assumptions, the derivative (1.4) reduces to

$$\frac{dy}{dP} = \frac{(I_r - S_r)}{L_r(I_y - S_y) - L_y(I_r - S_r)}\frac{M}{P^2} = \frac{\dfrac{1}{L_r}}{\left(\dfrac{dr}{dy}\right)_{LM} - \left(\dfrac{dr}{dy}\right)_{IS}}\frac{M}{P^2}$$

(1.5)

$$\{\lessgtr\}\, 0 \text{ if } \left(\frac{dr}{dy}\right)_{LM} \{\gtrless\} \left(\frac{dr}{dy}\right)_{IS}.$$

There is only one commodity in the model, which serves both as consumption good and, when held in the form of inventories, as capital stock. Its aggregate supply per unit of time, AS, is a simple function of the price level:

$$y = AS(P), y_P \gtrless 0. \tag{1.6}$$

We make no attempt to relate (1.6) to underlying factor markets and production function. It is simply a postulate of the model, describing the actual output levels attained both in $AD\text{-}AS$ equilibrium and, apart from temporary deviations, during adjustment processes. Later, in order to distinguish between the actual supply and effective demand for output, we use the symbols y_s and y_d, respectively.[5]

The model is closed to the rest of the world, and the stock of money is wholly of the outside variety.

Financial Elements and Dynamic Adjustment

The main distinction between the present study and the existing disequilibrium models (such as Korliras, 1975) lies in the specification of the financial markets. In their financial aspect, ex ante investment and saving are, respectively, a real flow supply S^f and flow demand D^f of securities:

$$I = S^f, S = D^f. \tag{1.7}$$

Subtracting one equation from the other, we obtain

$$I - S = S^f - D^f, \tag{1.8}$$

a Walras' law for flows.[6] We distinguish sharply between the flow security market, thus defined, and the stock or existing security market, which is the wealth complement of the money market. Given a real wealth total and the supply and demand for real balances, and letting D^E and S^E denote real stock security demand and supply, respectively, we can write

$$\frac{M}{P} - L = D^E - S^E, \tag{1.9}$$

which is a Walras' law for stocks. S^E is the capitalized value of earnings on the existing capital stock. Our prototype security may be thought of as either a purchasing power perpetual bond or, preferably, an equity instrument such as common stock. The real earnings payment on the security, whether interest income or dividends, is assumed to be constant at unity.[7]

We emphasize the distinction between stock and flow security markets. The flows are not merely the changes in the stocks. They are functions in their own right, determined fundamentally by growth variables (income, capital, wealth). The budget constraint for flow demand is income, itself a flow variable. The constraint for the stock demands is total wealth, a stock variable. It would thus make no more sense to add stock and flow excess demands within a single budget constraint than to add income and wealth.

Stock and flow security markets, though independently constituted, do, however, interact over time. There is, after all, only one variety of security (a perpetuity) and only one security price and yield. Together, the security stocks and flows form a total market in which supply and demand for a discrete period t are

$$S_t^T = S_{t-1}^E + S_t^f$$
$$D_t^T = D_{t-1}^E + D_t^f$$

(1.10)

which determine the price of securities or its reciprocal, the rate of interest, and its rate of change:

$$\dot{r} = \Phi(S_t^T - D_t^T) = \Phi\left[(S_t^f - D_t^f) - (D_{t-1}^E - S_{t-1}^E)\right],$$
$$\Phi' > 0, \Phi(0) = 0.$$

(1.11)

In view of (1.8) and (1.9) we can write:

$$\dot{r} = \Phi[(I_t - S_t) - \left(\frac{M}{P} - L\right)\left(\frac{M}{P} - L\right)_{t-1}].$$

(1.12)

For the present, and until section III, we shall assume that the securities market is stable and the speed of adjustment within any period is infinite. This assumption implies that the securities market equilibrates each period. Thus $S_t^T = D_t^T$ and, from (1.10),

$$S_t^f - D_t^f = D_{t-1}^E - S_{t-1}^E.$$

(1.13)

Also, from (1.8) and (1.9), or from (1.12) with the assumption of instantaneous stable adjustment,

$$I_t - S_t = \left(\frac{M}{P} - L\right)_{t-1}.$$

(1.14)

Equation (1.13) summarizes the financing of positive excess investment expenditures or, more generally, excess commodity demand, in the model. Starting from a position of *IS-LM* equilibrium, an excess of *I* over *S* takes the form of an excess flow (and hence total) supply of securities [(1.8) and (1.10)], which, by (1.11), raises the rate of interest and, by (1.13), stimulates an equal excess stock demand for securities and, by (1.9), excess supply of real balances. Thus asset holders, in order to purchase the excess flow securities (i.e., finance their excess stock security demand), draw down their balances, which are thereby transferred to investing units. By this transfer, excess desired investment is financed and is added to the prevailing level of total *effective* (financed) demand for output.

Figure 1

The Interaction of Stock $\left(\dfrac{M}{P} - L\right)$ and Flow (I − S) Security Markets and the Financing of Excess Investment Demand

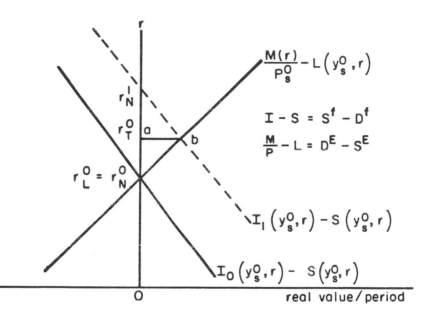

While the excess supply of real balances in (1.14) is dated along the pre-period $(t-1)$ functions, it persists throughout t, until, following its transfer to investing units, it is spent at the close of the interval. Thus both sides of (1.14) pertain effectively to the same period of time and we will henceforth omit the time subscripts. This is done in figure 1, a diagrammatic summary of the interaction of stock and flow excess security functions and the financing of excess commodity demand in a given interval. $I - S$, standing in for $S^f - D^f$, is a downward function of r, while $M/P - L$, equal to $D^E - S^E$, is a rising function. They are constructed for output supply level y_s^0. Initially, they meet at the zero quantity and a "market" rate of interest $r = r_L^0$ equal to the "natural" rate of interest r_N^0. The market rate, which is always the actually prevailing rate, will equilibrate the money (and stock security) market at the beginning of each period. The natural rate is the rate which will equilibrate the investment-saving (and flow security) market to establish long-run equilibrium. For a given output and price level, r_L is thus on the LM schedule, r_N on IS.

Following an increase in the I function from I_0 to I_1, $I - S$ shifts to the right, raising the natural rate to r_N^1, as indicated. During a succeeding brief interval, the new $I - S$ schedule meets $M/P - L$ at an increased market or "transfer" rate, r_T^0, at which the total securities market is in equilibrium: $S^T = D^T$. At r_T^0, excess real balances in the amount of ab are transferred from asset holders to spending units and added to the effective demand for output, y_d.

In the predisturbance equilibrium of aggregate supply and demand, effective demand for output is equal to de facto output:

$$y_s^0 = y_d^0 = C(y_s^0, r^0) + I_0(y_s^0, r^0) \tag{1.15}$$

where $r^0 = r_N^0 = r_L^0$. Following the increase in desired spending, the first adjustment interval, as described above, is characterized by

$$I_1(y_s^0, r_T^0) - S(y_s^0, r_T^0) = M/P_s^0 - L(y_s^0, r_T^0) \tag{1.16}$$

where P_s^0 is the initial prevailing price of output (that is, the supply price) and r_T^0 is the market (or transfer) rate that is the solution to (1.16). Since $S(y_s^0, r_T^0) = y_s^0 - C(y_s^0, r_T^0)$ and $y_d^1 = C(y_s^0, r_T^0) + I_1(y_s^0, r_T^0)$, we have, substituting in (1.16),

$$y_d^1 - y_s^0 = \frac{M}{P_s^0} - L(y_s^0, r_T^0) \tag{1.17}$$

or simply

$$y_d^1 = y_s^0 + \frac{M}{P_s^0} - L(y_s^0, r_T^0). \tag{1.18}$$

At the close of the interval, the excess commodity demand thus financed is applied to the supply of output, causing changes in prices, output, and the rate of interest (or any subset of these variables) until effective demand and output are again equal. In terms of (1.18), the end-of-period equilibrium is characterized by changes in y_s, P_s, and r_T, which cause the excess supply of real balances to go to zero while altering the separate y_s term in the equation directly. The movement of the variables depends, of course, on the shape of the AS function as well as the nature of the short-run output response.[8] These subjects are taken up in the following section. Assuming, for the present, that AS is upward sloped and the process is equilibrating, there will be a succession of intervals like the first, in which the excess of investment over saving (diminishing with each interval) takes the form of excess flow security supply which raises the market rate of interest, stimulating an excess supply of balances that are transferred to investing units whose expenditure, thus financed, raises prices and output until eventually $AD = AS$ and $r_L = r_N$.

II. THE BASIC STABILITY CONDITIONS

Two Varieties of Output-Market Adjustment

The stability conditions of alternative models are established by combining the effective-demand financing process described in section I with two fundamental output-market responses—one, Marshallian, the other, Walrasian. In the Marshallian response, the supply quantity of output and the corresponding supply price are momentarily fixed (as in the Marshallian short-period adjustment). This causes the de facto price level (the "demand price" in this case) to rise automatically, deflating effective demand to the supply level. The higher demand price is caused by a single period's excess effective demand and so cannot be sustained for more than an instant. But that is long enough to stimulate a Marshallian supply response to the excess of demand price, P_d, over the unchanged supply price, P_s:

$$\dot{y} = \Psi[P_d(y) - P_s(y)], \Psi' > 0, \Psi(0) = 0, \tag{2.1}$$

following which the supply price (once again the prevailing price) moves to a higher level given by the AS function.

In the Walrasian adjustment, the movement of the price level (the supply price in this case) is explained as an immediate response to the difference between the output quantities initially supplied and effectively demanded:

$$\dot{P} = \Theta\,[y_d(y_s(P), r(P)) - y_s(P)], \Theta' > 0, \Theta(0) = 0. \tag{2.2}$$

Following this, output moves automatically to the point on the AS schedule that corresponds to the higher supply price.

In both adjustments, we end at a higher supply quantity and price along the AS function. In the Marshallian case, the supply price adapts to the initially determined output level. In the Walrasian case, the supply quantity adapts to the initially determined price level.

The adjustments are illustrated in terms of four connected diagrams: figure 2(a), in which AD and AS are drawn; figure 2(b), the underlying IS-LM graph; figure 2(c), the prevailing saving-investment market; and figure

2(d), the corresponding money market. The initial (nonequilibrium) point in all four diagrams is A, at which, proceeding counterclockwise, the price level is $P_s^0[(a)]$ and output $y_s^0[(a)(b)]$, the market rate is $r_L^0 < r_N^0[(b)(c)(d)]$, and real balances are $M^0/P_S^0[(d)]$. Point A in (a) is on the AS curve below AD, a fact reflected in (b) in that A is on LM, drawn for price parameter P_s^0, but below IS; in (c) in that at A, $I(y_s^0, r_L^0) > S(y_s^0, r_L^0)$; and in (d) in that A is at the intersection of $L(y_s^0, r_L^0)$ and M^0/P_s^0. The existence of money market equilibrium implies that the preexisting securities market (which is not drawn) also clears at r_L^0.

Figure 2
The Financing of Excess Investment Expenditures Followed by Marshallian and Walrasian Output-Market Response

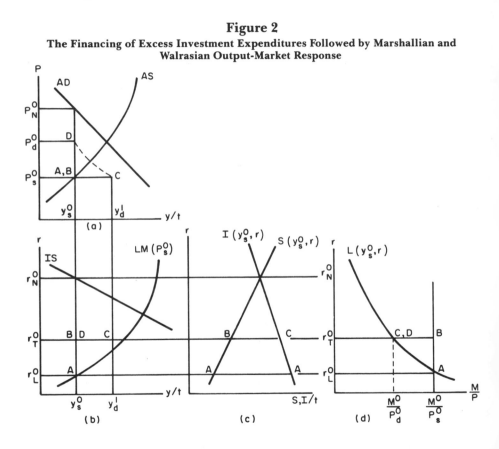

Since at A, $I > S$, we also have $S^f > D^f$. This, as we have seen, raises the market rate and finances the excess investment of a given brief interval. In (b) and (d) the increase in r to r_T^0 is shown as the vertical distance AB; the resulting excess supply of real balances and increase in effective demand to y_d^1 is the segment CB in (d) and BC in (a), (b), and (c).[9]

In the Marshallian adjustment, the price level in (a) rises to P_d^0 (point D), at which y_d has been deflated to y_s^0, while in (d) the supply and demand for money (at D) are again equal.[10] In (a), $P_d^0 > P_s^0$ (that is, D above B) evokes a positive output response, placing y_s of the next period on AS, somewhere to the right of y_s^0, and raising supply price accordingly. [11] (As noted above, in the face of continuing output flows, demand price, supported by only a single round of an excess rate of expenditure, remains above the newly determined supply price only momentarily.)

In the Walrasian adjustment, $y_d^1 > y_s^0$ in (a) (that is, C to the right of B) evokes a higher supply price directly, following which output moves at once to the corresponding point on the AS schedule.

The remainder of the path to equilibrium in either the Marshallian or Walrasian adjustments is simply a continuation along AS of the security and output-market interaction. $I > S$ ($S^f > D^f$) continues to be financed by raising the market rate, which channels money to investing firms, whose resulting expenditures, in one case, repeatedly raise demand price above the prevailing supply price, inducing output to expand, and, in the other case, raise supply price and then output directly.

Marshallian Stability Condition

The general Marshallian stability condition follows. We write (1.18) as a general expression and drop the s subscript of y_s:

$$y_d = y + \frac{M}{P_s(y)} - L(y, r_T). \tag{2.3}$$

Effective demand price is defined as

$$P_d(y) = \frac{M}{L(y, r_T)}, \tag{2.4}$$

where r_T satisfies (1.16), expressed in general terms:

$$I(y, r_T) - S(y, r_T) = \frac{M}{P_s(y)} - L(y, r_T). \tag{2.5}$$

We differentiate r_T in (2.5) with respect to y:

$$\frac{dr_T}{dy} = -\frac{I_y - S_y + \dfrac{M}{P_s^2} P_s'(y) + L_y}{I_r - S_r + L_r} \tag{2.6}$$

where $P_s'(y)$ is the derivative of AS with respect to y. Next, we differentiate (2.4):

$$\frac{dP_d}{dy} = -\frac{M}{L^2}\left\{L_y + L_r \frac{dr_T}{dy}\right\}. \tag{2.7}$$

Marshallian stability requires

$$P_d'(y) < P_s'(y) \tag{2.8}$$

in the neighborhood of equilibrium. Limiting our derivatives to this range in the following expressions, substitution of (2.6) in (2.7) simplifies P_d' to

$$P_d'(y) = -\frac{1}{\alpha}\left\{\frac{1}{L_r}\frac{L_r\left[\left(\frac{dr}{dy}\right)_{LM} - \left(\frac{dr}{dy}\right)_{IS}\right]}{\frac{M}{P_s^2}} + \frac{1}{I_r - S_r}P_s'(y)\right\}$$

where $\alpha = -\left(\frac{1}{L_r} + \frac{1}{I_r - S_r}\right)$. Substituting $P_N'(y)$, the derivative of AD with respect to y, for the large fraction within the braces, we have

$$P_d'(y) = \frac{-\frac{1}{L_r}}{\alpha}P_N'(y) - \frac{\frac{1}{I_r - S_r}}{\alpha}P_s'(y). \tag{2.9}$$

Finally, substituting (2.9) for $P_d'(y)$ in (2.8) and collecting terms, Marshallian stability is given by:

$$\frac{-\frac{1}{L_r}}{\alpha}[P_N'(y) - P_s'(y)] < 0, \tag{2.10}$$

which, since $I_r - S_r < 0 < -L_r$ (and thus $\alpha > 0$), is satisfied if

$$P_N'(y) < P_s'(y). \tag{2.11}$$

It follows that the price-output path is stable, provided that
(1) AS is upward sloped and AD is downward sloped [figures 3(a) and 3 (b)].
(2) AS and AD are both downward sloped and AD is steeper than AS [figure 3(c)].
(3) AS and AD are both upward sloped [AD because of $(dr/dy)_{LM} < (dr/dy)_{IS}$] and AD is flatter than AS [figure 3(d)].

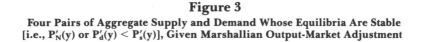

Figure 3
Four Pairs of Aggregate Supply and Demand Whose Equilibria Are Stable
[i.e., P$'_N$(y) or P$'_d$(y) < P$'_s$(y)], Given Marshallian Output-Market Adjustment

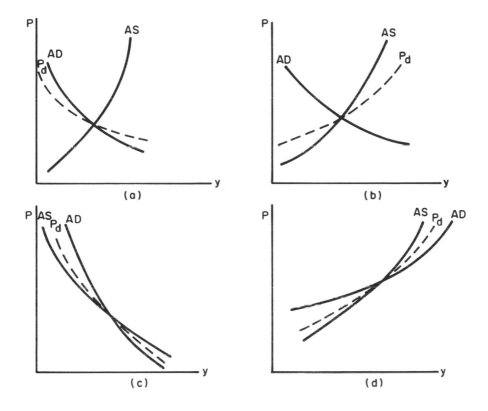

The path of effective demand price P_d, with which supply price P_s can be directly compared, is also drawn in each diagram. Since in AD-AS equilibrium, $y_d = y_s$, it follows that $P_d = P_s = P_N$ and P_d passes through each AD-AS intersection. Moreover, at any income, P_d lies between AD and AS. We establish this first by reference to figure 1, where, for $y^0 < y^e$ (equilibrium y), $r_L^0 < r_T^0 < r_N^1$. This is a general relationship. For $y > y^e$, the schedules intersect in the negative quadrant with a reverse ordering of the interest rates, but with r_T still in the middle.[12] Second, since

$$P_s = \frac{M}{L(y, r_L)}, P_d = \frac{M}{L(y, r_T)}, \text{ and } P_N = \frac{M}{L(y, r_N)},$$

it follows, for given y, that

$$P_d \gtreqless P_s \text{ if } r_T \gtreqless r_L, P_d \gtreqless P_N \text{ if } r_T \gtreqless r_N, P_s \gtreqless P_N \text{ if } r_L \gtreqless r_N. \quad (2.12)$$

The reader may verify that (2.12) is satisfied only when P_s, P_d, and P_N are ordered as r_L, r_T, and r_N, respectively. Thus P_d, like r_T, is always the middle variable.

The slope of the P_d curve, P_d', is, from (2.9),

$$\left\{ \begin{matrix} > \\ = \\ < \end{matrix} \right\} 0 \text{ if}$$

(1) $\dfrac{P_N'}{P_s'} \begin{matrix} > \\ < \end{matrix} \dfrac{-L_r}{I_r - S_r} < 0$ and $P_s' > 0$,

(2) $\dfrac{P_N'}{P_s'} \begin{matrix} < \\ > \end{matrix} \dfrac{-L_r}{I_r - S_r} < 0$ and $P_s' < 0$.

Thus in figures 3(c) and (d), P_d is unambiguously downward and upward sloped, respectively. In figure 3(a), P_d is downward sloped, unless, as in (b), AD (a downward schedule) is sufficiently flat in relation to AS. From (1.5) we know that AD tends to be flatter the smaller is $(dr/dy)_{LM} - (dr/dy)_{IS} > 0$.

Walrasian Stability Condition

To find the stability condition for the Walrasian output-market adjustment, we again write (1.18) in general terms, this time dropping the s subscript of P:

$$y_d = y_s(P) + \frac{M}{P} - L(y_s, r_T), \quad (2.13)$$

where r_T is the solution to

$$I(y_s, r_T) - S(y_s, r_T) = \frac{M}{P} - L(y_s, r_T). \quad (2.14)$$

Differentiation of r_T in (2.14) with respect to P yields

$$\frac{dr_T}{dP} = -\frac{(I_y - S_y + L_y)y_s'(P) + \dfrac{M}{P^2}}{I_r - S_r + L_r} \quad (2.15)$$

where $y'_s(P)$ is the derivative of AS with respect to P. The derivative of (2.13) is

$$\frac{dy_d}{dP} = y'_s(P) - \frac{M}{P^2} - L_y y'_s(P) - L_r \frac{dr_T}{dP}. \tag{2.16}$$

Walrasian stability requires

$$y'_d(P) < y'_s(P) \tag{2.17}$$

in the equilibrium vicinity. Again restricting derivatives to this region in subsequent expressions, substitution of (2.15) in (2.16) reduces y'_d to

$$y'_d(P) = (1 - \gamma)y'_s(P) + \gamma y'_N(P) \tag{2.18}$$

where $y'_N(P)$ is the derivative of AD with respect to P [(1.5)] and

$$\gamma = \frac{L_y(I_r - S_r) - L_r(I_y - S_y)}{I_r - S_r + L_r} = \frac{\left(\dfrac{dr}{dy}\right)_{LM} - \left(\dfrac{dr}{dy}\right)_{IS}}{\alpha}. \tag{2.19}$$

Replacing $y'_d(P)$ in (2.17) by (2.18) and rearranging terms, the Walrasian stability condition is

$$\gamma[y'_s(P) - y'_N(P)] > 0 \tag{2.20}$$

or, since $\alpha > 0$ by assumption,

$$y'_s(P) \gtreqless y'_N(P) \text{ as } \left(\frac{dr}{dy}\right)_{LM} \gtreqless \left(\frac{dr}{dy}\right)_{IS}. \tag{2.21}$$

This condition includes the traditional stability conditions derived from the *IS-LM* model (e.g., Modigliani, 1944; Bailey, 1971; Dernburg and Mc-Dougall, 1976; Chang and Smyth, 1972) as a special case where the *AS* curve is flat.

Four stable cases can be distinguished:

(1) *AS* is upward sloped and *AD* is downward sloped [figure 4(a)].

(2) *AS* and *AD* are both downward sloped and *AS* is steeper than *AD* [figure 4(b)].

(3) *AS* and *AD* are both upward sloped and *AS* is steeper than *AD* [figure 4(c)].

(4) *AS* is downward sloped and *AD* is upward sloped [figure 4(d)].

Cases (1) and (3) are the same as (1) and (3) of the Marshallian adjustment. The y_d paths are drawn in each of these Walrasian cases. From (2.18) we have

$$y'_d(P) \underset{<}{\overset{>}{=}} 0 \text{ as } y'_s(P) \underset{<}{\overset{>}{=}} - \frac{\gamma}{1 - \gamma} y'_N(P), \text{ given that } \gamma \in [0, 1]. \quad (2.22)$$

The signs of the inequality relating $y'_s(P)$ and $y'_N(P)$ are reversed in the event that $\gamma \in [0, 1]$. (2.22) is difficult to evaluate, owing to uncertainty as to the sign and relative magnitude of $- \gamma/(1 - \gamma)$. But assuming that γ is a positive fraction, it is clear that increasing the slope of AD relative to the price axis, say by increasing $(dr/dy)_{LM} - (dr/dy)_{IS}$, tends to make y_d in figure 4(a) a rising function.[13]

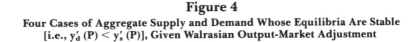

Figure 4
**Four Cases of Aggregate Supply and Demand Whose Equilibria Are Stable
[i.e., y'_d (P) $<$ y'_s (P)], Given Walrasian Output-Market Adjustment**

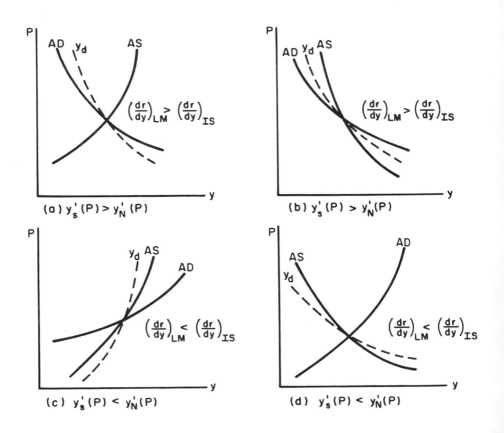

III. FINITE SPEED OF ADJUSTMENT IN THE SECURITIES MARKET

This section relaxes our assumption that the intraperiod interest rate is always in equilibrium. This will enable us to construct general adjustment paths of r and y, in the Marshallian case, and of r and P in the Walrasian case of output-market adjustment. We do so in terms of graphs of each pair of variables, the space of which is partitioned into phases of positive, negative, and zero change. We continue to assume that the intraperiod output-market adjustment speed is infinite, given the financing of demand that $\dot{r} \gtrless 0$ makes possible. Our stability analysis here is based on Olech (1963).

A by-product of our graphic dynamics is the construction of market equilibrium curves for securities, output, and money. While these curves resemble those of Patinkin's general equilibrium model (1965, pp. 258–264), they reflect our special assumptions of separate Walras' laws for stocks and flows, variable output (which is incorporated in the functions), and an interest rate dynamics based on the interaction of separate stock and flow security markets.

We begin with the Marshallian output response. The movement of the rate of interest and of output is described, in order.

Marshallian Output-Market Adjustment

The general interest rate response is given by equations (1.11) and (1.12). Since $\Phi' > 0$,

$$\dot{r} \gtrless 0 \text{ as } S^T - D^T \gtrless 0 \text{ or } [I(y, r) - S(y, r)] - \left[\frac{M}{P_s(y)} - L(y, r)\right] \gtrless 0, \quad (3.1)$$

where time subscripts have been dropped, in accordance with our period assumptions on page 247, and the dependence on y and r is made explicit. The path of $\dot{r} = 0$ is thus given by

$$I(y, r) - S(y, r) = \frac{M}{P_s(y)} - L(y, r), \quad (3.2)$$

the derivative of which, with respect to y, is

$$\left(\frac{dr}{dy}\right)_{\dot{r}=0} = -\frac{I_y - S_y + \left(\frac{M}{P_s^2}P_s' + L_y\right)}{I_r - S_r + L_r} \gtrless 0$$

$$\text{as } \frac{M}{P_s^2}P_s' + L_y \gtrless -(I_y - S_y) \quad (3.3)$$

since $I_r - S_r + L_r < 0$. The locus of $\dot{r} = 0$ is plotted as the upward sloped (dashed) curve RR in figure 5(a), an r-y diagram. Clearly, the slope of RR is positive if P'_s and L_y are sufficiently large relative to $- (I_y - S_y)$, and it is negative otherwise.

Figure 5(b), a graph of a given interval's excess investment and real-balance functions at an output y^0, is useful in showing the directional movement of r, as well as for deriving that of y. The intersection of the two functions at point A, for which the market rate is r_T^0, coincides with equilibrium in the total securities market: $S^T = D^T$. For all $r \gtrless r_T^0$, we have $S^T \lessgtr D^T$ and $\dot{r} \lessgtr 0$. The inequalities with respect to S^T and D^T are noted on the diagram. Point A is also entered in figure 5(a), where, at output y^0, it lies on RR. We conclude that at all points above and below RR, r tends to fall and rise, respectively. Several vertical arrows, showing this tendency, are drawn in figure 5(a) at outputs y^0 (points a–d) and $y^1 > y^0$ (points e–g).

Figure 5
Phase Drawings of r and y Under Marshallian Output Adjustment and Finite Speed of Adjustment in the Securities Market

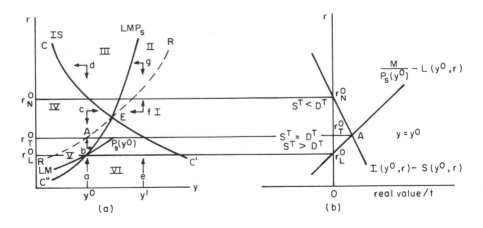

Equilibrium in the output market requires that $P_d = P_s$, which is satisfied if, at a given (y, r), the *effective* (that is, financed) investment-saving gap is zero. Consider interest rates below r_T^0, a region below RR in which $S^T > D^T$. Since the total demand for securities falls short of total supply, firms are unable to finance their entire desired investment. The amount they can finance is limited to voluntary saving plus the excess supply of real balances [equal, by (1.9), to the excess stock demand for securities], as indicated by a point on the excess real-balance line of figure 5(b). Since a portion of the investment-saving gap is financed, we get, via the Marshallian adjustment, $P_d > P_s$ and a rise in output. Now, at interest rate r_L^0 the excess supply of

real balances (excess stock demand for securities) is zero, effective investment is exactly equal to saving, and the output market is in "effective"
(though not intended) equilibrium. At interest rates below r_L^0, the desired
investment-saving gap is still positive, but the excess supply of real balances
(and the excess stock demand for securities) is negative and effective investment again is limited to voluntary saving.[14]

We summarize these tendencies in the output market by entering appropriate horizontal arrows in figure 5(a). At output y^0 between interest rates
r_T^0 (point A) and r_L^0, effective investment exceeds saving and output tends to
expand. This is indicated by the rightward horizontal arrow at b. Since r_L^0 is
the interest rate at which the money market is in equilibrium, it is shown in
figure 5(a) as lying on a brief segment of an LM schedule whose price level
parameter is $P_s(y^0)$. Below r_L^0 we have seen that effective investment is constrained by saving, and output has no tendency to rise. Thus at a, only the
arrow signifying the upward pressure of $S^T > D^T$ on the rate of interest is
drawn.

Next consider interest rates above r_T^0. Since $S^T < D^T$, firms are able to
finance all of any desired investment. It follows that the effective and intended investment-saving gaps are equal and the output market will be in
equilibrium only when the interest rate equals the natural rate, r_N^0. This
tendency, in the range r_T^0 to r_N^0, for $I > S$ to be fully financed and y to expand,
is shown in figure 5(a) as the rightward arrow at c. This point, at output y^0,
is above RR and below IS, on which r_N^0 lies.[15]

At interest rates above r_N^0, I is $< S$ and both demand price and output tend
to fall. There is no qualification to this tendency comparable to the financing
requirement of $I > S$. The contraction in expenditures represented by
$I < S$ is restrained only by income itself, and is immediately and spontaneously effective. Leftward horizontal arrows are thus entered in figure 5(a)
at all points above the IS schedule—at d for output y^0 and at f and g for
output y^1.

While RR, the locus of $\dot{r} = 0$, is relatively simple, the path of $\dot{y} = 0$ is
clearly more complex. We have seen for points below IS that $\dot{y}$ is > 0 at
interest rates in the region of positive excess supply of real balances—i.e.,
above the LM schedule. LM, when it is below IS, is thus a "southern" boundary to the region of expandable output. The precise path of this boundary
is derived by letting LM incorporate the relationship between y and P given
by the AS schedule. That is, as we move, say, to the right of y^0 in figure 5(a),
LM will shift as the price levels associated with each y along AS themselves
change. If $P_s' > 0$, LM will shift upward with each increase of output and
hence prices. The curve labeled LMP_s in the graph is an example of a net
upward path. The general expression for LMP_s is

$$\frac{M}{P_s(y)} = L(y, r) \qquad (3.4)$$

and its derivative is

$$\left(\frac{dr}{dy}\right)_{LMP_s} = -\frac{\frac{M}{P_s^2}P_s' + L_y}{L_r} \gtrless 0 \text{ as } \frac{yP_s'}{P_s} \gtrless -\frac{yL_y}{L}. \tag{3.5}$$

The intersection of LMP_s and IS, point E, is an equilibrium point for all markets of the model: investment-saving (and flow security), money (and stock security), and output. It corresponds to the intersection point of AD and AS.

We have noted that IS itself, along which $I = S$, is a locus of $\dot{y} = 0$. But while points below IS to the left of E correspond to $\dot{y} > 0$, points below IS to the right of E, falling as they do below LMP_s in the region of negative excess supply of money, correspond to $\dot{y} = 0$. Hence no rightward horizontal arrow can be added to point e.

The locus or boundary of $\dot{y} = 0$ is thus CE–EC'–EC''. At points above CE and EC', which together constitute the IS schedule, $\dot{y} < 0$. Within the vertical angle enclosed by CE and $C''E$, $\dot{y} > 0$. Within the angle enclosed by $C''E$ and EC', $\dot{y} = 0$.

The six regions in the r–y space, delineated by our functions, are numbered by roman numerals in figure 5(a).

Figure 6 graphs the r–y counterpart of the Marshallian cases of figure 3 plus one additional case. Figure 6(a) is identical to figure 5(a) and is the r–y graph of the standard case drawn in figure 3(a): AD and AS are downward and upward sloped, respectively, and IS is a downward schedule. In figure 6(a), LMP_s is drawn as a rising schedule, for which $P_s' > 0$ is a sufficient condition [(3.5)]. Paths, based on our previous equilibrium assumption about the securities market ($\dot{r} = 0$), are represented by the two boldface arrows lying on RR.[16] An illustrative path, based on finite adjustment speed, begins in region I at point a. It passes successively through the next four regions before reaching the equilibrium at E. Only region VI, in which output cannot rise, is inaccessible to this path, and thereby acts to hasten the approach to equilibrium. Notice that in passing from region I to II the path crosses RR, along which $\dot{r} = 0$, and thus becomes perfectly horizontal at that point. This would also be true in going from region IV to V. Similarly, in passing from III to IV the path crosses CE (a segment of IS), along which $\dot{y} = 0$ and is momentarily vertical. This would occur also in crossing $C''E$ (region VI to V) and EC' (region VI to I).

A path originating at b in region IV can approach equilibrium directly within the region or by crossing over only into region V. The paths emanating from c and d in region VI move vertically before assuming curved trajectories in adjacent regions.

Figure 6
Stable [(a)-(c)] and Unstable [(d)] Marshallian Output Adjustment Paths, Given Finite
Adjustment Speed in the Securities Market

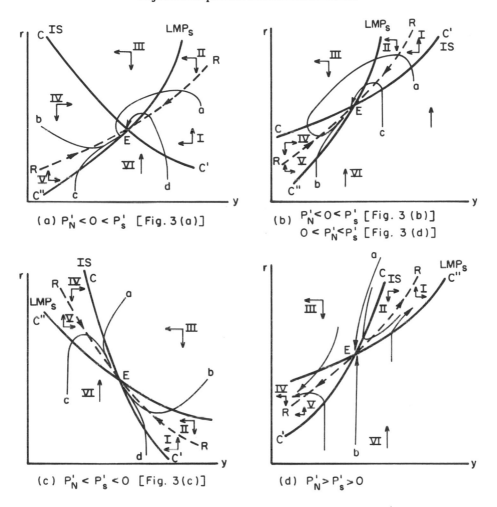

(a) $P'_N < 0 < P'_s$ [Fig. 3(a)]

(b) $P'_N < 0 < P'_s$ [Fig. 3(b)]
   $0 < P'_N < P'_s$ [Fig. 3(d)]

(c) $P'_N < P'_s < 0$ [Fig. 3(c)]

(d) $P'_N > P'_s > 0$

Figure 6(b) corresponds to figure 3(b), in which the slope of *IS* is positive
but less than that of any individual *LM* schedule. In figure 6(b), LMP_s is
drawn steeper than *IS*, and the adjustment paths are shown as converging
to equilibrium, which occurs if the speed of adjustment in the security market is sufficiently great relative to that of the output market.[17]

Figure 6(c) corresponds to figure 3(c), in which the slope of *AS* is negative
but greater (algebraically) than that of *AD*. $P'_s < 0$ generates a downward
LMP_s schedule, constructed so as to have a greater algebraic slope than that
of *IS*.[18] The paths are equilibrating.

In figure 3(d) the slope of *IS* exceeds that of any individual *LM* schedule. *AD* thus has a positive slope [(1.5)]. But the slope of *AS*, also positive, is greater than that of *AD*, and the model was shown to be stable [(2.11)]. In the *r–y* framework, we construct LMP_s steeper than *IS*, reflecting the relatively substantial value of $P'_s > 0$. Figure 6(b) is thus the counterpart to figure 3(d) as well as 3(b). However, the model of figure 3(d), unlike 3(b), has underlying *LM* schedules that are flatter than *IS*. But LMP_s is rendered steeper than *IS* by an *AS* schedule for which $P'_s > 0$ is sufficiently great.

The final Marshallian case is pictured in figure 6 (d). *IS* is steeper than LMP_s and the adjustment paths exhibit the saddle point property. Only the two stable branches, one southwest, starting at *a*, and the other an upward vertical path from *b*, converge to equilibrium. The boldface arrows again denote the instantaneous stable interest rate adjustment. While the path lies on *RR*, it moves away from equilibrium. Figure 6(d) could be a case in which $P'_N > P'_s > 0$.

It is clear by inspection of the four panels of figure 6 that in *r–y* space, Marshallian stability is satisfied if the slope of LMP_s exceeds that of *IS*. Moreover, the slope of *RR* also must exceed that of *IS*. The latter requirement follows from the fact that, at any income, *RR* lies between LMP_s and *IS*, as drawn. This is based on the ordering of interest rates revealed by

figure 1: as $y \gtrless y^e$, $r_L \gtrless r_T \gtrless r_N$.[19] Since r_L lies on LMP_s, r_T on *RR*, and r_N on

IS, *RR* occupies the intermediate ordinate position.

Finally, we can show that the global stability slope-requirement for LMP_s and *IS* implies our earlier stability condition, $P'_N < P'_s$ [(2.11)]:

$$\left(\frac{dr}{dy}\right)_{LMP_s} > \left(\frac{dr}{dy}\right)_{IS}$$

$$-\frac{\dfrac{M}{P_s^2}P'_s + Ly}{L_r} > -\frac{I_y - S_y}{I_r - S_r}$$

$$\frac{M}{P_s^2}P'_s > \left(\frac{I_y - S_y}{I_r - S_r}\right)L_r - L_y \qquad (3.6)$$

$$P'_s > \frac{(I_y - S_y)L_r - (I_r - S_r)L_y}{\dfrac{M}{P_s^2}(I_r - S_r)}$$

$$P'_s > P'_N$$

Q.E.D.[20]

Walrasian Output-Market Adjustment

We analyze the Walrasian output-market response under finite security-market speed of adjustment in r–P space. The functions are essentially analogous to those of the Marshallian case.

The RR curve plotted in figure 7(a) is derived by rewriting (3.2) as

$$I[y_s(P), r] - S[y_s(P), r] = \frac{M}{P} - L[y_s(P), r] \qquad (3.7)$$

Figure 7
Phase Drawings of r and P Under Walrasian Output-Market Adjustment and Finite Speed of Adjustment in the Securities Market

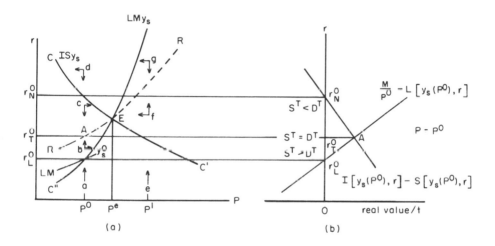

and differentiating (3.7) with respect to P:

$$\left(\frac{dr}{dP}\right)_{r=0} = - \frac{(I_y - S_y + L_y)y_s' + \dfrac{M}{P^2}}{I_r - S_r + L_r} \qquad (3.8)$$

which is $\left\{ \begin{matrix} > \\ = \\ < \end{matrix} \right\} 0$ if

$$(1) \quad \frac{M}{P^2}\frac{1}{y_s'} + L_y \begin{matrix} > \\ < \end{matrix} - (I_y - S_y) \text{ and } y_s' > 0$$

$$(2) \quad \frac{M}{P^2}\frac{1}{y_s'} + L_y \begin{matrix} < \\ > \end{matrix} - (I_y - S_y) \text{ and } y_s' < 0.$$

The underlying excess investment and real balance functions are drawn in figure 7(b) for a given price level, $P^0 < P^e$ (the equilibrium price), and output, $y_s(P^0)$, implied by the AS schedule. The relations between total security supply and demand indicate: (i) points above and below RR correspond to $\dot{r} < 0$ and $\dot{r} > 0$, respectively; (ii) at $P^0 < P^e$, effective investment exceeds saving, $y_d > y_s$, and, thus, $\dot{P}$ is > 0 for points lying between the output and money market-equilibrium curves; points above the former curve, at which $I < S$ and $y_d < y_s$, correspond to $\dot{P} < 0$, and points below the latter curve, at which intended excess investment is unfinanced and $y_d = y_s$, correspond to $\dot{P} = 0$.

Both the output and money market-equilibrium curves incorporate the $y_s(P)$ relation of AS. The former curve, designated ISy_s, is

$$I\,[y_s\,(P),\,r] = S\,[y_s\,(P),\,r] \tag{3.9}$$

and its derivative is

$$\left(\frac{dr}{dP}\right)_{ISy_s} = -\left(\frac{I_y - S_y}{I_r - S_r}\right) y_s' \tag{3.10}$$

which is $\left\{\begin{matrix}\geq\\<\end{matrix}\right\} 0$ if

$$(1)\ I_y - S_y \begin{matrix}\geq\\<\end{matrix} 0 \text{ and } y_s' > 0$$

$$(2)\ I_y - S_y \begin{matrix}\leq\\>\end{matrix} 0 \text{ and } y_s' < 0$$

or

$$(3)\ y_s' \begin{matrix}\geq\\<\end{matrix} 0 \text{ and } I_y - S_y > 0$$

$$(4)\ y_s' \begin{matrix}\leq\\>\end{matrix} 0 \text{ and } I_y - S_y < 0.$$

Notice in (3.10) that $y_s' > 0$ and $I_y - S_y < 0$ are solely responsible for the negative slope of ISy_s, as drawn in figure 7(a).[21] The real balance effect on saving, which could also produce this result, is not introduced until section IV.

The money market–equilibrium curve, labeled LMy_s, is

$$L\,[y_s\,(P),\,r] = \frac{M}{P}. \tag{3.11}$$

Its derivative is

$$\left(\frac{dr}{dy}\right)_{LM_{y_s}} = -\frac{\dfrac{M}{P^2} + L_y\,y_s'}{L_r} \gtrless 0 \text{ as } y_s' \gtrless -\frac{M}{P^2}\frac{1}{L_y}. \tag{3.12}$$

Further reasoning, analogous to that underlying figure 5, establishes that in figure 7(a) the locus-boundary of $\dot{P} = 0$ is CE–EC'–EC'' and that the phases of the regions at $P^1 > P^e$ have the indicated directional movements.

The drawings of figure 6 can also be used to illustrate dynamic paths under Walrasian output-market adjustment and finite adjustment in the securities market. For this purpose, figure 6 would be altered as follows: in each panel the horizontal axis is relabeled P, LMP_s is redesignated LMy_s, and IS becomes ISy_s. The caption under figure 6(a) would be changed to $y_s' > 0 > y_N'$; under 6(b) to $0 > y_s' > y_N'$ or $y_N' > y_s' > 0$; under 6(c) to $y_N' > 0 > y_s'$; and under 6(d) to $y_s' > y_N' > 0$. Thus figure 6(a) would be the r–P counterpart to figure 4(a); 6(b) to 4(b) or 4(c); 6(c) to 4(d); and 6(d) to a model in which AS and AD are both upward sloped, but AS is flatter.[22]

Inspection of the revised figure 6 would indicate that in r–P space Walrasian, like Marshallian, stability requires the slope of both LMy_s and RR to exceed that of ISy_s. (That RR must in any case lie between LMy_s and ISy_s at any price level can be established by reference to the relative positions of r_L, r_T, and r_N in figure 7(b).) Moreover, it can easily be shown that $(dr/dP)_{LMy_s} > (dr/dP)_{ISy_s}$ is consistent with the Walrasian stability rule, (2.21).[23]

IV. THE REAL BALANCE EFFECT

The presence of the real balance effect on consumption affects the stability of the system by causing (1) a change in the slope of aggregate demand [see (1.4)], and (2) in the Marshallian output-market adjustment, a change in the weight function used in deriving P_d'. These changes affect the speed of adjustment but not the stability conditions.

Consider first the Marshallian case. Although the effective demand price remains the same as that specified by (2.4), the transfer rate, r_T, derived from (2.5), is now determined by

$$I(y, r_T) - S\left(y, r_T, \frac{M}{P_s(y)}\right) = \frac{M}{P_s(y)} - L(y, r_T) \tag{4.1}$$

with

$$\frac{dr_T}{dy} = -\frac{I_y - S_y + L_y + (1 + S_M)\dfrac{M}{P_s^2}P_s'(y)}{I_r - S_r + L_r}.$$

This altered relation between r_T and y affects the magnitude of the weight function for P'_d in (2.10).[24] But the stability condition in (2.11), $P'_N < P'_s$, still holds.

In the case where the speed of adjustment in the security market is finite, the real balance effect affects mainly the *IS* relationship,

$$I(y, r) = S[y, r, M/P_s(y)],$$

which defines the upper portion of the $\dot{y} = 0$ locus. Each increase in y depresses $M/P_s(y)$, thereby raising S and causing a leftward shift in *IS*. The resultant relation between the natural rate, r_N, and y incorporates the *AS* relation between P_s and y, and is labeled ISP_s. Its slope is given by

$$\left(\frac{dr}{dy}\right)_{ISP_s} = -\frac{I_y - S_y + S_{\frac{M}{P}} \frac{M}{P^2} P'_s}{I_r - S_r} = \left(\frac{dr}{dy}\right)_{IS} - \frac{S_{\frac{M}{P}} \frac{M}{P^2} P'_s}{I_r - S_r} \qquad (4.2)$$

which is greater or less than the slope of its member *IS* curves as $P'_s \gtreqless 0$. Combining (4.2) and (3.5), we can rewrite the stability condition

$$\left(\frac{dr}{dy}\right)_{LMP_s} > \left(\frac{dr}{dy}\right)_{ISP_s}$$

as

$$\left(\frac{1}{L_r} - \frac{S_{\frac{M}{P}}}{I_r - S_r}\right)\left(P'_N - P'_s\right) > 0.$$

As in the case where the securities market is instantaneously equilibrating, the system is stable with $P'_N < P'_s$.

Consider next the Walrasian output-market adjustment. Although the real balance effect alters the relation between r_T and y, it leaves the weight function, γ, in (2.19), and therefore the stability condition in (2.21), unchanged. Its only impact is to alter the slope of *AD*.

In the case of finite adjustment in the security market, the real balance effect, while leaving LMy_s unaffected, tends to increase the steepness of ISy_s:

$$I[y_s(P), r] = S[y_s(P), r, M/P]$$

$$\left(\frac{dr}{dy}\right)_{ISy_s} = -\frac{(I_y - S_y)y'_s + S_{\frac{M}{P}}\frac{M}{P^2}}{I_r - S_r} < -\frac{(I_r - S_r)y'_s}{I_r - S_r}.$$

However, the stability condition (2.21) remains effective.[25] As in the case where the securities market is instantaneously equilibrating, a positive real balance effect affects the stability of the system only by causing a change in the slope of *AD*.

V. SUMMARY

Our global stability analysis of aggregate supply and demand incorporates stock-flow interactions in the security market and treats both Marshallian and Walrasian adjustment processes in the output market. Given our assumptions, among them $I_r - S_r < 0$, Marshallian stability requires the horizontal slope of aggregate supply to exceed that of aggregate demand. Walrasian stability requires the vertical slope of aggregate supply to be greater or less, respectively, than that of aggregate demand when the horizontal slope of *LM* is greater or less than that of *IS*. These results hold regardless of the speed of adjustment in the security market.

Our analysis is supplemented by *IS-LM* schedules that incorporate the aggregate supply relationship between price and output. While the resulting curves resemble Patinkin's general equilibrium model, they reflect our assumptions of variable output and an interest rate mechanism based on stock-flow interactions. The interest rate path is shown to be monotonic, if the security market is instantaneously equilibrating, but possibly cyclical if the speed of adjustment in that market is finite.

NOTES

The authors wish to thank James Quirk for valuable comments and suggestions.

1. Brownlee (1948) attempted an aggregate supply-demand exposition somewhat earlier. His supply function is based on the Keynesian rigid-wage assumption, but his demand curve is derived from the money market without reference to *IS*. Moreover, the demand for money is equal to all of income and is independent of the rate of interest. Given the money supply, this imparts a simple rectangular hyperbolic relation between *P* and *y*, which is taken as the aggregate demand curve. Brownlee (p. 228) asserts that the rate of interest is held constant by government action; but in that event, *LM* would be horizontal and demand vertical (see Marschak, 1951, p. 20.62).

2. Clower (1954) also interacted security market stocks and flows. His analysis described the adjustment of a stationary state and so omitted a flow demand originating in current saving. Horwich's framework, which we employ in this paper, contained both flow demand and supply security functions and is thus essentially that of a growing economy. Horwich also related the security markets to the money market and aggregate expenditures, as we do in section I(B) below.

3. Although our sign restrictions preclude it, the pathological case, $I_r - S_r > 0$, would add an alternative condition under which the inequality of (1.4a) holds:

$$0 \geq S_{\frac{M}{P}} > \frac{I_r - S_r}{L_r}.$$

$I_r - S_r > 0$ could occur for a sufficiently small $S_r < 0$. That this is not empirically implausible is shown by Webber (1970).

4. Again, $I_r - S_r > 0$ would add an alternative condition. For the inequality of (1.4b), it is

$$0 > \frac{I_r - S_r}{L_r} > S_{\frac{M}{P}}.$$

5. Aggregate demand, as represented in (1.3), is the sum of desired consumption and investment. The former is the unconstrained utility-maximizing level of consumption; the latter is the expected profit-maximizing level of investment that firms are willing to undertake if the supply of funds is not a constraint. Effective demand, on the other hand, is equal to effective consumption plus effective investment. Effective consumption is the consumption level which maximizes households' utility subject to the condition that income is equal to actual output (see Clower, 1965). Effective investment is the desired level of investment that firms are able to finance in the securities market. Finally, aggregate supply is the profit-maximizing level of output. Since we assume that the time path of the economy moves along the AS curve, AS is also effective supply.

6. See May (1970) for the argument that separate Walras' laws for stock and flow functions should be written. See also Foley and Sidrauski (1971, pp. 89–90), Perg (1974), and Horwich (1955, 1964).

7. If the security is a common stock, the rate of interest is, of course, the dividend-price ratio.

8. Hendershott and Horwich (1974) assumed two limiting cases, one in which output is fixed and the excess demand for output is choked off entirely by a rise in the price level, another in which prices are fixed and output rises to the level of effective demand. In the former case, the rate of interest is constant at r_T^0 and, with reference to (1.18), P_s assumes a value above P_s^0 such that the excess supply of real balances is zero and y_d again equals y_s^0. In the latter case of elastic output, y_s takes on a value equal to y_d^1; the excess supply of money is eliminated by increases in the demand for money both because of the rise in output and an induced fall in the rate of interest. The fall in interest is explained by the fact that r_T rose as part of the financing process *prior* to the excess expenditure, and that the resulting increase in output tends to increase L somewhat less than enough to maintain r_T at r_T^0 (ibid., p. 388).

9. Branson (1979, p. 178) identifies the excess demand at a nonequilibrium price, such as P_s^0, as the entire distance between point A and the abscissa of the AD curve, which he designates y_2. But this fails to take account of the income constraint provided by the actual level of output, y_s^0 (or y_0 in Branson's notation). Demand is effective when households are able to sell all of their desired factor services. At output y_s^0, this condition is met by demand level y_d^1 and not y_2. See Clower (1965). Dernburg and McDougall (1976, pp. 443–446) present a construction similar to Branson's, except that it is cast in terms of $IS\text{-}LM$ instead of $AD\text{-}AS$.

10. The effect of the short-period Marshallian adjustment on effective demand corresponds to one of the limiting cases described in note 8: output is fixed and the rise in prices is solely responsible for eliminating the excess supply of money and reducing y_d to the y_s^0 level.

11. Effective demand will rise equally with any induced increase in output, and y_d and y_s will be equal at the start of the next adjustment interval. While the

consumption component of effective demand will tend to rise less than output, investment expenditure will rise by the full difference between C and y_s, viz., the increase in *ex ante* saving. This is because the underlying conditions are those of disequilibrium in which $I > S$. Any increase in desired saving, a flow of funds directed at securities, will, at the going rate of interest, be absorbed immediately by a portion of the prevailing excess flow supply of securities (equal to desired investment) and converted fully to investment outlays.

The rise in output will also cause an instantaneous displacement of the money market equilbrium. The increase in y_s increases L; M/P also increases because of the fall in P (to the new P_s level, which, while it tends to be above P_s^0, is below P_d^0, the immediately preceding price level). Depending on the relative movements of demand and supply, the market rate will increase or decrease. However, this is a second-order movement of r, which in general will not be deflected from its equilibrating course.

12. If the model were unstable, the interest rate inequality would be reversed, but with r_T still the middle rate: for $y \lesseqgtr y^e$, $r_L \gtreqless r_T \gtreqless r_N$.

Notice also that since the ranking of interest rates depends only on the interest-rate slopes of $I - S$ and $M/P - L$, it is independent of $I_y - S_y$ and thus of the slope of IS.

13. The rule for the placement of y_d relative to the AD and AS schedules is more complex than it is for P_d. With reference to (2.22), we have three cases for the slope of y_d, and thereby its position relative to y_N and y_s. As $y_N' \lesseqgtr y_s'$,

$$y_N' \lesseqgtr y_d' \lesseqgtr y_s' \text{ if } 0 < \gamma < 1$$
$$y_d' \lesseqgtr y_N' \lesseqgtr y_s' \text{ if } \gamma > 1$$
$$y_N' \lesseqgtr y_s' \lesseqgtr y_d' \text{ if } \gamma < 0.$$

14. We are implicitly assuming that at $r < r_L^0$, saving goes entirely into the purchase of new, as opposed to existing, securities. For if any portion of saving were expended on existing securities (of which the excess supply is positive), funds would be diverted from new issues, causing investment spending and thus output to contract. Notice that in these circumstances, with the excess stock demand for securities negative, saving is the only potential source of investment financing. This is not the case at $r_L^0 < r < r_N^0$, at which the excess stock demand is positive. In this range, moreover, savers have no choice but to buy new issues.

15. Note the difference in the way in which I-S gaps are eliminated directly above and below the RR schedule. Below RR, a portion of the gap (the horizontal distance between the excess investment and real-balance lines) is simply not financed. The portion that is financed (the amount given by the excess supply of real balances) is suppressed by a sufficient increase in the effective demand price above the supply price. Above RR, I-S gaps are fully financed and are erased entirely by the increase of demand price.

16. If the interest rate adjustment is instantaneous and stable, the dynamic path moves vertically, directly to the RR schedule, and thence along it. More precisely, the period adjustment generates a series of discrete instantaneous back-and-forth movements between LMP_s and RR. See Hendershott and Horwich (1974, pp. 391, 395, 396). In the r–y diagrams on these pages, the locus corresponding to RR is traced out by temporarily shifting LM schedules.

17. $P'_s > 0$ is not only sufficient for LMP_s to be rising (3.5), but also for it to be steeper than any single LM schedule:

$$\left(\frac{dr}{dy}\right)_{LMP_s} \overset{\geq}{\underset{<}{}} \left(\frac{dr}{dy}\right)_{LM}$$

$$-\frac{1}{L_r}\left(\frac{M}{P_s^2}P'_s + L_y\right) \overset{\geq}{\underset{<}{}} -\frac{L_y}{L_r}$$

$$P'_s \overset{\geq}{\underset{<}{}} 0.$$

RR will also be upward sloped in the model of figure 6(b): in (3.3) the left side is > 0 and the right side is < 0. Note also that, by the Olech (1963) theorem, the stability of the system requires, in addition,

$$\Phi'\,(I_r - S_r) + \Psi'\,(I_y - S_y) < 0.$$

This second condition is satisfied if the IS curve is downward sloped or if the speed of adjustment in the security market is sufficiently great relative to that in the output market (e.g., $\Phi' \to \infty$).

18. By (3.5) we see that $P'_s < 0$ is not sufficient for LMP_s to have a downward slope. But the right side of (3.5) promises to be of such small absolute magnitude that P'_s does not have to be very much below zero to grant LMP_s a negative slope.

19. This inequality assumes the security market is stable. Otherwise it is reversed, but with r_T still in the middle. See page 253, including note 12.

20. Recall, however, that the dynamics underlying the P_N (or P_d) and P_s stability rule were based on the assumption of instantaneous and stable security-market adjustment. That is, the path in r–y space is on the RR schedule. The P_d function, accordingly, was derived on the assumption that effective demand is equal to the financing available at each r_T (RR) level. Thus when the market rates, under finite security-market adjustment in the region of $\dot{y} > 0$, deviate from RR, effective demand tends to be less than the levels generated at r_T: at $r > r_T$, more excess balances are offered, but excess desired investment, the spending constraint, is lower; at $r < r_T$, fewer balances are available and thereby limit the increased desired investment. The P_d function is pulled downward; P_d, as constructed in figure 3, is an upper boundary. In the region of $\dot{y} < 0$, $I - S < 0$ is effectively unconstrained, exerting an unqualified downward influence on demand price and thence output. See page 259. Thus when $r \gtrless r_T$, both $I - S$ and $\dot{y}$ are algebraically $\lessgtr$ than their values at r_T, and the relevant segment of P_d is lowered or raised, respectively.

21. In the absence of these output influences, IS, independent of P, would be a horizontal line in r–P space. Taking account of y_s (P) shifts IS vertically, up or down, and traces a nonhorizontal locus as P is varied.

22. Figure 6(a) could, for a sufficiently small absolute value of $y'_s < 0$, also be the counterpart to the model of figure 4(a) [cf. (3.12)].

23. The proof follows:

$$\left(\frac{dr}{dy}\right)_{LM_{y_s}} > \left(\frac{dr}{dy}\right)_{IS_{y_s}}$$

$$-\frac{\frac{M}{P^2} + L_y \, y_s'}{L_r} > -\frac{(I_y - S_y) \, y_s'}{(I_r - S_r)}$$

$$-\frac{M}{P^2}\frac{1}{L_r} > y_s' \left(\frac{L_y}{L_r} - \frac{I_y - S_y}{I_r - S_r}\right)$$

$$\frac{M}{P^2}\frac{1}{L_r} < y_s' \left[\left(\frac{dr}{dy}\right)_{LM} - \left(\frac{dr}{dy}\right)_{IS}\right]$$

$$y_N' \lessgtr y_s' \text{ if } \left(\frac{dr}{dy}\right)_{LM} > \left(\frac{dr}{dy}\right)_{IS}$$

$$y_N' \gtrless y_s' \text{ if } \left(\frac{dr}{dy}\right)_{LM} < \left(\frac{dr}{dy}\right)_{IS}$$

Q.E.D.

24. The weight function $\beta = -\dfrac{\frac{1}{L_r}}{\alpha} = \dfrac{I_r - S_r}{I_r - S_r + L_r}$, used in deriving P_d' [see (2.10)] is reduced to

$$\beta = \frac{I_r - S_r + S_{M/P}\, L_r}{I_r - S_r + L_r} > 0 \text{ if } \frac{I_r - S_r}{L_r} > S_{M/P}.$$

Contrary to the case of no real balance effect, a positive $I_r - S_r$ is consistent with a positive β and therefore with the stability condition $P_N' < P_s'$.

25.

$$\left(\frac{dr}{dy}\right)_{LM_{y_s}} < \left(\frac{dr}{dy}\right)_{IS_{y_s}}$$

$$\frac{\frac{M}{P^2} - L_y \, y_s'}{L_r} > \frac{(I_y - S_y) \, y_s' + S_M \frac{M}{P^2}}{I_r - S_r}$$

$$\left(-\frac{L_y}{L_r} + \frac{I_y - S_y}{I_r - S_r}\right) y_s' - \left(\frac{M}{P^2} + \frac{S_M \frac{M}{P^2}}{I_r - S_r}\right) > 0$$

$$\left[\left(\frac{dr}{dy}\right)_{LM} - \left(\frac{dr}{dy}\right)_{IS}\right](y_s' - y_N') > 0.$$

REFERENCES

Bailey, M. J. *National Income and the Price Level.* New York: McGraw-Hill, 1971.
Barro, R. J., and Grossman, H. I. "A General Disequilibrium Model of Income and Employment," *American Economic Review,* 61 (March 1971), 82–93.
Branson, W. H. *Macroeconomic Theory and Policy.* New York: Harper & Row, 1979.
Bronfenbrenner, M., and Holzman, F. "A Survey of Inflation Theory," *American Economic Review,* 53 (September 1963), 593–661.
Brownlee, O. H. "Money, Credit, and Monetary Policy," section 4 in F. M. Boddy, ed., *Applied Economic Analysis.* New York: Pitman, 1948.
_____. "The Theory of Employment and Stabilization Policy," *Journal of Political Economy,* 58 (October 1950), 412–424.
Chang, W. W., and Smyth, D. J. "The Stability and Instability of *IS-LM* Equilibrium," *Oxford Economic Papers,* 24 (1972), 372–384.
Clower, R. W. "Productivity, Thrift and the Rate of Interest," *Economic Journal,* 64 (March 1954), 107–115.
_____. "The Keynesian Counterrevolution: A Theoretical Appraisal," in F. H. Hahn and F. P. Brechling, eds., *The Theory of Interest Rates,* pp. 103–125. New York: Macmillan, 1965.
Dernburg, T. F., and McDougall, D. M. *Macroeconomics.* 5th ed. New York: McGraw-Hill, 1976.
Foley, D. K., and Sidrauski, M. *Monetary and Fiscal Policy in a Growing Economy.* New York: Macmillan, 1971.
Hendershott, P. H., and Horwich, G. "*IS-LM* as a Dynamic Framework," in G. Horwich and P. A. Samuelson, eds., *Trade, Stability, and Macroeconomics: Essays in Honor of Lloyd A. Metzler,* pp. 375–399. New York: Academic Press, 1974.
Horwich, G. "Open Market Operations, the Rate of Interest, and the Price Level." University of Chicago dissertation (March 1954). Summarized in *Journal of Finance,* 10 (December 1955), 508–509.
_____. *Money, Capital, and Prices.* Homewood, Ill.: Irwin, 1964.
Korliras, P. G. "A Disequilibrium Macroeconomic Model," *Quarterly Journal of Economics,* 89 (February 1975), 56–80.
McKenna, J. P. *Aggregate Economic Analysis.* New York: Dryden Press, 1955.
Marschak, J. *Lectures on Income, Employment, and the Price Level.* New York: Kelley, 1951.
May, J. "Period Analysis and Continuous Analysis in Patinkin's Macroeconomic Model," *Journal of Economic Theory,* 2 (March 1970), 1–9.
Modigliani, F. "Liquidity Preference and the Theory of Interest and Money," *Econometrica,* 12 (January 1944), 45–88.
Olech, C. "On the Global Stability of an Autonomous System on the Plane," J. P. LaSalle and J. B. Diaz, eds., vol. 1: *The Contribution to Differential Equations,* pp. 389–400. New York: Wiley, 1963.
Patinkin, D. *Money, Interest, and Prices.* New York: Harper & Row, 1965.
Perg, W. F. "The Dynamics of Interest Rate Adjustment in a Keynesian Macroeconomic Model," in G. Horwich and P. A. Samuelson, eds., *Trade, Stability, and Macroeconomics: Essays in Honor of Lloyd A. Metzler,* pp. 401–425. New York: Academic Press, 1974.
Pesek, B. P., and Saving, T. R. *Money, Wealth, and Economic Theory.* New York: Macmillan, 1967.
Rose, H. "Liquidity Preference and Loanable Funds," *Review of Economic Studies,* 24 (February 1957), 111–119.

Solow, R. M., and Stiglitz, J. E. "Output, Employment, and Wages in the Short Run," *Quarterly Journal of Economics*, 82 (November 1968), 537–560.

Webber, W. E. "The Effect of Interest Rates on Aggregate Consumption," *American Economic Review*, 60 (September 1970), 591–600.

Economics
Education

The Development
of Economics Education
through the Principles
of Economics Course
in the United States:
Its Goals, Content,
and Methodology

Dennis J. Weidenaar

Economics education has many dimensions, and the breadth of its scope is reflected in this volume. In addition, consider the following sampling of contemporary economic education activities. Largely through the efforts of Lawrence Senesh, the nation's first professor of economics education—appointed, not surprisingly, by E. T. Weiler—basic economic concepts have been introduced in the elementary social studies classrooms throughout the country.[1] At the other extreme, college- and university-level professors of education are now receiving economics instruction in institutes designed to meet their needs.[2] For over twenty years, the Economic Education Foundation for Clergy has instructed clergymen of all faiths in positive economics.[3]

During the past several years, economics instructional programs for employees have become common in many companies. Admittedly, many of them stretch the credibility of the term "economics education" beyond the breaking point, frequently turning out to be advocacy programs. Nonetheless, there are several programs which are reasonably objective and do convey basic economic principles.

In addition to Lawrence Senesh's activities, Marilyn Kourilsky at the University of California, Los Angeles, has developed a whole series of learning programs for elementary school students, namely, the Kinder-economy, the Mini-society, and the Max-economy.

Teacher workshops in economics have become summer traditions, coordinated by members of over 100 college and university economics departments, seeking to add to the skills of the classroom teacher whose education has been devoid of formal economics instruction.

For over twenty-five years, the Joint Council on Economic Education and its affiliated state councils and university centers have sought to upgrade the level of economics taught in the schools by producing curricular materials, sponsoring workshops, and recruiting entire school systems to cooperate in such ventures.

But underlying all of these activities and surpassing each of them, in terms of the value of inputs used and sheer perserverance, has been the lowly principles of economics course. This is the vehicle by which the vast majority of the educated public has acquired its first and, in many cases, last contact with formal economics education.

The principles of economics course—the early training ground of budding economists, the path to wealth for a fortunate few textbook authors, the department head's justification for new positions, and the last holdout from the cutting edge of the discipline of economics—provides a fascinating study of the development of economics education. I believe it is accurate to say that virtually all practicing economists received their introductions to the profession through the portals of principles of economics courses and, quite likely, exercised their newly won economics understanding in the confines of principles of economics classes.

In addition to the role this course has had in the careers of practicing economists, the person whom we are honoring in this symposium has made a significant contribution, both as professor and dean, to the development and success of this important course.

In 1952, E. T. Weiler wrote a principles of economics text with the title *The Economic System*.[4] It was revised and published in 1957 as *The American Economic System*.[5] It was well received and adopted by the best schools in the country. But, alas, there simply were not enough of the best schools to perpetuate it. Anyone who has used the text will immediately recall the detailed and useful modifications to the circular flow diagram introduced by Weiler, and his emphasis on general equilibrium and on how prices and money payments serve as a communications system. His concern for the student, as well as his rigor, are reflected in the preface to the first edition, where he states: "A textbook must, however, serve two masters. Not only must it fairly represent our intellectual heritage; it must also be thoroughly comprehensible to the student."[6]

Upon his promotion from the deanship to the position of Krannert Distinguished Professor of Management and Economics, Weiler again threw himself headlong into teaching and developing materials for the principles of economics course, culminating in the publication of another textbook, *Economics: An Introduction to the World around You*,[7] an exploit which I have had the enriching experience of sharing with Weiler.

Given this background, it is fitting that we survey the historic development of this course—the mainstay effort in economics education—and the object of an immense contribution by E. T. Weiler.

The members of the American Economic Association exhibited a keen interest in economics education in its earliest days. In an organizational meeting in 1886, Richard T. Ely stated: "One aim of our association should be the education of public opinion in regard to economic questions and economic literature. In no other science is there so much quackery and it must be our province to expose it and bring it into merited contempt."[8]

In the fourth annual meeting of the association, Francis A. Walker, its president, and author of a widely used principles of economics textbook, created a standing committee on the teaching of political economy.[9]

The interest the association displayed—like the booms and busts its members so intently study, waxed and waned over time. In an attempt to view in an organized way the goals, content, and methodologies exercised in the principles of economics course over the last century, it is useful to identify several time periods (albeit artificial) that reflect different thrusts and interests, and examine these periods in terms of the content, methodology, and goals of economics education as expressed in the principles course. Following the guidance of Lawrence Leamer (cited in note 8), the following periods emerge as reasonable phases in the development of economics education as reflected in the typical college courses.

Phase I, 1865–1900. This is a period in which political economy emerged as a legitimate discipline in American colleges and universities, as the receding shadows of the Civil War left a wake strewn with economic problems.

Phase II, 1900–1930. This period was characterized by increased collegiate enrollments and emphasis on commercial education, not unlike the current interest in consumer economics.

Phase III, 1930–1960. The dissatisfaction with the economic system during the early part of this phase was reflected in the content and the way economics was taught. The latter part featured the introduction of employment theory into the principles course.

Phase IV, 1960 to the present. This period featured the blending of educational technology with concern for evaluating its effects.

I will begin with the most recent period, which shares with the 1865–1900 era the distinction of being the most active period in economics education. This period, 1960 to the present, features a number of events that occurred simultaneously—some less successful than others—leading to a general increase in support and prestige for economics education and greater interest in the introductory college course.

An incomplete recitation of events during this period, in more or less chronological order, would include:

1. A conference convened to study the principles of economics course, culminating in the publication of *The Teaching of Elementary Economics* (Holt, Rinehart, and Winston), edited by K. A. Knopf and J. H. Strauss, in 1960.

2. The national television course, "The American Economy," starring Professor John R. Coleman of Carnegie-Mellon University, filmed in 1962.
3. The Elkhart Project, introducing economics to elementary school children, conducted by Lawrence Senesh.
4. A program conducted by the Stanford Graduate School of Business, held in the summer of 1966, titled "New Developments in the Teaching of Economics," and subsequent publication of the proceedings, edited by Keith G. Lumsden. Its main emphasis was on the methodology in teaching economics rather than on the content.
5. The operation of year-long master's-degree programs in economics for in-service social studies teachers, conducted at the University of Missouri, Ohio University, and Purdue University.
6. The series of summer institutes held at the University of Chicago for college teachers of economics, sponsored by the General Electric Foundation.
7. Publication by the Psychological Corporation of the "Test of Understanding of College Economics" in 1968. Development of this test was recommended by the Committee on Education of the American Economic Association. Its preparation was supervised by a committee appointed by the Joint Council on Economic Education.
8. Four annual workshops for economic educators in economics education research, 1969–1972, at Carnegie-Mellon and Purdue universities.
9. The birth of the *Journal of Economic Education* in 1969.
10. The application to economics of educational innovations such as programmed learning, television, computer-assisted instruction, and personalized systems of instruction.
11. Introduction of different textbook approaches and formats, including the paperbound "cafeteria" approach; the explicit introduction of calculus; reemphasis on the problems approach; and the radical economics viewpoint.
12. The growth of state councils and university centers for economics education.
13. The increased mandating of economics courses for high school students.
14. Creation by the Joint Council on Economic Education of the *Master Curriculum*, a guide to the economic concepts that are appropriate for precollege economics education.
15. Preparation and dissemination of the film/videotape *Tradeoffs*, a series of vignettes that teach basic economic concepts.

The period of the late '60s to the present, more than any previous period, was characterized by attempts to evaluate the effectiveness of alternative methods of presenting economics, primarily at the principles level.[10] This emphasis came about for several reasons. The unveiling of a nationally normed measure of college-level economic understanding that bore the imprimatur of some of the profession's most respected economists was quickly, and in many cases unthinkingly, adopted as the criterion of economic understanding. This test, affectionately referred to as "the TUCE" (Test of Understanding of College Economics), came just as the "canned" multiple regression computer programs became available to virtually everyone affiliated with a university. It also coincided with the inauguration of the new *Journal of Economic Education.*

With the TUCE score as a dependent variable, computer regression programs ready to run, and a journal soliciting articles, the teaching methodology used in the classroom became the focus of study. Concurrently, programmed learning, television, and personalized systems of instruction entered the scene. A decade of frantic economics education research activity was initiated, with results that can be summarized in one sentence. As far as TUCE is concerned, nothing makes any difference except sex. The conclusion is that no statistically significant difference is evident in the economics understanding of college students, whether exposed to television, programmed learning, different instructors, different textbooks, different hours, etc. The only variable that shows statistical significance consistently is sex. Females score lower than males.

However, the most interesting study, and one whose results seem to contradict the TUCE findings, was conducted by Philip Saunders. He sought to test the Stigler hypothesis (proposed at the 1962 American Economic Association meetings) that asserted—given an adequate sample of college alumni (preferably men five years out of college), equally divided between those who have never had a course in economics and those who have had a conventional one-year course—an examination on current economic problems (not on textbook questions) will reveal no difference in the performances of the two groups. The results (without going into the details of the study) showed that the average scores of alumni with only a principles course, compared to those with none, was higher by 3.7 points out of 33. The difference is statistically significant at the .001 level. Whether 3.7 points out of 33 is large or small is debatable. One measure of its magnitude is that it would take a difference of over 300 points in combined SAT scores to approach the difference in scores associated with having taken an introductory economics course.[11]

Now that there is some evidence that all those valiant efforts in the principles of economics course have not been completely in vain, let us trace the developments in the introductory economics course since the Civil War.

What has changed since political economy became a legitimate discipline in the colleges and universities of America? In particular, what can we say about what is taught, how it is taught, the content, and the goals?

PHASE I: 1865–1900

The real impetus to formal incorporation of political economy into the curriculum came shortly after the Civil War. L. Lawrence Laughlin wrote a little book in May 1885 (the same year in which the American Economic Association was organized) titled *The Study of Political Economy*. In it, he attributed the rise in the popularity of economics directly to the Civil War:

> In fact, it is now unquestionable that a new interest in economics and finance has already arisen, and the cause of it seems to be very clear. The Civil War was, so to speak, the convulsion which brought into existence a desire for the study of political economy in the United States. The country was stirred to its depths by economic questions: for they entered into the political issues of exciting campaigns. The war issues thus did for the United States—in a different way, of course—even more than the corn-law agitation did for England. They actually gave birth to new motives for study. There never has been a time in our history when there was so evident a desire to get light on the economic problems of the day as now.

The most frequently cited aim of economics education was its value as a mental exercise. There was no shortage of ideas on how best to teach economics. Again, I quote Laughlin:

> The key to efficient teaching [of political economy] is to connect principles with actual facts: and this process can go on in the beginner's mind only through experience. By experience I mean the personal (subjective) effort of each one to realize the working of the principle for himself in the facts of his own knowledge.
> The relative advantages of lectures and recitations for political economy have never to my knowledge been openly discussed. An experience with both methods of teaching leads me to think that the lecture system, pure and simple, is so ineffective that it ought to be set aside at once as entirely undesirable. The disciplinary power to be gained by the study is almost wholly lost to the student by this method of teaching.

His recommendations could have been written today. They include:

1. Recitation.
2. Writing questions on the chalkboard.
3. Using newspapers.
4. Using charts and diagrams.
5. Using graphs.
6. Testing for applications, not facts.

He also urged his students to write in their textbooks and form discussion clubs of three or four people.

Had you been a student in the post–Civil War period, your economics text would most likely have been one of the following: Smith's *Wealth of Nations*, Ricardo's *Principles of Political Economy and Taxation*, Mill's *Principles of Political Economy*, Bowen's *Principles of Political Economy*, Rogers' *A Manual of Political Economy for Schools and Colleges*, Cairnes' *Leading Principles of Political Economy*, or Walker's *Political Economy*.

The content of your course would have included a section on the character and logical method of political economy, followed by units organized into production, exchange, distribution, and consumption. Production would have focused on the factors of production. Exchange would have dealt with the theory of value, international exchange, and money. Distribution would have covered the returns to the productive resources: rent, interest, wages, and profits. The consumption section would likely have been brief, discussing the morality of different wants, among other things. The problems that would have been raised in class dealt with the silver question, industrial cooperation (monopolies), pauperism, trade unions and strikes, the national banking system, metallism, taxation, protectionism, socialism, the public land system, and the regulation of freight and passenger fares on the railways.

PHASE II: 1900–1930

By 1900, many new textbooks had been written and your course may have used one or more of the following: Marshall's *Principles of Economics*, Ely's *Outlines of Economics*, Davenport's *Outlines of Elementary Economics*, Seligman's *Elements of Political Economy*, Fisher's *Elementary Principles of Economics*, and Taussig's *Principles of Economics*. As you can see from the titles, the term "political economy" was shed for "economics."[12]

The goals of the introductory course in economics were thoughtfully expressed by A. B. Wolfe of Oberlin College at a conference on the teaching of elementary economics in 1909. Wolfe suggested the following goals.

a. Students should acquire a general knowledge of the organization and processes of the business world sufficient to enable them to read the newspapers—even the financial page—with something approaching intelligent comprehension, and gain the power and willingness to see something outside the economic class to which they belong and the business or industry which they know a little about.

b. Students should get the beginnings of an intelligent interest in politico-economic questions and policies.

c. Students should have their inherited and habitual prejudices shaken up; should begin to acquire the elements of the judicial fairmindedness and critical cautiousness of which we all ought to have more when dealing with practical economic issues.

d. Students should gain a stimulus to a desire for economic justice throughout society and a background upon which to view various large and small schemes of social reform.

Ideally, the content would include extended treatment of money, banking, and present American monetary problems, with a background of the history of currency and banking in this country. This would entail:

Knowing the organization of the U. S. Treasury.

Knowing the organization of a typical bank.

Knowing the relation of banking to speculation.

International trade, with concrete discussion of the tariff and its history.

Transportation and the theory of railway-rate making, of the processes of the ICC.

Theory of monopoly and a study of the rise, organization, and economics influence of industrial corporations, including outline knowledge of two or three great railway systems and trusts, such as the Standard Oil Company and the United States Steel Company.

Business organization in a limited sense: marketing, accounting, production, etc.

Labor problems should be given a large share of attention.

Much time on the study of public revenue, especially taxation.

Agricultural economics, including irrigation and conservation.

It was also suggested that one use economics history throughout the course, not just as a preface, and the student should know about the Industrial Revolution and the place in economic theory of the Mercantilists, Physiocrats, Smith, Ricardo, Senior, Malthus, Mill, Cairnes, Jevons, Marshall, the Austrian School, and half a dozen contemporary American economists.

The methodology should be:

1. Effective presentation of facts and principles.
2. Personal discussion of these facts and principles with the student in order to clear up difficulties, ensure comprehension, etc.
3. Drilling the student in reproducing and applying economic principles.
4. Testing the student as to the correctness, fullness, and adequacy of his knowledge and his capacity to apply it.

The content in this period includes the organization of production, value and exchange (including supply, demand, and elasticity), money and banking, international trade, distribution of wealth, labor, and taxation. The primary problems dealt with trusts, public ownership, railway rates, and socialism.

The goals of economics education shifted from mental discipline to broader goals. In 1899, the American Economic Association published *Economics as a School Study* by Frederick R. Chow. His report notes that "economics helps people to understand the great individual world in which they live. To most men the industrial world is the only one that exists, it is their whole being. Now economics turns the light of scientific investigation on the phenomena of this world."[13] By this time, economics was creeping into the high schools and a debate raged as to whether economics was an appropriate discipline for that group of students. Among the adherents were Ely, Taussig, and Laughlin, all of whom had written textbooks. They expressed concern, however, over the poorly prepared teachers, and especially about the capacity of pupils, but they felt that the available textbooks were adequate. President Capen of Tufts stated: "The subject is so broad and so profound and has so many ramifications, requiring so much knowledge on kindred subjects before it can be thoroughly digested and applied, that I sometimes doubt the wisdom of trying to teach it to immature minds."[14]

The approach of the authors of some of the better-known textbooks is instructive. Irving Fisher addressed part of the preface in his economics textbook to the methods of writing economics textbooks.[15]

Of the many possible methods of writing economics textbooks, there are three which follow well-defined (though widely different) orders of topics. These are "historical," "logical," and "pedagogical."

> The historical method follows the order provided by economic history.
> The logical approach begins with a classification of economics in relation to other studies, explains its methodology, and then proceeds by means of abstract examples, from the simplest imaginary case of "Robinson Crusoe economics" to the more complex conditions of real life.
> The pedagogical approach begins with the student's existing experience, theories, and prejudices as to economic topics, and proceeds to mold them into a correct and self-consistent whole.

The order of the first method, therefore, is from ancient to modern, that of the second from simple to complex, and that of the third, from familiar to unfamiliar. The third order is the one here adopted.

Taussig made no bones about the content of his text. In the preface of his two-volume work he stated:

> No one can understand economic phenomena or prepare himself to deal with economic problems who is unwilling to follow trains of reasoning which call for sustained attention.
> Though not written on the usual model of textbooks and not planned primarily to meet the needs of teachers and students, the book will prove of service I hope in institutions which offer substantial courses in economics. The fact that it is addressed to mature persons, not to the immature, should be an argument in favor of its use rather than against it.[16]

PHASE III: 1930–1960

Economics education fell to its lowest state during the early part of this period, the 1930s. The principles course became a whipping boy for the economic events which troubled the nation. The profession—the American Economic Association—relegated concern for economics education to periodic roundtable discussions where the problems of teaching were dealt with in a "bull session" manner, each participant calling upon his personal experiences as providing the guidance for future teaching. The profound concern in 1935, for example, was the extent to which economics students should follow developments in the New Deal by reading current magazines as supplements to the textbook. After considerable debate, in which Frank Knight suggested we not rely on the "pink weeklies" entirely and John R. Commons urged that students find out what the science of economics was and what are its laws, H. L. McCracken summarized the debate by stating that there are two views:

> One is that classical principles of economics are still the basic principles and the automatic forces of supply and demand will be the major forces operating to bring about a recovery. The other is that the economic order had come to such a pass by 1933 that a considerable amount of government intervention was necessary, and any realistic attempt to teach economic principles must reckon with that fact.[17]

In 1940, in another roundtable discussion, four criticisms were leveled against the introductory economics courses in American colleges: (1) they have no clear objective; (2) they lack any semblance of unity, having become hodgepodges of unrelated subjects; (3) they are so overcrowded that adequate treatment of content is impossible; (4) college students, admitted to them, are without the necessary background.

However, help was on the way. In 1942 a 212-page introductory economics book, with the title *The Social Framework*, written by J. R. Hicks (and adapted for American readers by A. G. Hart), changed both the order and the content of most principles courses. I quote from the preface of this work:

> I have written this book because I have come to hold a particular point of view about the right way to arrange economics for elementary study. Until lately the problem of how to begin the study of economics reduced itself to a dilemma: either one might begin with economic theory—which meant in practice the theory of supply and demand—or one might begin with descriptive economics, the practical problems of industry and labor. [He then cited difficulties with each approach].
>
> As a result of the developments in economic knowledge which have taken place during recent years, we are now in a position to resolve this dilemma. . . . It is now possible to mark out a preliminary stage in economic study, which is wholly concerned with topics which are obviously interesting and important, and which is yet systematic enough to give some of the mental discipline necessary for study on a scientific level.
>
> This change has come about because the chapters on definitions, which formed so indigestible a portion of the old textbooks, have been kindled into life by the work of economic statisticians and also by some of the newer developments of economic theory. They have grown into a distinct branch of economics, a branch which is being pursued with very special success at the present time, and which is, nevertheless, particularly suited to serve as an introduction to the science in general. If we want a name for it, it might be described as Social Accounting, for it is nothing else but the accounting of the whole community or nation.[18]

This approach of Hicks was popularized by Samuelson in his first edition (1948), and the rest is history. He justified the inclusion of this new material as follows:

> Over the past few years, several thousand civilian and armed-forces students—largely studying engineering or business—have been introduced in the M.I.T. required beginning course to such topics as saving and investment and income determination. The tentative verdict of the more than two dozen instructors that have participated is that introductory analysis of income determination is easier and more interesting than introductory value and distribution theory.[19]

Although Samuelson popularized employment theory, credit should be given to Lorie Tarshis, who in 1947, a year earlier than Samuelson, published a principles book, *The Elements of Economics*, that had an entire section on national income and employment.[20]

The books which became widely used during this era were R. T. Bye, *Applied Economics;* Fairchild, Furniss, and Buck, *Elementary Economics*; K. Boulding, *Economic Analysis*; S. Slichter, *Modern Economic Society*; J. Ise, *Economics*; and R. T. Bye, *Principles of Economics*.

The approaches and principles of economics books, following in Hicks', Tarshis', and Samuelson's wake, are common knowledge to you, and this brings us to the fourth era, 1960 to the present.

The principles of economics course has now been standard fare in the undergraduate curriculum for about a century. In review, what has changed? The goals articulated have varied from honing the intellect to helping one understand the world in which one lives. The goals have been attacked for being too broad *and* too narrow. Few would quarrel, however, with A. B. Wolfe's statement of 1909, which I quoted earlier. The conclusion: There has been little, if any, change in basic goals.

The methodology? To the extent that most large public universities rely on large lecture sessions for the introductory courses, I suspect that more lecturing occurs in principles courses today than in 1885—and a good deal less of the hard-nose recitation that accompanied virtually every class in that earlier time. This has likely reduced the intensity of economics understanding. The new education technologies lack this instructor–student interaction in which the creative ideas of the student can be applied and identified with the instructor's knowledge and experience. Television, programmed learning, and personalized systems of instruction cast the student into a passive mode.[21] Computer-assisted instruction allows interaction, but only in narrowly defined, preordained channels of thought.

What about content? I have not focused on the process by which new economic ideas, relations, and principles are molded into the principles course. It is clear that the major ideas in the mainstream books change only slowly. Given the nature of the market for new textbooks, in which each author seeks to differentiate his product, the lag which occurs between the identification of new ideas and concepts and appearance in the textbook is more a demand than a supply phenomenon. Authors and publishers are quick to incorporate new concepts which will give their salespersons something to sell—in addition to five colors, pictures, cartoons, and biographical sketches of famous economists. The demanders, however, are far more tradition-bound, and here is the lag. The textbook-publishing landscape is strewn with textbooks that never survived the first edition.

The conclusion: Little has changed over the past 100 years. Certainly, the pedagogical techniques are much the same. The goals have changed but little, although mental discipline is not as highly regarded. Even the content today bears astonishing similarity to the turn of the century, except for the prose.

NOTES

1. Lawrence Senesh initiated the Elkhart Project, in which elementary school children were introduced to basic economic concepts. This project culminated in the publication of the learning package *Our Working World*, which spans grades one through six and is published by Science Research Associates (1973 revised edition).

2. In the summer of 1976 the first Institute in Economics for College and University Social Studies Educators was held at Purdue University. In 1978 and 1980 similar such programs were conducted.

3. The Economics Education Foundation for Clergy, now operating out of Washington, D.C., was founded at Purdue University in 1957.

4. E. T. Weiler, *The Economic System: An Analysis of the Flow of Economic Life* (New York: Macmillan, 1952).

5. E. T. Weiler and W. H. Martin, *The American Economic System: An Analytical Approach to Public Policy* (New York: Macmillan, 1957).

6. Weiler, *The Economic System*, p. viii.

7. D. J. Weidenaar and E. T. Weiler, *Economics: An Introduction to the World around You* (Reading, Mass.: Addison-Wesley, 1976).

8. Quoted from the article by Lawrence Leamer, "A Brief History of Economics in General Education," which provides a fascinating review of the early economics courses and approaches (*American Economic Review*, 402 [1950], 22).

9. Ibid, p. 22.

10. A recent paper by Professor Burton A. Weisbrod notes that 77 percent of the articles devoted to exploring the effects of different teaching approaches, appearing in the *Journal of Economic Education* and the economics education section of the annual papers and proceedings issues of the *American Economic Review*, are on the college principles course (*American Economic Review*, Feb. 1979).

11. P. Saunders, "The Lasting Effectiveness of Introductory Economics Courses," Final Report, NSF Grant GY7208, 1973 (mimeo).

12. See A. B. Wolfe, "Proceedings of a Conference on the Teaching of Elementary Economics," *Journal of Political Economy*, 17, no. 10 (Dec. 1909), 676.

13. Frederick R. Chow, "Economics as a School Study," *Economic Studies*, III: 183.

14. Ibid., p. 199.

15. Irving Fisher, *Elementary Principles of Economics*, (New York: Macmillian, 1913), p. viii.

16. F. W. Taussig, *Principles of Economics*, (3d ed.; New York: Macmillan, 1921), p. vii.

17. "The New Deal and the Teaching of Economics," *American Economic Review*, supplement vol. XXV, no. 1, March 1935, pp. 11–12.

18. J. R. Hicks and A. G. Hart, *The Social Framework of the American Economy*, (New York: Oxford University Press, 1945), pp. xi–xii.

19. Paul A. Samuelson, *Economics* (1st ed.; New York: McGraw-Hill, 1948), p. vi.

20. Lorie Tarshis, *The Elements of Economics* (Boston: Houghton Mifflin, 1947).

21. Paden and Moyer concluded, in a study of the relative effectiveness of live lectures, programmed learning, and televised lectures, "that students taught by television and programmed learning are less likely to rate the course as 'effectively taught' and more likely to find it 'difficult to concentrate' than students with live instruction." D. W. Paden and M. E. Moyer, "The Relative Effectiveness of Three Methods of Teaching Principles of Economics," *Journal of Economic Education*, 1, no. 1 (Fall 1969), p. 45.

Perspectives on Economics

Leonid Hurwicz

For economics this is an era of contradiction and paradox. Following two postwar decades of self-satisfaction with the behavior of the economy and the state of the discipline, we are now experiencing the simultaneous evils of inflation and unemployment as well as profound dissatisfaction with the economy's distribution of income. While college students crowd economics classrooms, expecting to hear solutions or hoping to develop their own, many academic economists are either less convinced that they have the answers or are less convincing to their own colleagues when they present diagnoses and prescriptions.

In this climate we are naturally led to reconsider both the substance and methodology of our science. Not surprisingly, macroeconomics is in the center of attention. So-called Keynesian models,[1] oversimplified for classroom use, had led some to think in terms of a sharp dichotomy between a regime of less than full employment in which money, wages, and prices remain virtually constant and a full employment economy in which prices vary in proportion to wages.

There had been much optimism concerning the potential for reconciling high levels of employment with price stability. This optimism was, in part at least, generated by oversimplified models and seemed to be confirmed by much of the U.S. postwar period. However, it was seriously undermined by the inability of Great Britain and other West European countries to halt the upward movement of prices and wages and has yielded more recently to widespread professional pessimism.

This reversal of attitudes has been reinforced by the simultaneity of high unemployment rates and rapid price increases in the U.S. in the last few years. Given the presence of exogenous forces such as the oil embargo and weather impact on food supply, this "stagflation" might have been classified as an aberration unrepresentative of the economic system had not our discipline been intellectually prepared for such a coincidence by the Phillips

Reprinted with permission of the Joint Council on Economic Education, National Council for the Social Studies, and Social Science Education Consortium, Inc., from *Perspectives on Economic Education* (Donald R. Wentworth, W. Lee Hansen, and Sharryl H. Hawke, editors), Proceedings of the National Conference on Needed Research and Development in Precollege Economic Education held 12–14 February 1976 in New Orleans, Louisiana, and funded by the National Science Foundation.

curve doctrine. This doctrine states that as unemployment falls, the rate of inflation rises even before "full employment" is reached. Initially developed on the basis of empirical observations, the Phillips curve has lately been supplied with explanatory theoretical models of individual behavior. It appears to face the policymaker with the choice between unacceptably high levels of inflation or unemployment.

Some argue that our present difficulties result in part from the success of our earlier full employment policies, particularly in the 1960s. Others argue that economics faces a more basic problem—the inherent variability of human behavior patterns and institutions. I shall not try to assess the merits of each of these explanations. However, I do feel that recent experience should make an economist more modest about understanding of the causal relations in the macroeconomy and about having a solid scientific basis for policy recommendations likely to produce results commensurate with claims often made for them.

Economics as a discipline need not be apologetic for having encountered phenomena which are not amenable to satisfactory explanation in the light of earlier theories. After all, physicists and astronomers have just recently discovered new evidence contradicting the heretofore accepted theories of how and why the sun shines! Nor must we plead guilty for failing to find remedies that would make our economy attain performance levels corresponding to popular aspirations. These levels may be outside the realm of possibility, given the various constraints under which we operate. Medical experience teaches that toxic side effects may be an unavoidable accompaniment of therapy.

There is, however, a legitimate question: Is economics, as a discipline, making appropriate efforts in the right direction to fill the gaps and, where necessary, radically restructure its approach? This question has many ramifications: empiricism versus theory, the role of mathematics in economic analysis, the problems and limitations of competitive markets, institutional aspects, and policy issues. Without attempting to do justice to all, I shall try placing some of these issues in a more systematic framework and then concentrate on those closest to my principal area of interest—the design of economic systems.

ISSUES AND PROBLEMS IN ECONOMIC ANALYSIS

Empirical Observations, Theory, and Mathematics

Whether economists are trying to prescribe remedies or merely to develop an understanding of the economic process, they are—or should be—dealing with the real world of economic phenomena, just as physicists deal with the world of physical phenomena. Problem formulations suggest themselves to the economist from observations or debates among policymakers, reformers, or even utopians who are motivated by their notions about actual or potential economic performance. No doubt the basic stimulus and often the framework of economic analysis come from the empirical side. However, in trying to answer policy questions, one is forced to conjecture the likely consequences of hypothetical actions, typically in circumstances where many causal factors are variable but beyond control. A scientist's reaction is to construct a model encompassing the essential features of the phenomena and to examine the consequences of policies under consideration within the framework of the model. But such a model hardly puts the scientist in a position to draw immediate policy conclusions.

Although the model is necessarily a simplified version of reality, it should be tested to determine how well it explains observed phenomena. In the field of macro-models of the U.S. economy such testing is routine, and if the fit is not good enough, an attempt is typically made to improve the model. We witness here a remarkable degree of interaction between empirical observation and theory. Highly sophisticated mathematical tools are involved both in model construction and in statistical procedures used to test hypotheses underlying the model. Furthermore, these procedures provide quantitative estimates of the direction and magnitude of effects of the policies under consideration. In addition, projections are obtained to serve as bases for forecasts of economic variables. Whether the models and econometric techniques used in generating the estimates and forecasts are correct, or at least good enough for purposes of policy, is a matter of controversy. The error margins are undoubtedly larger than we would like them to be. Still, econometric macro-models are widely used both by public and private bodies.

Econometrics could not have attained its present state without the use of mathematical techniques. This is particularly evident in developing justifications for the choice of algebraic form of, say, the equation explaining investment behavior. But perhaps the most important role mathematics has played here is in helping the economist analyze the operation of a system with simultaneous and complex feedback effects; these effects are a fundamental feature of interdependence of economic phenomena and are difficult to grasp without the use of mathematics.

On the other hand, I do not believe that the "power of resolution" (to use the microscope analogy) of the econometric macro-models is sufficient to distinguish between the alternative hypotheses explaining, say, the Phillips curve. Here again there is an analogy from physical science: to explain the ocean currents, one must draw on knowledge developed not only from observing those currents but also from laboratory experiments performed on a small scale with high accuracy. For the economist, micro-analysis becomes an essential adjunct of macro-analysis.

Unfortunately, a real integration of these two major branches of analysis, although advocated and attempted in different ways for about three decades, is far from accomplished. For one thing, there is as yet no accepted body of theory concerning the behavior of the individual economic unit, be it a household or a firm. But even if this were available, there would remain the major unsolved problem of aggregation, that is, the problem of explaining the behavior of observable aggregative variables such as GNP and the price level, given the behavior of the individual units.

Competitive Equilibrium and Beyond

The persistence of such a gap between understanding the behavior of individual units and explaining the movements of the aggregative variables may seem surprising since much of economists' recent thinking has been based on a model whose goal is to build up the behavior of the whole system from postulates concerning the behavior of individual units. This model is known under various labels—general equilibrium, neoclassical, and Arrow-Debreu. In its narrowest interpretation, it postulates perfectly competitive (price-taking) behavior on everyone's part and deals only with the system when at rest (in equilibrium). Putting these two features together, it is a theory of perfectly competitive equilibria. *Competitive equilibrium* (short for "perfectly competitive equilibrium") is defined as a position of the economy in which all parties, firms as well as households, behave as if their actions would have no effect on the prevailing prices and wages,[2] consumers/workers maximize satisfaction subject to the requirement of balancing the household budget, firms maximize profits, and aggregate supply equals aggregate demand.

A basic proposition concerning competitive equilibrium is that, under certain conditions discussed below, it is guaranteed to be *optimal*, meaning that there is no feasible reallocation of resources that could raise anyone's satisfaction without lowering that of someone else.[3] The conditions under which the optimality of competitive equilibria is guaranteed are imposed upon the economic environment. By *economic environment* we mean those aspects of the economy taken as given by the economist—including preferences and behavior patterns of household and firms, technology, and resource endowment. In contrast to the notion of economic environment, we speak of the economic *mechanism* or *system* as the set of "rules of the game" and institutions that can be changed by the society's decisions. Perfectly competitive mechanisms are a special category in the class of market mechanisms.

To guarantee the optimality of a competitive equilibrium, two conditions are imposed on the economic environment: (1) Absence of externalities, also called "external economies and diseconomies of scale" and "third party costs and benefits." Pollution is a prominent example of an externality. (2) Absence of indivisibilities. A river dam is an example of an indivisible good.

The sort of equilibrium encountered in this neoclassical model clearly rules out a host of phenomena observed in real Western-type economies. In particular, like the classical economics criticized by Keynes in the 1930s, it leaves no room for involuntary unemployment. This is so because, by definition, involuntary unemployment means an excess supply of labor at prevailing money wages and prices, while—also by definition—at a competitive equilibrium there can be no excess supply of any good, including labor, at prevailing wages and prices. Therefore, if one believes that involuntary unemployment often exists, one must look beyond the model of competitive equilibrium. One must also look beyond competitive equilibrium to deal with problems of monopoly.

There are two not incompatible approaches that can be taken when the hypothesis of competitive equilibrium is abandoned. One approach retains the notion of equilibrium but in a sense much broader than competitive equilibrium. In this broader sense, equilibrium is simply any position which has a tendency to persist once having been reached. Thus there is nothing contradictory about equilibrium with involuntary unemployment or monopolies; it is only that such equilibrium is not a competitive equilibrium. Among terms synonymous with this more general notion of equilibrium are "position of rest" and "stationary position." The study of systems in stationary positions is called statics. The second approach involves abandoning the emphasis on statics and focusing on the movements of the system, that is, its dynamics.

From Statics to Dynamics

In recent years there has been so much focus on competitive equilibria that an outside observer can be forgiven for believing dynamics and other than perfectly competitive statics to be alien to the science of economics. But, in fact, both of these "nonclassical" directions have considerable history behind them, and currently there is evidence of renewed interest.

Ours is not the first generation faced with economic disequilibria. In the nineteenth century observers noted the wide swings in economic activity of the capitalist economies (the "trade" or "business cycle"). Not surprisingly, the Great Depression of the 1930s following the boom of the 1920s made many economists feel that the dynamics of the economy, its oscillations and instabilities, are of primary importance and that the economy would rarely and only for short periods find itself in a position of equilibrium. Therefore, it would be irrelevant whether the claims concerning the optimality properties of such equilibria were correct.

Thus, the 1930s witnessed a flowering of literature devoted to economic fluctuations and possible instability phenomena present in the capitalist economy. Some of the earlier attempts at explaining business cycles were widely felt to be unsatisfactory. First, they relied excessively on external causal factors such as sunspots, central bank actions, and government policies. Second, they tended to explain each phase of the cycle by changed behavior patterns peculiar to that phase, without explaining the causes of these changes. A need was felt for the development of *endogenous* theories explaining the phenomena observed during each phase of the cycle as resulting from the accumulated consequences of earlier ones, with strong variation in the economic variables (investment, employment) despite the constancy of behavior patterns such as fraction of income saved or the relationship of investment decisions to variations in aggregate consumption.

Although many of the elements of new theories were developed in intuitive or verbal terms, mathematics again turned out to be the natural tool for integrating these elements into simple, yet powerful, theoretical structures. The mathematical techniques were sometimes largely geometric, as in the models constructed by Kalecki and Kaldor, or based on the framework of difference and differential equations (Tinbergen, Frisch, Kalecki, Le Corbeiller, Samuelson). Those of Frisch allowed explicitly for the important role played by exogenous random disturbances and thus laid a foundation for the construction of statistical (econometric) models incorporating the insights from business cycle theory (Tinbergen, Haavelmo, Koopmans, Klein).

The endogenous business cycle theories and other branches of economic dynamics help to explain why the economy may undergo wide fluctuations away from equilibrium even in the presence of stabilizing forces. But many observers point to the presence of significant unemployment not only during downswings but even during periods of stability. In their view the problem is not merely one of disequilibrium but also one of persistence of "bad equilibria." Thus the issue of dynamics versus imperfect statics reappears.

It might seem that the reversion in the 1950s to perfectly competitive statics was a step backward from the concern with dynamics in the 1930s and 1940s. If so, this step was perhaps necessary to ground the analysis firmly in two important respects: (1) *completeness*—treating the economy as a whole and taking into account all relevant feedbacks—a "general equilibrium" approach as opposed to "partial equilibrium," and (2) *behaviorism*—making assumptions about individual human behavior rather than about movements of "anonymous" aggregates such as price level and GNP. Furthermore, once the statics of perfect competition were analyzed in this manner, the dynamic study of stabilities and instabilities of competitive equilibrium followed within a few years, in the late 1950s. Then in the 1960s, general equilibrium analysis of imperfect markets was initiated.

The ideas underlying these models of the 1950s and 1960s go back to the writings of Walras in the 1870s. Indeed, in currently accepted terminology, "Walrasian" is applied to what we have been calling perfectly competitive equilibria.

It is perhaps depressing that it took economics until the early 1960s to "clean up" the Walrasian inheritance. The reasons for this lag are manifold, among them the fact that the requisite mathematical tools, especially the so-called "fixed-point" theorems, did not become available until well into the twentieth century. But if there is still such a lag now, it is not in the realm of research—where studies of imperfect markets abound—but rather in teaching and popular expositions. Therefore, at present there is little excuse for limiting one's horizons to the framework of Walrasian perfect competition.

Externalities, Increasing Returns, and Equilibrium

Even a casual inspection of the theoretical results concerning competitive equilibria is bound to alert one to the highly restrictive assumptions used in obtaining these results. Rigorous mathematical formulation reinforces this awareness. Foremost among limiting assumptions is the absence of externalities. When externalities are in the picture, competitive equilibria are no longer guaranteed to be optimal. Those familiar with the reasoning used in demonstrating the optimality of competitive equilibria are not likely to rely exclusively on "forces of competition" unless they have escaped the daily reminders of such externalities as air and water pollution, airport noise, crime, drug use, and highway crowding.

Faced with externalities, some economists favor a solution which views the externality as an additional ("negative") commodity and finds the appropriate negative price (for example, an effluent charge); if not laissez-faire, this solution still uses the price mechanism. Thus the mechanism remains of a modified Walrasian type, although there is a state interference with the activities of individual economic units. Yet theory warns us that devices of this type may fail because there may be no position of competitive equilibrium in such a system.

It should be realized that not all systems have equilibrium positions. If they do not, they are doomed to eternal motion—downward, upward, or cyclical—unless they get transformed into other systems that do possess equilibria. Whether a given economic mechanism does or does not have positions of equilibrium depends on two factors: the nature of the *mechanism* and the characteristics of the *economic environment*. Consider, for instance, the mechanism of perfect competition,[4] in which firms maximize profits, consumers maximize their satisfactions, and both treat prices as unaffected by their decisions.[5] This mechanism may lack any position of equilibrium when the economic environment is characterized by technologies with increasing returns ("decreasing costs") where output grows more than in proportion to input.

I suppose only an economic theorist would view such economies of scale as troublesome! Others would feel that it is wonderful to be able to increase output more than in proportion to the increase in inputs. The trouble is that the perfectly competitive entrepreneur is supposed to take prices as given and to ignore adverse price changes that would result from the expanded scale of operations. Thus, with increasing returns, he sees his imaginary profits growing without limit as he expands and finds no scale of output at which to stop. Therefore, there is no position of perfectly competitive equilibrium. However, there may well exist positions of *imperfectly* competitive (perhaps monopolistic) equilibrium.

Even though equilibrium positions may exist in an economy, the economy may be in other positions most of the time, like the pendulum of a grandfather clock. Nevertheless, we shall see below that the issue of existence of positions of equilibrium is important in analyzing the workings and viability of a system. We therefore ask, When can one be sure that the mechanism of perfect competition does possess positions of equilibrium? As can be seen from the preceding example of economies of scale (increasing returns), this depends on the economic environment. To guarantee the existence of competitive equilibria, it is usually assumed that the economic environment is free of economies of scale and indivisibilities and that all goods and services have diminishing marginal utility. These and other more technical requirements for competitive equilibrium were specified in basic theorems on the existence and optimality of competitive equilibria by Kenneth Arrow and Gerard Debreu in the early 1950s, extending the early work of Walras in the 1870s and Abraham Wald in the 1930s.

Monopoly and Oligopoly

What happens if some of these environment characteristics are absent and the perfectly competitive mechanism has no equilibrium positions? The example of increasing returns suggests an answer since the presence of increasing returns creates a tendency toward monopoly, thus making it extremely unlikely that firms would ignore the effects of their actions on market prices. Assuming freedom of economic actions, an environment characterized by increasing returns eliminates competitive behavior. Thus, a mechanism (perfect competition) incapable of equilibrium under given environmental conditions is displaced by another mechanism (monopoly) which does possess positions of rest. Of course, these new monopolistic equilibria may well be inefficient or nonoptimal.

The presence of economics of scale is only one among many reasons for expecting the emergence of monopolies. Others are well known. They include various barriers to entry: control of resources, patents, regulation, financial limitations, and other organizational devices designed to keep potential entrants out.

Those who tend to identify mathematical economics with the study of perfect competition may be surprised to hear that the rigorous analysis of monopolistic and oligopolistic markets was initiated by the "founding father" of mathematical economics, Augustin Cournot, as early as 1838. Economic theorists after Cournot had not lost awareness of the monopoly and oligopoly phenomena and, perhaps with the exception of Schumpeter, considered them to result in social waste—that is, in inefficiency and non-optimality. Yet until the 1930s little progress was made in the analysis of these phenomena. Pure monopoly was probably regarded by many as rare or unimportant, by others as presenting a political but not an intellectual challenge, since the behavior of a monopolistic firm was easily analyzed. With regard to oligopoly, on the other hand, no consensus could be reached as to the proper analytical framework. The solution proposed by Cournot was criticized by many, but alternative models proposed by the critics (such as Bertrand) failed to find general acceptance.

The 1930s saw a resurgence of interest in monopoly phenomena, although mainly in the context of partial equilibrium theory, devoted to the study of individual industries without taking into account systemwide repercussions and feedbacks. Chamberlin utilized the Cournot-Bertrand analytical framework to study, under the label of *monopolistic competition,* the implications of product differentiation (possibly resulting from advertising) when free entry is assumed. Joan Robinson looked into related phenomena, including market discrimination, and called them *imperfect competition.* Some of Chamberlin's conclusions for the markets with many small sellers of closely related goods—the "large numbers" case—especially the zero profit claim, were properly criticized, but much of his analysis is correct and of practical interest. Yet Chamberlin's monopolistic competition has not been integrated into modern "general equilibrium" analysis, perhaps partly because it was viewed as a rather harmless and insignificant phenomenon. Unfortunately, there has been little work on the welfare loss aspect of the "large numbers" monopolistic case, and it is difficult to see clear policy conclusions.

The situation with regard to the "small numbers" cases—especially oligopoly and bilateral monopoly—is very difficult. Static analysis easily shows that nondiscriminatory monopoly equilibria are inefficient and nonoptimal. Indeed, under increasing returns, social waste is likely to occur, given the requirement that price should cover average (unit) costs. But—as seen by Schumpeter—a purely static analysis is not an adequate basis for policy conclusions, especially when applied in the realm of research and development.

Remedies for Monopolistic Waste

During the 1930s not everyone was willing to accept social waste resulting from monopoly as unavoidable. Some saw "socialism" as a solution, but meaningful economic content had to be put into this term. The relevant version of "socialism" is that proposed by Lange and Lerner since, despite a radical departure from capitalism in institutional structure, it proposed a state-operated price and output policy that amounted to a simulation of competitive markets, including profit maximization by firms, but with profits going to the state. It may seem paradoxical that socialism should be advocated as a means of providing a social mechanism for the enforcement of perfect competition, in part on the ground that capitalism leads to monopoly and oligopoly rather than competition. However, the proposal is theoretically viable if one is prepared to adopt the assumptions guaranteeing the possibility and the optimality of competitive equilibria. But we saw earlier that these equilibria would typically fail to exist in the presence of economies of scale (increasing returns) which are likely to account for the monopolies the socialist system wants to supplant as wasteful. Hence, it was necessary to go beyond competitive market rules and find principles for the behavior of firms with increasing returns that would be neither monopolistic nor competitive.

Marginal cost pricing turned out to be such a principle. Operating on this principle, a firm is required (as in the world of perfect competition) to treat prices parametrically—that is, to ignore its own effects on the market—and to minimize the total cost of producing a given output. But unlike a market firm, whether monopolistic or competitive, it must renounce the desire to maximize profit; instead, it must bring its output to a level where the resulting marginal cost will just equal the prevailing announced price. Should this create excess demand or supply, the price will be adjusted in the proper direction just as in a competitive economy. For firms with decreasing returns, this behavior turns out to be equivalent to profit maximization, but for firms with increasing returns a deficit will be generated. In a socialist economy, this deficit could presumably be covered out of profits generated by other firms or out of taxes.

However, even without socializing the whole economy, marginal cost pricing could be viewed as increasing the efficiency of the system. It was advocated in this spirit by Hotelling in the United States, in particular for the railroads, in the mid-1930s. Of course, here too the problem of deficit would have to be resolved, perhaps through a tax-supported subsidy from the state. After World War II many countries, both in Western Europe and in areas of the Third World, nationalized industries with increasing returns; hence, the issue of appropriate pricing policies to be followed by nationalized enterprises gained in importance. Marginal cost pricing, as well as other more complex pricing rules designed to minimize waste under these conditions without incurring deficits, have been tried in various countries.

DESIGNING ECONOMIC SYSTEMS

In my view, the importance of the Hotelling-Lange-Lerner[6] ideas on marginal cost pricing lies not in the specific contents of their proposals which are open to a variety of technical and practical criticism. Rather, they are important because they open a new path for economic analysis: the use of tools of theoretical analysis in exploring, in a normative spirit, alternatives to existing institutional arrangements.

These analytical explorations have shown that not all proposals for alternative economic systems are Utopian. Hayek and von Mises had questioned whether even theoretically a socialist economy could generate the information required to make it work. The Lange-Lerner solution and the ensuing debate laid a foundation for the systematic study of whole classes of resource allocation mechanisms or systems. Instead of being a *given*, the *mechanism* becomes the *unknown of the problem*. In this spirit, the economist can view the problem as one of designing a mechanism maximizing certain social disiderata, such as efficiency, equity, and freedom—subject to behavioral and information constraints.

This approach differs from the traditional economic analysis which mostly focuses on idealized[7] versions of systems that either exist or have existed in the past. While the study of historically observed systems is essential in *positive* economics, more is needed for *normative* purposes. Of course, classical welfare economics is done in a normative spirit, pursuing the desirable as distinct from the actual. However, much of traditional normative economics deals with the desirability of specific actions, such as whether to build a certain dam, or with the choice of appropriate levels of certain control parameters, such as foreign exchange rates or discount rates; this might be called *action-normative* economics. By contrast, in designing a new mechanism we deal with the comparative desirability of alternative operating rules and organizational structures including those that have never been tried; this might be called *system-normative* economics.

As is usual with such distinctions, there are borderline cases that qualify under both headings. Thus lowering import duties constitutes an adjustment of control parameters and qualifies in the action-normative sphere. But bringing them down to zero level produces conditions of free trade and may be viewed as a change in operating rules, that is, in the system-normative sphere.

System-normative issues are before us virtually all the time. Most recently they have been conspicuous in the environmental domain. New institutional structures, such as environmental control agencies, have been created, with operating rules that call for vastly increased information flow (impact statements) prior to decision making. Typically, such requirements decrease the autonomy of individual units, both public and private. In the past, important system changes occurred in the financial sector, again involving new organizational structures, such as the Federal Reserve System and the Federal Deposit Insurance Corporation, and radically modified operational rules.

The preceding examples involve important but still very partial system changes, superimposed on existing structures and touching only selected sectors of the economy. But there are system models differing from existing reality in a manner that touches all sectors and virtually all dimensions of economic activity. The differences can be as far reaching as those between medieval feudalism and nineteenth-century market capitalism or as those between socialism Swedish style and socialism Soviet sytle.

Centralization versus Decentralization

If one is persuaded that designing alternative systems and mechanisms is an important task for economics, there is a danger of designing an economic Utopia. It is pointless to postulate an omniscient and all-powerful central authority. There are limits to enforceability of rules. Information relevant to economic decision making is widely dispersed throughout the economy, and its transmission between units is often costly or impossible. For these and other reasons, centralization of economic decision making may be either infeasible or extremely wasteful. On this point, much debated during the 1930s, there was substantial agreement between an advocate of socialism (Lange) and an opponent (Hayek). In addition, there may be preference for decentralization on ethical and other noneconomic grounds, such as civil liberties and the value of self-expression. On the other hand, it must be recognized that there are circumstances where centralization is feasible and decentralization would result in inefficiency. In any case, it is of great importance to see whether economic systems designed to cope with various obstacles (such as externalities or increasing returns) are decentralized.

Naturally, whether a system qualifies as decentralized depends on the definition. In our context it seems reasonable to define decentralization in such a manner that a market system would qualify as decentralized. It is essential, however, not to identify decentralization with market mechanism; that is, there should be room for nonmarket systems that are decentralized. Hence, in situations where the competitive mechanism fails to operate satisfactorily, one need not automatically resign oneself to the alternative of centralization of inefficiency; there remains to be explored the third possibility, a system which is both decentralized and efficient but decentralized in a manner different from the competitive mechanism or even any market mechanism.

In defining decentralization, it is convenient to distinguish two aspects: (1) decentralization of authority and incentive structure, and (2) informational decentralization.

With respect to authority structure, decentralization means a high degree of autonomy in decision making by individual units—firms and households. But if a unit is free to choose among many alternative actions, the movements of the economy as a whole can be predicted only if enough is known about the behavioral laws or patterns underlying choices made by the unit. Classical economics has typically assumed maximization of profits and utilities to achieve behavioral determinacy of its model. A system is usually designed in the expectation that the economic units will behave in a specified way. One must ask, however, whether given the rules of the system, this expected behavior would be consistent with the known individual behavior patterns as determined by incentives to which they are known to respond. If the answer is affirmative, we say the system is *incentive-compatible*.

On the informational side, it would not make sense to define (informational) decentralization as complete absence of communication. Our definition is inspired by (but not synonymous with!) the model of perfect competition and its informational advantages discussed by Hayek. In a perfectly competitive market an individual unit (firm, household) can make appropriate decisions as to output, consumption, or trade without any direct knowledge concerning the other units' technologies, preferences, and so on—provided it has received the signals summarizing the relevant information, namely, prices or aggregate excess demand or supply.

Our concept of informational decentralization tries to capture this attribute of a perfectly competitive market while abstracting from its other properties. In particular, it is independent of the nature of signals exchanged between participants. In a perfect market, prices constitute such signals. In other economic systems, quantity targets, or input-output matrices may constitute the signals. Let us refer to the universe of signals available in a system as its language. Informational decentralization is then defined *relative* to that language. There are several conditions that would qualify a system as informationally decentralized. I shall confine myself to two, to which I give what may seem somewhat strange labels, "privacy" and "anonymity." A system is said to be *privacy-preserving* if a unit is able to make appropriate decisions having only that information about other units which has been transmitted *according to the operational rules of the system* and without using signals other than those of the system's language. A system is called *anonymous* if the unit receiving signals need not know the source of origin, as for instance when all one knows is the *aggregate* of bids made by others.

Other things being equal, an informationally decentralized system is easier to operate than one that is not decentralized since it enables participants to make decisions without having to find out the characteristics of other units and without having to keep track of "who said what," as long as the totality of signals received is known. On the other hand, "other things" are not always equal. In particular, systems differ with regard to the size and complexity of their languages and also the complexity of decision rules (algorithms). In may be advantageous to trade a degree of informational decentralization for smaller or less complex language or rules of behavior.

The above definition stresses the negative aspect of privacy—what one *need not* know about others. The reverse of the coin is a positive feature, namely, that a privacy-preserving system leads to decision making where actions pertaining to a given economic unit are based on that unit's signaling and responses. This is good if we assume that a unit is the best source of information about itself. However, reliance on the unit as an exclusive source of information about itself provides an opportunity for misrepresentation.[8] Hence the system is not likely to work well unless it is incentive-compatible.

Ideally, the reward structure implicit in the system should be such as to encourage behavior corresponding to the true state of affairs within each unit. There has been a good deal of research recently in the area of concocting such reward structures, but it appears that in many situations this is impossible. One is then faced with the choice of either condoning a certain amount of misrepresentation and consequently sustaining a corresponding loss of social welfare (as compared with ideal truthful behavior required by the rules of the system), or sacrificing a degree of informational decentralization by instituting audit and control systems designed to discourage misrepresentation. The latter solution also involves social cost since it requires the diversion of resources into the control process; insofar as it involves an invasion of privacy of economic units, it may also be viewed as undesirable in terms of human values.

Some System Designs

At this point it will be helpful to have some illustrations of "artificial" systems produced in the spirit of design. These systems are often radically different from anything previously tried or observed, yet they are not Utopian. Although far from ready for adoption in their present form, they constitute potentially fruitful steps toward the discovery of better functioning economic systems.

The marginal cost pricing scheme for dealing with increasing returns, which has been discussed above, is perhaps the simplest of the "artificial" systems. In modified form, it has already been applied by nationalized enterprises in certain countries. However, marginal cost pricing rules are difficult to implement because they lack incentive compatibility. To remedy this difficulty, alternative proposals have been made which preserve the incentive of profit maximization.

If profits are to be maximized under increasing returns, we cannot require that firms treat prices as given parameters. If we did, we would be back under a regime of perfect competition which, as seen above, will lack equilibrium. But there is nothing sacred about the parametric price regime. One can substitute for it an arrangement under which a firm will be facing not a given price to be paid independently of the number of units purchased, but rather a price *schedule* where the unit price varies with quantities purchased or sold according to a specific formula which takes account of supply and demand and is calculated so as to yield efficient resource allocation when firms maximize their profits. This is analogous to the situation under monopoly where the firm also faces a schedule, the demand curve, with prices varying according to quantities sold. However, under our "designed" system, the schedules faced by the firms are not the same ones that would have been faced by a monopolist.

This type of system—a variant of which was proposed by Arrow and Hurwicz—is very close to qualifying as informationally decentralized because the schedules can be devised with only a minimum of technological information on the part of system designers, and the firms themselves follow rules that are privacy and anonymity preserving. Also, there is less difficulty with incentives because it is possible to build some form of profit sharing into the system. However, there are other difficulties, including the possibility of malfunction when the economy starts from a position far removed from an equilibrium.

As another example of an "artificial" system, let me mention a rather different informationally decentralized mechanism which would tend to converge to optimal resource allocations. This system, proposed by Hurwicz, Radner, and Reiter, is called the B-process, where B stands for "bidding." The essence of the process is that individual buyers and sellers, both firms and households, make bids which include the terms on which they are willing to buy and sell. Under certain rules and assumptions specified by the authors of this system, successive rounds of bids converge toward a final Pareto-optimal solution, in which all the mutually advantageous transactions have been made and no one can be made better off without someone else being made worse off.

The B-process is informationally decentralized, preserving privacy and anonymity. Its incentive properties have not yet been studied thoroughly, although it is clear that the system moves toward improvement of the participants' position. A most important characteristic of the process is that it converges to optimality, even with increasing returns or indivisibilities, where perfectly competitive equilibria might be nonoptimal or nonexistent.

So far we have seen examples of processes designed to remedy the weaknesses of the perfectly competitive process resulting from factors *internal* to an economic unit, such as increasing returns or indivisibilities. Similarly, there are "artificial" systems designed to remedy difficulties due to interrelations *between* economic units. An instance of this type of problem is the financing of the production of a public good, that is, a good or service where consumption by one person does not diminish its availability to others. Examples are national defense and classical music radio stations. Under ordinary market conditions there arises what is known as the free rider problem—everyone trying to get the service supplied at the expense of others. This leads to a misallocation of resources. Various remedies have been proposed. The best-known of these is Lindahl's, with payments based on the declarations of individuals as to the value of the public good to themselves. This system is informationally decentralized. It is optimal if the declarations of individuals accurately reflect their valuation of the public good, but the incentive structure encourages misrepresentation. Other schemes have been proposed. As an example, in a system suggested by Groves and Ledyard, participants indicate the desired level of public services—knowing the formula that determines their own payments given their own and others' bids. At equilibrium, an optimal allocation results. This and other processes I am familiar with satisfy the requirements of informational decentralization but have other weaknesses: they are either subject to manipulation or require some subsidization.

Potentials and Limitations of System Designs

By analyzing various alternative systems we sometimes discover that optimality cannot be achieved, given realistic assumptions concerning individual incentives and the difficulties of transmitting information from where it originates to where it is needed. Such results are negative, but only in a formal sense. In fact, they should play as constructive a role in designing economic systems as the law of energy conservation does in guiding the design of physical systems: they should make us aware of the unavoidable trade-offs and so steer us away from unrealistic goals.

It may well be that no economic system can guarantee complete efficiency with decentralization and incentive compatibility in an economic environment having externalities, indivisibilities, and public goods. If so, we are faced with a fundamental problem that has only recently begun to be studied: How can one design a decentralized incentive-compatible system with the highest degree of efficiency? We have as yet little idea as to the "efficiency coefficient" one can expect under the best feasible design, except that it will be below 100 percent. Nor do we know how much could be gained by abandoning the requirement of complete decentralization.

In all such calculations, it is not enough to look at the system's efficiency in providing goods and services from resources utilized for *production* purposes, since every system also uses resources in its own *operation*. For instance, the market system uses brokers while a centrally planned system uses planners. Both types of persons constitute human resources diverted from the production of goods and services into the operation of the system. This, of course, does not make them socially useless, since no mechanism will work without some use of resources to make it work. Thus, to properly assess systems, one should use a *net efficiency rating* which takes into account the fraction of social resources used to operate the mechanism. One can think of such a net efficiency rating as a ratio, with the economy's net output in the numerator and the totality of resources used (both for production and for system operation) in the denominator.

It is clear that our analysis, although theoretical, deals to a considerable extent with factors usually called institutional. These factors enter the analysis in several ways. For example, they appear in connection with incentive structures. Recent contributions to the study of incentives have been made by Keren and Stiglitz, who compared the performance of systems under which labor is rewarded through a wage, on a piece rate basis, or through renting. Criminal law enforcement has been studied in a similar manner by examining the effects of incentive—or rather disincentive—aspects of different penal systems.

Institutional factors play an important part in our concept of net efficiency since the cost of operating a system and, in fact, its feasibility is crucially dependent on legal and other institutions which determine the flow of information, the liability structure, the required intensity of enforcement of rules, and so forth. One is almost tempted to say that the "right institutional framework" is a major unknown. In any case, once we are in the area of system design, theory is needed for institutional analysis, and institutions constitute a major element of the theoretical structure.

BROADENING HORIZONS

A general systematic study of economic systems is still a formidable undertaking, and we have made no more than a beginning. But a significant broadening of our vision can already be discerned. An important body of recent literature is, for instance, devoted to the performance of an economy such as Yugoslavia where worker-managed enterprises predominate. A start has been made in analyzing Soviet-type economics. And last, but not least, "general equilibrium" models of capitalist economies are no longer confined to the perfectly competitive framework.

Significant advances have been made in models of capitalist economies with aspects of both monopoly and oligopoly. Both statics and dynamics of "complete"[9] systems containing significant monopoly aspects have been studied by Negishi, Arrow, and Hahn. There is as yet no "complete" model comprehensive enough to allow for the unrestricted presence of oligopolies. The latter is perhaps the next item on the economist's agenda, but the difficulties faced are formidable. Partial equilibrium contributions in the realm of oligopoly with free entry have provided important building blocks by Bain, Sylos-Labini, and Dewey. Important contributions have also come from abstract game theory developments.

Another avenue of progress involves noncompetitive patterns resulting from uncertainty concerning others' actions. Such uncertainty, together with transaction costs and monetary phenomena, has been used by Benassy, Varian, Hahn, and Futia to define a "neo-Keynesian" notion of effective demand. This newly defined effective demand may explain certain aspects of involuntary unemployment—without abandoning the assumption of rational behavior on the part of either entrepreneurs or workers.

A more radical departure drops the assumption that economic units try to maximize profits or satisfaction. Instead, the assumption is that these units are satisfied so long as they are above a certain "aspiration level" but go into action when falling below this level. Such behavior is called "satis-ficing," and has been studied by Simon, Radner, and Rothschild.

MANAGING THE FUTURE

An important shortcoming of the competitive model which we have not yet dealt with explicitly is its treatment of the future. The competitive model is inadequate as a basis for formulating policies to cope with cyclical swings in unemployment and prices and issues of economic development and growth.

Our major linkages to the future are (1) current decisions to invest in plant and equipment to produce goods and services in the future, and (2) current plans of firms and households to buy goods and services in the future. Many of the problems of a competitive system stem from miscalculations about the relationships between future supplies and demands. These problems could be handled within the competitive framework if for all goods and services there existed comprehensive futures markets similar to the futures markets which do exist for many commodities. But such universal futures markets do not in fact exist. Hence the resulting system does not qualify as truly competitive; it may be called an *incomplete market* system. In the absence of futures markets, investment decisions must be made on the basis of expectations about future prices and demands, expectations which may turn out to be very inaccurate. Consequently, in such an incomplete market system, there is no basis for asserting that decisions—taken in the absence of comprehensive futures markets—will be either efficient or optimal.

One theoretical attempt to get around this difficulty is based on the assumption that buyers and sellers, observing the discrepancies between their predictions and their experience, will modify both their forecast formulas and decision principles so that in time their expectations will tend to be confirmed by subsequent experience. In my view, this *rational expectation hypothesis* requires such a long time perspective as to have at best limited applicability to problems involving capital formation and cyclical fluctuations.

An alternative approach to dealing with the future is a system called *indicative planning* which is practiced to some extent in France. Such "planning" involves exchanges of information concerning the intentions and expectations of the various economic decision makers but includes no commitments or coercion. In principle, it could lead to the elimination of inconsistent expectations among the participants. Also, given the statements of intentions and plans, one could calculate the likely forms and levels of capital formation, simulating a complete futures market. For instance, should the extrapolations indicate excess supplies of future services generated by the planned capital expansion, the expansion plans could be scaled down until a prospective balance develops.

In my view, however, indicative planning fails as a substitute for the absent futures markets. Statements of intentions are not reliable as binding contracts that would have been entered into if the futures markets existed. Nor do I see any reason to think of the intention statements as mutually self-enforcing. The resulting uncertainty would induce as least some participants to depart from stated intentions to protect themselves against the consequences of just such a departure by others. What the indicative planning system lacks is the element of guarantee.

The provision of guarantees is possible through various social mechanisms, although perhaps at the cost of introducing a degree of centralization. Guarantees offer still another approach to the problem of managing the future—an approach still in its infancy as far as research and theory are concerned. In practice, however, such guarantees are familiar in forms such as home mortgage and student loan guarantees and even in the New York City rescue operation. Particularly in times of economic stress, there are many pressures for guarantees of many kinds and these guarantees, once instituted, may persist even when the economic stress is lessened. Examples are farm price parity, indexation of wages, and ceilings on prices, wages, and interest rates. The debates that ensue usually center on their administrative feasibility and costs or their effects on income distribution. A more fundamental issue is, To what extent can and should we provide guarantees against the vicissitudes of the economic process given the difficulty of either controlling or predicting its path?

In the foregoing survey, I have tried to show that the horizons of contemporary economic analysis are by no means limited to the abstract perfectly competitive model, nor even to market-type phenomena. Economics has responded to criticisms of its simplistic theories by building into its models such aspects of reality as uncertainty, time structure, externalities, economies of scale, sensitivity to incentives, and monopolistic or manipulative behavior.

I have emphasized the efficiency and optimality aspects of economic systems, while neglecting the distributive aspects, primarily because my own work has been in the former area. There has been recent analytical work on the concepts of fairness and equity in economic systems and on the extent to which a trade-off between fairness and efficiency may be unavoidable. We have also become more aware of the importance of income distribution even in the perfectly competitive models. Developments in the area of social welfare and choice functions have provided economics with natural tools for incorporating distributive value judgments into normative theory. In my view, however, the distributive aspects, although not ignored, have not as yet been integrated into the general framework of economic analysis to an extent comparable with efficiency aspects.

That formal theoretical analysis has lagged behind economic reality cannot be denied. But in the 1950s this lag was about eighty years; at present I would estimate it at between five and ten years. The perfectly competitive model is only a small, though technically important, part of the field. Theoretical work is progressively intertwining theoretical postulates, empirical observations, and institutional elements into one integrated structure amenable to analytical treatment. At the same time, applied policy analysis, using tools such as cost-benefit calculations and econometric models, makes systematic use of the available theoretical tools. I optimistically expect the methodological quarrels based on schools of thought committed to particular techniques or tools to pass into well-deserved oblivion. Economic analysis, which in the past regarded as the only legitimate objects of study a few traditional systems and the manipulation of policy parameters (such as the rate of money growth) is moving toward a creative and imaginative role in designing social mechanisms and institutions superior to those now existing.

Economics is far from having complete answers to our era's complex questions. We still lack satisfactory explanations for some observed phenomena, and we often lack remedies—even when the disease has been diagnosed. However, there has been more progress than we tend to claim in the present skeptical period, although perhaps less than we were inclined to claim a decade ago. Progress in understanding is bound to lead to sounder policy prescriptions, albeit with a greater admixture of humility. I do not believe the students crowding our economics classes are wasting their time.

NOTES

The author wishes to express his appreciation to W. Lee Hansen, Irving Morrissett, and Lawrence Senesh for valuable comments and suggestions. Research for this paper was aided by National Science Foundation grant GS 31276X.

1. I say "so called Keynesian" because Keynes himself, in a chapter of his *General Theory* called "The Theory of Prices," stressed the role of "bottlenecks" and increased wage demands in creating what he called positions of "semi-inflation" despite existence of unemployed resources. He thus avoided the oversimplifications vitiating some of his followers' work.

2. Such behavior is called price-taking (as opposed to price-setting); it is also called parametric treatment of prices because prices are viewed as fixed parameters.

3. This notion of optimality is referred to as "Pareto-optimality." In the literature the term "efficient" is often used as a synonym for "optimal." Our usage of "efficient," however, will be confined to the sphere of production; we speak of efficiency if aggregate outputs are maximized given the aggregate inputs or if aggregate inputs are minimized given the aggregate outputs.

4. The competitive equilibrium encountered above is a position of rest of this mechanism.

5. Although, in fact, prices will be affected by these decisions.

6. There were, of course, precursors. With regard to the marginal cost pricing idea, credit is given Dupuit who proposed it in connection with the financing of public works in 1844. Lindahl's proposal (1919) for resource allocation involving public goods was an important early step in the direction of designing novel mechanisms.

7. By "idealized" I mean simplified for purposes of analysis rather than made to appear better than they are, although the latter type of idealization is not rare.

8. Asking for contributions for a public good, such as police protection, is a case in point: the responses of individuals are likely to indicate a lower value than they actually place on the public good.

9. A model is called "complete" if it takes into account the various indirect feedbacks; thus, a general equilibrium model is complete in this sense, while partial equilibrium analysis is not.

Closing the Gap between Frontier Thinking and the Curriculum in Economics

Lawrence Senesh

The history of economic education is closely related to the period of the Weiler administration. In 1953 the Joint Council on Economic Education approached Dr. Frederick Hovde, then president of Purdue University, to develop a statewide economic education program centered at Purdue University. President Hovde, probably because of his commitment to the philosophy of a state university, identified himself with the cause of improving the economic literacy of youth and adults. He called on the Division of Continuing Education to undertake the task of establishing a statewide network. Dr. Olin Davis, with the support of labor, agriculture, business, and government, organized the Indiana Council for Economic Education. President Hovde at the same time called upon Dr. Weiler to accept the responsibility for the academic program. Dr. Weiler brought together a committed group, made up of Professors Jay Wiley, Richard Kohls, John Hicks, and, later, myself. Our task was to civilize the natives in the wilderness of Lake Oliver, where the summer workshops were held. (We civilized everyone but the mosquitoes.) The gospels of Lord Keynes and Adam Smith spread. We not only preached the gospel, we practiced it. We went into the elementary classrooms. We developed middle and upper management programs with private and government grants. We conducted nationwide leadership programs, and with the help of a Carnegie grant, I developed a K–12 design in economic education.

Our efforts culminated in a MAT program in economic education, supported by the late John Best of Elkhart, Indiana.

My particular interest in the area of economic education was always to "humanize" economic theory. This was the whole idea of *Our Working World,* a set of twenty-four publications covering grades 1–6. I wanted to liberate economic principles from the confines of college textbooks and to relate the fundamental ideas of economics to children's experiences, with increasing depth and complexity as the children matured.

Economic educators have two important jobs:

First, the economic educator must build a bridge which establishes an organic relationship with the other scientific disciplines. Economic analysis

311

is too narrow to explain economic phenomena. For example, economic development is a process of great complexity. It involves change in the character, values, knowledge, and activity of virtually everyone within a society. It involves change in the inputs and outputs of all processes of production. It involves change in the character and quality, as well as the quantity, of human artifacts. It involves change in human organizations and institutions. When we have reduced all this to a single number, such as the growth of GNP per capita, we have eliminated a very large part of reality in the pursuit of simplicity.

The recognition of this inter-relatedness and the revelation that God did not create the academic departments led me to a commitment to structure the knowledge of the five social science disciplines. With a team of social scientists, working on a National Science Foundation grant, we undertook this work at Purdue University. And I am still committed to this task.

The second important task of the economic educator is to lure frontier thinkers out of their fur-lined niches. The National Science Foundation supports thousands of research projects, but very few see the daylight and enter the public domain. It is the task of the economic educator to close the gap between the frontier thinker and the hinterland. Putting the cutting edge of knowledge into the public domain as early as possible will accelerate the demonopolization of knowledge and help increase the social competence of a large segment of society.

It has been my privilege to work cooperatively with many frontier thinkers, and very recently with three: Profs. Kenneth Boulding, Alfred Kuhn, and Leonid Hurwicz. All three of these fine analytical scientists are interested in minute details, without losing sight of the universe and humanity.

Kenneth Boulding, Alfred Kuhn, and I received an NSF grant to build a bridge between general-system theory and the curriculum.[1] We worked together a whole summer, and later we met sporadically to compare notes. In our deliberations, Boulding and Kuhn were the frontier thinkers and I was the representative of the first graders. Boulding and Kuhn probed the frontier; I probed how to relate the fundamental ideas of the general system to the experiences of the child. I made a great discovery: knowing and ways of knowing are inseparable. The more one internalizes an idea, the more eloquent and clear the communication of that idea becomes. The secret of pedagogical success is primarily clarity of thinking, from which clarity of communication emerges.

So frontier thinkers and economic educators have a common interest: to bring knowing and ways of knowing into harmony. Recognition of this common interest of scientists and science educators could be a key to a beneficent Pandora's box, from which human wisdom finally could escape to enrich the quality of human decisions in a free society.

My interest in general-system theory was awakened on the school playground in Brooklyn the day after the astronauts landed on the moon. Cutting across the schoolyard, I noticed children playing astronauts. One child made the countdown: "Ten, nine, eight, seven, six, five, four, three, two, one, liftoff!"

Another child announced: "All systems go!"

A third and a fourth child communicated with each other through a makeshift microphone, holding their hands to their mouths. You could hear "Contact," "Roger." I said "Roger" too, because the children stirred my imagination and saved my day in the third grade classroom, where I was headed to give a demonstration lesson on city planning.

In the classroom, the dialogue between the children and me went like this:

"How many of you watched the astronauts take off from Cape Kennedy and land on the moon?" (The children raised their hands.)

"What did the Houston announcer say which confirmed a smooth takeoff?" ("All systems go!")

"What did this statement mean?" ("It meant that man and machines were working together well at that moment to put the astronauts on the moon.")

"Can you describe the tasks of some of the people and machines which had to work together?" ("The computers had to be working and the computer specialists had to analyze the printouts; weathermen had to decide whether it was good enough weather for takeoff; communication equipment had to be in good order and radio men had to operate it; the rockets and boosters were to function; etc.")

"What would happen if any one part would fail?" ("It would affect the other parts.")

"If something goes wrong, who will make it right?" ("Sometimes the machine, computer, or thermostat; sometimes the people in the Space Center or the astronauts.")

"So, boys and girls, we can say that a system is made up of many parts; that the entire system has a goal—to put the astronauts on the moon; that the parts must interact to reach the goal; that if something goes wrong, the machine or people must correct the errors."

"Now children, let us study the city of New York. Is the city a system?" ("Yes.")

"Why?" ("Because it is made up of many parts, of many smaller systems.")

"Name some of them." ("Road system, transportation system, communication system, sewage system, electrical system, school system, housing system, public health system, business system, legal system, recreation and playground system, water system.")

"These are the systems that work together within a larger system to accomplish goals. What are these goals?" ("A beautiful city, a healthy city, a safe city, a city with a livelihood for everyone.")

"Can we say about New York City, 'All systems go!'?" ("No.")

"Why not?" ("Unlike the moon-landing space program, where the goal has been reached, the goals of New York City are to build a beautiful and safe city, a city where people who are looking for a job can find one; but these goals have not been realized yet.")

The children had discovered that the various components of the system do not work properly together to accomplish these goals. For example, the educational system and the business system are illmatched to make a large number of youths employable. The housing system, the business system, and the transportation system in many neighborhoods are badly coordinated to get breadwinners to their working places cheaply and quickly. The same dissonance may apply to the school system, housing system, park system. Frequently, changes create service dislocations which may become a permanent defect of the system. As an example, the children acted out what could happen to the family system, the business system, and the school system if the city decided to tear down old houses where poor families lived and replace them with big buildings for high-income families and expensive offices. Students may also act out what would happen to the business system, the school system, the playground system, the transportation system, and the sewage system if New York City decided to build a housing project for many hundreds of low-income families. The task of planning is to find out how the subsystems of a city must work together to help the city reach its goals.

At the close of the project, I asked the children to prepare a mobile from clothes hangers. Hanging from the end of each arm was a subsystem. If the children touched any one subsystem, the other subsystems were affected, bringing the system nearer to or further away from the goals of the system: the achievement of beauty, health, safety, and livelihood.

This experience in Brooklyn generated the request for and the approval of an NSF grant for the purpose of translating general-system theory into the curriculum.

The first task of a science educator is to identify the fundamental ideas of the disciplines or the subdisciplines. The purpose of the identification is to take an inventory of the core ideas of the discipline so that the science educator sees the scope of the knowledge and the shape of its frontiers. Without such identification, the educators will be inclined to teach the so-called "minimum" concepts and will sacrifice the integrity of the disciplines. Chart 1 presents the fundamental ideas of the general-system disciplines.

Chart 1
The Fundamental Ideas of the General-System Disciplines

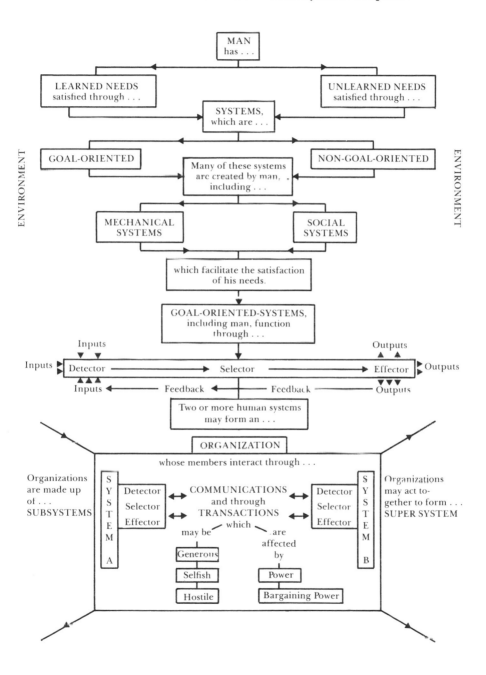

The second task is to relate those fundamental ideas or the concept to youths' experiences on every grade level with increasing depth and complexity. Let me illustrate my point.

SOME OF THE CONCEPTS OF GENERAL-SYSTEM THEORY AND THEIR CURRICULUM APPLICATIONS

Concept: A system is made up of two or more parts which interact.

To help young people discover systems, students should look around, study their textbooks and picture magazines to identify living or nonliving things that are made up of parts working together to "get something done." They will discover, through the thermostat, the heating system; through the water faucet, the water system; through the lights, the electrical system; through the drain, the sewage system; through buses, automobiles, trucks, subways and airplanes, the transportation system; through the mailboxes, telephones and televisions, the vast communication system; and through the streams and their tributaries, the river system.

Students should collect objects or cut out pictures representing systems, such as a vacuum cleaner, computer, dishwasher, anthills, clock, family, tree, vegetable, church, Salvation Army, school, post office, pond, stove, wilderness, farm, library, dogs, cats, and human beings. All of these living and nonliving things are made up of parts which interact to do a job. The class will discover that some of the systems are simple systems (a clock), while others are complicated and made up of many subsystems. Such complicated systems are the transportation system, made up of the many different means of transportation; the family, made up of many human beings; and the anthill, made up of many ants.

Concept: The system created by human beings may be a mechanical or a social system.

The class will pick out from the system pile those systems which have been constructed by human beings. Then two classroom committees divide the "man-made" systems into two groups: one group is made up of objects (freezer, clock, heating system, etc.) and the other group is made up of human beings (Salvation Army, church, family, etc.). Systems made up of objects are called "mechanical" systems, ranging in capability from replacing human labor to replacing the human brain. Systems made up of human beings are called "social" systems, which group human beings to accomplish various tasks, ranging from producing and distributing resources to rendering social justice to society. Mechanical and social systems alike may be used for the betterment, or the disintegration, of society.

Concept: Systems may be goal-oriented or non-goal-oriented.

Students will select from the system pile those objects and cutouts which are goal-oriented: human beings, church, school, Salvation Army, plant, cat, dog, post office, family refrigerator, etc. Then the students will explain, one by one, the goals of these systems and how the system corrects itself if some disturbance obstructs achievement of its goals. The teacher may raise his arm, holding in his hand the symbols of two systems: a picture of a wilderness and a picture of a farm. The classroom discussion will reveal the following findings: wilderness is created by nature and a farm is created by human beings. If a tornado causes serious damage to the wilderness, there is no guarantee that the wilderness will restore itself to its original state. The trees are goal-oriented systems, but there is no common goal to a wilderness system. If a tornado causes serious damage to a farm, the farmer (who is part of the system) will restore the farm to its original state of producing the greatest amount of food at lowest cost. The farm is a goal-oriented system. Students should discuss why human interference is necessary to make a nature-made system into a goal-oriented or cybernetic system. Using arguments similar to those of the farm and the wilderness, students should discuss why a pond is a non-goal-oriented system while the air-conditioning system is a goal-oriented or cybernetic system. What are the consequences if the pond is affected by an outside influence, such as pollution, or if the air conditioning system is affected by changing temperature?

Concept: Some systems are capable of learning, while others are not.

The class may discuss the following questions: "Are human beings a part of nature?" ("Yes.") "Are human beings a system?" ("Yes, human beings' organs interact.") "Is a human being a goal-oriented system?" ("Yes.") "What are his goals?" ("To change the natural environment or build his/her environment for improving the human condition.") "What is the difference between beavers and human beings as a goal-oriented system?" ("Human beings, through learning, develop many different organizations and lifestyles of settlement which they can improve upon through invention and innovation. The beavers' ability to learn is limited. Therefore, the lifestyles and organization of the beaver colony are static.")

Concept: There is a dynamic interaction between human beings and the environment.

To help students understand the interaction between social systems and nature, students may study chart 2, "Interaction between the Social System and the Ecological System."

Concept: Man and all other goal-oriented systems achieve their goals by the built-in mechanism of the detector, selector, and effector.

The detector mechanism acquires information from the environment. The selector mechanism evaluates the information and chooses the preferred action in conformity with the goals. The effector mechanism puts the preferred choice into action.

Chart 2
. Interaction between the Social System and the Ecological System

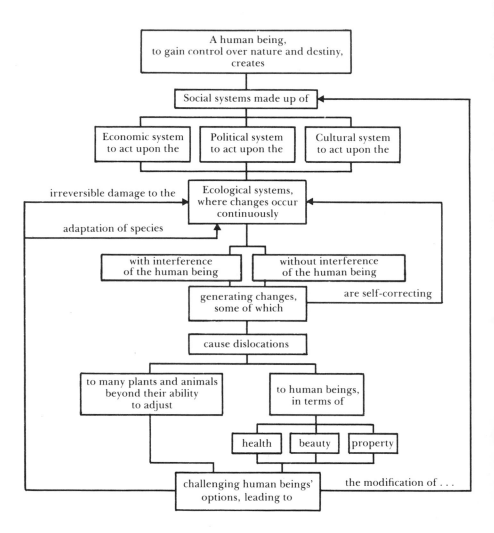

The students may develop the following activities:

Detector: Jimmy discovers that to get a good job, he must have good training and education.

Selector: Jimmy is determined to get a good job. He studies the various options by which he can get better training and education. He selects the one best suited to him.

Effector: Jimmy begins the training best suited to him.

The class may practice the above sequence of detector-selector-effector, using other examples. The class may be divided into committees, which will all use the same examples and then compare notes. They will discover considerable differences in the way the committees evaluate the environment, identify the options, and choose among the options. The reasons for the differences may be differences in values (negative response to the sight of poverty), lack of sharp observation, lack of information, or differences in perceptions of reality. For example, people receive different signals concerning the energy shortage or the quality of the environment.

Concept: When two or more systems work together, they form a super-system or an organization. These systems work together through communication and transactions. The transactions may be generous, selfish, or hostile.

Generous transactions are those in which one party is motivated primarily by concern for the other party's welfare. Selfish transactions are those in which the parties are concerned only, or primarily, with their own welfare—as in buying and selling—and are indifferent to the welfare of the other party. A hostile transaction is one in which one party tries to hurt another, even though the action may hurt the doer—for example, in maintaining a boycott. Students may act out sociodramas demonstrating these transactions: a mother feeding her baby or a person giving money to a beggar. The students may discuss why these transactions are generous transactions and whether or not they are important in our society. Students may discuss the following example.

Al has some marbles. Bob has a pocket knife. Al would like to have a pocket knife and is willing to give up not more than eight marbles for the knife. Bob would like to have some marbles instead of the pocket knife and is willing to give up the pocket knife for no fewer than four marbles. Al is indifferent to Bob and Bob is indifferent to Al. Both are selfish. The transaction between them may take place between the range of four to eight marbles for the pocket knife.

Why is this transaction a selfish transaction? What determines the maximum number of marbles Al is willing to give up for the knife? What determines the minimum number of marbles Bob is willing to accept for the knife? What are the techniques Al may use to increase his bargaining power?

Are selfish transactions important to our society? (Yes, because most people are motivated by self-interest.)

Al becomes hostile to Bob. Now he is not willing to give more than two marbles for the pocket knife. Bob is still willing to give up the pocket knife for not less than four marbles. Why is this a hostile transaction? Under these conditions, can the transaction be completed? Can you make up stories in which people are involved in hostile transactions? How do hostile transactions affect families, cities, countries, and the world?

> **Concept:** An important concept in understanding the functioning of a system is equilibrium. Equilibrium is a stable balance between two or more forces.

Students may recognize systems in equilibrium in the following situations:

A river with stable water level: the rate of water inflow and the rate of water outflow are in balance with each other.

A refrigerator with a stable temperature: there are two forces, one which works to keep the temperature of the refrigerator low, and the outside temperature, which tends to keep the temperature of the refrigerator high. These forces are in balance with each other when the refrigerator works properly.

When the family income equals intended expenditure and saving, the budget is in balance or equilibrium.

When the population of a country is in a stationary equilibrium, the number of people born each year is equal to the number of people who die each year.

When a family follows customs and traditions and acts and thinks alike from year to year, there is a balance or equilibrium in the family.

A factory, given the taste and income of the buyers and given price and technology, will be in equilibrium as a production system.

> **Concept:** If the equilibrium of a system is disturbed, different systems respond to such disturbances differently.

How does the water level of a river respond during the melting season? Is there any mechanism to maintain a stable water level? How does the cooling system of a refrigerator respond to changing temperature? How does the family respond if they spend more than they earn? What may happen to the population of a country if the rate of growth is increasing? Is there anything in the system which could control a population explosion? How does the traditional family react if their ways of life are challenged by increased equal job opportunities for women? How do nonconventional families react to the same challenge? What happens with the equilibrium of the factory if new innovations challenge its market? In discussing these questions, students will discover that some systems, such as the river and population, have no built-in mechanisms to correct deviations from an equilibrium. Other systems, such as the refrigerator, have mechanisms built in to cope with deviations. Still other systems, such as the factory or the nonconformist family, have a learning capacity which enables them to identify new goals and establish an equilibrium different from that of the past.

Concept: In a social system, inertia plays an important role in keeping the system in equilibrium.

The students should try to find examples of how customs keep a system in equilibrium; for example, how the habit of drinking coffee in the United States assures the stability of income of coffee producers and the coffee industry.

Concept: Science and technology and changing value preferences perpetually challenge the equilibrium of the economic system. Some systems make adjustments quickly; others do not.

The students may discuss how the following forces affect the equilibrium of systems:

The invention of the automobile and its impact on the urban system.

The expanded welfare system and its impact on charitable organizations.

The impact of longevity on the family system.

The impact of the assembly line on the design and location of factories.

Concept: Changes in one system may affect other systems.

The students may discuss the following questions:

What will happen if big corporations come to a city? How does this event affect other systems? What adjustments must be made to keep the city a pleasant place to live?

What would happen if the river system would flood a city? How would this event affect the various systems in the city?

What would happen if the size of families increased or decreased? How would the change in family size affect the school system or the business system?

Concept: Some changes reinforce; other changes counteract.

A student panel may discuss how, in the past, economic growth begot economic growth and poverty begot poverty. Students may discuss how, in traditional societies, such as the Amish, the acceptance of technology may break down the culture, and how the breaking down of the culture attracts more technology.

The students may also discuss the built-in mechanisms in our economic system which counteract a depression (unemployment insurance, social security).

The students may discuss how the river system has, up to a certain point, a self-cleaning capacity.

Concept: Changes in a system create costs or benefits to the society.

The class may collect newspaper articles illustrating such relationships. The headlines might be: "Oil Leaks off California Coast," "Billboards Approved in Yellowstone National Park," "Grand Canyon for Power Generation."

After discussing what social costs or benefits are brought about by these changes, the students should consider who ought to pay the costs and who should enjoy the benefits of these changes.

Concept: The goals of the economic system depend upon the dominant values of the society.

A U.S. history class may investigate the changing goals of the American society. They may discover that the result of the Jefferson–Hamilton debate was our commitment to economic freedom: the promotion of the sovereignty of producers and consumers in such a manner that anyone in this group, exercising freedom, is not abridging the freedom of others. The Great Depression committed our economic system to economic stability and family security. The fear of postwar depression in the 1940s resulted in the Employment Act of 1946. The recent preoccupation with pollution has generated a new goal: quality of life.

By studying the goals of our history, the class will be able to identify seven goals incorporated into our economic system: efficiency, growth, stability, security, freedom, justice, and quality of life. The class may be divided into six committees, each studying the following questions:

How would you rank each goal in relationship to other goals?

What are the forces which strengthened or weakened our preference for each goal?

What are our records in reaching each goal?

How does each goal reinforce or conflict with other goals?

What are the future courses of each goal?

This is the summary of my transplant operation from the minds of frontier thinkers Kenneth Boulding and Alfred Kuhn into the hinterland of the curriculum. If the operation proves to be successful, I hope the patient will not die.

My other recent association, aimed at building the bridge between frontier thinking and the school curriculum, has been with Professor Leonid Hurwicz of the University of Minnesota. In 1976, he and I attended a National Science Foundation–sponsored conference in New Orleans on needed research and development in precollege economic education. During that conference, Professor Hurwicz presented a paper, "Perspectives on Economics,"[2] in which he addressed himself to the following questions:

What should we look for in an optimal economic system? (An optimal economic system is one which responds most sensitively to the private and social preferences of society, and satisfies these preferences in such a way that no further reallocation of resources can take place to raise the satisfaction of some without lowering the satisfaction of others.)

What are the operating characteristics of the competitive market system and how can its deficiencies be corrected?

If a system is to be modified to move toward optimality, what must the system designer watch for?

The late professor, R. A. Gordon of the University of California, responded to the paper.[3] He severely questioned its appropriateness. Professor Gordon was puzzled as to "how a survey of this sort will help in teaching economics at the pre-college level. I suspect a good many people at this conference cannot understand some of the literature he discusses (I know I cannot), and what the teacher of pre-college economics would be able to do with most of the concepts and analytical tools he surveys is beyond me."

The dialogue between Hurwicz and Gordon raised an important issue: the role of the economic educator in placing frontier knowledge into the public domain. Professor Hurwicz' presentation convinced me more than ever of the importance of narrowing the ever-widening gap between science and society. Free society is doomed to death if frontier ideas become the monopoly of a small group of experts. The cutting edge of knowledge, regardless of its visible merit or its immediate relevance, has to become a part of dialogues in the schools and in the community. This conviction led me to a working alliance with Leonid Hurwicz. After listening to his presentation, I requested a series of conversations with him. These stimulating dialogues helped me build the bridge between a creative mind and the school curriculum. In the following pages I attempt to make some of the concepts, identified by Professor Hurwicz, operational for instructional use. I have not tried at this stage to relate the activities to any particular grade level.

SOME OF THE CONCEPTS OF AN OPTIMAL ECONOMIC SYSTEM WITH CURRICULUM APPLICATIONS

Concept: An optimal economic system should incorporate social goals that reflect the value system of the society in order to provide a proper tradeoff with efficiency.

Students may read the opening of the Declaration of Independence and the Preamble to the United States Constitution. They may discuss how the philosophical commitments declared in the two documents have shaped the goals of our social system. The class may be divided into six committees. Each will present a historical episode to the class to demonstrate that some periods have brought us nearer to these goals and others have taken us further away from them.

Students may have a classroom discussion titled "What do we want our economic system to accomplish?" The random answers may be classified into seven goals: efficiency, economic growth, stability, security, freedom, justice, and quality of life. The students may discuss what the goals mean, how these goals are involved in social issues, and how some of them reinforce while others conflict with each other.

The students may study the following historical episodes: the Jefferson–Hamilton debates, the bank wars of the Jacksonian period, the emergence of Populism in the 1890s, the Great Depression of the 1930s, the recognition of pollution and its threat to health in the 1960s, inflation, and the formation of the international oil cartel, OPEC, and its consequences.[4] Students will identify the goal awareness which emerged during each of these periods.

Throughout the academic year, the students may investigate those political demands which challenge or reinforce the goals of our economic system. For example, to cope with the problems of pollution and develop a comprehensive energy policy, modification of the existing market system may be necessary, which may challenge the goals of economic growth and economic freedom.

The Preamble of the U. S. Constitution commits our political system to "promote the general welfare." Students may discuss how the promotion of general welfare is reflected in the economic system. They may also discuss how government revenue and expenditure policies, such as the progressive income tax, subsidized school tuition, urban renewal, national health insurance, and public works may help or hinder employment, upward mobility, and equalization of income.

Students who are interested in history may study the differences between feudalism and market capitalism. They may investigate the forces which contributed to the decline of feudalism and the rise of capitalism. (Status gave way to mobility, spiritual reward to monetary reward, and the strict rules of the manor and guilds gave way to competition.)

The students may study the Harris survey of the public's possible willingness to be restricted in consumer behavior. The survey, a stratified sample of 1,497 persons, was conducted by Louis Harris and Associates between 30 August and 6 September 1975 (see table 1).

Table 1
Public's Willingness to Restrict Consumption (Harris Survey)

	Willing	Not Willing	Not Sure
Have one meatless day per week	91%	7%	2%
Stop feeding all-beef products to pet animals	78	15	7
Do away with changing clothing fashions every year	90	7	3
Wear old clothes even if they shine, until they wear out	73	22	5
Prohibit the building of large houses with extra rooms that are seldom used	73	19	8
Make it cheaper to live in multiple-unit apartments than in single homes	57	34	9
Eliminate annual model changes in automobiles	92	5	3
Sharply reduce the amount of advertising urging people to buy more products	82	11	7

SOURCE: "Harris Survey," Chicago *Tribune*, Dec. 4, 1975.

The students may discuss how the responses may reflect changing values and how these changing values may affect the goals of our economic system.

Concept: Attainment of the social goals is limited by the environment (resources and technology) and by institutional constraints; therefore, the notion of optimality is conditioned by the perceived constraints.

To help students understand the difficulty of achieving, simultaneously, two of the most important goals of the American economy, economic growth and stability, senior high school students may study President Carter's economic goals for 1981 (table 2).

Table 2
Economic Goals for 1981

	1977	1981
	Calendar Year	
GNP[a]	1,330.0	1,621.0
Annual rate of increase	5.1	4.9
GNP inflationary rate—annual rate (percent)	5.9	4.3
Unemployment rate (percent)	7.0	4.8
	Fiscal Year	
Federal receipts[a]	259.4	355.0
Federal outlays[a]	293.9	330.7
Deficit (−)	34.5	24.3
As percentages of GNP		
Receipts	19.5	21.9
Outlays	22.1	20.4

[a]Millions of constant (1972) dollars.

SOURCE: The Macroeconomic Goals of the Administration for 1981: Targets and Realizations, August 5, 1977, p. 1, table I. Joint Economic Committee. U.S. Government Printing Office. 95th Congress, 1st session.

After the students have studied table 2 and the targets for 1981, they may discuss to what extent the targets are compatible with each other. The class may invite an economist from a nearby college to discuss what attempts are made today to decrease unemployment and, at the same time, balance the budget and stabilize the general level of prices.

Some economists have made the following predictions. Students should discuss how these predictions (if they come true) would affect President Carter's 1981 predictions.

Predictions

The rising cost of energy will serve as an incentive for business to switch from capital- to labor-intensive methods of production.

Population trends and the energy shortage are likely to reduce school and highway construction.

Continued increase of oil imports will cause our foreign debt to grow, with little hope of increasing our exports. As a result of this, the international value of the dollar will drop.

Home building, buying on the installment plan, the borrowing by state and local governments will all decrease because of high interest rates.

The students may discuss the consequences to our present way of life if economic growth should slow down because of the energy shortage and environmental hazards. On the assumption that our economy will have a constant stock of wealth and a constant population, what will the way of life be in such an economy? The students may consider the following statement of John Stuart Mill:

> It is scarcely necessary to remark that a stationary condition of capital and population implies no stationary state of human improvement. There would be as much scope as ever for all kinds of mental culture, and moral and social progress; as much room for improving the Art of Living and much more likelihood of its being improved, when minds cease to be engrossed by the Art of Getting On. Even the industrial arts might be as earnestly and as successfully cultivated, with this sole difference, that instead of serving no purpose but the increase of wealth, industrial improvements would produce their legitimate effect, that of abridging labor.[5]

To help students understand the relationship between taxpayers' priorities and government spending, each student will receive 100 chips, each representing one dollar. At the front of the classroom on a long table, there should be twelve baskets, each representing one of the following areas of government spending: national defense, foreign aid, space research, alternate energy research, housing, highway construction, mass transportation, environment, education, health care, old-age insurance and welfare for the needy, and conservation of resources.

The class is divided into six committees. Each committee studies two of the twelve budgetary items and prepares the pro and con arguments related to the contribution of items to general welfare. The arguments will be prepared by each student on his or her own time. After discussion of these arguments, students distribute the 100 chips among the twelve baskets. A committee will count the chips and prepare a report on the social priorities of the class. Another committee, with the help of the public librarian, will prepare a statement on how the federal government distributes the revenues among these twelve items. The class will then compare the pattern of social priorities presumed by the class and those presumed by the government. They may discuss the following questions: What are the similarities and differences between the priorities of the class and the government?

What are the reasons for the differences? Should the people follow the priorities of the government, or should the government follow the priorities of the people? The class may repeat the exercise, but the report and the best possible options may be discussed in small groups, before each individual decides how to divide his or her 100 chips.

To help students understand how global events may challenge our economic goals, the class may read the *Declaration and the Programme of Action on the Establishment of a New International Economic Order,* adopted by the United Nations General Assembly in its sixth special session, 1974. The Declaration states:

> We . . . proclaim our united determination to work urgently for the establishment of a new international economic order based on equity, sovereign equality, interdependence, common interest and cooperation among all States, irrespective of their economic and social systems, which shall correct inequalities and redress existing injustices, make it possible to eliminate the widening gap between the developed and the developing countries and peace and justice . . . The prosperity of the international community as a whole depends upon the prosperity of its constituent parts.

Students may discuss how such a new international economic order could be carried out and how it may affect U.S. economic goals.

Concept: In measuring efficiency of a system, the cost of private and public maintenance to operate the system should be deducted from the value of the output: "For instance, the market system uses brokers while a centrally planned system uses planners. Both types of persons constitute human resources diverted from the production of goods and services into the operation of the system. This, of course, does not make them socially useless, since no mechanism will work without some use of resources to make it work."[6]

The class may investigate how much local businesses spend on advertising and other sales promotion necessary to expand the market for their products. In their search they may also discover that running a business requires support systems maintained from taxes: street lights, streets and sidewalks, a police system to protect private property, and the court system to uphold the sanctity of contracts. The classroom discussion should bring out that the size of expenditures necessary to maintain support systems depends on the efficiency of the enabling legislation and the degree to which government officials and private citizens observe the law.

The class may also discuss President Carter's plans for voluntary measures to control inflation and the energy shortage. They may discuss the costs and benefits of voluntary measures, compared to the effectiveness and cost of punitive measures.

Students in the lower elementary grades may name the systems that support the functioning of the corner grocery store (police, fire protection, road paving, snow clearance, etc.).

Students in the elementary grades may act out the following sociodrama. The city council in a little town decides it should have big industries so that the city may grow and earn tax money. Industrialists come to town. They are happy with the town, but they demand a bigger supply of water and electricity, more roads, and better schools. The mayor and the city council suddenly realize the great costs of having an industry in their town.

Concept: Strength of the competitive market system. Its incentive structure depends on the pursuit of self-interest by labor and management.

A central aspect of an optimal economic system is an incentive structure that leads both labor and management to produce goods and services at the lowest possible cost and in a product mix corresponding to consumer preferences. The most powerful management incentive is the expectation of profit. The traditional view is that the profit motive stimulates efficiency; but this may not work as well when ownership and management are separated. In fact, there is much separation of corporate management from ownership.

This separation may cause business managers in medium- and large-size firms to engage in what is called "satisficing" behavior. They satisfy their stockholders with an adequate but less than optimal profit margin, while they stimulate their own egos by elegant offices, large supportive staffs, and other perquisites of their positions. Since power and prestige tend to accompany bigness, a corporate executive may expand production to a point well beyond that of maximum efficiency and profit. This behavior leads to inefficiency; therefore, a new or additional incentive structure, independent of the market, may be needed that will tame management's ambition for bigness for its own sake.

The class may study the effectiveness of different incentive schemes for labor and try to gauge the relative effectiveness of various economic and noneconomic rewards such as wages, piece-rate payments, profit sharing, and worker-managed enterprise. They may study how the development of loyalty to the company, as in Japan, and openness of communication between management and labor affect employee incentives.

The development of the incentive system within the firm encounters great problems. It is difficult to measure the potentialities of the members of the labor force to increase their efficiency through the incentive system. Potentiality is a latent quality, hardly observable. In some cases, a small incentive may result in high worker efficiency. In other cases, a great incentive program may bring forth little measurable result.

Concept: Strength of the competitive market system: the decentralization of information.

To help students understand the importance of decentralized information in a competitive system, students should inquire how much information the farmer needs in making production decisions. Students should find out that market price and the farmer's production costs are the two most important pieces of information. The interaction between market demand and supply will establish a price equilibrium, which in turn will again affect the farmer's decision.

To demonstrate the chain reaction of changing demand and supply, students may follow (in the newspapers) price changes in raw materials, wages, interest rates, and finished goods. Through a logical process, they may follow how such initiating changes will affect related markets. Students may act out interrelated markets in the following way:

Narrator: In October 1973, the government of Peru decreed an indefinite halt to all exports of fish meal and fish oil. Ecological changes caused a mysterious shift in the pattern of ocean currents, causing anchovies and related species to vanish from coastal waters. Anchovies are used to make fish meal and fish oil, of which Peru is the world's largest supplier.

U.S. Feedmill Owner: The world anchovy supply has dropped. I have to compete with other feedmill owners for that depleted supply by paying higher prices for it. Since fishmeal is an important ingredient of cattle feed, I have to raise cattle feed prices.

U.S. Cattle Rancher: I have to pay a higher price for cattle feed, so I have to raise the price of beef. I shall also try to feed my cattle more soybeans, which are cheaper than feed containing fishmeal.

U.S. Housewife: The cost of living goes up and up, and our incomes buy less and less. I hope we soon get a pay raise.

U.S. Farmer: Since feed prices are high, this year I'll plant more soybeans on my fallow land. I can even raise my price for soybeans, as long as it remains lower than the price of other feed. So I had better order more chemical fertilizer for the soybeans.

U.S. Chemical Fertilizer Manufacturer: Farmers want more of my fertilizer, so I will need more natural gas to produce more fertilizer. That will make my costs go up, so I will have to raise the price for my fertilizer.

U.S. Natural Gas Producer: Since fertilizer manufacturers want more of my natural gas, I shall produce more; that raises my cost, so I will raise my price.

Japanese Importer: Japan must replace the declining supply of anchovy meal with soybeans from the United States, which will increase the demand and market price for soybeans, and will also increase the volume of soybeans leaving the United States and entering Japan.

Narrator: Demand and prices for U.S. soybeans are skyrocketing.

U.S. Government Official: Our cattle ranchers are facing higher soybean prices, due in part to increased demand for them from Japan. We shall control the export of soybeans to Japan, which will decrease the demand for soybeans and bring the prices down.

The class may discuss the distortions which can take place as information is transmitted from one place to another in a nonmarket situation.

The class may interview a public official to find out how governments on the local, state, and federal levels prepare their budgets. How do the different government departments determine the amount of funds they need? Do the departments "pad" their budgetary requests? What can civic organizations do to prevent agencies from overstating their requests, in good faith or intentionally? Students should discuss to what extent the inaccuracy of the budget requests is due to centralized systems of information.

To help students understand the importance of information decentralization to safeguard truth, the class should compare how the different media report a single event. The class may discuss the reasons for the differences.

The issue of decentralized versus centralized information is closely related to the debate over capitalist versus socialist economies.

In the middle of the 1930s, two economists, Ludwig von Mises and Oskar Lange, engaged in a long series of dialogues on the merits and demerits of socialism. Von Mises was an Austrian economist, born in 1881. Oskar Lange was a Polish economist, who, after a career in the United States, returned to Poland after World War II.

Von Mises criticized socialism because, according to him, it did not contain a rational method of pricing. Socialism lacked adequate incentives to spur men to work hard, to undertake risks, and to introduce innovation.

Lange attempted to refute this criticism. He argued that a socialist economy could do everything as well as a capitalist economy, if not better, thanks to the centralization of information.

There is very little, if anything, about this dialogue in high school or college textbooks. Comprehension of this dialogue would help people understand the changing nature of the socialist economies in Eastern Europe. Much work must be done to put the analytical work of Lange and von Mises into the public domain.

The class may be divided into two committees. One committee would represent the ideas of von Mises and the other, the ideas of Lange.

According to von Mises, the competitive system has three virtues:

1. The producers own the factors of production, and producers and consumers have free choice.

2. Many producers compete with each other for raw materials, labor, and capital, using and combining these resources as economically as possible.

3. Many producers compete in the market for customers. Competition compels them to keep up with the latest innovations and maintain prices at the level of the cost of production.

Von Mises argued that public ownership of raw materials and capital makes the best allocation of resources impossible. He argued that raw materials and capital goods are not traded on the market. If they are not traded, they have no price; if they have no price, their relative importance cannot be measured. Economists of the von Mises school argue that in a socialist economy, the government must make thousands or even millions of calculations for every economic decision.

The other class committee would represent Mr. Lange, whose arguments are:

1. The consumer is free to express preferences through demand prices.
2. People have the freedom to choose occupations. Income from labor is equally distributed and modified inversely by the value attached to safety and pleasantness of the job.
3. The planning authority assigns values to the raw materials and capital goods. These values act like market prices. Producers combine these factors to achieve minimum production costs. The planning authority, like the market, makes price adjustments if demand does not equal supply. The methods of trial and error for determining prices are characteristic of both the socialist economy and the market economy.
4. The quantity produced by each firm would be increased to the point where the cost of producing an additional unit equals price.
5. The right prices are determined in both systems by the interaction of demand and supply.

Mr. Lange argued that the socialist economy is superior to the private enterprise system because:

1. The central authority has more information for decision making.
2. Bad decisions can be isolated and need not penetrate into the entire system.
3. With equal distribution of income, the demand of different consumers for commodities at the same price represents an equal urgency of need.
4. Income from capital goods is distributed as social dividends to individuals according to the criteria of equity (for example, size of family, age, etc.).

But Mr. Lange had a serious concern in 1938, which should be a part of the classroom discussion: "The real danger of socialism is that of the bureaucratization of economic life."[7]

The Mises–Lange dialogue may be dramatized or translated into simulations (but it is imperative that awareness of the socialist economy, as presented by Lange, not be confused with Marxism). As a follow-up activity, the class may study how "participatory socialism" works in Yugoslavia (a different but related type of system).

Concept: Weaknesses of the competitive market system: possible inefficiencies where externalities and indivisibilities are significant.

The class may study externalities in their own communities. "Externalities" are costs and benefits that affect or spill over onto parties that are not involved in a given exchange. Spillover costs occur, for example, when a chemical manufacturer or meat-packing plant dumps wastes into a lake or river, when a petroleum refinery pollutes the air with smoke, or when a paint factory creates distressing odors. In each case, society gives up something (clean water, clean air), but the firm does not have to pay this cost. Therefore the production cost is smaller to the firm than it is to the society, and the firm will therefore produce more and charge a price below the true production cost. When spillover costs are significant and not accounted for, the market will overallocate resources to the production of the good or service. Students may have a mock hearing of the city council to decide the need for additional legislation.

Spillover benefits occur in the area of private health, as when communicable diseases are controlled; in the area of education, which may assure not only higher income for individuals but benefits for the entire society, such as political stability. In each case, society receives benefits, but the providers are not fully compensated for them. Therefore, when spillover benefits are important and not accounted for, the market will underallocate resources to that commodity. Students may have a debate on the statement "Be it resolved that preserving health should be a fundamental public responsibility to the individual."

Concept: Weaknesses of the competitive market system: possible inefficiencies generated in the process of allocating the benefits of public goods. Public goods are those goods which are consumed by any number of persons simultaneously, without the necessity of dividing or diminishing the quantity in any way and without affecting or limiting the pleasure or usefulness they offer to their simultaneous users.

National defense, the services of a lighthouse, and radio and television programs are public goods.

The problem every economic system faces is how to distribute the benefits of such public goods to assure maximum welfare.

The tools to establish welfare criteria were pioneered by Vilfredo Pareto (1848–1923) and developed by others. According to the Pareto criterion, an economic system reaches an optimum when resources are allocated in such a way that no party can be made better off without making other parties worse off. In certain cases, such as public goods, a competitive or price-taking system may fail to achieve the Pareto optimum. In such cases, some alternative economic arrangements may be able to achieve a Pareto-superior position.

Although Pareto occupies an important place in advanced economic theory, very seldom is reference made to him in introductory college courses in economics. Since his ideas are important, economic educators must find a way to relate his welfare models to the young people's experience. I offer the following story to illustrate this point.

The Pareto Kids' Dilemma

Once upon a time there was a poor country where practically no one could read, write, or count, but where every family had a radio. The people decided that since they could not afford to build a neighborhood school, they would use some of their common funds to build themselves a radio station to learn what they would have learned in school.

The economic advisor told them that the *construction cost*, the cost of building and equipping the radio station, would be $100. The station manager told them that the *operating cost*, the cost of running the station, would be $10 a year. The people asked their lawmakers to approve the funds to construct the station, to develop the programs, and to run the station for one year.

The radio station was built and opened with a grand public ceremony, which no one attended, except the little girl who was to cut the ribbon. All the listeners—children and adults—were at home, waiting for the educational broadcasts to begin.

During the first year, the radio station was a great success. The general welfare was very much improved; people learned many things they would have learned in school. The output of the radio station truly was a *public good*, for it was something that everyone shared, and the amount received by anyone was not lessened in any way by the large number of people who shared and enjoyed it.

People agreed that this was the optimum—the best situation for the general welfare. The listeners were well off because they could listen to the educational programs and learn things. Listeners were also well off because, once a program was produced, the cost of additional listeners was zero. But there was one serious problem. When the year was up, there would be no money.

The manager spent many sleepless nights wondering what to do. When the end of the year came and there was no more money, there was nothing to do but close the station. "Yet," said the economic advisor, speaking from the business point of view, "it is very wise to close the station since there is no money to run it with." But from the people's point of view, closing the station would be a great blow to the general welfare.

"We must do something to have the radio station operating again," people said. "Let's ask our lawmakers to give the radio station $10 for the operating cost for another year," someone suggested.

But the lawmakers said that there was no money in the treasury which could be spent for operating the station, and there would not be for many years to come.

"There must be another way to operate the radio station," people said to themselves. The people wondered if those who wanted to listen to the radio programs would pay a fee.

"If enough people would pay the fee agreed upon, we could collect the operating cost of $10," and because many people wanted to pay the fee, the $10 was collected. These people knew that they had to give up other things they could have bought with the money. But they felt that the listening pleasure far outweighed the sacrifice of paying the fee.

"But how about those who do not pay the fee and still listen to the programs? They should not be allowed to listen to the programs," some said. "How can we prevent them from listening?"

A scientist said, "I can solve the problem with a new invention. It is a radio scrambler. It mixes up the radio program when the radio waves leave the station. If people turn their radios to listen, all they will hear is the program all scrambled up. But to every person who pays the radio station the fee, I will give a device to put in his radio to unscramble the program for him."

In this way the problem of fees for the radio station was solved. The radio station went back on the air and began to broadcast the educational programs again, but all scrambled up. The people who paid the fee were happy because now they could again listen to the radio with their unscramblers, but the people who did not pay the fee were very sad.

But the situation that was created was less than the best for the community. It was less than optimal. It did not assure the greatest welfare of the community. Why? The addition of more listeners to the program would produce greater consumption without additional cost to the radio station and without interfering with the listening pleasure of the other listeners. If the people who were now excluded would be permitted to listen free of charge, they would be better off without making anyone else worse off.

People who cared for the general welfare wanted to change the system. Some of these people argued that the radio station was underutilized since people whose participation would not cause sacrifice to anybody were excluded from listening. Other people in this group argued that excluding people from pleasure, who did not cause inconvenience to anybody, caused unnecessary unfairness and disappointment and unnecessarily created an uneducated group in the society. So the feeling grew that it would be better if everyone could again listen to the radio.

"It's all very well that everyone can listen," said the station manager, taking the scrambling device out of the station, "but remember what will happen if no one pays the operating cost." So the people started thinking about where the revenue would come from to run the radio station.

"If it is necessary to have revenue," someone ventured to say, "but no one wants to be excluded from listening, perhaps we can raise the revenue by people giving what they feel the program is worth to them. Maybe we can collect enough revenue that way."

"Yes," chimed in another, "but people should be honest and give what they think the programs are worth to them."

And thus it came about that the people gave what they could, in accordance with the value they placed on the education which the radio provided. Those who could not afford to pay anything listened to the programs free. When the collection was counted, they learned that enough money had been collected to keep the radio programs going.

"You see," said the economic advisor, "we have achieved greater welfare than before because people who could pay less or nothing are now allowed to listen without making those who listen and pay for it worse off."

Most of the people thought that this system was a just system, but some people felt otherwise. These people, who were not quite as open-hearted, were not, as it turned out, quite as open-handed. They suspected that some of their neighbors, who listened to the radio programs just as much as they did, and who were just as wealthy as they were, were giving less than the programs were honestly worth to them.

"Why should such people, who pay less than the program is worth to them, listen to the radio programs at our expense?" they asked each other. "I am not such a fool. Why should I be honest if they are not?" And so it turned out that one year, not long after the collection was counted, there was not enough revenue to pay the operating cost of the radio station for another year. The station had to close down again.

But shortly thereafter, somebody had a bright idea. "Why don't we cover the operating cost from businesses that would like to advertise their products on the radio?" And so a businessman paid the radio station for the advertising, which covered the $10 operating cost. Because the advertising made the listeners better informed, they could buy more wisely. The businessman hoped he would sell more merchandise, which would recover the advertising costs and, also, earn him extra profit.

The radio station opened again and everybody listened to the program at no charge. The listeners were better off than before, without making anyone else worse off—everyone had moved to a Pareto-superior position. The total welfare was improved. But how do we measure welfare?

There are many things which are difficult to measure in terms of money. For example, it is difficult to express how much pleasure or pain is worth in terms of money. Therefore it was difficult for the children to decide how much they would benefit in terms of money if they learned to read, write, and count by listening to the radio. They found out that it would cost $32 per year (which they didn't have) to hire a bus that would take them to the nearest village to attend school. So the benefit of literacy at home was $32. But the children found one disadvantage: advertising on the radio during the educational programs slowed them down and learning took much longer. They estimated that the extra time needed for them to learn kept them away from work and made them lose $26 in wages. In this case, they figured that the benefit they would gain from the radio station would be only $6.

The adults made similar calculations. Since they were partially educated before the programs began, they figured it would cost them only $20 per year to hire a bus to go (less often) to the nearest school. So the adults gained a benefit of $20 from learning at home. But the adults also gained an additional welfare of $5 from the information they gained from advertising. They became better-informed consumers.

However, the longer time it took them to learn, because of advertising, meant a sacrifice of $22 in lost wages.

The members of the community figured out how their welfare would change if the radio station would operate with advertising, compared to the station's not operating at all:

	Change in Welfare
The station owner's welfare did not change, since he collected $10 from the businessman, the amount necessary to run the station. The owner was just as well off as before.	$ 0
The businessman's welfare increased, because his increasing sales ($12), due to the advertising, were larger than his payment to the radio station ($10).	2
The children's welfare increased, because their benefit from avoiding the bus ride by studying at home ($32) was larger than their sacrifice of time and wages lost while listening to the advertising ($26).	6
The adults' welfare increased, because their benefit from avoiding the bus ride by home study ($20), plus their gain as wiser consumers ($5), was larger than their sacrifice of time in listening to the advertising ($22).	3
Total welfare increased by	$11

The community concluded that operating the radio station with advertising is a Pareto-superior position, compared to not operating the station at all, because children and adults were better off without making anyone else worse off.

But as time passed, more and more of the children and adults became irritated by the advertising because it took them so much longer to learn. But eliminating advertising meant taking over the operating costs of the radio station by the listeners. So the children decided (out of sheer goodness of heart) that the businessman had to be compensated for the losses he suffered by taking his advertisements off the radio. The benefits of increased social welfare *with* advertising had to be compared to the increase in social welfare *without* advertising.

The community agreed on the following. The adults would pay $10 to the radio station to operate the programs. They also agreed to endure the loss of $5 in welfare by being deprived of the information received by the advertising. And the children agreed they would pay the businessman $2 to operate the programs without advertising.

Now the community had all the information necessary to figure out in which case the social welfare would be higher: programs without advertising or programs with advertising. "But who is smart enough to make this determination?" the people asked.

"I," said a young boy, "I am a member of the Pareto Kids, an economics club, and we have determined the total welfare gained in both cases in the following way":

	Change in Welfare
The station owner's welfare would not change, since in both cases he would collect the same amount of money necessary to operate the radio station.	$ 0
The businessman's welfare would not change, since in both cases he would gain the same amount ($2).	0
The children's benefit from home study was $32 without advertising. But the children would compensate the businessman $2 for the profit he lost.	30
The adults' benefit from home study without advertising was $20. The adults paid the operating cost of the station, which was $10, and lost $5 in welfare due to the loss of information.	5
Net gain in welfare without advertising	$35
Net gain in welfare with advertising	$11

"So, my friends," said the members of the Pareto Kids, "in the first case we gained $11 in total welfare by having the radio station operating with advertising. Running the radio station with advertising raises total benefit by $11, whereas running the radio station without advertising results in a $35 gain in welfare. Operating the radio station without advertising is Pareto-superior to operating the radio station with advertising, because adults and children are better off without making anybody worse off."

"What a marvelous group of children the Pareto Kids are," said the proud parents. But one parent said, "Let us give another task to the Pareto Kids. What would happen if the station operated by charging a subscription rate of $5 to cover the operating costs of the station for a while?"

The children frowned because they didn't have enough money for that. To hide their prejudice and to demonstrate their objectivity, one Pareto Kid spoke up. "If that is what you parents want, then we children would get more and more stupid while some adults get smarter and smarter. Let us compare the operation of the radio station by subscription to operation of the radio station without advertising.

"Adults would be worse off, because some adults for whom the program was not worth $5 or who could not afford $5 would be excluded. The radio station would be better off if it had more than two subscriptions. The businessman would be worse off because the children would not compensate him for his loss of profit. The children would be worse off because they would not be able to listen to the radio because they could not pay the price. Putting a price on listening by subscription would be unfair to us."

When the Pareto Kid had finished his argument, the parents had tears in their eyes. The children were crying too. One parent said, "We cannot deprive our children of education. We will continue to run the radio station without advertising."

"You are right," said the children, "because this is Pareto-superior to all other possibilities."

"What a marvelous social benefit the radio programs have been," said the economic advisor. "I wish Pareto's ghost could be here to listen to our Pareto Kids. But who needs Pareto's ghost when we have found the best possible solution?"

Everyone agreed.

> **Concept:** A weakness of the nondiscriminatory market system, whether competitive or monopolistic, in which each consumer pays the same price, is that it may be unable to yield optimal solutions. The following story will attempt to illustrate this concept.

The Bridge Story

Three "bridge users" (farmers) visit the only bridge builder in the area and ask him to build a bridge across a small stream where their farms are located. The bridge builder estimates the construction cost of the bridge to be $120.

Bridge user A is willing to pay $75 for a bridge-crossing permit. This means that if he has to pay *as much* as $75 for a permit, he will be exactly as well off as if he didn't have a permit. If he pays less than $75, he is better off than if he didn't have a permit.

Similarly, bridge user B has a maximum price of $50, at which he is as well off as without a permit, and below which he is better off. For bridge user C, the maximum price is $25.

The willingness of the users to pay for the bridge-crossing permit is summarized by schedule 1.

Schedule 1

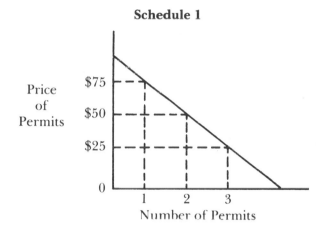

The bridge builder sits down to set the price for the bridge-crossing permit, using table 3.

Table 3
Setting the Price for Bridge-crossing Permits

Price	No. of Permits Sold	Total Revenue	Cost of Bridge	Profit (+) or Loss (−)
$75	1	$75	$120	− $45
$50	2	$100	$120	− $20
$25	3	$75	$120	− $45

The class may discuss the following questions. How many permits can the bridge builder sell if the price is $75, $50, $25? At what price can the bridge builder maximize his revenue? ($50 per permit produces the most revenue, $100.) Can the bridge builder afford to build the bridge under the present market conditions? (No. The highest market revenue, based on a price of $50, is insufficient to cover the construction cost of the bridge. The bridge cannot be built without price discrimination—i.e., charging each user a different price.)

The builder and the potential users of the bridge are unhappy because even the best single market price makes it impossible to bring the buyers and sellers together. An innovative approach, called the "*B* process," developed by Professors Hurwicz, Radner, and Reiter, enables the parties to come together.[8] They make the following recommendations.

Each member of the party puts in his/her hat six slips of paper, indicating the proposed revenues and prices. The bridge builder indicates on his slips the revenue he would be satisfied with, which cannot be below $120 but can be above. Bridge user A indicates on his slips the prices he would be willing to pay, which cannot be higher than $75, but of course may be less, which would please him. Bridge user B indicates on his slips the prices which he would be willing to pay, which cannot be above $50, but may be below. Bridge user C indicates on his slips of paper the prices he would be willing to pay, which are at most $25.

Each bridge user is free to push the odds in his favor by putting in the most slips (loading), up to six, for his lowest prices. But if everyone loads his hat in this way, the process of negotiation will break down. The following are examples of the kinds of proposals the bridge builder and the bridge user may make.

The bridge builder places in his hat the following revenue proposals, which are all greater than what the market would have allowed him to make:

Proposed Amount	Number of Slips
$120	1
125	2
130	3

Bridge user A places in his hat the following price proposals that he is willing to pay for a permit, which are no more than he offered on the market:

Proposed Amount	Number of Slips
$70	3
60	3

Bridge user B places in his hat the following price proposals that he is willing to pay for a permit, which are no more than he offered on the market:

Proposed Amount	Number of Slips
$50	1
45	2
40	3

Bridge user C places in his hat the following price proposals that he is willing to pay for a permit, which are no more than he offered on the market:

Proposed Amount	Number of Slips
$25	2
10	4

A referee pulls a bid from each hat. At the end of the first round, the result is checked to see whether or not an agreement will be feasible. For example, in round 1 the referee might have drawn from each hat the following proposals:

Proposal from	Amount on Slip
Bridge builder	$125
Bridge user A	60
Bridge user B	45
Bridge user C	10

The bridge builder is asking for $125 but the users, together, are offering only $115. So with this bid an agreement cannot be made; hence the referee must try again. The outcome of the second round of bidding may be:

Proposal from	Amount on Slip
Bridge builder	$120
Bridge user A	70
Bridge user B	40
Bridge user C	10

The bridge builder is asking for $120 and the users are offering $120! At this point, the parties agree. This is only one of many feasible outcomes.

Students will discover that this position is Pareto-superior to the market solution because all the users are better off than they would have been if the bridge had not been built, without making the bridge builder worse off.

Concept: Weaknesses of the competitive market system: The system needs to incorporate externalities in such a way that, for example, the marginal cost of damage to the environment is equal to the marginal cost of preventing or correcting these environmental externalities.

To illustrate the problem of externalities, students can make a survey of their community and report on externalities that are causing deterioration of the environment. They may invite local political leaders and other speakers to report on the ways the political system copes with environmental externalities. They may discuss those externalities or other costs which have been caused by forces outside the community: natural disasters and the impact of the immigration of people from rural areas.

The teacher may discuss the following case with the class. An industry moves into a town. It causes great damage to the environment. A negotiation starts between city officials and the industry. The industry is willing to clean up the environment, but there are certain questions to be decided: Should the industry restore the environment to the same state it was in before the industry moved in? Should the industry limit the cleanup to the point that the cost will not exceed the benefit from the last unit of cleanliness, since there is a point beyond which the additional costs far exceed the additional benefits? Should the industry improve the environment to such an optimal level and give a cash compensation to the members of the community for the loss of the original state?

To help students understand that externalities may be caused by outside forces that are beyond the community's control, students may study such issues as: How does the immigration of low-income groups affect the fiscal problems of a city? How can natural disasters affect the welfare of a community?

The class may discuss how communities can deal with such problems. Does the federal government give assistance to compensate for any of the externalities mentioned above? Why should an area, hit by a natural externality, be entitled to federal assistance, but not an area hit by a social externality?

I discussed the issue of externalities with Prof. Vernon Smith of the University of Arizona, who referred me to one of his articles dealing with the problem of waste disposal.[9] I asked him to help me keep on the track while I related his idea to the first graders' experiences. Here is the result.

1. The children drink a popular beverage from a tin container.

2. Drinking a "good" produces a private "bad" for the child, since he has no further use for the container.

3. Drinking a "good" also produces a social "bad" for society because the discarded can reduces the beauty of the landscape.

4. It costs the city 5¢ to clean up after each child who throws away a can.

5. The city goes to the can manufacturer and says: "Your cans cost us 5¢ each to pick up. Also, a street full of litter is not good for health and beauty. You must pay us 5¢ for each can you produce, and you get a credit for each old can you recycle." The factory agrees.

6. The can manufacturer advertises that he will pay 5¢ for every returned empty can. Used cans, which in the hands of the children were private "bads," now become private "goods."

7. The can manufacturer raises the price of an empty can that he sells to the soft drink manufacturer by 5¢, who in turn increases the price of one can of a soft drink by 5¢.

8. The child must pay a higher price for the drink, but he is compensated 5¢ for every used can he returns to the can manufacturer.

9. The can manufacturer is not worse off, since he receives a 5¢ credit for each old can he recycles.

10. Society, on net, is better off, given that children and adults take pleasure in a cleaner environment.

Concept: Weaknesses of the competitive market system: The system needs to assure that the public benefits from the economies of scale through government regulation.

To help the class discover that competitive firms with increasing returns to scale move toward monopoly, students may study table 4.

Table 4
Production Schedule of Competitive Firms with Increasing Returns

Factory 1		Factory 2	
No. of Workers	Lamps Produced	No. of Workers	Lamps Produced
0	0	0	0
1	1	1	1
2	4	2	4
3	9	3	9
4	16	4	16
5	25	5	25
6	36	6	36
7	49	7	49
8	64	8	64
9	81	9	81
10	100	10	100

Assume there are four workers. When will the workers produce lamps more efficiently (and thus produce as many lamps as possible)? If workers are divided between two factories or if all are hired by one factory? Why is it that the total labor force, working in only one factory, can produce more efficiently? (Increasing returns to scale.) Given that it is less efficient for the workers to be divided between two factories than concentrated in one factory, what are the lamp-producing firms likely to do in order to cut production costs and to maximize profit? (The firms merge and close down one factory.)

What is the disadvantage to society if an industry is monopolized? (The monopoly can cut production and set the price far above the cost of production.)

Sometimes it is said that capitalism leads to monopoly rather than to more competition. The class may discuss the validity and the significance of this statement. (It depends on whether there are increasing or decreasing returns. A firm with increasing returns to scale tends toward monopoly. A firm with decreasing returns to scale has no such tendency.)

Thus, when increasing returns are present, as in electric utilities and telephone companies, government plays a role as a regulator of the monopoly. Government tries to ensure that the company produces as much as consumers will take at a price no greater than cost.

> **Concept:** Weaknesses of the competitive market system: The economic system needs public policies involving transfer payments to assure higher minimum standards of living and to lessen inequalities.

This concept, to be taught correctly, should be placed in the larger context of the "grants economy" developed by Professor Kenneth Boulding.[10] In the process of translating the system concept into the curriculum, we distinguished between selfish, generous, and hostile transactions. Transfer payments are generous or hostile transactions, and the resources applied to such transactions and their optimum allocation represent the grants economy. For our purpose, it is the generous transactions that are important.

Students may write creative stories of generous transactions in the family, neighborhoods, the nation, and between nations. Classroom discussion may bring to light that the motivation for generous transactions may be the individual's identification with the group, the community at large, the nation, and the world.

Generous transactions may be acted out in the classroom, for example, a person gives a coin to a beggar or to the United Fund. In these sociodramas, the students may also discover that giving means making a sacrifice, without being directly compensated.

Professor Boulding also emphasizes that generous transactions or grants are complementary to the selfish transactions or to the exchange economy, in which the motivation for giving up something is to get something in return. Selfish transactions or the exchange economy can be seen in schools, where students swap things with each other, and in stores and offices, where people sell goods or services for personal gain.

Within the grants system, grants are either coerced or noncoerced. Examples of noncoerced grants are giving to the poor, to hospitals, etc. Coerced grants represent the vast welfare programs of local, state, and federal governments, financed by taxes. In a democratic society, even the coerced grants are quasi-voluntary, because individuals in effect coerce themselves when they vote for a school bond issue or when their representatives vote income tax or property tax legislation.

Grants complement three areas of the exchange economy:

1. The exchange economy, guided by the profit motive, determines what goods and services the economy should produce. The grants economy complements this area by producing goods and services which are in the social interest, but the exchange economy, for one reason or another, does not produce such goods and services. Students may discuss such programs as social security, tax support of the arts and humanities, and defense industries.

2. The exchange economy distributes income to the owners of talent or property, according to their productivity. Society frequently does not accept the decisions of the exchange economy. Students may explain how, in the United States, society's attitudes have changed toward government grants to the poor—from punitive "poor laws" to recognition that a minimum standard of living is a fundamental public responsibility. Students may also discuss how governments, through the grants economy, help groups such as farmers, large families, etc. Students may study the educational budget of the federal government and the various educational programs that may help to eliminate poverty in their own communities in the future.

3. The exchange economy sets aside resources so as to promote economic growth by guiding basic technological change. The grants economy complements this trend. Students may study the roles of private foundations and the National Science Foundation in distributing funds for the improvement of education, research, and development.

The big problem that the grants economy faces is proper allocation in order to assure maximum social return. Students may investigate how political pressure groups exercise their power to influence the distribution of government grants at the expense of the general welfare. Students may also investigate how local foundations distribute grants and the priorities established by these foundations.

Professor Boulding thinks there is a maldistribution of grants within and between nations and the rest of the world, and between grants to improve the standard of living and grants to pay for defense. Students may discuss how grants for defense may be cut by the peaceful management of conflict between nations, so that more resources may be allocated for improvement of the standard of living.

Concept: Weaknesses of the competitive market: The system needs policies that are designed to minimize uncertainties.

An economic system faces many uncertainties. Generally speaking, they may be divided into two types. One type of uncertainty is external to the system: war, earthquake, drought, etc.

However, many uncertainties are generated by the economic system itself. Firms and households must make decisions today that affect their futures. Such decisions involve firms' plans to invest in new capital equipment and plant expansion or to introduce a new product, or the decision on the part of a family to sign a mortgage for a new home. Since no one can predict the future with absolute accuracy, economic decisions that are made today, based on imperfect information about the future, may result in inefficient resource use in the future. A firm may decide to expand its plant size, only to discover that demand for its product will have fallen a year from now. Alternatively, it may decide *not* to introduce a new product, only to find, a few years later, that the product would have met a substantial consumer demand. Cities, needing loans to finance public services, may sometimes find that lending institutions refuse to provide loans because they are uncertain about the cities' future ability to pay. Or it can happen that the community, in a referendum, refuses to approve a school bond issue to build new schools. The development of a suburban neighborhood may be stopped because the construction firm did not receive accurate signals from the developers of the transportation system that would connect the suburban development to the inner city. Uncertainty arises from the fact that one economic agent does not know what the other economic agent may do.

Economists are studying ways to lessen future uncertainties. One way is through private insurance, which operates on the principle of sharing risks. Another way is to eliminate the sources of uncertainties by making the decisions of the authorities binding. Laws concerning firm safety regulations and speed limits reduce the source of uncertainties relating to the physical hazards of death and disability.

There are two forces which undermine the operation of the private insurance principle. One is moral hazard, which is when insurance, by its very existence, encourages the behavior it insures against. For example, because they are insured, people may be more careless in protecting against fires or more prone to commit accidents. The other undermining force applies when the magnitude of uncertainties is so great that it is not feasible to spread the risk—for example, drought, earthquakes, floods. In these cases, public policy plays an important role in lessening the uncertainties.

The class may study the following problem: How can the American family be protected against the economic uncertainties of unemployment and against the physical uncertainties of death of the breadwinner, old age, and disability?

The class may be divided into five committees. One committee may investigate how the uncertainties can be mitigated by the individual effort of proper nutrition, increasing earning capacity through education, budgeting, saving, and private insurance programs.

The second committee may investigate how uncertainty may be lessened through business programs such as private pension plans, insurance programs, etc. The third committee may investigate how the uncertainties can be mitigated by government programs, such as social security. The fourth committee may collect statistical data which measure the scope of uncertainties. The fifth committee may investigate how historical forces (such as greater longevity, increasing dependence on cash income, inflation, and improved technology) aggravate uncertainty.

To find out the uncertainties the businessman faces, the students may interview business executives and learn how they protect themselves against such uncertainties.

Students should interview lawyers to find out how excessive insurance claims can jeopardize the operation of the insurance principle.

The negative aspects of totally removing uncertainties could be easily acted out in the classroom in connection with a science fair. After students have presented their inventions and their potential commercial applications, the classroom may discuss the problems of incorporating some of these inventions into the market economic system. What would happen with many of these innovations if there were no risk takers in a world of uncertainty? If the government guaranteed a profit to every producer?

Concept: The designers of the economic system should discover whether the system contains an incentive structure which relies not only on market incentives but also on incentives that are generated independently of the market.

The class may make a number of surveys: Why people have chosen one job over another; why a businessman chose to go into one business rather than another; why a saver put his savings into one form rather than another.

During the surveys, the students may discover that sometimes the incentive for choosing a job was not only high salary but also love of nature, pleasure in working with people, pride in helping the poor, pride in serving the country or the world.

The class may invite people from the community, known for their commitment to generous transactions, to explain the reasons for their commitment. Students in senior high school may identify the career of their choice and explain the reasons for their choice.

To help students understand the relationship between job security and incentive, they may organize a debate on the statement "Be it resolved that the tenure of the teaching profession should be abolished."

To help students understand that nonmarket incentives must have a scarcity value, the class may decide on a certain recognition system for quality work. The teacher deliberately places the qualifications for reward on such a level that many students will receive awards; thus respect for this reward will decline. The teacher will discuss with the class the result of the experiment.

An exercise in the classroom itself could involve the establishment of special incentives to study a particular subject in one classroom, while a "controlled" class studies the same material but with no special incentives for learning, and relate the findings to the economic system. In the process of evaluating the results, the class may find that the special incentive structure may work better with some individuals than with others within the experimental class. The class may discuss the reasons for the results.

Students may have a panel on the following topic: How can the school system build an incentive system that will stimulate students to develop their potentialities?

Students may invite successful blue- and white-collar workers or craftspeople to talk about their occupational commitments and to explain the forces that stimulated them to excellence.

Students may invite talented young people who participate in the various branches of the performing arts to find out what qualities people must have to be motivated for excellence in these fields. How does the environment or the qualities of these young people differ from that of the students in the classroom?

Professor Hurwicz suggests that the areas discussed in his paper, most of which I attempted to relate to the school curriculum, are of special importance in understanding how economic systems should be adapted to achieve conditions of optimality and in designing new economic arrangements for our own society. One way in which these concepts can be used by economists is in modifying general-equilibrium models of the economic system. Only in this way can the full effects of alternative policies be assessed.

Economists are becoming highly aware that improvements in macroeconomic analysis must be tied to a better understanding of microeconomics. These two fields of economics have been largely separated in the past, mainly because economists did not know how to build the total picture of the economy from individual households and firms. As economists realize the importance of integrating the two fields of study, they are returning to the tool of the general-equilibrium model.

A general-equilibrium model of the economy is a set of equations that relate the prices, inputs, and outputs of all resources, goods, and services in the economy to the available quantities of these resources and to the preferences of the consumers. The model shows that any change in the economy will be felt in every other part of the system, if only very slightly. In the general-equilibrium view, the economic system, in a state of equilibrium or rest, might correspond to a quiet pond. When a rock is dropped into the pond, waves will be generated that will eventually reach every part of the pond. After a while, the pond will return to its quiet, or equilibrium, state. However, the pond will not be quite the same; some reeds will have moved slightly because of the waves and now find themselves in a new position, and a lily pad or two will have been displaced. In much the same way, any economic event that disturbs the equilibrium of the economy will be felt throughout the system.

In theory, a general-equilibrium model should include all of the economic relationships in the system, so that economists can predict, on the macro-economic level, the results of microeconomic changes in the economy. In practice, such a model would be much too complicated to be constructed. Relationships are difficult to identify, and in any event are constantly changing. Yet such models, in simpler forms, can be helpful to economists as they attempt to visualize how macroeconomics and microeconomics are related.

It is very important that students develop a systems awareness of their economy. In the lower grades, the teacher may initiate the following discussion. If we assume that a factory moves into our neighborhood, bringing with it 100 families, how will such a new external force affect our housing, educational, business, political, transportation, and cultural systems? After the discussion, the teacher should introduce an imperfection that disturbs the outcome. For example, the factory is a paper mill that emits bad smells. In the process of discussion, students will discover that many components of the economic system do not respond to the market, and government policy will be necessary to make the system work.

To help students gain insight into the broad impact of an economic event, they may complete the following exercises:

The government decides to produce B-1 bombers. The total expenditures would be approximately $35 million. The main contract has been given to one giant corporation, located in California. The class may be divided into ten committees, each discussing the impact of this project upon one area assigned to the committee.

Committee 1 will discuss the impact of the project on the total airplane industry and airlines: cost of the factors of production, price of airplanes, air fares of commercial airlines, amount of savings needed for new investment in the airlines, etc.

Committee 2 will investigate the impact of the project on related industries such as rubber, steel, glass, aluminum, copper, and alloys.

Committee 3 will investigate the impact of the project on energy resources.

Committee 4 will investigate the impact of the project on the demand for capital goods in the airplane industry.

Committee 5 will investigate the impact of the project on the community where the industry is located in terms of size of population, demand for housing and transportation, retail trade, public investment, and land use.

Committee 6 will investigate the impact of the project on other communities from which workers will be attracted.

Committee 7 will investigate the impact of the project on gross national product and the distribution of income.

Committee 8 will investigate the impact of the project on national priorities, externalities, distribution of social benefits, and net efficiency.

Committee 9 will investigate the impact of the project on the character of the competitive system.

Committee 10 will investigate the impact of the project on resource allocation in other great powers and in the developing countries.

After these reports, the students can discuss the importance of developing such universal general-equilibrium models for decision making. If decision makers could see the broad consequences of their decisions, perhaps many costly failures could be avoided. The challenge to the future is to adapt the general-equilibrium model to reality.

Economists are indeed expanding the frontiers of knowledge in their discipline. It is the responsibility of the economic educator to be aware of these new dimensions in economic science and to translate them into learning experiences in the classroom. Only in this way will the teaching of economics be made relevant to the lives of students and contribute to an understanding of economics that is the best and most advanced that social science can provide. However, to discover frontier thinking and translate it into the classroom is a painstaking and painful process. The economic educator cannot do this without entering into dialogue with the frontier thinker. As a result of this alliance, the frontier thinker discovers that knowing and ways of knowing are often two sides of the same coin and that a clearer formulation of ideas emerges from such an alliance. The economics profession should establish opportunities for the interaction of frontier thinkers and economic educators. Thank God, there are many brilliant innovators in the profession who are not only interested in making their contribution known to their fellow frontier thinkers but have a keen desire to put their ideas into the public domain. The economics profession must attempt to establish an information channel through which the best and most promising ideas are communicated to economic educators, who can then relate the frontier thinking to the experience of youth and to the concern of society. This paper is such an attempt.

NOTES

I would like to express my appreciation to Dr. George Horwich and to Dr. Robert McNown of the University of Colorado for reading my manuscript and for helping me clarify some concepts for young students.

1. *System Analysis and Its Use in the Classroom,* published by Social Science Education Consortium, Inc., Boulder, Colorado (1973), 58 pp.

2. Leonid Hurwicz, "Perspectives on Economics," in Donald R. Wentworth et al. eds., *Perspectives on Economic Education* (New York: Joint Council on Economic Education, 1977, pp. 21–40 (reprinted in this volume).

3. "Response to Professor Hurwicz," ibid., pp. 41–42.

4. See the article by George Horwich, "Energy: The View from the Market," *Focus on Economic Issues,* Indiana Council for Economic Education, Purdue University, 1977, esp. fig. 2.

5. John Stuart Mill, *Principles of Political Economy with Some of Their Applications to Social Philosophy,* pp. 753–755 in Volume III of *Collected Works of John Stuart Mill* (Toronto: University of Toronto Press, 1965).

6. Leonid Hurwicz, "Perspectives on Economics", *op. cit.,* p. 37.

7. Oskar Lange and Fred M. Taylor, *On the Economic Theory of Socialsim* (New York: McGraw-Hill, 1956), p. 109.

8. Leonid Hurwicz, Roy Radner, and Stanley Reiter, "A Stochastic Decentralized Resource Relocation Process: Part 1," in *Econometrica,* 43, no. 2 (Mar. 1975), 187–221, and "Part 2," 43, no. 3 (May 1975), 363–393.

9. "Dynamics of Waste Accumulation: Disposal versus Recycling," *Quarterly Journal of Economics,* 86, no. 4, 600–616.

10. Kenneth Boulding, *The Economy of Love and Fear: A Preface to Grants Economics* (Belmont, Calif.: Wadsworth Publishing Co. 1973).

Four
Memoirs

ON FORGETTING
ECONOMICS WITH
EM WEILER

Edward Ames

Although universities are called centers of higher learning, they are better described as centers of higher forgetting. It is our duty to show respect for our ancestors, and universities rightly maintain libraries for this purpose. But scholarship progresses by learning what our forebears did *not* know, and by forgetting what they thought they knew but did not. A major part of Em Weiler's work at Purdue, to which this collection pays tribute, consisted in allowing his faculty to forget what they had been taught, because they knew better than to perpetuate it.

If one of the other contributors to this volume were writing this memoir, his examples of higher forgetting would be different from mine, but they would tell a similar story. In the days I speak of, we had the sadistic practice of oral examinations. As a frequent sufferer through these painful scenes, I watched (say) the integration of monetary analysis with national income theory through the halting explanations of George Horwich's students, and the development of simultaneous equations methods through those of A. L. Nagar's and R. L. Basmann's. By teaching a "topics in" course with James Quirk and Rubin Saposnik, I watched the purple prose of their dittoed course notes trace out the early draft of their book on general equilibrium and welfare. By countless arguments with Lance Davis and Jonathan Hughes, and later by collaboration with Nathan Rosenberg, I saw the rise of the "New Economic History." Each of these experiences marked a deliberate effort to forget the ideological controversies of the post-Keynesian period, the myopia of ordinary single-equation regression techniques, the question-begging of the "old welfare economics," the unsupported jump from historical observation to economic conclusion. Each fit of forgetfulness was justified, because better work could (and was being) done. This is a memoir, not a bibliography, and I shall be impressionistic rather than exhaustive.

Purdue was my fourth graduate school, and when I arrived, as an untenured associate professor in 1954, I had a lot to forget. After graduating from college, I proceeded to the U.S. embassy in the Soviet Union, where I did economic research. I have forgotten nearly all of it. Though I can still put together a card index system of notes, I no longer can bring to mind the economic geography and budget finance with which my mind was once cluttered. I *do* remember that I got a liking for assembling evidence.

In this period of my life, I may have exerted my greatest individual impact on the economics profession, for I may have retarded the advance of economics by as much as four years. In 1943 Kantorovich published his second paper on the "transportation problem." It certainly crossed my desk in Moscow (for we received the journal). By then I had completed my formal training in mathematical economics (one year of calculus and one semester of mathematical economics). It was my duty to translate important papers and make them available to Washington (where Koopmans was also working on the transportation problem, as his Collected Works show). Had I not failed in this duty (obviously, I did not understand a word of Kantorovich), Koopmans' *Activity Analysis* might have been published before I finished my next graduate school, and I could then have learned something useful while earning my degree.

After I returned to the United States, I went to my second graduate school (and even picked up a degree). I completed my course work in the summer of 1947. In 1948 came Samuelson's *Foundations,* followed shortly by Arrow's *Social Choice and Individual Values,* and by the Koopmans volumes on activity analysis and econometrics (that monstrous "Monograph 10"). Within five years, everything I had learned was completely antiquated.

In particular, Schumpeter (one of my teachers) was fond of saying, "When Ibsen wishes to show that his heroine, Hedda Gabler, was capable of stirring up infinite trouble out of desperate boredom, he had only to have her speak (in her opening scene) of her recent honeymoon with an economic historian." Surrounded, as I later was, by Basmann, Flanders, Horwich, Quirk, Reiter, and all those other eminent economic historians of the *Purdue Faculty Papers in Economic History,* I certainly changed my opinion about this part of economics.

In 1951 I reentered graduate school, this time in the International Division of the Federal Reserve Board. At this time I decided that most of my views about the Soviet economy had been misguided, and I began the process of forgetting which led to publishing my 1965 book on the Soviet economy. In terms of my present story, I should remark only that my "big boss" was Arthur Marget. A dedicated warrior in the battle for the convertibility of European currencies, he was also the author of an important book on monetary theory. In his staff meetings, he could often not control himself, and would relate the latest "inflationist and controllist" heresies of the International Monetary Fund or the State Department, referring back to analogous controversies taken by British economists of the post-Napoleonic period. So it was here that I learned of the connection between theory and public policy.

Now Em Weiler had been Marget's student, and he was hiring when I went into the job market in 1954. At the Fed I was told: "Marget says Weiler was his best graduate student—and there is only one other person he says that of." Let us keep the record straight: Em offered me $1,000 less than I was earning in Washington and $500 less than another, more celebrated department. (They made real dollars back in those days.) I will not deny that Em drove a shrewd bargain. (That is all right. In the longer run, he did well by me.)

I came to my fourth graduate school, Purdue, in the hope that I would be allowed to forget what I had learned before. This hope was certainly realized. It is worth remembering that as late as 1959—when we admitted our first regular class of graduate students—respectable microeconomics programs were built around Alfred Marshall's *Principles of Economics.* Marshall's genius lay in his ability to construct a seemingly simple, clear, and authoritative sentence beneath which lay as much dirt as would be covered by the gross national product of Tabriz and Ispahan. Reputations were made, in microeconomics, by parsing and construing one of Marshall's sentences into book length. The nearly unanimous view (away from Purdue) was that a grounding in Marshall was necessary and sufficient for the aspiring theorist.

The Purdue economists felt that their main task was to forget Marshall. Respectable theorists considered them dangerous lunatics. In the first place, there was no way to teach the calculus to graduate students. Even if there were a way, who would want to? After all, Marshall had revealed economic theory. When I reached this point in my draft, I asked myself just what we proposed to do instead of Marshall. As I recall those early days, the "new economics" consisted of Hicks-Samuelson methods (considered old-fashioned by today's graduate student) and linear programming (which we now bequeath to the business school).

The "new economics" gave us power to do new things. For a century, engineers had been making stuff most successfully, but economists had no way to transform an engineering process into a production function. Vernon Smith, in the late 1950s, showed us how to do it. Charles Howe (for one) applied the notion to river transportation. His model, among other things, provided that when the keel of a river boat touched the bottom of the waterway, all output ceased! Jonathan Hughes and Stanley Reiter (salt-water rather than fresh-water sailors in land-locked Indiana) used the formulae of naval architecture to devise a measure of the carrying capacity of British steamships before 1860. The National Science Foundation had not yet declared economics a science, but we certainly felt close to science.

This "new economics" was fun because it was useful. It was a new toy and not a new ikon. We did not justify it by referring to the nineteenth-century canon. We were not, in short, like those macroeconomists of the 1970s who

stitch Lagrange multipliers to their tattered ideological banners, hoping
thereby to swell the ranks of their supporters. We liked the unpolluted air
of the economic frontier, and modesty was not our strongest virtue.

(There is a widespread, malicious myth that Purdue economists were all
mathematicians. Even if our emphasis on economic history did not make
this an unlikely tale, one might point to Lawrence Senesh, one of the contributors to this volume. One of the very best introductions to economics is
the second-grade textbook developed in his Elkhart project. I treasure my
copy and wish it had been offered in 1928. I have not seen Senesh's high
school material, which is probably beyond my capabilities.)

The Purdue program of the late 1950s, I think, made its mark on several
fields, notably economic history, macroeconomics, and econometrics. In theoretical economics, Em Weiler's program helped lay the basis for a longer-
term development, which is only now emerging to a clear form. Here, the
contributions of our students (of whom Kamien, Ledyard, Schwartz, and
Wood are represented in this volume) are as significant as those of their
teachers. (Naturally, we can take full credit for our students' work, just as
Em Weiler can take full credit for ours.)

When I went to Purdue in 1954, it was generally held that economic
theory applied only to market economies. The work of Kantorovich, Frisch,
and Tinbergen on planning was generally unknown, and I was considered
mainly certifiable when (in 1957) I presented a first (and pretty crude) try
at a general-equilibrium model of the Soviet-type system to the American
Economic Association. Imagine, then, my delight when I realized that Leonid Hurwicz (who has been, all along, an honorary member of the department) had shown that there were economic systems which had the
theoretical advantages of the market economy but did not have prices! The
new theory of economic systems began to emerge in the early 1960s, notably
in the Purdue seminars (referred to locally as "the Strange Ones"), and now
is in grave danger of becoming academically respectable. It has nevertheless
enabled me to begin forgetting what I learned in Purdue, my fourth graduate school.

Here I am, writing about everyone in Purdue economics except Em
Weiler. What, then, about his part in this unique experience? Not every
department chairman and dean has a Festschrift in his honor. (Indeed,
faculties generally believe that deans pollute the environment and endanger
laboratory animals.) Many Purdue economists, including myself, believing
imitation to be the sincerest form of flattery, have gone elsewhere to become
administrators and to set up new programs.

It would be easy to dwell on Em's talents as a fund raiser. If I say these
were not his main contribution, I do not suggest that his faculty was ever
reluctant to accept money that he raised. But I would point out that Em's
department was poor to a high degree when he brought his faculty together,

and he did not tempt them from other jobs by waving greenbacks in front of them.

When I arrived in Lafayette, there was a tradition that the Economics Department would not issue a new pencil unless one turned in the stub of an old one. It is certainly true (here I invoke the statute of limitations) that several years later Em had to reimburse Jonathan Hughes for travel expenses in postage stamps, all his other accounts having been overspent. On more than one occasion, I was asked to speak as follows about departmental research to moneyed representatives of such institutions as the Ford or National Science foundations: I was to be very brief in discussing projects which they were financing and to emphasize all the papers emerging from the projects they had turned down. In this sense, we were disdainful (at least in public) of worldly wealth. In the mid-1960s we shared in Em's new riches, but I for one have remembered the leaner years. This memory has encouraged me, in the 1970s, with the thought that we may once again know a period of prosperity. Prosperity is better.

Em's personal contribution to his program lay mainly in his relation to his faculty. In the Purdue scheme of things, departments had *heads*, not *chairmen*, and these could be (and were) thought of as military dictators. Em's procedure was to listen to faculty say what they wanted to do, to order them to do it, and then to hold them responsible for performance (for which he came to be known among some as a very devious person). I think that the only time I gave expression to fulsome personal flattery was after a meeting with high Purdue administrators: I remarked that Em alone had referred to us as *faculty* rather than as *instructional staff*. We knew the difference.

From one point of view, departmental growth was unplanned. Thus, economic history (one of our great successes) came into the program only because Davis and later Hughes insisted that it must be there. "That behavioral science stuff" appeared because Smith moved into the experimental testing of market behavior. The topological magic shimmered into the advanced courses when Reiter told us that time had to be provided for it. And so on. Em evidently realized quite soon that to be an original scholar it was necessary to be a little mad. He also realized an equally important point: this necessary condition is not sufficient.

One's central task in Em's department was to find something to do which was useful. Different people had quite different tasks. I never was quite sure what my own might be. This served me right: my only fixed teaching assignment was a one-semester course for first-year graduate students. This course trained students in the formulation and testing of crude hypotheses; the central problem for students was to find out what the course was about. It was poetic justice, therefore, that my task in the department was to define my own job and then explain it to Em. In fact, most of my teaching consisted of pinch-hitting for people who went on leave. My resumé shows that I wrote papers in half a dozen widely scattered subject areas. Eventually, in the Purdue administrative terminology, where Horwich was "our monetary guy," Quirk "our welfare theory guy," Reiter became "our far-out guy," and so on, I became "our versatile guy" (and even, when Em was in a mood for flattery, "our philosopher"). On this basis, I won tenure, promotion, glory, etc., and I kept very busy indeed.

This curious administrative procedure assumed that if faculty were kept busy enough doing things which they considered important, not only would useful research be done but students would be exposed to enough subjects at sufficient depth to teach them the tricks of the trade. Em's table of organization came after the fact, not before it, and was subject to constant revision. Em's administrative secret seems to be simple enough: find out what people want to do, and make sure that they actually do it. In this way, he sorted out talkers from doers, and avoided squeezing people into badly shaped holes.

Amid the intellectual turmoil of his faculty, Em was not a lump of wet clay, waiting to be molded into someone else's shape. He made frequent, forceful proposals, and we discussed them at length, breadth, and depth. Because he became the Dean of a School of Industrial Administration, he necessarily involved us in basic questions involving the relation between basic and applied economics. These questions are never finally resolved from an intellectual point of view, but they should concern all professional economists. They may be resolved by academic mayhem if people are not taught to think before they shoot.

Em managed to embed a theoretical Ph.D. program into an undergraduate economics program, and the resulting economics department into a business school without mayhem. He did so by insisting that solutions to administrative problems should be consistent with the principles of good scholarship. One does not advance theoretical economics by insisting on its sanctity relative to applied economics. One does not advance applied economics by pointing to the toil-stained hands of the applied economists. Em made the various parts of his school discuss the entire enterprise as a common undertaking and eventually led them into an attitude of mutual tolerance and even respect, for the only parts of economics which may be worth remembering are those which combine the work of the theorist and the empiricist, and the act of combination is still one of the arts.

Even while wearing his deanly toga, then, Em Weiler dealt in fundamental economic questions and not mere academic politics. Even when invoking the "publish or perish" rule, he qualified the "publish" by the saving clause, "whatever you consider most important." We may have forgotten a great deal of economics, but we have not forgotten our experiences in his department, nor the part which he played in making it succeed.

A NOTE ON EARLY CLIOMETRICA

Jonathan Hughes

The years of one's career pass quickly and, unexpectedly, one finds himself a senior man in the field, and his early work is considered to be a collection of artifacts. It is now twenty years since Stan Reiter and I did the work on "The First 1,945 British Steamships"—an inexact title, as it turned out. At the 1976 AEA convention in Atlantic City, a younger colleague (Knick Harley, a decade and a half younger) was asking me how things were back in the olden days when the world was young and the first cliometrica were being written. In the interest of the history of economic history, here is a short memoir.

I arrived at Purdue in the fall of 1956, after laboring a year and a half in the New York Federal Reserve Bank. Purdue was my choice between only two alternatives, and I chose it primarily because Lance Davis was there and had convinced me with stories of "rolling hills." Lance was a born recruiter. Lance and I had been in classes together at the University of Washington in 1950 and 1951, before I had gone off to Oxford, and he had gone to Korea (Navy) and then to Johns Hopkins. One of our teachers in Seattle had been acting instructor Douglass North.

Oxford in the early 1950s had not been the sort of place where the latest electronic aids to scholarship were emphasized. I knew of only three desk calculators there: one of them, in the Institute of Statistics, was operated very slowly by two young ladies who apparently had been hired for that purpose; one in the Medical School; and an interesting manually operated speciman at Nuffield College. Most of my quantitative work had therefore been done by hand. When I got back in the United States in January 1955, I made a fruitless trip to Cambridge (Massachusetts) job hunting, and while there was excited by descriptions of the new "IBM machines" related to me by Harvard graduate students. These persons included Andy Brimmer and John Meyer, both of whom had come east from the University of Washington. I also met Harvard graduate student Henry Rosovsky on that trip, which sets the time lapse in human perspective.

At Purdue, Lance told me of his adventures with these machines, some of them at Harvard in the previous summer. One of my new colleagues was Stanley Reiter, then known mainly as a statistician. He was jointly appointed in Economics, Mathematics, and Statistics, and thus had knowledge of and access to the building that housed Purdue's collection of these mechanical wonders. We had not only the IBM machines but also a big UNIVAC, which, it seemed, we didn't know how to use. Stanley took me over there and showed me everything: what it did, how it worked.

As it happened, there had been a hiatus in Oxford while the examiners read my thesis, and I spent some of that time back in the Radcliffe Camera looking at titles of things I had never got to read and writing down the more interesting ones. I left England on the *Queen Elizabeth* the evening of my examination; so I did not actually get to pursue many of the volumes whose titles I had written down. But I did look briefly into a parliamentary paper with an apparently inclusive title, which began: "A RETURN, in Tabular Form, With Consecutive Numbers, of the whole of the Steam Vessels Registered in the United Kingdom on or before the 1st day of January 1861. . . ."

I remembered that it was a long, long paper, and included physical dimensions of the ships as well as the details of registry, dates of "build," nature of propulsion, and so forth. So as Davis and Reiter talked about the possibilities in economics and economic history of data processing techniques, I wondered about the steamships. We did not know, until after the resulting paper was in print, that the title referred only to those steamships still afloat in 1861. As it turned out, this fact made less difference for our empirical results than we at first feared.

Our initial problem was money. We didn't have any. My salary was then $5,400 a year, and moving from New York to Indiana had wiped me out. Stan was also broke. We could not travel anywhere to consult archives or whatever. Such times were still in the future. Instead, we wrote to the New York Public Library and asked them how much a photostatic copy of the document would cost, and were told it would be $18. We managed to get that much together, received the document, and started out. Stan had to learn some marine engineering to figure out how to measure transport capacity from the numbers we had. It involved taking a cube root, and he had also to devise a "routine" for the machines to do it. They had only done square roots before. A lady employee of the Purdue Statistics Laboratory "wired the boards" for us free. Stan knew how to sort and punch cards, and he taught me, so we could do most of the labor ourselves once the main part of the set-up operations was completed. We worked at night and on weekends with the machines. We could repair and correct the punchcards on a machine that worked like a typewriter. But the bulk of the cards, 1,945 of them, had been produced by the laboratory staff, and that had to be paid for. It came to $90 and we did not have it.

In those pre-Sputnik days, there was little money around for people like assistant professors Hughes and Reiter. We went to our boss, Emanuel Weiler, with our problem. A few days later he told us that "department funds" would be provided. We later found out that Em had given us the department's accumulated supplies money. Our department secretary, Miss Stover, a wispy Hoosier maiden lady, had for some twenty-odd years saved up small change from departmental monetary affairs and that is what launched the steamships. I don't think she ever forgave Stan and me. Miss Stover was not reticent with her opinions about department affairs, so Em Weiler's role at the beginning of our little revolution has probably been underrated.

We had the main data diagrammed for us in India ink by a professional draftsman, and wrote up our results. I could not imagine where we could publish anything that *looked* like our paper did, with those big diagrams and all those numbers. Stan said he would try Allen Wallis and *The Journal of the American Statistical Association*. Wallis wrote back, indicating an interest in seeing the thing, and we mailed it off. He sent it out to referees. When he wrote to Stan to tell him that JASA would take the paper, he said he wanted to congratulate us not only for starting a new discipline but "a new way of academic life." A wise man.

Our paper came out in June 1958, to join other papers in quantitative economic history by Meyer and Conrad (Apr. 1958) and Lance ("Sources of Industrial Finance," which had come out in the winter of 1957, ahead of either of these, and which Lance had been working on in 1956, when Stan and I were doing the steamships).

After these papers appeared, Arthur Cole had become intrigued by it all, and by his conversations with Lance about it, and he urged Lance to do something with the ledgers in Baker Library of sterling bills purchased over most of a century by a Philadelphia metals-importing firm. The steamships had whetted my appetite, and when Lance asked me to help out with the Trotter papers I agreed to try. This work was to become the paper on dollar-sterling exchange rates.

Professor Cole had the ledgers mailed to us, free, but we still had no funds for assistance; so Lance and I spent many weary months doing all the dog work on the bills of exchange. We *did* get the machine-time paid for, less dramatically than had been true of the steamships, and we even had a pair of fairly dubious "research assistants" laid on at one point. We finished off that work in due course, and Hrothgar (now Sir John) Habakkuk, who had been kept apprised by overseas airmail letters of the project's development, asked for our results for the *Economic History Review*. That made, in all, five papers produced by 1959 at Purdue: three by Lance as sole author, one by him and me, and one by me and Stan.

By then, fame and fortune had begun to come our way. Carter Goodrich asked us to come to the meetings of the Economic History Association in the fall of 1960 in Philadelphia to explain to everyone else what he called *La Loi Lafayette* (Purdue is in West Lafayette, Indiana) was all about. We produced a survey paper for this occasion, "Aspects of Quantitative Research in Economic History," in which Stanley was seized by the inspiration to call our new stuff "cliometrics."

With that much achievement, Lance believed we had a case for some academic imperialism, and he got some support from Purdue. We received some of the department's Ford Foundation seed-money grant, and the first "Clio" meetings were held in December 1960 at Purdue. We had a paper on research, using data processing methods to collate information of Sumerian clay tablets, by John Snyder of Indiana University. Quirk and McRandle presented parts of their fantastic paper on the German fleet before 1914. We did not give finished papers then, but discussed our work in progress, with each man briefly explaining his work, and then opening the meeting for discussion by all the members. It was a small group. Henry Rosovsky introduced Bob Fogel to the group and he showed us the work he had been doing on railroads, using econometric techniques. I had never heard of Fogel before Lance invited him.

A year later we met again at Purdue, and invited "the terrible Harvard twins," graduate students Fishlow and David. The future of economic history was now beginning to change before our eyes.

We did not think of the punch cards as documents of any value and they were put in the basement of our building. Some years later, when I wanted the steamship cards, I phoned Lance. He tried to find them and discovered that the janitors who presided over the Biology Annex, where the Purdue Economics Department had been housed, had thrown them all out.

Such, in brief, were the simple beginnings as I perceived them. No doubt the other hot-eyed young men of the old Purdue Cliometrics Society—now aging establishment figures—would have similar tales to tell. But how could any of us describe convincingly to our younger colleagues the *spirit* of those early meetings? I never again saw anything in the academic world quite like it: the candor, warmth, enthusiasm, intellectual generosity, and comradeship of young men who found themselves to be pioneers.

"IT'S JUST LIKE NEW YORK!"

Morton I. Kamien

Early in the spring semester of 1960 at CCNY, our math stat professor, Lenny Cohen, announced that the economics department at Purdue was looking for graduate students interested in mathematics and economics and that those who were interested should sign up for an interview. The emphasis seemed to be more on mathematics than economics because the economics department hadn't heard about this impending interview and the economics faculty members didn't appear to know very much about Purdue.

My math stat classmate Gene Silberberg hadn't decided what he was going to do after graduation, and so I persuaded him to sign up with me for an interview with Purdue. John Hughes and Stan Reiter were supposed to be the interviewers (Stan didn't make it to New York because of illness), and it was in the course of this interview that John, having been at Columbia, assured me that Lafayette was just like New York. Now this was very important to me because I had to assure my father and my future in-laws that we were not going off into the wilderness. After all, in our circle of friends no one had heard of Purdue or Lafayette. And saying that it was in Indiana didn't help dispel the image of a wilderness. I did meet an acquaintance on the subway who told me that Purdue was the home of the Boilermakers. *Boilermakers?* So, having the assurance of a professor (a compelling authority in my home) that Lafayette was just like New York—understandably somewhat smaller—was a great relief.

Several weeks after the interview with John, I received a letter from Purdue offering tuition plus $1,500 for living expenses. It was like a miracle. Imagine, getting paid to go to school. Besides, I had really done terribly during the first semester of my junior year and I wasn't sure I could get into graduate school at all. My next best alternative, Brown, offered to admit me and said I might get financial aid if somebody else turned it down.

My wife, Lenore, and I arrived in Lafayette about the third week of August 1960. There was a banner in front of the administration building welcoming the "steamfitters" (boilermakers, steamfitters—it seemed to make sense). Where else would the steamfitters be but at the home of the Boilermakers? We moved into a one-room apartment on Ross-Ade Drive, shopped at Sears and Krogers, found out you didn't have to lock your front door or your car doors, and that a cherry soda in Lafayette was what we called an ice cream soda in New York. Lenore taught in Frankfort, as a result of which we came to know Elsa and Frank Sterner.

The economics department was housed in Stanley Coulter Annex. Our entering class included Nancy Schwartz, Gene Silberberg, Enid Barnett, Steve Suzuki, Chuck Lave, Jim Boisseau, Bruce Cohen, Bill Wendt, Bill Jean, JoAnn Lysic, Chiou-Shaung Yan, Bill Gigax, Harold Reid, Dave Harold, John Wood, and John Powers, who joined us in the spring semester. Our class first met in a small room on the second floor that must have been used for chemistry classes at one time. It had three rows of seats at successively higher levels and no windows. It was very hot and there was a very old electric fan on the desk that really wasn't doing much good. We were greeted by Em Weiler, John Day, Ron Stucky, and Jay Wiley. Afterward we went to Jay Wiley's office to get our course schedules approved. Jay sent Gene and me over to the math department to see Meyer Jerison, a CCNY graduate, to calm our fears about being here. Art Messenger was in charge of teaching assignments and I was assigned to assist Roland Thomas.

John Hughes taught Econ 685, and on the first day of class he looked at me and said "It's just like New York, isn't it?" and laughed, as only he can. We were overwhelmed by his reading list. We read John Neville Keynes' essay on economics as a science and our first assignment was to write a paper on that subject. I remembered reading R. G. Hawtrey's *The Gold Standard in Theory and Practice* for this course.

Duncan McDougall taught Econ 607. We used Hick's *Value and Capital*, Leftwich's *The Price System and Resource Allocation,* and *The Framework of the Pricing System* by Phelps Brown, a copy of which I still have.

Lance Davis taught Econ 616 in a room on the first floor behind the staircase. The topic for that year was whether there should be federal aid to higher education. We wrote papers each week that we had to defend before the class, if called on. We dealt with the question of the value of a college degree, a question that has become the subject of intense investigation more recently. It was a tough course, but I heard that when Ed Ames taught it the year before, the topic was the economy as seen from the standpoint of a horse. (I always wondered from which end the perspective was to be taken.) Sometimes the class would end early, around 4:30 p.m. instead of 5 p.m., so that we could watch the Purdue Marching Band and the Golden Girl rehearsing behind our building.

John Hughes threw a party for the graduate students. We were greeted by his giant St. Bernard when we got to his farmhouse and then by John, resplendent in a red and blue plaid vest. John told us we were in the best Ph.D. program in economics anywhere, with the possible exception of Oxford. By this time I had discovered that my classmates, like me, were "high risk" students. But this was the same guy who three months before had told me Lafayette was just like New York.

That winter I attended a Purdue Quantitative Institute Seminar for the first time. It was held in a large room on the second floor of the library, arranged like a conference room, with the participants sitting around a rectangle of tables and students sitting in a row of chairs up against the wall. Abba Lerner, Franco Modigliani, Jerome Rothenberg, Hirofumi Uzawa, Jacob Marschak, John Chipman, and Martin Beckmann, were there. The conference didn't begin until after a short man with a long, old coat and a very full briefcase arrived. I heard someone say, "Leo is here, we can start now." I knew of Leo Hurwicz because I had read his article on game theory as an undergraduate. I believe Jim Quirk and Rubin Saposnik presented their paper on stochastic dominance at that time, and there was talk about Uzawa having found a more direct method of proving one of their results on his flight out from California.

Each speaker had about an hour and a half to present his paper. Leo asked a lot of "clarifying" questions. This caused others to ask questions and the speaker and others to offer answers. This seemed to give rise to a lot of confusion, at which point Jacob Marschak, with a few very simple, straightforward remarks, would clarify what was going on. The speaker would resume, and soon Leo had another clarifying question and the process would repeat itself.

The familiar accents and the arguing made me think that maybe this was what John had in mind when he said Lafayette was just like New York. There was also Vernon Smith, with a motorcycle jacket and blond hair combed back in a D.A. style that reminded me of New York, but the accent wasn't right. The lesson of the conference was that not all the problems of economics had been solved and that even the great men didn't always agree. This was very encouraging, for it meant there would still be something to write about when it came time to do a thesis.

What started out as a reading course in Samuelson's *Foundations* turned into a regular course in the summer of 1961, taught by Jim Quirk. I remember Jim in his orange, ankle-high boots with thick yellow, rubber soles, gray workman's pants, flannel shirt covered by a gray sweatshirt, and sunglasses always perched on top of his head. Jim posed a problem in that course that led to my first published paper.

In the second year, Rubin Saposnik taught Dorfman, Samuelson, and Solow. That's where we learned about Kuhn-Tucker and the Turnpike theorem. George Horwich taught Econ 611. That was before his book was out. Where other authors put the interest rate on the vertical axis, George put its reciprocal. I always thought that this was like economics as seen by a man standing on his head. When I later taught from Gale's book, I thought it was like linear programming as seen by a man lying on his side. Ed Ames and A. L. Nagar taught econometrics. There was no text then, so we studied out of Hood and Koopmans, and Theil. The identification problem and two-stage-least-squares were the rage then.

June Flanders invited us to her house for dinner on Yom Kippur. June and Harley introduced us to Lafayette's famous Chinese restaurant; it was out in one of the shopping centers then. It was from Harley that we found out about MooShui Pork. There were lots of parties, beers at Harry's Chocolate Shop, and coffee in the second-floor lounge in the library. A big event was Jim Quirk's Dixieland Jazz Band, playing at the Merou Grotto with Dick Ruppert on the washboard. We took qualifiers in June. Three days of written exams and a two-hour oral. Nate Rosenberg, Lance Davis, Jay Wiley, and Jim Quirk administered the orals. Why did the U.S. price level decline from 1870 to 1900? Hint from Lance Davis: "What were the Silver Purchase Acts about?"

I took a seminar taught jointly by Ed Ames, Jim Quirk, and Rubin Saposnik, with Lance Davis sitting in, at the beginning of my third year. Steve Suzuki, Nancy Schwartz, and Hugo Sonnenschein were my classmates. We got off to a slow start, trying to resolve whether it would make a difference in a general-equilibrium model if eggs were sold individually or by the dozen. I believe that it was in this course that Hugo's work on excess demand functions began.

It was decided during that year that there were enough students to justify teaching Econ 660, Mathematical Economics. Stan Reiter was the instructor and the text was Debreu. Stan was working with Gordon Sherman on a computational method for solving the traveling salesman problem that he called "discrete optimizing." He lectured on this work during the first few sessions. I had never seen anybody develop a new computational procedure before, and so I thought to myself that this is what it must have been like when Newton invented the calculus. I was overwhelmed by the notation. There were double and triple summations, subscripts and superscripts, Roman and Greek symbols. While I was being overwhelmed, Tom Muench raised his hand and pointed out that there should be i's in certain places where there were j's. I thought, Wow.

There are many more things to tell and people to recall, both from the preceding classes and the succeeding ones. John Hughes, of course, had tricked me. Lafayette is *not* just like New York. But then I've never returned to live in New York after Purdue. I'm older and wiser now. Yet if John came and told me that there was a place just like Purdue, I believe I might get tricked again.

EXPERIMENTAL ECONOMICS AT PURDUE

Vernon L. Smith

This memoir is about many people connected with Purdue and with Em Weiler, but mostly it is about me and a continuing struggle of escape from the prison of conventional patterns of economic thought.

I arrived in West Lafayette in the summer of 1955. I had turned down an offer from Princeton at $3,750 per year, because I was already poor enough, and a good offer from Carnegie Tech, because somehow Carnegie seemed too structured. Whatever Purdue was, it wasn't that! In the next two to three years I found myself in the company of Ed Ames, Lance Davis, George Horwich, Chuck Howe, John Hughes, Jim Quirk, Stan Reiter, Rubin Saposnik, Larry Senesh, and, of course, Em Weiler. Many of us had only one thing in common—a very subverting sense of considerable dissatisfaction with our own graduate education, whether it was at Chicago, Harvard, Stanford, or wherever, and with the state of economic knowledge. This was the glue that bound—that allowed each of us to be encouraged to "do our own thing" (before that phrase became part of the language) by Em Weiler. Em, I think, had no prevision at all as to which direction that collection of renegades should go, but he had an intuition that maybe something would emerge out of a process that did not try to prevent things from happening.

Out of this menagerie many successful (and unsuccessful) cultural experiments emerged: a remarkable graduate program, an honors undergraduate program, the Quantitative Institute Seminars, cliometrics, and—for me—experimental economics.

Experimental economics at Purdue started in the late fall of 1955. In those days it was common to teach twelve hours, and I was teaching four sections of principles—the hardest job I have ever had. Not surprisingly, I had insomnia one night, and for reasons that utterly escape me, in the dead of night I found myself thinking about the classroom demonstration that Ed Chamberlin used to perform with the Harvard graduate students to "prove" the impossibility of pure competition. I didn't take Chamberlin's course, because I decided after sitting in on the first two meetings that I had had a superior course on imperfect competition from Dick Howey at the University of Kansas. But I did observe and participate in Ed Chamberlin's little "experiment." The scuttlebutt among the Harvard graduate students was that the whole exercise was sort of silly; and being at a peer-impressionable age, I recall being in agreement with this rather harsh and, I think in retrospect, inaccurate conclusion.

So there I was, wide awake at 3 a.m., thinking about Chamberlin's "silly" experiment. He gave each buyer a card with a maximum buying price for a single unit, and each seller a card with a minimum selling price for one unit. All of us were instructed just to circulate in the room, engage a buyer (or seller), negotiate a contract, or go on to find another buyer (or seller), and so on. If a buyer and a seller made a contract, they were to come to Chamberlin, reveal the price of the exchange, turn in their cards, and he would post the price on the blackboard for all to see. When it was all over, he would reveal what had been the implicit supply and demand (without-income-effects) schedules, and we would learn the important lesson that supply and demand theory was worthless in explaining what had happened; namely, that prices were not near the equilibrium, and neither was the quantity exchanged.

The thought occurred to me that the idea of doing an experiment was right, but what was wrong was that if you were going to show that competitive equilibria are not realizable operationally under conditions of incomplete information, then you should choose an existing institution of exchange that might be informationally more favorable to yielding competitive equilibria. Then, when such an equilibrium failed to be approached, you had a more powerful result. This led to two ideas: (1) Instead of having the subjects circulate and make bilateral deals, why not use the double oral auction procedure, used on the stock and commodity exchanges? After all, it would seem that these markets would come closest to that which is surely unattainable: competitive equilibria. (2) Since Marshall had talked about a competitive equilibrium as simply a tendency, conditional upon the supply and demand flows remaining stationary for a "long enough" period of time, why not conduct the experiment in a sequence of trading "days" in which supply and demand were renewed to yield functions that were "daily" flows? These two changes seemed to be the appropriate modifications to do a more credible job of rejecting competitive price theory, which after all, was for teaching, not believing (everyone at Harvard knew that, and you just knew, deep down, that those Chicago guys also knew it). So, I thought, in the spring semester (1956), to keep myself from repeating again, four times over, the textbook supply-and-demand song-and-dance, I would first take a class period to run this new experiment. I will run it on the class before they are contaminated by any discussion of supply and demand or of competitive markets.

The following January, I carried through on my insomniacal plan. The experiment I ran is labeled "Chart 1, Test 1" on page 113 of "An Experimental Study of Competitive Market Behavior" in the *Journal of Political Economy* (April 1962). I am still recovering from the shock of the experi mental results. The outcome was unbelievably consistent with competitive price theory. If these results were to be believed, what was being knocked down was Chamberlin's hypothesis of the unattainability of supply-and-demand equilibria. But the results *can't* be believed, I thought. It must be an accident, so I will take another class and do a new experiment with different supply-and-demand schedules.

I performed the experiment labeled "Test 2" in the 1962 article. Wham! It converged remarkably fast. How can this be? These subjects do not have knowledge of the market supply-and-demand schedules of the experiment. They do not even know, as yet, what "supply" and "demand" might mean. Then an explanation occurred to me. Why didn't I think of it before? Both of these experiments used symmetrical supply-and-demand curves—consumers' surplus is equal to producers' surplus—these were just special cases! The next semester, I ran an experiment with the asymmetrical design labeled "Test 7" in the 1962 article. It took a little longer, but it converged! This early series of experiments continued until 1960.

Meantime I was doing "serious" research on engineering production functions, their characteristics, and how these characteristics affected investment and production theory. I was also teaching it, and the Purdue graduate students had named it "enginomics." That had all started because I wasn't sure I believed all that stuff about production functions and how there were diminishing returns with all those guys tramping around in the cornfields with their rakes and hoes. I thought that there ought to be a better case for factor substitution, or there was no case at all.

By 1961 I had gotten that bone out of my throat, and thinking I now knew what could be believed about production and investment theory, I published *Investment and Production*. Also in 1961, I went to Stanford as a visitor. There I ran several experiments, received some strong encouragement from Bill Capron and (if my memory serves me) Mo Abramovitz, and I discovered that there was nothing unusual about Purdue students as experimental subjects. I also got convergence with the Stanford students. Although there were some wise guys at Stanford who thought these experiments were trivial, I thought they might be wrong, although it was probably the case that they were smarter than I.

A really important event at Stanford was my meeting Sydney Siegel, who was a fellow that year at the Center for Advanced Study in the Behavioral Sciences. I knew Syd only six weeks before, very inconveniently, he died. (I have never forgiven him. What a great experimental scientist!) I showed him my work. He was skeptical, too, but it was different; his was the skepticism of a scientist, not a wise guy. He had ideas, suggestions, and challenges for me that emanated from a deep commitment to the science of behavior. Through his cutting criticism came excitement and implicit encouragement. I learned much from Syd on what experimental science is all about. I eventually read most of his work. We were both delighted to find someone else thinking along similar lines for economics—although he was doing bilateral bargaining, duopoly, and triopoly experiments with Larry Fouraker, while I was doing larger-group competitive-market experiments and was more interested in studying institutions and market efficiency than in studying the effect of numbers. I often thought how well Syd would have fitted in with the Purdue crowd. I even wondered how come he turned out to be such an individualist without knowing Em Weiler.

Whatever the exact genesis, I got up the courage to write a paper reporting on all the experiments I had done from 1956 to 1960. It wasn't easy. People had been skeptical that there was a trick, some simple reason why the experiments worked that had *nothing* to do with economics or theory or that overused, undefined thing that economists call the "real world." But there were also those who consistently encouraged me—John Hughes and Em Weiler, in particular. I had gotten arrogant enough to give a seminar on the subject at Northwestern, about 1957. I had the feeling that they had no idea what I was up to, that I hadn't articulated very well what I was doing, and that they did not really believe any of it. But the seminar must not have been as bad as I thought, since they later asked if I would entertain an offer to come to Northwestern. I guess they figured, "Well, he does other things too." I didn't go to Northwestern, although I certainly was tempted.

In 1960 I wrote up my results and thought that the obvious place to send it was the *Journal of Political Economy.* It's surely a natural for those Chicago guys, I thought. What have I shown? I have shown that with remarkably little learning, strict privacy, and a modest number, inexperienced traders converge rapidly to a competitive equilibrium under the double oral auction mechanism. The market works under much weaker conditions than had traditionally been thought to be necessary. You didn't have to have large numbers. Economic agents do not have to have perfect knowledge of supply and demand. You do not need price-taking behavior—everyone in the double oral auction is as much a price maker as a price taker. A great discovery, right? Not quite, as it turned out. At Chicago they already knew that markets work. Who needs evidence?

So I shipped two copies of the first draft of "An Experimental Study" off to the *JPE,* soon to be "edited by Harry Johnson in cooperation with other members of the Economics Department of the University of Chicago." (Before the episode initiated by that action was over, I would wonder how appropriate was the word "cooperation.") Harry and I went through three referees (Harry revealed that he had been a fourth, just prior to his becoming the new editor.) I wrote detailed comments on each referee's comments and, in the end, big independent Harry, after a long period of waiting, simply "ran over" a couple of those referees. In a letter to me, dated October 13, 1961, Harry wrote:

If you feel that your paper stands up against their criticisms or that the revisions you suggest are the only concessions that you think it is necessary to make to them, just send the article to me as revised, and I will publish it. If the referees feel strongly enough to write up their criticism as comments, and these comments are worth publishing, you will have the right to rejoin. But somehow, I don't think that we will have much trouble that way. . . . I have learned something about my referees from this experience. As you may suspect, this is a very difficult job inasmuch as one has to keep evaluating everyone, including oneself."

So the paper was published, and I won't forgive Harry for dying either.

There was laughter, there were tears, in all those years—with Em helping us achieve whatever might be our individual aspirations. Me too, Mort. If Em or his representative came and interviewed me again, and said there was a place just like Purdue, I would go. Maybe you can't go home again, but it sure would be worth a try.

Contributors

Edward Ames, Professor of Economics, State University of New York at Stony Brook

H. Stuart Burness, Professor of Economics, University of New Mexico

Lance E. Davis, Professor of Economics, California Institute of Technology

George Horwich, Professor of Economics, Purdue University

Charles W. Howe, Professor of Economics, University of Colorado

Sheng Cheng Hu, Professor of Economics, Purdue University

Jonathan Hughes, Professor of Economics, Northwestern University

Leonid Hurwicz, University Professor of Economics, University of Minnesota

Robert A. Huttenback, Chancellor and Professor of History, University of California, Santa Barbara

Morton I. Kamien, Harold L. Stuart Professor of Managerial Economics, Northwestern University

John O. Ledyard, Professor of Economics, Northwestern University

James P. Quirk, Professor of Economics, California Institute of Technology

Stanley Reiter, Morrison Professor of Economics and Mathematics, Northwestern University

Nancy L. Schwartz, Professor of Managerial Economics, Northwestern University

Lawrence Senesh, Professor of Economics, University of Colorado

Vernon L. Smith, Professor of Economics, University of Arizona

Dennis J. Weidenaar, Professor of Economics, Purdue University

John H. Wood, Professor of Finance, Northwestern University

Author Index

Abramovitz, M., 371
Adderly, C., 160, 167
Adler, A., 222
Alchian, A., 232, 236
Aliber, R. Z., 237
Ames, E., ix, 39, 149, 186, 355–360, 366, 367, 368, 369
Amihud, Y., 106
Andersen, L., 234, 236
Ando, A., 235, 236
Aranson, P., 79
Arrow, K., 149, 297, 304, 306, 356
Ashton, T. S., 174
Attwood, T., 233, 234
Ayllon, T., 38, 39
Ayres, R., 150
Azrin, N., 38, 39

Bailey, M. J., 242, 255, 272
Bain, J., 306
Barnett, E., 366
Barnett, H., 135, 149
Barro, R. J., 219, 232, 235, 236, 242, 272
Basmann, R. L., 39, 355, 356
Bass, F., ix
Battalio, R., 39
Becker, G. S., 234, 238
Beckmann, M., 367
Benassy, J. P., 306
Best, J., 311
Bewley, T., 22
Binswanger, H. P., 141, 144, 149, 150
Bloch, E., 236
Boisseau, J., 366
Boulding, K., 287, 312, 322, 344, 345, 351
Bowen, H., viii
Brady, D., viii
Branson, W. H., 268, 272
Brechling, F., 237

Breen, W., 231
Brimmer, A., 361
Brobst, D., 137, 149
Bronfenbrenner, M., 272
Brown, G., 140, 150
Brown, P., 366
Brownlee, O., 242, 267, 272
Brunner, K., 231, 234, 237
Buck, N., 287
Burness, H., 130
Bye, R. T., 287

Cairncross, A., 155, 166
Cairnes, J. E., 284
Camacho, A., 40
Cantillon, R., 195, 196, 197, 203, 237
Capron, B., 371
Carleton, W. T., 231, 237
Carlson, K., 234, 236
Carter, J., 325, 327
Chamberlin, E., 298, 369, 370, 371
Chang, A., 130, 242, 255
Chang, W. W., 272
Chipman, J., 367
Chow, F. R., 284, 288
Chow, G. C., 233, 237
Christensen, L., 140, 142, 150
Churchill, W., 191
Clapham, J. H., 174
Clarke, E. H., 83, 105
Clower, R. W., 219, 232, 237, 267, 268, 272
Cohen, B., 366
Cohen, L., 365
Cole, A., 175, 182, 183, 363
Coleman, R., 280
Commons, J. R., 286
Conn, D., 38
Corry, B. A., 232, 236, 237
Cotta, A., 38, 40
Cournot, A., 297, 298

Cropper, M. L., 41, 47, 52
Culbertson, J. M., 232, 237

d'Arge, R. C., 150
Daly, H., 132, 150
Darby, M., 133
Dasgupta, P., 41, 53, 138, 150
David, P. A., 364
Davis, L. E., 54, 169, 355, 362, 365, 366, 368, 369
Davis, O., 79, 311
Day, J. S., ix, 366
De, S., 231
Deane, P., 175, 182, 183, 185
Debreu, G., 297
Dernburg, T. F., 242, 255, 268, 272
Dewey, D., 306
Dobbs, M., 184
Dorfman, R., 367
Downs, A., 55, 79
Dupuit, J., 310

Easter, K., 149
Edelstein, M., 156, 166
Edgeworth, F. Y., 6
Eisner, R., viii
Ely, R. T., 279, 283
Engels, F., 173

Fairchild, F. R., 287
Feis, H., 178, 186, 187
Ferejohn, J., 54, 55, 58, 79
Field, B., 140, 150
Fieldhouse, D. K., 152, 166, 178
Fiorina, M., 54, 55, 58, 79
Fischer, S., 235, 236
Fisher, A. C., 41, 53
Fisher, I., 201, 204, 207, 232, 235, 237, 283, 285, 289
Fishlow, A., 364
Flanders, J., 356, 368
Fogel, R., 175, 185, 364
Foley, D. K., 268, 272
Fouraker, L., 372
Frankel, M., 185, 186
Freud, S., 178, 221, 222
Friedman, M., 191–241
Frisch, R., 295, 358
Furniss, E. S., 287
Futia, C., 23, 306

Galbraith, J. K., 169
Garver, G., viii
Gershoy, L., 181

Gigax, W., 366
Gilbert, R. J., 41, 53
Goodrich, C., 363
Gordon, R. A., 323
Gordon, R. J., 220, 238
Gramm, W. P., 133, 150
Gramps, W., ix
Green, J., 22, 23
Green, L., 39
Greene, W., 140, 142, 150
Gregory, P. R., 140
Griffin, J. M., 140, 150
Grossman, H. I., 219, 232, 236, 242, 272
Groves, T., 83, 106, 305

Haavelmo, T., 295
Habakkuk, H., 363
Hagen, E., viii
Hahn, F. H., 237, 306
Hansen, A., viii
Hansen, W. L., 309
Harberger, A. C., 235, 238
Harley, K., 361
Harold, D., 366
Harris, L., 325
Hart, A. G., 236, 238, 286, 289
Hartwell, R. M., 171, 172, 174, 181
Hawke, G., 176, 185
Hawtrey, R. G., 207, 238, 366
Hayami, Y., 141, 144, 150
Hayek, F. A., 203, 207, 232, 233, 235, 238, 300, 301, 302
Heal, G., 41, 53, 138, 150
Heller, W., 214, 215, 238
Hendershott, P. H., 242, 268, 272
Hicks, J. R., 169, 180, 187, 204, 206, 232, 238, 286, 287, 289, 311
Higgs, H., 237
Hinich, M., 54, 78, 79
Hobsbawm, E., 168–187
Hobson, J. A., 152, 154, 155, 163, 166, 178
Hoffman, W. G., 173, 183
Holzman, F., 272
Hood, W. C., 367
Horwich, G., 231, 267, 272, 242, 350, 355, 356, 359, 367, 369
Hotelling, H., 299
Houthakker, H. S., 150
Hovde, F. L., 311
Howe, C. W., 41, 53, 357, 369

Howey, R., 369
Howson, S., 232, 239
Hu, S. C., 130
Hughes, J. R. T., 183, 355, 357, 359, 361–364, 365, 366, 369, 372
Hume, D., 198, 206, 219, 232, 239
Humphrey, D. B., 139, 150
Hurwicz, L., viii, 20, 22, 23, 37, 38, 40, 312, 322, 323, 348, 350, 351, 358, 367
Hutchison, T. W., 231, 232, 239

Imlah, A., 183
Ise, J., 287

Jean, W., 366
Jerison, M., 366
Jevons, W. S., 133, 237, 284
Johnson, R. W., ix
Johnston, J., 233, 239
Jordon, J. L., 236

Kagel, J. H., 38, 40
Kalai, E., 22
Kaldor, N., 295
Kalecki, M., 295
Kamien, M., ix, 41, 53, 358, 365–368
Kaminow, I., 236, 239
Kantorovich, L., 356, 358
Kazdin, A. E., 38, 40
Kemp, M. C., 41, 47, 53
Keran, M. W., 234, 239
Keren, M., 306
Keynes, J. M., 133, 169, 191, 196, 199, 201, 202, 203, 205, 207, 208, 219, 220, 225, 232, 236, 239
Kindleberger, C. P., 169, 180
Klein, B., 236, 239, 295
Klemm, W., 39
Kneese, A., 150
Knight, F. H., 286
Knopf, K. A., 279
Kogiku, K. C., 150
Kohls, R., 311
Koopmans, T. C., 53, 239, 295, 356, 367
Korliras, P. G., 242, 245, 272
Korody, M., 105
Kourilsky, M., 277
Kramer, G., 79
Krannert, H. C., ix
Kraynick, R., 149, 150
Kregel, J. A., 232, 239

Krutilla, J., 143, 150
Kuhn, A., 312, 322
Kuznets, S., 175, 184, 185

Lange, O., 298, 299, 301, 330–332, 351
Laughlin, L. L., 282
Lave, C., 366
Law, J., 239
Leamer, L., 279
Le Corbeiller, P., 295
Ledyard, J. O., 78, 106, 305, 358
Lehfeldt, R. A., 155, 166
Leijonhufvud, A., 219, 232, 235, 239
Lenin, V. I., 178, 186
Lerner, A. P., 83, 106, 298, 299, 367
Lieberman, C., 236, 240
Lindahl, E., 304, 310
Lind, R., 149
Lippman, S., 22, 23
Locke, J., 195, 232, 239
Loury, G., 22, 41, 47, 53
Lucas, R. E., 232, 235, 239
Luce, D., 22, 23
Lumsden, K. G., 280
Lysic, J., 366

McCall, J., 22, 23
McCracken, H. L., 286
McDougall, D. M., 242, 255, 268, 272
McKelvey, R., 80
McKenna, J. P., 242, 272
McNown, R., 350
McRandle, J., 364
Magill, M., 22
Maizels, A., 186
Malthus, T. R., 284
Marget, A., viii, 356, 357
Marschak, J., 242, 267, 272, 367
Marsden, J., 150
Marshall, A., 193, 199, 200, 201, 204, 205, 207, 208, 216, 233, 239, 283, 284, 357
Martin, L. R., 149
Martin, W. H., ix
Marx, K., 152, 169, 170, 172–175, 180, 221, 222
Mattingly, G., 179
May, J., 268, 272
Mayhew, H., 173, 174, 184
Meiselman, D., 193, 210, 214, 215, 216, 225, 235, 238
Meltzer, A. H., 231, 232, 237, 239
Messenger, A., 366

Meyer, J., 361
Mill, J. S., 177, 186, 193, 198, 199, 205, 206, 207, 208, 212, 239, 284, 326, 351
Mints, L., 207, 209, 224, 239
Mitchell, B. R., 182, 183, 185
Mitchell, W. C., 192, 194, 195, 231, 239
Modigliani, F., viii, 234, 236, 242, 255, 272, 367
Moroney, J. R., 139
Morrisett, I., 309
Morse, C., 135
Mortenson, D. T., 232, 235, 240
Moyer, M. E., 289
Muench, T., 368
Murnighan, J. K., 100, 106
Muth, J. F., 220, 240

Nagar, A. L., 355, 367
Negishi, T., 306
Nichols, D. A., 144, 150
Nicolson, H., 181
North, D., 185

Olech, C., 257, 272
Ordeshook, P., 54, 55, 78, 79, 80
Osborne, D., 231

Paden, D. W., 289
Page, T., 132, 149, 150
Paish, G., 178
Paley, W. S., 134, 135
Pareto, V., 332, 333
Patinkin, D., viii, 235, 240, 242, 257, 272
Perg, W. F., 268, 272
Pesek, B. P., 272
Pessemier, E., ix
Peterson, F. M., 41, 53
Phelps, E. S., 232, 233, 235, 236, 240
Pigou, A. C., 199, 202, 207
Pingry, D., 150
Plott, C. R., 92, 106
Pollak, R. A., 24, 26, 40
Poole, W., 236, 240
Popper, K. R., 221, 240
Powers, J., 366

Quirk, J. P., 130, 150, 267, 355, 356, 359, 364, 367, 368, 369

Rachlen, R., 39
Radner, R., 23, 304, 307, 351
Raffer, H., 22, 23

Rapping, L. A., 232, 235, 239
Rawls, J., 132, 150
Real, L., 160
Reid, H., 366
Reid, M., viii
Reiter, S., 22, 23, 39, 40, 304, 351, 356, 357, 359, 361, 362, 365, 368, 369
Rendleman, R., 231
Ricardo, D., 198, 199, 232, 240, 284
Ridker, R., 136, 150
Riker, W., 55, 80
Robertson, D. H., 207
Robinson, J., 298
Roosa, R. V., 226, 240
Rose, H., 242, 272
Rosenberg, N., 138, 149, 150, 186, 355, 368
Rosovsky, H., 361, 364
Rostow, W. W., 174, 175, 185
Roth, A. E., 100, 106
Rothchild, M., 22, 23, 307
Rothenberg, J., 367
Rotwein, E., 232, 240
Rubinstein, J., 130
Rudé, G., 181
Ruttan, V., 141, 144, 149, 150

Samuelson, P. A., 182, 231, 240, 287, 289, 295, 356, 367
Saposnik, R., 355, 367, 369
Sargent, T. J., 235, 240
Saunders, P., 281, 288
Saving, T. R., 272
Sayers, R. S., 233, 240
Schmeidler, D., 22, 23
Schumpeter, J. A., 164, 166, 174, 175, 178, 184, 186, 232, 240, 297, 298, 356
Schwartz, A. J., 185, 191, 192, 193, 194, 196, 210–216, 221, 231
Schwartz, N. L., 41, 53, 358, 366, 368
Segal, H., 162, 167
Seligman, E., 283
Senesh, L., 277, 280, 288, 309, 358, 369
Senior, N., 284
Shackle, G. L., 233, 240
Shannon, H. A., 166
Shapley, L., 22, 23
Sherman, G., 368
Shubik, M., 22, 23
Shultz, G. P., 237
Sidrauski, M., 268, 272

Siegel, S., 186, 371
Silberberg, G., 365, 366
Simon, H., 307
Simon, M., 162, 167, 178, 186
Simons, H. C., 207, 208, 209, 224, 226, 228, 233, 236, 240
Slichter, S., 287
Smith, A., 198, 199, 202, 241, 284, 311
Smyth, D. J., 242, 255, 272
Snyder, J., 364
Solow, R. M., 132, 138, 242, 273, 367
Sonnenschein, H., 22, 368
Spiegel, H. W., 151
Sraffa, P., 241
Stalin, J. V., 170
Starleaf, D., 236, 241
Stigler, G., viii
Stiglitz, J., 144, 151, 242, 273, 306
Strauss, J. H., 279
Stucky, R., 366
Suzuki, S., 366, 368
Sylos-Labini, P., 306

Taggart, R., 231
Tam, M. Y., 38
Tarshis, L., 287, 289
Taussig, F. W., 283, 285, 289
Taylor, F. M., 351
Taylor, W. R., 38
Teigen, R. L., 231, 241
Theil, H., 367
Thomas, R., 366
Thornton, J., 39, 198, 206, 232, 241
Tinbergen, J., 295, 358
Tobin, J., 215, 216, 231, 232, 234, 241
Truman, H., 134
Tsao, C., 106
Tse, J., ix

Tullock, G., 55, 80

Uselding, P. J., 151
Uzawa, H., 367

Varian, H., 306
Veblen, T., 169
Veeck, B., 155
Vickers, D., 231
Vickrey, W., 106
Vignola, A., 106
von Mises, L., 300, 330, 331

Wald, A., 297
Walker, F. A., 279
Wallace, N., 235, 240
Wallis, W. A., 363
Walras, L., 295, 297
Walters, A. A., 232, 241
Walton, R., ix
Wantrup, S. V., 147, 150, 151
Webber, W. E., 268, 273
Weidenaar, D. J., ix
Weiler, E. T., vii, 277, 278, 288, 311, 355, 356, 358, 363, 366, 369, 372
Weisbrod, B. A., 288
Wendt, W., 366
Wentworth, D. R., 350
Whinston, A., 150
Wicksell, K., 199, 204, 233, 241
Wickstrom, B., 38
Wiley, J., 311, 364, 366
Williams, A., 84, 105
Williams, F., 106
Winkler, R. C., 38
Wolfe, A. B., 283, 288
Wood, J., 358, 366

Yan, C. S., 166